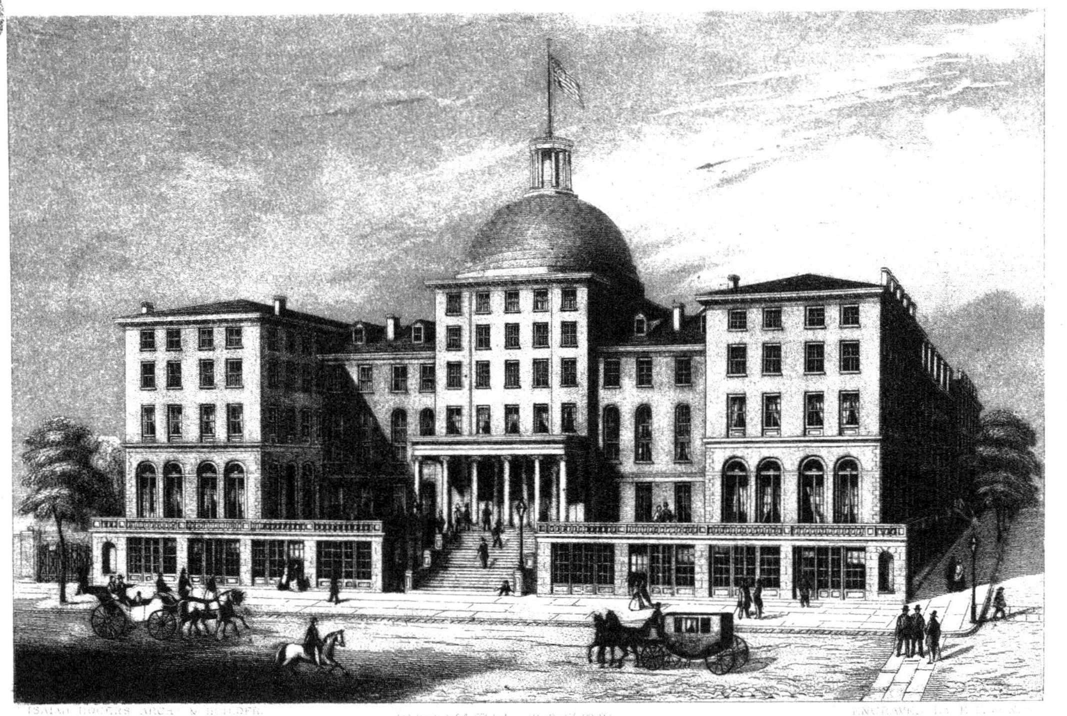

ISAIAH ROGERS ARCH. & BUILDER.

BURNET HOUSE,

CINCINNATI. [illegible] COLEMAN, PROPRIETOR.

ENGRAVED BY [illegible]

SKETCHES AND STATISTICS

OF

CINCINNATI IN 1851:

BY CHARLES CIST.

CINCINNATI:
WM. H. MOORE & CO., PUBLISHERS,
118 MAIN STREET.
1851.

E. MORGAN & CO.,
STEREOTYPERS, PRINTERS AND BINDERS,
111 MAIN STREET.

PREFACE.

I AM well aware that a large proportion of my readers will not deign to read this, or any other preface, but there are those who know, as I do, that it is impossible to derive as much benefit from the volume itself, as it is capable of imparting, unless the reader obtains some general idea of its character and nature, and other attendant circumstances from the preface. These last will, for these reasons, give it a perusal.

Ten years have elapsed since "Cincinnati in 1841," the predecessor of these pages, made its appearance. It was received with a degree of favor beyond its merits, and has served, together with kindred publications from other and earlier pens, to render this great western metropolis known not only through our great republic, but in Great Britain and even on the continent of Europe; more than four hundred copies having been sent across the Atlantic by residents here, to their friends and relatives in the land of their fathers. I trust that the present volume, comprehending, as it does, a wider range of subjects and of greater importance to persons at a distance, will be found as fully in advance of its predecessor as the city which it portrays, is of Cincinnati in 1841. I could ask no more rapid improvement, or higher success.

One great perplexity, in publications of this sort, consists in the difficulty, if not impossibility, of putting it into the shape which the various classes of readers think that it should assume. If some trifle or other has been omitted, in which an individual has a personal, professional, or pecuniary interest, he feels that the value of the volume is greatly impaired, for all such persons find it difficult to comprehend that what is thus of interest to them, probably interests very few others; and that if every topic were presented to public notice, which each individual might deem of importance, no single volume, however large, could embrace the entire subject. If I had not known, in early life, the unreasonableness of individuals on this point, a circumstance that occurred to me a few years since, would have fully enlightened me.

I had been preparing for publication, a directory, and in the progress of the work, called upon an honest German up Walnut street, who was extensively engaged in the manufacture of bratwurst, knackwurst, leber wurst, and sour-krout. I had taken down his address. "When you got dat book out," said he, "you brings me one, and I pays you for it." I promised to do so, accordingly.

By some unaccountable neglect of my transcriber of names, the dealer in wurst and sour-krout was left out of the directory, and having ascertained that fact, I did not trouble myself to deliver a book, which I knew this individual would not take on finding himself left out, as he readily would by turning to it in search of the name—the universal practice of purchasers.

Several months had elapsed, when one morning rising Main street, and just opposite Ephraim Morgan's store, I discovered my German friend. Stopping short, and in a very angry tone, he accosted me, with "Why you not put my name down in your *correctory?*" "Well, I don't know; is it not down?" was my remark. "No," replied he, very indignantly, "Your correctory not wort one cent. How do people knows where he kits his sour krout?"

I shall make no further application of the story than to say, that I must expect every man who has his sour-krout left out, will also be apt to pronounce this volume "not worth one cent."

It behooves me, however, to refer to what is in, rather than what has been left out. The articles on Geology and Magnetism, by Professor Locke; on Medical Topography, by Dr. Drake; on Meteorology, by Professor Ray; on Education, and Transportation and Travel, by E. D. Mansfield, as well as articles on the culture of the strawberry and grape by Robert Buchanan, have been obtained from the fountainheads of knowledge in these lines, respectively, and will commend themselves to the reader as of high value. The article, Cincinnati—its Destiny, from the pen of S. H. Goodin, of our city, will not fail to make a strong impression upon those who desire to contemplate the great future of Cincinnati. The residue of the volume is, with few exceptions, my own, and claims no higher merit than accuracy, as far as attainable.

One great design of this publication, being to illustrate Cincinnati in whatever aspect it might be contemplated, biographies of individuals who have been selected as types of the industrial and professional classes, constitute one of its features. The subjects of these articles, are persons who have by industry, energy, integrity, perseverance and business tact, achieved the position—in most cases, at the head of their respective classes—which they now occupy. Many of these individuals have fought the great battle of life, without aid or even sympathy in the darkest hour of that struggle, and their history enforces the great lesson to new beginners, that few things are impossible to the resolute will, the patient and untiring purpose, and the direct and straightforward principle.

A large share of this publication is taken up with the statistics of manufactured and industrial products. I cannot persuade myself, however, that the extent of this department is greater than the importance of the subject demands, taking into view the great fact which these tables establish, that the products of manufacture here, constitute more than one-half the business operations of Cincinnati, and the profits not less than three-fourths of the rewards of industry in all its branches. These tables afford indisputable evidence that the raw material consumed in our manufacturing operations does not as an average exceed 54 per cent, or thirty out of fifty-five millions dollars, the entire value of our industrial products, leaving 46 per cent. or more than twenty-five millions of dollars, as the revenue derived to Cincinnati from this department of business. It is believed that this mode of exhibiting the value of manufactures to a community, at any rate presents the subject in a clearer light than it has heretofore been shown.

I take this opportunity of saying, that my statistics will be found to differ in most points of a corresponding nature, from the national census of 1850, to which I am indebted for nothing but the tables of population and nativities in Cincinnati, and the census table for Ohio. I leave the question, which is more worthy of credit, to the public, simply adding, that this is one great reason why my manufacturing table enters so largely as it does, into details. Many of the marshals' assistants here, did their duty faithfully, but the stupidity or worse, of others, shut out a variety of details necessary to the fullness and accuracy of the aggregate.

CINCINNATI, July 10th, 1851.

TABLE OF SUBJECTS.

CINCINNATI IN 1851.

I. PHYSICAL CHARACTERISTICS.

SITE.

A WELL-DEFINED circle of hills—three miles in its diameter, and of remarkable regularity of outline, bisected east and west by the river Ohio, and north and south by Mill creek and Licking river—marks the site of Cincinnati, as its precise centre. The Ohio, at this point, makes in its course a bold, abrupt sweep, in the immediate curve of which, and on its northern edge, lies the city, which is, therefore, when approached by water, hardly visible until its entire panorama bursts upon the eye. The territory it embraces, including its north-east suburb—Fulton—may be not inaptly compared, in shape, to the old-fashioned harp, the curved side of which is formed by the Ohio; the upper edge, by Mill creek; and the straight edge, by the northern line of the city, brought down at the north-east at an acute angle to the base of the instrument.

Cincinnati is immediately opposite Covington and Newport, in Kentucky.—Its latitude was determined, by Colonel Jared Mansfield, in his topographical surveys, 39° 6′ 30″ north, and its longitude 7° 24′ 45″ west. It is nearly central between Pittsburgh, at the head of the Ohio, and Cairo, at the junction of that river with the Mississippi, being about 465 miles from each point. Its distance by land traveling is—from Columbus 115; Indianapolis 120; Lexington 90; Nashville 270, and Pittsburgh 298 miles. By steamboat conveyance—from Louisville 138; St. Louis 655; Natchez 1335, and New Orleans 1631 miles. By stage route it is 572 miles from Washington; 551 from Baltimore; 600 from Philadelphia, and, via Lake Erie and the Erie canal, 950 miles from New York.

The upper plane of Cincinnati is 540 feet above tide water at

Albany, and 25 feet below the level of Lake Erie: low water-mark of the Ohio river here being 432 feet above tide water at Albany, or 133 feet below Lake Erie. The descent of the upper part of Cincinnati to low water-mark is therefore 108 feet.

The platform of the city was originally formed of three levels or terraces, all sloping from the Ohio northwardly. The first of these extended from the bluff bank of the river to the base of the gravelly hill, which ranged nearly parallel with what is now Third street. The second of these terraces stretched to the hills immediately north of the old Corporation line; and the third, embraced the yet higher elevations, which comprise the principal part of the XIth and XIIth wards of Cincinnati, and form the city boundary at its northern edge or line. The grade of these terraces has been for years changing, to conform to the general improvement of the city, and now affords the regular and facile ascent and descent required for heavy draughts, as well as to permit the safe discharge of water from the upper table of Cincinnati.

The best views of Cincinnati may be obtained from various points of the hills along its northern edge. Those whose residence on the immediate coast of the Atlantic renders the dashing of its billows along the shore a familiar sound, will recognize at once, while standing on one of these hills, in the sounds of city life blended and harmonized by distance, the peculiar and well known music of ocean waves bursting on the shore,—one of the grandest, and at the same time of the sweetest, among the harmonies of nature.

BOUNDARIES AND DIVISIONS

CINCINNATI is bounded—north and north-east by Mill creek and Fulton townships; the Ohio river forms its southern and eastern boundaries; and Mill creek lies on its west. It is divided into sixteen WARDS, whose limits and boundary lines are as follows:

I.—Beginning at the intersection of Main and Third streets; running thence eastwardly, along Third to Symmes street; thence north-eastwardly, along Symmes and High streets, to the old Corporation line; thence due west, along said Corporation line, as far as the point of intersection of East Sixth street; thence south-westwardly, along East Sixth street, to Main street; thence southwardly, along Main street, to the place of beginning.

II.—Beginning at the intersection of Race and Third streets;

running thence eastwardly, along Third street, to Walnut street; thence southwardly, along Walnut street, to Pearl street; thence eastwardly, along Pearl street to Main street; thence northwardly, along Main street to Seventh street; thence westwardly, along Seventh street to Race street; thence southwardly, along Race street, to the place of beginning.

III.—Beginning at the intersection of Main and Third streets; running thence eastwardly, along Third street to Symmes street; thence north-eastwardly along Symmes and High streets, to the old Corporation line; thence east, along said line to the Ohio river; thence down the Ohio river, with the meanders thereof, to the foot of Main street; thence northwardly, along Main street, to the place of beginning.

IV.—Beginning at the intersection of John and Third streets; running thence, eastwardly, along Third street to Walnut street; thence southwardly, along Walnut street to Pearl street; thence eastwardly, along Pearl street to Main street; thence southwardly, along Main street, to the Ohio river; thence down the Ohio river, with the meanders thereof, to the foot of John street; thence northwardly, along John street, to the place of beginning.

V.—Beginning at the intersection of Western Row and Seventh street; running thence, eastwardly, along Seventh street to Main street; thence northwardly, along Main street, to the Miami canal; thence westwardly, along said Miami canal to Plum street; thence westwardly, along the continuation of South Canal, or Grandin street, to Western Row; thence southwardly, along Western Row, to the place of beginning.

VI.—Beginning at the intersection of Fifth and Smith streets; running thence, southwardly, along Smith street, to Third street; thence eastwardly, along Third street, to John street; thence southwardly, along John street, to the Ohio river; thence down the Ohio river, with the meanders thereof, to the foot of Fifth street; thence eastwardly, along Fifth street, to the place of beginning.

VII.—Beginning at the intersection of Western Row and Liberty street, or the old Corporation line; running thence east, along said Liberty street, or old Corporation line, to Race street; thence southwardly, along Race street, to the Miami canal; thence westwardly, along and across the Miami canal to Plum street; thence westwardly along the continuation of South Canal or Grandin street, to Western Row; thence northwardly, along Western Row, to the place of beginning.

VIII.—Beginning at the intersection of Baymiller and Catharine streets; running thence eastwardly, along Catharine street, to Western Row; thence northwardly, along Western Row, to Liberty street, or the old Corporation line; thence east, along the said Liberty street, or old Corporation line, to Piatt street; thence southwardly, along Piatt street to Clark street; thence eastwardly, along Clark street, to Baymiller street; thence southwardly along Baymiller street, to the place of beginning.

IX.—Beginning at the intersection of Main and Hunt streets; running thence eastwardly, along Hunt street, to the Lebanon turnpike road; thence north-eastwardly, along the Lebanon turnpike road, to Liberty street, or the old Corporation line; thence east, along Liberty street, or the old Corporation line, to Main street; thence southwardly, along Main street, to the place of beginning.

X.—Beginning at Race street, where it intersects the Miami canal; running thence eastwardly, along the said Miami canal to Main street; thence northwardly, along Main street, to Liberty street, or the old Corporation line; thence east, along the said Liberty street, or the old Corporation line, to Race street; thence southwardly, along Race street, to the place of beginning.

XI.—Beginning at the intersection of Vine street and Liberty street, or the old Corporation line; running thence east, along said line, to the point where the same is intersected by the west line of Fulton township; thence north-eastwardly, along the said line, to the northern boundary of the city; thence west, along the said northern boundary line, to the Vine street road: thence southwardly, along the Vine street road, to the place of beginning.

XII.—Beginning at the intersection of Vine street and Liberty street, or the old Corporation line; running thence west, along said line to Mill creek; thence up Mill creek, with the meanders thereof, to the northern boundary of the city; thence east, along the said northern boundary line, to the Vine street road; thence southwardly, along the said road, to the place of beginning.

XIII.—Beginning at the intersection of Main and Sixth streets; running thence eastwardly and north-eastwardly, along Sixth street, to the old Corporation line; thence west, along the said old Corporation line, to the Lebanon turnpike road; thence south-westwardly, along the said Lebanon turnpike road, to a point where it intersects Hunt street; thence eastwardly, along Hunt street, to Main street; thence southwardly, along Main street, to the place of beginning.

XIV.—Beginning at the intersection of Smith and Third streets; running thence eastwardly, along Third street, to Race street; thence northwardly, along Race street, to Seventh street; thence westwardly, along Seventh street to John street; thence southwardly, along John street, to Sixth street; thence westwardly, along Sixth street, to Smith street; thence southwardly, along Smith street, to the place of beginning.

XV.—Beginning at the intersection of Catharine street and Baymiller street; running thence southwardly, along Baymiller street, to George street; thence south from George street to Sixth street; thence westwardly, along Sixth street, to the Whitewater canal; thence southwardly, along the Whitewater canal, to the crossing of Fifth street; thence eastwardly, along Fifth street to Smith street; thence northwardly, along Smith street, to Sixth street; thence eastwardly, along Sixth street, to John street; thence northwardly, along John street to Seventh street; thence eastwardly, along Seventh street, to Western Row; thence northwardly, along Western Row, to Catharine street; thence westwardly, along Catharine street, to the place of beginning.

XVI.—Beginning at the foot of Fifth street; running thence eastwardly, along Fifth street to the Whitewater canal; thence northwardly, along the said Whitewater canal, to Sixth street; thence eastwardly, along Sixth street, to a point south of Baymiller street, where it intersects George street; thence north to George street; thence northwardly, along Baymiller street, to Clark street; thence westwardly, along Clark street, to Piatt street; thence northwardly, along Piatt street, to the old Corporation line; thence west, along said line, to Mill creek; thence down Mill creek, with the meanders thereof, to the Ohio river; thence up the Ohio river, with the meanders thereof, to the place of beginning.

GEOLOGY.

Cincinnati is situated in that part of the "geological column" of rocks commonly known, among the learned, under the name of the "Lower Silurian Formation," a place in general below, but nearly contiguous to, the coal-measures, but in particular at Cincinnati, considerably removed from the coal by the interposition of several layers of different sorts of rocks. Our blue limestone at Cincinnati is, however, very different in its character from the Silurian Formation of England, being infinitely more abundant in fossils, most of which are of a different species. The country in the immediate vicinity of Cincinnati seems, in a remote period of *geological* history, to have been a level terrace about 600 feet above low water of the Ohio, and nearly 1200 feet above the Atlantic ocean. This terrace, now modified by the valleys or channels excavated by the streams, is composed of alternate layers of blue clay-marl, and a blue or lead-colored fossiliferous limestone. The stone is nearly pure carbonate of lime, but sometimes passing more or less into a soft shale or slate. The marl contains lime and is effervescent with acids, but still exhibits the external characters of a tough clay somewhat indurated. Through these strata the streams appear to have worn their present channels to the depth of five to six hundred feet, having left, at various heights above their present beds, their ancient alluvion of clay, sand, and gravel, often inclosing logs of wood and not unfrequently the remains of elephants and mastodons. The larger streams are now found meandering through alluvial plains called "bottom lands," extending from half of a mile to four miles in width. These alluvions present at the surface a rich, black, fertile mold, from six inches to two or three feet deep, well wrought in the native condition, by the natural cultivators, the earth-worm and the mole. Beneath this mold are several feet, eight to twelve, perhaps, of amber-colored clay-loam, supported often by a substratum of clay, sand, or granitic gravel. The black mold and amber loam above described, extend over the high terrace, but often with a diminished thickness, and without the gravelly substratum, resting immediately on the limestone in situ. It constitutes a soil of proverbial fertility, but from the quantity of clay which it contains, it is adhesive when too wet, and stiff and impenetrable when too dry. This amber-colored loam imparts its tinge to the waters of the Ohio during its floods, and has given origin to the poetical name of the "Amber Stream." The descents into the valleys, although steep, are generally rounded and covered with fertile soil. As the rocks, although they sometimes "crop out," never form high cliffs, the waved and hilly outline seen from below is rather beautiful than picturesque.

Cincinnati itself is built on an ancient alluvial plain, lying in two levels called the "upper and lower bottoms." The lower level, fifty to sixty feet above extreme low water of the Ohio, presents a deep loam; the upper level, seventy or eighty feet higher than the lower one, beside the black mold and amber loam, has a substratum of sharp quartzose sand and coarse granitic gravel, intermingled with limestone pebbles. Imbedded in this gravel have been found several bones and teeth of elephants. Wells and deep pits, either in the upper or lower level, are often filled with "choke damp" or carbonic acid, so as to prove fatal to the incautious laborer who attempts to descend; this is especially apt to be the case, after such places have remained covered during the night.

The layers of blue limestone are from the thinnest possible to twenty-two inches or possibly two feet in thickness, compact or somewhat granular, semicrystalline, strong and durable and well calculated for many economical purposes, such as affording lime for mortar, "metal" for roads, stones for pavements, and for foundations, and even a handsome dark marble for interior architecture. They are often literally filled with marine fossils, such as corallines, trilobites, encrinites, orthocerites and various univalve and bivalve shells. People ordinarily mistake these for petrifactions of objects now found in the country, but they are all the products of a primitive ocean. The blue limestone of Cincinnati is the lowest rock which occurs within several hundred miles, and occupies a space at least a thousand feet in thickness. Although its layers lie apparently in an exact level, yet they decline both to the east and to the west so as ultimately to disappear under other strata, and finally with those strata, under the two great coal-fields which commence between one and two hundred miles on both sides of the city. The strata intervening between the blue limestone and the coal formation, begin to be found at the surface between forty and one hundred miles from our city, concealing that limestone from view. Proceeding upward, they are, in thickness, as follows:—

1st. Blue fossiliferous limestone of Cincinnati, ... 1000 ft.
2d. Cliff-limestone, ... 200
3d. Bituminous shale, ... 250
4th. Fine-grained sandstone used for building in Cincinnati, ... 350
5th. A coarse pebbly or conglomerate sandstone which includes shale, limestone, iron, salt, and coal, . 2000

As the limits of this article do not permit a separate description of these formations, the reader is referred to Professor Locke's report to the legislature of Ohio on the geology of the south-western part of the state, and to Dr. Owen's report, including Dr. Locke's also, to the Congress of the United States, on the geology of the mineral lands of Iowa, Wisconsin and Illinois. It was stated in the survey of the last named region, that its rocks, including the immense treasures of iron, zinc, lead, and copper, were identical with the cliff-limestone of Ohio, showing itself at the Yellow Springs, at Dayton, Columbus, and West Union in Ohio, and at Madison in Indiana, at all of which places it is more or less metalliferous.

The blue fossiliferous limestone of Cincinnati, after plunging under the great coal-field of Illinois in company with the cliff-limestone, reappears at Dubuque, where it is diminished to a few feet in thickness, while the superincumbent cliff-stone, filled with veins of lead ore, is developed into a stratum of six hundred feet in height. The blue limestone extends to Prairie du Chien, to the falls of St. Anthony and some distance up the river St. Peter's, but in a layer of only twenty feet or less. At Prairie du Chien it is raised some hundreds of feet above the water of the Mississippi, and exhibits underneath it a renewal of the cliff rock, but with fewer fossils. From this brief sketch every geologist would anticipate our local advantages. Situated in the centre of the inexhaustibly fertile region of the blue limestone *with its alternations of enriching marl*, midway between the two largest and most easily wrought coal-fields in the world, and also between inexhaustible beds of excellent iron ore, with every facility of natural water communication, so that even the treasures of the Mississippi mines come to our doors almost spontaneously; with a fine climate and with every material for the foundation and the superstructure of a city, it must be from a wanton abuse of the benevolent munificence of our Creator if we fail to continue to be prosperous and happy.

The natural waters of the vicinity of Cincinnati, are such as might be anticipated from the geology. The wells and springs afford clear, cool, "limestone water," viz.: water holding carbonate of lime in solution. The waters of the Miamis, especially when low, contain lime to such an extent as to be too hard for washing. This might be expected, as they have their origin and course through limestone rocks. The proper cliff-limestone is often magnesian, and sulphate of magnesia is not an uncommon ingredient in waters from particular localities, as at Pace's wells. The waters of the Ohio, flowing chiefly over the sandstone and shales of the coal-measures, until within seventy or eighty miles of our city, are but slightly impregnated with mineral matter, and are so soft as scarcely to coagulate a solution of soap. Although rather bland in taste, the "hydrant water" of our city, raised from the Ohio, is reputed to be healthy, and less liable to disagree with strangers accustomed only to soft water, than that of springs or wells.

MAGNETISM.

POPULAR ELEMENTARY DEFINITIONS.

The elements of terrestrial magnetism consist simply of the *force, power,* or *intensity* with which the earth attracts the magnetized needle, and of the *direction* in which that force acts; but from the vast importance of the horizontal or compass-needle, both in navigation and surveying, and from the facility of suspending and experimenting with the same, it is customary to estimate certain elements of the needle in that position, although it is seldom the direction—never in our latitude—in which, if allowed to move freely in all directions, it would place itself. The quantities sought to be measured are usually four:

First. The declination "variation," or direction of the horizontal needle, as it respects the true astronomical north or south points.

Second. The force or *intensity* with which the horizontal needle is attracted by the earth, and held in its direction: this is called the *horizontal intensity.*

Third. The *dip,* or true course in which a needle, perfectly free to move in all directions, would finally rest and be held by the earth's attraction.

Fourth. The force or *intensity* with which the needle, in the direction of the dip, is attracted by the earth: this is called the *total intensity.**

MAGNETICAL DECLINATION OR VARIATION.

Most persons are aware that the compass-needle does not everywhere point to the true north, but varies in its direction in different places on the earth's surface, in such a manner that it either points east of it, directly toward it, or west of it. The force with which the earth attracts or pulls such a needle, so as to hold it in its direction, and cause it to *vibrate* if it be moved out of that direction and be suffered freely to return, is called the horizontal intensity, and is

* To avoid a circumlocution of language, the earth's attraction is named without expressing particularly the mutual attraction between the earth and needle.

measured by the quickness of the vibrations. Thus, when there are a greater number of vibrations of the same needle, in the same time, the horizontal intensity is greater, being as the squares of the numbers of such vibrations. A vibrating needle used for determining the intensity, is a "magnetical pendulum," acted upon by magnetism as a clock pendulum is by gravitation.

MAGNETICAL DIP.

Make a needle of tempered steel, with pivots at the sides, so that it can turn like a cannon, and point up or down; balance it so nicely that it will stay in any position in which you place it: this must be done while the steel has no magnetism. Next, magnetize that needle by "touching" it with magnets, as directed in the books on magnetism. Lastly, place the pivots in proper supports, exactly crosswise of the line in which the compass-needle points: it will no longer remain balanced, especially in the horizontal position, but, in the latitude of the United States, the north end will turn down, nearer to a perpendicular than to a level. This turning down, or out of the level, is called the *dip;* it is measured by the number of degrees which the north end descends from a level line. The dip increases as we travel northward, until at a point north of the western part of Hudson's Bay, it points directly downward. At or near the equator there is no dip, or the dipping-needle lies level; and south of that point, the south end of the needle descends, as does the north end in the northern hemisphere.

Now, whatever direction the dipping-needle takes, it is held there by a magnetical force of the earth, which when it is moved out of that direction, draws it back again, and causes it to vibrate like a pendulum, and finally, to settle at the proper dip. If the force be greater, the vibrations will be quicker: this force is called the *total intensity*, and is not usually ascertained by the vibrations of the dipping-needle, but is deduced by calculations from the horizontal intensity, and the dip at any locality. This force, on the whole, increases as we proceed northwardly; but the horizontal intensity, in consequence of the increase of the dip, diminishes in the same direction. At the magnetic pole, where the dip would be 90 degrees (viz.: the dipping-needle perpendicular) the horizontal intensity would be nothing, and the common compass-needle would point in one direction as soon as in another—the magnetical force of the earth pulling it, at all points, directly downward upon the supporting pivot.

Now, to measure these four quantities, in different localities, as accurately as possible, has been a part of my labors in the late brief survey of a part of our territories.

Some sorts of iron ores have an influence on the magnetic needle, and change either its direction or its intensity. The effect of such ore increases directly as the quantity or mass, and diminishes as the squares of the distance increase; and although the mass may be large, yet, from the effect of depth or distance, the indication may be too slight to be observed, unless by the most delicate instruments, skillfully used. By means of these, we may be guided to vast mineralogical treasures; for, however desirous we may be to discover gold and silver mines, iron is the more useful metal. In Iowa, one magnetical node has been discovered, which may be produced by a "*subterraneous* iron mountain." Independently, however, of any economical views, it will be a matter of gratification to the scientific world to receive a small contribution to their fund of magnetical knowledge; for an effort is now making to collect and embody as many accurate magnetical observations as possible, in order the more fully to determine the changes, distributions, and general laws of this wonderful force, and to make it still more subservient to the purposes of general utility.

TERRESTRIAL MAGNETISM AT CINCINNATI.

MAGNETICAL DECLINATION OR VARIATION.

In 1825, Mr. Gest, the city surveyor, and Dr. Locke, found the compass-needle to point 5° 15′ east of due north. In 1840, the above quantity had diminished to 4° 46′ east of due north. In 1846, the variation had been reduced to 4° 01′, and at the present time it is probably somewhat less.

MAGNETICAL DIP.

Since March, 1840, Dr. Locke has made monthly observations on the dip and horizontal intensity. The following table exhibits his results, as regards the dip, up to January, 1841.

Each of the twelve observations on the following page, is the mean of sixteen single observations, including all of the possible reversals of the dipping apparatus with two needles

LINE OF EQUAL DIP OF LONDON.

This line, which, in 1837, was by observation 69° 23′, passes more than a degree south of Cincinnati, and advancing westward, passes through Princeton, in Indiana, lat. 38° 23′ north, long. 87° 30′ west, and crosses the Mississippi river about fifteen miles south of St. Louis, in Missouri.

This line of equal dip had an adventitious interest, from the fact, that the lines of equal magnetic dip, are also lines of equal mean temperature. Thus the mean temperature of Princeton, Indiana, would be presumed to be nearly equal to that of London.

TABLE OF MAGNETICAL DIP OBSERVED MONTHLY AT CINCINNATI.

Day.	Hour.	Dip by needle No. 1.	Dip by needle No. 2.	Mean.
1840.	h. m. h. m.	° ′	° ′	° ′
March 6,	2 30 to 3 30 P. M.	70 27.250	70 27.562	70 27.812
April 21,	9 46 to 10 40 A. M.	70 29.687	70 28.000	70 28.844
May 21,	10 35 to 11 35 A. M.	70 24.450	70 24.937	70 24.694
June 22,	11 34 to 12 30 M.	70 28.062	70 27.437	70 27.750
July 18,	5 30 to 6 30 P. M.	70 29.062	70 27.937	70 28.500
July 19,	11 30 to 12 30 M.	70 25.625	70 25.812	70 25.718
August 18,	10 00 to 11 00 A. M.	70 27.375	70 27.500	70 27.437
Septr. 24,	9 00 to 10 45 A. M.	70 29.200	70 29.200	70 29.200
October 22,	9 30 to 10 30 A. M.	70 29.000	70 28.375	70 28.687
Novem. 20,	10 15 to 11 15 A. M.	70 25.187	70 25.437	70 25.313
Decem. 23,	11 00 to 12 00 M.	70 27.250	70 26.812	70 27.031
Jan. 23, 1841,	11 00 to 12 00 M.	70 24.937	70 24.750	70 24.844

Mean of 192 observations............................70° 27′.152.

MAGNETIC INTENSITY.

CINCINNATI AS THE BASE OF REFERENCE OF A MAGNETICAL SURVEY OF THE UNITED STATES.

BESIDE the determinations of magnetical dip made at Cincinnati, and quoted above, Dr. Locke has made a survey of the magnetism of a large portion of the United States. His labors were continued for about ten years, viz.: from 1838 to 1848; and were extended from the south part of Kentucky to the north side of Lake Superior; and from the State of Maine to some distance beyond the Mississippi. During the progress of the work, he made the garden of Nicholas Longworth, Esq., of Cincinnati, the base or standard of comparison of the magnetic forces. The magnetic force of the earth at Cincinnati, he called 1000; and proceeded to compare the force at all other places with that assumed quantity.

Finally, Dr. Locke, at the request of Col. Sabine, R. A., Secretary of the Royal Society, extended his researches to the magnetical observatory of the British Government at Toronto in Canada. By these, and by observations made by Capt. Lefroy, R. A., at several places in the U. S., where Dr. Locke had observed, the force at Cincinnati and throughout Dr. Locke's whole survey has been compared with that of all the similar surveys throughout the world. The following table exhibits a comparison of the horizontal force, or the magnetical force with which a compass-needle is held and also the total magnetical force with which the needle of the dipping compass is held at the several places named.

This epitome of Dr. Locke's survey is abstracted from Col. Sabine's work in the Philosophical Transactions, Part III, for 1846. London. The results are arranged in three parts:—

1st. A general line of observations from Lexington, Ky., through Cincinnati to Isle Royale, on the north side of Lake Superior.

2d. A line along the Atlantic coast, from Washington city to the State of Maine.

3d. A line along the Mississippi from St. Louis in Missouri, to Prairie du Chien in Wisconsin.

The first of the numerical columns refers to the horizontal magnetic force at Cincinnati, assumed as 1000; the second, to the total force at Cincinnati, also assumed as 1000.

FIRST LINE.—LEXINGTON TO ISLE ROYALE.

LOCALITY.	HOR. FORCE.	TOTAL FORCE
CINCINNATI	1000	1000
Lexington, Ky.	1012	985
Columbus, O.	966	996
Cleveland, O.	880	1016
Detroit	816	1011
Mackinaw	716	1039
Sault St. Mary	669	1037
Ontonagon R.	686	1039
Lapointe	705	1044
Isle Royale	646	1052

SECOND OR ATLANTIC LINE.

Washington	948	988
Baltimore	932	991
Philadelphia	917	995
New York	883	994
New Haven	839	988

LOCALITY.	HOR. FORCE.	TOTAL FORCE.
Portland	753	989
Mt. Washington	729	991
Bethel, Me..	727	996
THIRD OR MISSISSIPPI LINE.		
St. Louis	1042	997
Davenport	939	1012
Dubuque	881	1013
Prairie du Chien	876	1019

In the preceding table, the horizontal and total forces at Cincinnati are arbitrarily assumed as 1000. The absolute ratio of the horizontal force at Cincinnati to the total force, is near 1 to 3, being on August 21, 1843, 1000 to 2986.

It will be seen by inspecting this table, that in general, as we are proceeding northwardly, the horizontal magnetic force by which a compass-needle is held in its direction, is diminishing, while the total force by which the dipping-needle is held in its direction, is increasing. Thus the compass force at Isle Royale, would be less than two-thirds; 646 to 1000, of what it is at Cincinnati; while the whole force *in the dip or true magnetic direction*, would be greater than at Cincinnati: as 1052 to 1000.

This diminution of the horizontal or compass force, is caused by the distance to which the horizontal-needle is forced out of the natural magnetic direction—the dip—until, when the dip should be perpendicular the horizontal force would be nothing, and the surveyor's and the mariner's compass would be useless; the needle pointing in one direction as readily as in another.

Though there have been other laborers in the field of terrestrial magnetism in the U. S., yet none have approached so near to a general survey of the country, in this particular, as Dr. Locke of our own city. The scientific magnetic chart of the U. S., as filled up by Col. Sabine in the work to which reference has been made, is almost entirely based on his observations.

The last series of the labors of Professor Locke in this department, has been lately published as a part of Dr. Jackson's survey of the geology of Lake Superior, by the Department of the Interior, under Hon. Secretary Ewing.

Baron Humboldt made observations near the equator in South

America, and assumed the magnetic force at his station to be one (1.) Other observations have since been compared very extensively with his, until we have reached a station where the total magnetism of the earth is near twice as much as that assumed unit. The intensity of the total magnetic force at Cincinnati, according to Humboldt's unit, is 1.796; and the greatest intensity known on the earth is by the same scale 1.878. Dr. Locke found the total intensity at Isle Royale in Lake Superior, to be 1.876, scarcely differing at all from the highest magnetic force yet found, being little over 1 in 1000 less.

It is interesting to observe the coincidence of the results obtained by Captain Lefroy and Dr. Locke, where they happened to observe at the same places. These gentlemen have never seen each other; they used different instruments, and observed at different times, noting, each, the various equations required for temperature, &c.; nor was it known by anybody what the results would be, until the observations were finally reduced by Col. Sabine in England. The following are some of them:—

PLACES	TOTAL INTENSITY OF MAGNETIC FORCE.	OBSERVER.
Detroit	1814	Lefroy
	1815	Locke
Cleveland	1828	Lefroy
	1824	Locke
Toronto	1836	Lefroy
	1836	Locke
Princeton, N. J.	1783	Lefroy
	1783	Locke
Albany	1797	Lefroy
	1792	Locke
New Haven	1773	Lefroy
	1774	Locke
Cambridge	1774	Lefroy
	1777	Locke

It is worthy of notice that the stronger magnetic pole is north of the U. S., and about 20° this side of the true astronomical pole. This spot has been examined by Capt. Henry Ross, nephew of Sir James, who there found the direction of the dipping needle to be perpendicular. This point is also the convergent point of compass-needles, and causes the variation to be toward the west in eastern situations; and toward the east in situations in general westward of the meridian of this pole of convergence. The pole of greatest force is still further southward, lying in general between Lake Superior and Hudson's Bay, varying very little from one of these points to the other.

Thus, in general, on the meridian of 90° west, and, of course, lying N. of the U. S., there are three great poles: 1st. The pole of magnetic intensity of forces, about 50° N. lat. 2d. The pole of magnetic dip and convergence, or the pole of declination, about 70° N. lat. 3d. The astronomical pole, at 90° N. lat. The singular fact, that the point of greatest magnetic attraction of the earth is not near the pole of magnetic dip and convergence, was first ascertained by Col. Sabine, who ventured to predict its situation. In 1844, Dr. Locke made experiments within the limits of this region of high magnetism, and communicated them to the American Philosophical Society.

Some idea of the range of magnetic intensity from Lake Superior to Hudson's Bay, may be formed, from the observations of Capt. Lefroy, from the one point to the other. These observations commence within 16 miles of those of Dr. Locke on Lake Superior, and are here thrown into four groups. The mean of the four, compared with Dr. Locke's, at Isle Royale, may be thus stated:—

PLACE.	TOTAL INTENSITY.	OBSERV.	REMARKS.
Isle Royale	1889	Locke	Mean of 11 obs.
Lapointe, Lake Supr.	1875	Locke	
1st Group, N. L. Supr.	1860	Lefroy	
2d " "	1867	Lefroy	Mean of 13 obs.
3d " "	1870	Lefroy	Mean of 10 obs.
4th Group, reaching to Hudson's Bay.	1865	Lefroy	Mean of 5 obs.
Cincinnati	1796	Locke.	Added for comparison.
Toronto	1836	Locke.	

It seems from the above that there is a special magnetic intensity about Lake Superior, even exceeding that between the lake and Hudson's Bay; still, the increase of the intensity generally, at distant places, may point to a locality north of the lake, say lat. 52°, as the centre of greatest magnetic force.

Oncken's Lithography, 214, Walnut Str. Cin. O.

ST. PETER'S CATHEDRAL.

MEDICAL TOPOGRAPHY.

On the 26th of December, 1788, when the third landing for the permanent settlement of Ohio was made, where Cincinnati now stands, there were already in the Interior Valley of North America—between New Orleans and Quebec—more than thirty towns. In sixty years, the encampment of twenty-six men, by the side of a beaver pond, beneath a dense forest of beech trees, has grown into a city, which has a more numerous stationary white population than any other within the Great Valley; and, in permanent inhabitants, ranks as the fifth city of the United States. Such an unrivaled growth would, perhaps, justify an ample notice of its condition, even if the medical historian were not identified with it in feeling, interest, and early recollections.

The site of the city, on the right bank of the Ohio river, consists of two plains or bottoms; one near the river, comparatively narrow, and composed of argillaceous alluvion; the other in its rear, six or eight times as broad, diluvial, and made up, like the higher or second terraces generally, of pebbles, gravel, and sand, with a covering of loam and soil. The lower plain widens as it stretches down the river, and its back part, on the settlement of the town, was a narrow, shallow, and heavily-timbered pond or swamp, overflowed by ordinary spring floods of the river, which ascended upon it along the marshy rivulets by which that tract was partially drained into the Ohio, below the town. In 1793 the whole of the lower plain was submerged; and in 1832 and 1848 the inundation was repeated, upon every part which had not been raised, with materials washed by the rains, or hauled from the adjacent higher terrace. For many years after the settlement of the village, the drainage of both terraces was into the low grounds of this bottom, where it accumulated in part upon the surface, and partly in the numerous pits, formed by the manufacture of brick. From these foul accumulations, in summer and early autumn, a constant escape of gas through the superincumbent water could be perceived. The extent of this tract, lying to the west or windward of the village, was sufficient to generate a great many cases of autumnal fever, chiefly of the remittent type, not a few of which every year prove fatal.* Had its surface been but a few feet lower, so that it could not have been reclaimed,

* Drake: Notices concerning Cincinnati, 1810.

the nuisances in which it abounded must have exerted a retarding influence on the progress of the city. But for the last twenty years the work of transformation by draining, filling up, and building over, has been steadily advancing, and with it a corresponding improvement of autumnal health.

From the lower plain to the upper and older, the ascent is between fifty and sixty feet. With the growth of the town, the front margin of the latter, which was originally a bluff bank, has been graded to a gentle declivity, and the removed material used, as already intimated, to raise the back part of the lower bottom; so that the drainage of the city is now chiefly by the streets directly into the river.

The upper terrace, as was the case with the lower, slopes gently back from its southern or river margin, and at the average distance of a mile, terminates against the base of the Mount Auburn range of blue Silurian limestone hills, whence, during rains, there descend upon it several torrents, which coalesce and flow nearly in the same direction with the river. To the east this terrace is terminated by the narrow valley of a hill-torrent, called Deer creek. Up this valley, in early times, the back-water of the river, when in flood, ascended for half a mile; and on its recess left a deposit of silt, which, however, was to the summer-leeward of the town, and therefore never produced much effect on the health of the people. Beyond this ravine stands Mount Adams, between the base of which and the eastern margin of the city terrace the low ground has been raised above the highest river floods, a culvert has been formed for the creek, with streets extended across it, and the new surface built upon. The ravine, higher up, has a rocky bed and no bottom-lands.

The Western canal from Lake Erie, generally called the Miami canal traverses the back part of the upper terrace, from north-west to south-east, and descends into the Ohio by a series of locks through this valley, but does not seem to have generated fever.

We must now turn to the western margin of the terraces. In stretching off in that direction down the river, both become wider and sink lower, until they are lost in the broad alluvial valley of Mill creek, which stream; once a great river, joins the Ohio one mile and a half below the centre of the city. Its banks are of mud, and portions of them are overflowed by river freshets. The work of elevation, by the transfer of gravel and pebbles from the upper terrace, is, however, going on with the rapid extension of the city in that direction; so that the time seems to be at hand when the whole tract will be redeemed from all but the extraordinary floods which happen at distant periods, and of which there have been but three since the first settlement of the city. From that date down to the present time, the inhabitants of this locality have been subject to autumnal fever, while those farther east remained exempt.

The Whitewater canal, from Indiana, which is conducted up the river bank, crosses Mill creek by an aqueduct, and traversing the lower terrace, terminates in a basin of stagnant water in the southwestern part of the city, contributing, no doubt, to the prevalence of fever in that quarter.

The river shore, from the mouth of Deer creek to the mouth of Mill creek, a distance of two miles and a half, presents but few nuisances. At the former point the stream has thrown out a quantity of silt, which, in low water, is laid bare to a limited extent; from that spot to the other, the shore is free from natural sources of insalubrity, much of it being sloped and graveled down to low water. In front of the mouth of Mill creek there is a deposit of silt, enveloping the trunks and limbs of trees, of which a considerable extent is exposed in summer and autumn, and, lying to the windward of the city, may be regarded as the most permanent nuisance around it. Below the *embouchure* of Mill creek, for two miles, and above that of Deer creek for four miles, there is no alluvial bottom, and the river presses against the base of the limestone hills.

Let us now contemplate, as a whole, the locality we have been surveying in detail. *First:* As a general fact, where a tributary enters the Ohio, there is much low bottom; but here, two join it, on opposite sides, and the extent of drowned land is very little. It has elsewhere been intimated that Mill creek, during the diluvial period, was a great river; and then it was, that an immense quantity of drift, in the form of sand, gravel, pebbles, and bowlders, was heaped up in this locality to such a height that nearly all the terraces are above the ordinary freshets of the Ohio. *Second:* The area of these terraces, including both sides of the river, is about six square miles; and their extent, taken in connection with their elevation above the river gives this locality an advantage over every other, from the sources to the mouth of the river. *Third:* As a consequence of this topography, there is no other spot on the banks of the Ohio, where so great a number of persons could reside with as little exposure to the causes of intermittent and remittent fever. *Fourth:* From observations continued through forty-eight years, it may be stated, that while, in early times, autumnal fever, occurring every year, was seldom, except in some very limited spots, a violent and frequent disease, it has regularly diminished; and that parts once infested have become exempt. So true is this of the central portions of the city, in latter years, that when a case of intermittent fever happens there, it is generally found that the patient had sojourned in the country. Of remittent fever, so much cannot be said, as occasional cases still appear on streets which are entirely exempt from the other variety. *Fifth:* The estimated population, within a circle having a radius of a mile and a half, is about one hundred and twenty thousand; and the extraordinary growth, which has assembled such a number in so short a time, must undoubtedly be ascribed, in part, to the slight prevalence of autumnal fever; by which we are instructed, that medical topography has an intimate connection with the progress of population and civil improvement.

Cincinnati has extended (chiefly by a single street), nearly four miles up the Ohio, with the river close on one side and the hills as close on the other; the bank rising above high water. This extension comprehends the villages of Fulton, Lewistown, and Pendleton. Beyond the last to the mouth of the Little Miami river, two miles further up, there is a broad, alluvial plain, on which once stood the village of Columbia, the second settlement in the State of Ohio, made November 18th, 1788. Much of this bottom, especially that nearest the Miami, is subject to inundation in the spring of the year, and the inhabitants, chiefly agriculturists, are subject to autumnal fever; which, however, is much less prevalent and violent than it existed in 1803, and for many years afterward, when the locality was *in transitu* from dense woods to cultivated fields.

Up the valley of Mill creek, which is equal in width to that of the Ohio (although in summer there is scarcely the feeblest current of water), autumnal fever is an annual endemio-epidemic. This valley is not without second, and even third bottoms or terraces, which are elevated and dry; but it has also broad and low alluvions, on which the overflows of the stream and the spring rains leave sloughs filled with the decaying vegetation of its deep and fertile soil. To these surfaces we should ascribe the fever, which, limited to them in its origin, extends far beyond them in its spread; as it frequently reaches, not only to those who reside on the older terraces, but, also, the inhabitants of the neighboring bluffs. The malignant intermittents of the south are not, however, often met with in this locality, nor ever have been; and the chief mortality is from the remittent type, in its progress becoming typhous.

The hill-lands around Cincinnati are, in all directions, of the same height and character. In some places there are gently undulating table lands; but in general the country is rolling, and presents a countless number of knobs or tuberosities, covered with rich soil, resting on a clay or loam bed, embellished with numerous country seats. Permanent springs are scarce, and much of the well-water is of an inferior quality. Ponds, swales and swamps are of course, unknown; yet autumnal remitting fever, tending to a continued type, occurs more or less every year, and sometimes proves fatal.

For many years after the first settlement of Cincinnati, the people supplied themselves with water from wells, and also from the river, as is still the case in Newport and Covington. But to these methods succeeded the present hydraulic system. The water is thrown by a forcing-pump into reservoirs, exposed to the sun and rains, whence it is distributed, through iron and lead pipes, over the city. It often comes to the consumers turbid. The silt which it deposits in the reservoirs, a portion of which remains in suspension and is swallowed with the water, no doubt varies considerably in its composition. A single analysis, of a specimen thrown out of the reservoir in the spring of the year, was made by Dr. Raymond, and gave the following results in one hundred parts:

Alumina	49.84
Silex	38.30
Carbonate of lime	2.00
Do. iron	1.15
Phosphates of alumina and iron	0.52
Carbonate of magnesia, a trace	0.00
Vegetable mold (humus)	3.50
Other organic matter	4.69
	100.00

In general, during every flood, the water when distributed is turbid.

For a long time after the settlement of Cincinnati, its only fuel was wood, but this, to a great extent, has been superseded by bituminous coal, from the Apalachian Basin. At present, the amount consumed is greater than in any other locality in the Interior Valley, save Pittsburgh, perhaps. This results, not merely from the great number of inhabitants, but also from the multiplication of their manufacturing establishments. From the better ventilation of this locality, its atmosphere is, however, much less laden with the fumes of burning coal, than that of Pittsburgh.

Cincinnati stands in Lat. 39° 6′ N., and Long. 84° 29′ 30″ W. The elevation of the surface of the river at low water, above the level of the sea, is four hundred and thirty-one feet; that of the lower plain about four hundred and ninety; that of the upper five hundred and forty-three; that of the surrounding hills, on an average, not far from eight hundred and fifty feet.

The population of the city presents many varieties of physiology. The original settlers were from various states of the Union; and the armies of Harmar, St. Clair, and Wayne, during the Indian wars, left behind them a still greater variety of persons. The subsequent immigration, although largely from the Middle and Northern Atlantic States, has been, in part, from the more Southern. In latter years it has been composed, still more than from either, of Europeans. The most numerous of these are Germans, next Irish, then English, Scotch and Welsh. Very few French, Italians, or Spaniards have sought it out. Lastly, its African population, chiefly emancipated slaves and their offspring, from Kentucky and Virginia, is large: and although intermarriages with the whites are unknown, the streets present as many mulatto, griffe, and quadroon complexions, as those of New Orleans. Thus the varieties of national physiology are very great.

A comparative view of the facility or otherwise with which these heterogeneous elements become swallowed up in the absorbing and fusing process, now and for the future in progress, which is destined to render the Anglo-American race paramount throughout this great continent, would be sufficiently curious, although too extensive a subject to be brought into discussion here. It may suffice to say, that of all classes of foreigners, the German soonest assimilates to the great mass. It takes but one generation to obliterate all the distinctive marks of this race—even of its language, usually a most tenacious feature. On the contrary, the Irishman, whose dialect does not differ much, except in accent and tone, from ours, retains his family identity for several generations. So, also, but in a less degree, with the English and Scotch.

METEOROLOGY.

In the following article, it is proposed to give a summary of the meteorological observations made at Woodward College in this city (Lat. 39° 6′ N., Long. 84° 22′ W.) during the sixteen years beginning with 1835 and ending with 1850. It is most conveniently presented under the following divisions: TEMPERATURE, WIND, RAIN, WEATHER, and HEIGHT OF THE BAROMETER.

TEMPERATURE.

The first of the following Tables is deduced from observations made at least three times daily, viz.: at or a little before sunrise, at 2 P. M., and at 9 P. M. In meteorological reckoning the day commences at sunrise, and terminates at sunrise of the following morning; the mean temperature of each day is the average temperature of the whole 24 hours, and is found by adding together the temperatures of the two extreme periods of the day, twice the temperature at 2. P. M., and twice the temperature at 9 P. M., and dividing the sum by 6. Supposing the temperature to increase or decrease gradually between each observation, the result is mathematically accurate, and is more worthy of confidence than the common method of taking the mean of the greatest and least temperature. This rule is commonly called De Witt's Rule, and is used by the academies in the State of New York.

TABLE I.

MEAN TEMPERATURE OF CINCINNATI FOR 16 YEARS.

Yrs.	Jan.	Feb.	Mar.	Aprl.	May.	June.	July.	Aug.	Sept.	Oct.	Nov.	Dec.	Whole Year.
	°	°	°	°	°	°	°	°	°	°	°	°	°
1835	34.6	24.5	40.1	50.5	65.3	71.2	71.7	69.1	59.1	55.8	43.3	31.4	51.3
1836	30.6	28.8	36.1	55.6	65.8	70.4	75.8	71.6	69.3	46.2	38.7	30.6	51.6
1837	30.1	36.6	41.8	48.3	62.5	70.1	75.3	72.4	64.9	55.8	48.1	35.5	53.5
1838	36.4	20.9	48.4	50.5	56.7	73.1	79.2	77.7	66.3	50.6	39.0	28.2	52.2
1839	38.0	37.0	44.9	60.2	66.0	69.5	76.2	73.5	61.1	60.3	37.3	30.6	54.5
1840	25.7	42.0	47.7	57.4	63.2	70.8	75.4	74.7	61.8	54.3	40.9	32.4	53.9
1841	32.0	32.5	44.7	51.2	62.1	75.1	79.1	76.4	67.8	51.2	44.2	36.3	54.4
1842	36.7	36.4	52.4	57.7	60.8	69.0	75.6	71.4	66.6	52.2	35.1	33.8	54.0
1843	35.8	26.6	28.8	51.3	62.8	70.4	73.8	70.3	69.3	47.7	40.6	36.2	51.1
1844	31.7	37.4	44.4	64.1	66.8	71.6	78.5	72.6	65.7	49.5	44.2	36.3	55.2
1845	37.9	40.1	44.5	59.9	61.6	72.6	73.4	73.0	64.1	50.2	40.3	24.8	53.5
1846	35.2	31.5	44.2	57.1	67.0	68.2	75.9	76.4	70.7	52.8	45.7	39.8	55.4
1847	30.8	36.8	40.2	55.7	62.7	69.2	74.4	70.5	64.1	53.2	44.9	34.3	53.1
1848	36.7	36.9	42.3	53.7	66.5	71.8	73.8	74.6	62.2	54.0	39.8	41.1	54.4
1849	32.3	32.2	46.5	52.6	63.9	73.9	73.7	73.5	65.3	53.3	49.9	31.6	54.1
1850	36.6	35.6	41.2	49.0	58.9	73.3	81.6	78.3	66.0	53.4	46.4	34.6	54.6
	33.8	33.5	43.0	54.7	63.3	71.2	73.5	73.5	65.3	52.6	42.4	33.6	53 5

From this table we deduce the mean temperature of the four seasons as follows:—

Winter—Dec. Jan. Feb. 33°.6. Summer—June, July, Aug. 73°.5.
Spring—Mar. Apl. May, 53°.7. Autumn—Sept. Oct. Nov. 53°.4.

An inspection of the above table also shows the following, among other particulars:—

1st. February, on the average, is the coldest month of the year.* It is not, however, always the coldest of the winter months.

2d. July is always the warmest month of the year.

3d. June is the least variable month of the year, in regard to its mean temperature, the range being 6° .9; therefore its general character in regard to temperature, can be predicted with more certainty than that of either of the other months.

4th. March is the most variable month of the year, in regard to its mean temperature, the range being 23° .6; its general character, therefore, in regard to temperature, can be predicted with less certainty than that of any other month.

5th. The mean temperature of October is nearly the same as that of the entire year.

6th. The range of the mean temperature of the year is about 3°.5. In regard to the four seasons, we notice further; that the coldest winter in the above period was in 1845–6, of which, the mean temperature was 30° .5; and, that the warmest winter was that of 1844–5, of which, the mean temperature was 38° .1. This gives for the range of the mean temperature of winter, 7° .6.

The coldest spring was that of 1843, of which, the mean temperature was 47° .7; the warmest spring was that of 1844, of which, the mean temperature was 58° .4. This gives for the range of the mean temperature of spring, 10° .4.

The coldest summer was that of 1847, of which, the mean temperature was 71° .4; the warmest summer was that of 1850, of which, the mean temperature was 77° .7. This gives 6° .3, for the range of the mean temperature of summer.

The coldest autumn was that of 1842, of which, the mean temperature was 51° .3; the warmest autumn was that of 1846, of which, the

---

* Of the 54 military posts of the United States, embracing various latitudes from 24° 20′ to 47° 15′ N., at 8 posts, December was the coldest month of the year; at 30 posts, January; and in 16 posts, February. At 5 posts, June was the warmest month of the year; at 43 posts, July; and at 6 posts, August.—See Army Reports.

mean temperature was 56°.4. This gives 5° .1 for the range of the mean temperature of autumn.

A comparison of these results shows, that of the four seasons, autumn is the most stable, and spring the most variable in its temperature.

TABLE II.

MINIMUM TEMPERATURE OF EACH MONTH IN 16 YEARS, AT CINCINNATI.

Years.	Jan.	Feb.	Mar.	A.	M.	June.	July.	Aug.	S.	O.	N.	Dec.	Whole Year.
1835	3°	—17	1	21	40	45	48	46	33	29	3	9	—17 Feb. 8th.
1836	0	— 7	—4	25	38	52	55	48	40	27	15	3	— 7 Feb. 3d.
1837	5	8	20	26	39	52	57	52	42	26	22	7	+ 5 Jan. 3d.
1838	8	—10	11	28	36	53	59	62	39	30	14	—4	—10 Feb. 22d.
1839	13	5	2	32	36	46	54	47	31	32	2	8	+ 2 March 4th.
1840	—1	0	21	27	42	47	50	7	41	19	18	7	— 1 Jan. 2d, 19th.
1841	—7	4	18	30	37	53	59	9	42	25	25	18	— 7 Jan. 18th.
1842	9	— 5	25	27	36	45	56	53	40	27	8	0	— 5 Feb. 17th.
1843	2	— 2	1	26	41	38	50	53	48	19	22	15	—2 Feb. 7th, 16th.
1844	—1	15	20	28	45	54	65	56	38	26	15	8	— 1 Jan. 29th.
1845	19	8	18	20	34	51	49	50	40	25	11	—6	— 6 Dec. 20th.
1846	10	0	20	27	43	46	57	64	44	28	15	19	0 Feb. 26th.
1847	—3	5	14	26	36	47	54	52	38	27	19	2	— 3 Jan. 8th.
1848	—4	17	5	31	40	50	58	61	40	36	25	24	— 4 Jan. 10th.
1849	16	3	28	28	45	57	59	57	43	34	24	2	+ 2 Dec. 31st.
1850	7	0	22	25	36	44	65	60	44	31	25	11	0 Feb. 4th.
Least.	—7	—17	—4	20	34	38	48	46	31	19	2	—6	—17

TABLE III.

MAXIMUM TEMPERATURE OF EACH MONTH IN 16 YEARS, AT CINCINNATI.

Years.	Jan.	F.	M.	A.	May.	June.	July.	Aug.	S.	O.	N.	Dec.	Whole Year.
1835	66°	56	70	83	91	95	93	89	86	82	76	63	95° June 13th.
1836	61	62	71	91	89	95	99	95	93	80	68	55	99 July 23d.
1837	53	66	73	89	95	95	96	94	90	80	75	73	96 July 15th.
1838	69	51	85	85	87	93	97	100	91	84	65	54	100 Aug. 9th.
1839	66	70	79	83	94	94	96	95	88	88	61	48	96 July 25th.
1840	55	75	75	91	89	93	96	93	85	82	71	58	96 July 16th.
1841	54	58	83	82	93	99	98	96	93	76	72	64	99 June 12th.
1842	65	69	85	90	88	95	92	93	94	84	77	69	95 June 22d.
1843	67	58	59	88	93	97	98	92	92	77	68	60	98 J'y 1st, 16th, 27th.
1844	56	70	72	89	89	90	94	93	89	76	75	64	94 July 6th, 14th.
1845	62	70	77	93	91	94	95	92	86	76	68	51	95 July 21st.
1846	67	55	69	88	91	91	96	92	92	81	73	66	96 July 10th.
1847	67	60	72	86	88	92	92	90	89	83	75	60	92 July 18th.
1848	60	60	86	84	90	91	90	92	86	75	59	73	92 Aug. 14th.
1849	60	69	73	88	87	92	92	92	91	74	80	60	92 J'e 22, J'y 13, A. 5.
1850	61	72	71	86	89	95	96	93	90	83	77	65	96 July 6th.
Gr'tst.	69	72	86	93	95	99	99	100	94	88	80	73	100°

An examination of tables II and III, shows that the extreme range of the thermometer at Cincinnati is 117°: and that the greatest range in any one year is 100°.

That in 16 years the least temperature has occurred seven times in February, six times in January, twice in December, and once in March.

That in the same period, the greatest temperature has occurred eleven times in July, four times in June, and three times in August.

TABLE IV.

MONTHLY RANGE OF TEMPERATURE AT CINCINNATI IN 16 YEARS.

Years.	Jan.	Feb.	Mar.	Apr.	May.	June.	July.	Aug.	Sept.	Oct.	Nov.	Dec.	Wh. Yr.
1835	63°	73°	69°	62°	51°	50°	45°	43°	53°	53°	73°	54°	112°
1836	60	69	75	66	51	43	44	47	53	53	53	52	106
1837	48	58	53	63	56	43	38	42	48	54	53	66	90
1838	61	61	74	57	51	40	38	38	52	54	51	58	110
1839	53	65	77	51	58	48	42	48	57	56	59	40	94
1840	56	75	54	64	47	46	46	36	44	63	53	51	97
1841	61	54	65	52	56	46	39	37	51	51	47	46	106
1842	56	74	60	63	52	50	36	35	54	57	69	69	100
1843	65	60	58	62	52	59	48	39	44	58	46	45	99
1844	57	55	52	61	44	36	29	37	51	50	60	56	91
1845	43	62	59	73	57	43	46	42	46	51	57	57	101
1846	57	55	49	61	48	45	39	28	48	53	58	47	96
1847	70	55	58	60	52	45	38	38	51	56	56	58	95
1848	64	43	81	53	50	41	32	31	46	59	34	49	96
1849	44	66	45	60	42	35	33	35	48	40	56	58	90
1850	54	72	49	61	53	54	31	33	46	52	52	54	96
Mean.	57	62	61	61	51	45	39	38	49	54	55	54	

From this table, we discover that the months having the greatest range of temperature, are February, March, and April; and those having the least range, are August, July, and June.

TABLE V.

GREATEST CHANGE OF TEMPERATURE WITHIN 24 HOURS, IN EACH MONTH AT CINCINNATI, FOR 16 YEARS.

Years.	Jan.	Feb.	Mar.	Apr.	May.	June.	July.	Aug.	Sept.	Oct.	Nov.	Dec.	Wh. Yr.
1835	33°	37°	37°	37°	35°	31°	32°	30°	33°	31°	30°	28°	37°
1836	27	35	32	43	46	33	38	28	30	32	36	30	46
1837	27	25	32	40	42	31	30	35	22	31	32	31	42
1838	29	31	30	37	38	31	28	28	37	35	34	36	38
1839	25	35	31	38	35	35	39	33	35	40	29	19	40
1840	31	38	41	38	33	30	25	27	32	35	40	33	41
1841	21	30	30	37	36	33	30	28	30	35	31	21	37
1842	35	30	43	43	43	34	28	29	34	41	44	34	44
1843	31	31	32	34	36	38	34	32	29	38	28	26	38
1844	28	31	33	37	33	28	25	26	32	31	35	27	37
1845	32	38	39	43	42	32	30	33	31	39	35	32	43
1846	29	29	35	40	32	30	24	23	27	33	32	25	40
1847	22	27	33	42	38	30	25	25	29	7	29	30	42
1848	28	27	40	40	38	30	23	20	27	29	22	29	40
1849	21	28	32	32	34	30	24	30	34	34	34	21	34
1850	30	29	31	36	36	35	21	22	27	34	32	22	36
Mean.	35	38	43	43	46	38	39	35	37	41	44	36	46

The greatest changes, and those felt most sensibly, take place from noon or afternoon of one day to sunrise next morning—the thermometer falling.

The least changes generally occur in the summer and autumnal months; and the greatest in the winter and spring.

TABLE VI.

WIND

The following table contains the average course of the wind for each month in the year, the wind or breeze denoted as being from that one of the principal points to which its origin most nearly approaches.

	N.	N. E.	E.	S. E.	S.	S. W.	W.	N. W.
Jan.	2.0	1.7	2.0	0.3	1.1	8.0	12.0	3.9
Feb.	1.5	1.6	1.8	0.6	1.4	6.1	9.6	5.6
March	3.1	2.8	2.7	1.0	2.1	6.3	6.8	6.2
April	2.8	2.8	2.6	0.8	2.0	6.3	8.1	4.6
May	3.5	3.0	2.8	0.4	1.7	5.7	8.4	5.5
June	1.5	1.5	2.3	0.8	2.0	7.5	9.0	5.4
July	2.9	3.8	1.6	2.0	3.4	5.9	7.0	4.4
August	2.2	4.1	4.0	1.0	2.6	7.5	4.8	4.8
Septr.	2.5	3.4	2.8	0.5	1.6	7.8	5.4	6.0
October	2.5	3.0	1.1	0.6	1.6	6.8	9.4	6.0
Novem.	1.7	3.0	0.8	0.2	1.7	7.5	9.8	5.3
Decem.	1.6	2.0	2.6	0.5	1 3	7.8	10.5	4.7
	27.8	32.7	27.1	8.7	22.5	83.2	100.8	62.4

From the above table it will be seen that westerly winds prevail annually, on an average, about 246 days, or two-thirds of the year; that easterly winds prevail about 68 days, or less than one-fifth of the year; that the wind is from the north about 28 days, or one-tenth of the year; and from the south, about 22 days, or one-sixteenth of the year.

The above table is deduced from the observations of the 10 years* ending with 1850, and is the result of about 7000 separate observations. It coincides very nearly with the result of the six years' observations terminating with 1840.

* Except in regard to July and August. I was occasionally absent from the city during these months, and could not supply the course of the wind from the tables of other observers in the city, as I frequently did that of the temperatures from the tables of my friend, John Lea, Esq.

TABLE VII.

AMOUNT OF RAIN AND MELTED SNOW AT CINCINNATI FOR 16 YEARS.

Year.	Jan.	Feb.	Mar.	Apr.	May.	June.	July.	Aug..	Sept.	Oct.	Nov.	Dec.	Year.
	IN.	IN.	IN.	IN.	IN.	IN.	IN.	IN.	IN.	IN.	IN.	IN.	IN.
1835	3.82	1.75	1.86	3.37	7.57	7.34	2.46	6.54	3.23	4.35	6.66	3.20	52.15
1836	2.97	4.34	4.18	4.54	9.01	2.14	7.42	5.54	4.77	3.71	4.41	4.36	57.39
1837	0.80	3.43	3.70	2.00	3.79	4.38	3.83	5.91	3.14	4.16	2.52	5.05	42.71
1838	1.90	1.64	0.56	4.77	8.57	7.55	2.47	3.76	0.71	3.55	3.12	0.85	39.45
1839	4.56	2.75	2.69	2.38	4.46	1.96	2.97	0.56	3.24	0.13	2.20	1.72	30.62
1840	1.13	4.68	3.65	4.78	6.08	6.84	4.45	3.73	1.56	4.74	2.50	3.20	47.34
1841	5.55	0.82	2.34	4.75	2.16	1.51	5.33	2.71	2.94	2.46	4.92	5.56	41.05
1842	2.75	6.09	3.02	2.97	3.04	5.67	2.35	4.22	2.95	1.90	3.76	2.57	41.29
1843	3.51	3.54	2.97	6.15	3.54	4.52	2.92	5.89	6.73	4.16	4.26	3.00	51.19
1844	3.10	1.04	4.50	3.13	7.00	6.16	3.50	3.65	1.26	4.32	3.18	1.10	43.65
1845	3.03	1.66	5.46	1.08	1.89	11.50	3.06	6.88	7.51	2.03	1.68	0.60	46.38
1846	3.59	3.23	2.26	3.51	5.17	7.53	3.93	6.10	2.50	2.19	4.26	9.25	53.52
1847	4.71	4.06	5.37	2.12	4.30	7.63	8.25	3.20	3.87	9.57	3.95	8.15	65.18
1848	4.58	2.81	6.72	0.55	5.13	1.86	6.95	3.90	1.53	3.62	2.60	9.43	49.68
1849	6.48	2.04	4.70	3.65	3.61	4.90	8.90	4.41	2.68	3.86	2.42	5.32	52.97
1850	5.20	6.28	6.62	4.27	1.86	5.00	6.30	7.20	2.22	1.05	2.54	6.22	54.76
Mean.	3.60	3.14	3.79	3.38	4.82	5.41	4.69	4.64	3.18	3.49	3.50	4.35	48.02

The above gives for the quantity of fluid in the four seasons, tho following results:—

Winter . . . . . . Dec., Jan., Feb. . . . . 11.09 inches.
Spring . . . . . . Mar., April, May . . . . 12.00 "
Summer . . . . . June, July. Aug. . . . . 14.74 "
Autumn . . . . . Sept., Oct., Nov. . . . . 10.17 "

This shows that summer is the wettest, and autumn the driest season of the year.

A further inspection of the table, shows that the wettest month of the year is June, and the driest September (taking into account that it is two days longer than February).

The greatest quantity of rain in any month was 11.5 inches, in June, 1845; the least quantity in any month was one-eighth of an inch, in Oct., 1839.

The most marked drouth in the above period, was in 1850. From September 18th to November 26th—68 days, only 1.6 inches of rain fell.

The greatest quantity of rain in any one year, was in 1847; the amount being 65.18 inches, which was about 17 inches above the mean; the smallest quantity in any one year was 30.62 inches, which was about 17 inches less than the mean.

TABLE VIII.

DEPTH OF UNMELTED SNOW AT CINCINNATI, FOR 11 WINTERS.

Winter.	Nov.	Dec.	Jan.	Feb.	Mar.	April.	Total.
	IN.	IN.	IN.	IN.	IN.	IN.	IN.
1839–40	0.0	7.0	6.3	0.0	0.0	0.0	13.3
1840– 1	1.0	10.4	8.0	2.0	3.0	0.0	24.4
1841– 2	1.0	0.0	0.0	7.8	0.0	0.0	8.8
1842– 3	1.5	3.1	12.1	7.6	2.7	1.3	28.3
1843– 4	1.0	2.8	3.8	1.5	1.2	0.0	10.3
1844– 5	1.0	1.9	2.5	4.6	0.0	0.0	9.0
1845– 6	4.3	0.5	2.6	15.7	0.5	0.0	23.6
1846– 7	7.2	0.8	8.4	3.1	8.6	0.0	28.1
1847– 8	0.0	20.6	7.0	0.0	2.5	0.0	30.1
1848– 9	1.5	4.0	1.0	7.4	0.0	0.0	13.9
1849–50	0.0	18.0	10.0	19.0	3.0	0.0	50.0
Mean.	1.7	6.3	5.6	6.2	2.0	0.1	21.8

This table shows that the amount of snow during the year, is a very variable quantity, ranging from 9 to 50 inches. It also shows, that frequently November and March, and sometimes both, are without snow; and that only once in ten years, has any snow fallen in April.

WEATHER.

We have divided the days into three classes. Those that were clear, or of which the greater part was fair, are denominated *clear and fair days;* those partly clear, but of which the greater portion was cloudy, are denominated *variable days;* and those that were nearly or entirely cloudy, are denominated *cloudy days*. The following is the average number of days of each kind in a year, deduced from the observations from 1840 to 1850, except that the average number for July and August are deduced from the observations alone of 1841,—43,—45,—49, and 50.

Clear and fair days 146.3
Variable days 140.6
Cloudy days 78.3

This result is the same for the number of clear and fair days as the average from 1835 to 1840.

The least number of clear and fair days in any one of the last sixteen years was 107; this was in 1843, and the mean temperature of this year was only 51°.1; or more than 2° below the annual mean. In 1850 the number of cloudy days was only 62, and the mean temperature of this year was more than 1° above the annual mean.

The following table contains the average number of days of each kind of weather, for the several months of the year, according to the preceding classification.

TABLE IX.

	Clear and Fair Days.	Variable Days.	Cloudy Days.
January	10.7	7.8	12.5
February	10.0	9.2	9.0
March	10.8	11.2	9.0
April	12.4	12.6	5.0
May	13.0	14.4	3.6
June	11.9	15.3	2.8
July	14.6	13.6	2.8
August	12.8	15.8	2.4
September	15.9	11.2	2.9
October	14.7	10.8	5.5
November	10.8	9.8	9.4
December	8.7	8.9	13.4

According to this table the greatest amount of clear and fair weather occurs in June, July, August, September, and October; and the greatest number of cloudy days in December and January.

BAROMETER.

TABLE X.

Year.	Mean height Inches.	Min. height Inches.	Max. height Inches.	Range.
1835	29.353	28.70	29.89	1.19
1836	29.345	28.66	29.82	1.16
1837	29.291	28.54	29.81	1.27
1838	29.347	28.72	29.91	1.19
1839	29.357	28.66	30.04	1.38
1840	29.348	28.53	29.86	1.33
1841	29.314	28.42	29.96	1.54
1842	29.326	28.61	29.84	1.23
1843	29.302	28.48	29.92	1.44
1844	29.309	28.71	29.78	1.07
1845	29.328	28.83	29.85	1.02
1846	29.297	28.64	29.94	1.30
1847	29.294	28.57	29.91	1.34
1848	29.291	28.47	29.86	1.39
1849	29.519	28.65	30.05	1.40
1850	29.273	28.50	29.92	1.42
	29.318	28.42	30.05	1.63

The above table contains the mean height, the minimum and maximum height, and the range of the barometer at Woodward college, which is situated about 150 feet above low water of the Ohio, and about 17 feet above the level of Lake Erie.

From the table it will also be seen, 1st. that the mean height in any given year, differs but little from the annual mean height; 2d. that the range of the minimum height for different years is .41 of an unit; that the range of the maximum height for different years is .27 of an inch; and 3d. that the extreme range is 1.63 inches.

The following table presents the mean height of the barometer for each month, during the preceding period; also the minimum and maximum heights that have occurred in each month, in the same period.

TABLE XI.

Months.	Mean height. Inches.	Min. height. Inches.	Max. height. Inches.	Mean height for the Seasons.
Jan.	29.344	28.57	30.05	
Feb.	29.312	28.50	30.01	
Mar.	29.310	28.48	29.94	Winter.....29.335 inches.
Apr.	29.289	28.42	29.76	
May	29.243	28.59	29.63	Spring......29.281 "
June.	29.271	28.84	29.59	
July.	29.329	28.91	29.61	Summer....29.316 "
Aug.	29.348	29.05	29.62	
Sept.	29.341	28.73	29.72	Autumn.....29.348 "
Oct.	29.362	28.66	29.91	
Nov.	29.342	28.61	30.04	
Dec.	29.350	28.47	30.04	

An examination of this table gives the following results: The mean height of the barometer is the lowest in May, and the highest in October; the former being .075 below, and the latter .044 above the mean for the year; the range being .119. The minimum height of the barometer occurs when the sun is north; and the maximum height when it is south of the equator. The month nearest to the mean height, is July. Of the four seasons, autumn and winter are above, and spring and summer below the mean height for the year. Spring is the lowest, and autumn the highest of the whole; the difference between them being .067. The mean height for the summer is nearly the same as the mean height for the year.

The barometric heights were corrected for capillarity and reduced to the temperature of freezing water.

II. PERSONAL STATISTICS.

POPULATION—CENSUS OF 1850.

CINCINNATI.

WARDS.	WHITE.	COLORED.	TOTAL
1	6411	434	6845
2	8026	187	8213
3	7567	101	7668
4	10,394	563	10,957
5	5122	161	5283
6	9229	401	9630
7	9167	178	9345
8	14,328	96	14,424
9	9889	816	10,705
10	12,887	145	13,032
11, 12	19,246	90	19,336
	112,266	3172	115,438

HAMILTON COUNTY.

TOWNSHIPS.			
Fulton	3323	—	3323
Spencer	1655	1	1656
Columbia	2411	5	2416
Anderson	3014	36	3050
Mill creek	6180	107	6287
Storrs	1666	9	1675
Green	3947	1	3951
Delhi	1942	—	1942
Sycamore	3727	4	3731
Symmes	1115	—	1115
Colerain	3105	20	3125
Miami	1513	44	1557
Whitewater	1514	53	1567
Crosby	2480	8	2488
Springfield	3598	34	3632
	153,356	3494	156,850

Drawn by Capt. Jon^a Heart U.S.A. 1790.

Oncken's Lithography, Cincinnati, O.

FORT WASHINGTON.

As the population of Cincinnati in 1840 was 46,338, the census returns for 1850, manifest an increase, for the last ten years, of one hundred and fifty per cent. The increase from 1830 to 1840, was ninety per cent. Our city may therefore be ranked among those cities of the United States, whose growth is not exhausting their elements of progress. It would be doing injustice to the actual increase in population of Cincinnati, to omit the fact, that the recent national census was taken at a period when the cholera was raging in the midst of us. Not only did we sustain a loss of 4832 deaths on this score, but the population returns were farther reduced from the still greater numbers put to flight by the approach and arrival of that pestilence. For weeks every vehicle of conveyance was filled with these fugitives, who, in most cases, did not return in time to be included in the enumeration of inhabitants. There can be no just reason to doubt, that but for these drawbacks, Cincinnati would have yielded within its corporate limits alone, the population of 130,000 inhabitants, which it now comprehends, by including that of its suburbs and immediate adjacencies.

The following comparative table will afford a contrast of the progress in the population of Cincinnati, with that of other cities in the Ohio and Mississippi valley.

	CINCINNATI.	PITTSBURGH.	LOUISV.	NEW ORLEANS.
Census of 1800	750	1565	600	9650
" 1810	2540	4768	1350	17,242
" 1820	9602	7243	4012	27,176
" 1830	24,831	21,412*	10,306	46,310
" 1840	46,338	36,478*	21,214	102,296
" 1850	115,438	67,871*	43,277	120,951

These successive census returns for Cincinnati, embrace its corporate limits merely. If we include Covington, Newport, Fulton, Storrs, and other adjacencies, which may with as much propriety be reckoned with Cincinnati, as suburbs and adjacent villages are included with Philadelphia, our population will reach 150,000 souls.

At the same time, it must be observed, that Cincinnati derives less from its immediate neighborhoods, on the score of population, proportionally, than most other cities. While we have hardly more than one-fourth of the population put down to Philadelphia, the number of inhabitants within our corporate limits, is little less than that of

* Including Alleghany city.

those within that city; and, while the adjacencies included with Pittsburgh swell her population to 80,000, our inhabitants number one hundred and fifty per cent. more than hers, computing city limits alone.

The colored population, in 1826, amounted to 690 persons—the white inhabitants being at that date, 15,540. They were, therefore, as one in twenty-four of the entire population. In 1840, they had so far increased as to form one in twenty, or more exactly 2258, of the 46,382 persons returned in the census of Cincinnati of that period. They are now 3172 in 115,438, or one in thirty-six of the population. It is a significant fact, that in Columbus, the colored race form 1233 out of 17,867 inhabitants; or one in fourteen, although our city must afford a greater variety, as well as a greater extent of employment congenial to the habits and qualifications of the race.

It will be found on comparing the population progress of Cincinnati with that of other places, for the last ten years, as exhibited by a view of the census of 1840 and 1850, that there is no place of equal or greater magnitude in the United States, whose ratio of increase has been as large. Nor is there any whose absolute increase is so great, except Philadelphia and New York cities,—the one concentrating the most extensive mining and manufacturing operations in the United States, and the other being the great receptacle of its foreign commerce, as well as one of its most important manufacturing points.

NATIVITIES—UNITED STATES.

State	Number	State	Number
Ohio	33,258	Mississippi	201
Pennsylvania	5005	North Carolina	178
New York	3331	Illinois	166
Virginia	2370	Rhode Island	147
Kentucky	2223	District of Columbia	138
Maryland	1663	South Carolina	131
New Jersey	1546	Georgia	128
Indiana	1256	Missouri	107
Massachusetts	1166	Michigan	97
Connecticut	500	Alabama	63
Louisiana	406	Arkansas	32
Vermont	316	Iowa	28
Maine	255	Texas	10
Tennessee	251	Wisconsin	8
Delaware	220	Florida	1
New Hampshire	217		55,468

NATIVITIES—FOREIGNERS.

Germany	30,628	Russia	12
Ireland	13,616	Norway	11
England	3690	Spain	10
France	820	Isle of Jersey	7
Scotland	771	" Man	6
Wales	444	Greece	5
Canada	338	Brazil	4
Italy	171	Africa	4
Switzerland	154	Portugal	3
Prussia	130	New Brunswick	2
Holland	94	China	2
Poland	77	Guatimala	2
At Sea	38	Isle of Wight	2
Nova Scotia	29	" Guernsey	1
West Indies	27	" France	1
Sweden	20	Newfoundland	1
Denmark	18	Turkey	1
Belgium	16	Australia	1
Mexico	15		51,171

Unknown, principally natives of the United States. . . . 8799

The proportion of natives of the United States to foreigners, in the respective wards of Cincinnati, may be thus stated;

	I.	II.	III.	IV.	V.	VI.
Foreigners	2698	3058	3879	4513	1584	3383
Natives	3804	4499	3294	5840	3313	5860
Unknown	343	656	495	604	386	387
	6845	8213	7668	10,957	5283	9630

	VII.	VIII.	IX.	X.	XI. XII.	Total.
Foreigners	3471	4610	5504	5569	12,935	51,171
Natives	5526	9516	4571	4875	4339	55,468
Unknown	350	298	630	2588	2069	8799
	9345	14,424	10,705	13,032	19,336	115,438

The Irish constitute the largest share of foreigners in the First, Third, Fourth, and Seventh Wards, as the Germans do in the Fifth, Sixth, Eighth, Ninth, Tenth, Eleventh, and Twelfth Wards of the city. These two classes of foreigners are nearly balanced as respects numbers, in the Second Ward. The residue of our foreign population is, to a considerable extent, distributed equally throughout the city. The central wards contain the larger proportions of native population; while, as a general rule, the Irish reside contiguous to the river, and the Germans occupy our northern territory. These last, to a great degree, own the property they occupy, and the high price of ground in the active business regions, together with its pre-occupation for other purposes than sites for dwellings, has concentrated them along the northern line of Cincinnati.

In 1841, the elements of population stood, by estimate :—

Americans	54	per cent.
Germans	28	"
Great Britain	16	"
Other foreigners	2	"
	100	

It will be seen that the present constituent proportions of the community, as determined by the recent census, correspond exactly to the estimate of 1841.

The additions to the native column since 1840, by births here, do not, therefore, more than counterbalance the foreign immigration during the same space of time.

Although the nativities under the division "Unknown," if ascertained, would render the number of natives of the United States greater than that of foreigners, yet the proportion of these last to the mass of population, is greater here than in any large city of the United States, except Boston among the atlantic, and St. Louis of the western cities.

To the industry of foreigners, Cincinnati is indebted in a great degree, for its rapid growth. Their presence here has accelerated the execution of our public improvements, and given an impulse to our immense manufacturing operations, without which, they could not have reached their present extent and importance.

OCCUPATIONS, TRADES, AND PURSUITS.

Occupation	Number
Agents	94
Apple-butter makers	3
Architects	10
Artists	25
Artific. flowr. makers	4
Attorneys at law	176
Auctioneers	19
Auditor	1
Author	1
Awning makers	9
Astronomer	1
Bakers	421
Bandbox makers	2
Basket "	37
Barkeepers	189
Bedstead makers	7
Bellows "	3
Barbers	227
Beef curers	4
Billiard-table keepers	2
Billiard-table maker	1
Bill posters	2
Bishop	1
Blacksmiths	713
Blacking makers	2
Blind "	17
Block "	3
Boardinghouse keepers	127
Bonnet pressers	5
Boatmen	950
Boat builders	4
Bookbinders	136
Bookfolder	1
Bookkeepers	90
Booksellers	43
Boot & shoe makers	1569
Box makers	24
Brass founders	7
Brass finishers	4
Brewers	126
Boiler makers	69
Brush "	67
Brick "	143
Britannia ware merchants	8
Bricklayers & plasterers	809
Brokers and bankers	61
Bristle dressers	7
Broom makers	1
Bucket "	5
Builders	7
Butchers	672
Cabinet makers	485
Carpenters	2318
Carmen	17
Carters	54
Carders	8
Carriage drivers	42
Cap makers	15
Caulkers	8
Chandlers	82
Carriage makers	51
Card maker	1
Carvers	23
Candy manufacturers	7
Chair makers	303
" painters	4
Chocolate maker	1
Chemists	9
China manufacturers	2
City Gauger	1
" Criers	4
" Weigher	1
" Marshal	1
Civil engineers	5
Cistern builders	6
Cigar makers	170
Circus riders	2
Clerks	1583
Club-room keepers	3
Clergymen	97
Clothiers	22
Coopers	868
Coffee-house keepers	327
Coffee roasters	2
Copper smiths	56
Collectors	27
Cooks	142
Confectioners	136
Coroner	1
Coke maker	1
Corkmakers	2
Composition roofers	14
Coach makers	95
" painters	3
" trimmers	29
Constables	16
Cellar diggers	20
Congressmen	2
Comb makers	8
Coal merchants	13
Contractors	3
Coffin makers	3
Clock "	10
Colporteurs	4
Cotton spinners	12
Cutlers	13
Dairymen	5
Daguerreotypists	40
Dancing masters	2
Dentists	32
Deputy marshal	1
" auditor	1
" sheriffs	7
Draughtsmen	6
Draymen	482
Druggists	153
Distillers	18
Dyers	19
Dress makers	23
Drovers	3
Editors	26
Edge tool makers	41
" " grinders	9
Engineers	240
Engravers	55
Engine builders	3
Express messengers	2
Farmers	61
Feed store keepers	8
Flour dealers	4

Fruiterers......... 4
File cutters........ 8
Figure maker...... 1
Finishers.......... 264
Farriers........... 7
Fishermen......... 2
Foundrymen....... 162
Furniture dealer.... 1
Fur dealer......... 1
Flouring millers... 2
Florists........... 2
Faucet makers..... 2
Ferryman......... 1
Fringe makers..... 6
Fortune tellers..... 2
Forgeman......... 1
Furnacemen....... 29
Gardeners......... 88
Gasfitters.......... 8
Gas pipe makers... 2
Gas maker........ 1
Gilders............ 11
Gentlemen......... 11
Glass makers...... 2
" stainer...... 1
" cutter....... 1
" blowers..... 8
Glove makers...... 6
Glue " 3
Grate " 1
Grocers........... 533
Gaugers and measurers......... 8
Gold pen makers... 2
Gold beaters....... 3
Goldsmiths....... 18
Gold hunter....... 1
Gunsmiths........ 21
Hackmen.......... 3
Ham curers........ 12
Harness makers.... 22
Hat-box maker.... 1
Hair spinners...... 6
Hatters........... 184
Hostlers........... 26
Horse dealers...... 8
" shoer....... 1
Hucksters......... 53
Hotel keepers...... 79
House movers...... 2
Hod carrier........ 1
Hose & belt makers. 4
Inspectors......... 8
Iron workers...... 3
Ironmonger....... 1
Ice dealers........ 4
Ink makers........ 3
Iron founders...... 13
" rollers........ 12
" safe makers... 6
Jackscrew maker.. 1
Japaners.......... 9
Judges............ 2
Jewelers.......... 37
Laborers..........7864
Loafer............ 1
Last makers....... 6
Linseed oil makers. 5
Lard " " 34
Lamp makers...... 3
Letter carriers...... 4
Locksmiths....... 110
Livery stable keepers 45
Lightning rod makers............ 3
Landlords......... 69
Leather dressers.... 8
Looking-glass frame makers........ 4
Lumber merchants. 10
Lithographers..... 10
Lath maker........ 1
Molders.......... 512
Merchants and traders..........1550
Marble workers.... 6
Machinists........ 255
Miniature painters.. 2
Millers............ 53
Milliners.......... 8
Mill-stone makers.. 9
Mustard " .. 1
Mineral water makers............ 9
Magistrates........ 6
Mayor............ 1
Maltsters.......... 3
Millwrights....... 30
Musicians......... 82
Match makers...... 6
Music dealers...... 2
Musical instrument makers........ 6
Math. and astr. inst. makers........ 23
Morocco dressers... 9
Museum keeper.... 1
Milkmen.......... 5
Metal roofer....... 1
Mattress makers.... 5
Market-masters.... 3
Nurses............ 9
Nailers........... 13
Nail cutters........ 4
Nail makers....... 8
Naval officers...... 4
Nine-pin alley keepers........... 2
Newspaper publishers........... 9
Newspaper carriers. 23
Oilcloth makers... 14
Overseers......... 4
Organist.......... 1
Organ builders.... 12
Opticians.......... 4
Oil makers........ 3
Optical inst. maker. 1
Plumbers......... 39
Plaster Paris worker 1
Pattern makers.... 92
Paper " 3
Paper box makers.. 2
Paper bag " ... 1
Plane " ... 43
Pencil " ... 1
Plow " ... 14
Piano " ... 15
Pocket-book makers 3
Penny postmen.... 4
Physicians........ 278
Printers........... 298
Painters & glaziers. 589
Peddlers.......... 311

Occupation	Number
Pilots	130
Paper hangers	45
Pavers	51
Porters	129
Publishers	6
Perfumers	4
Potters	37
Polishers	7
Portrait painters	11
Professors	11
" Languages	8
" Chemistry	2
" Math'ics	1
Pump makers	5
Pork packers	13
President Gas Co.	1
Produce dealers	10
Paper stainer	1
Pyrotechnist	1
Patent medicine makers	4
Pleasure garden keepers	1
Picture frame maker	1
Press maker	1
Priests	25
Parlor grate maker	1
Policemen	28
ROPE makers	57
Recorder	1
Rectifier	1
Reporter	1
Rigger	1
SILVER platers	4
Silversmiths	54
Soap and candle makers	11
Scale makers	21
Sash "	12
Stove "	28
Starch "	10
Saw "	3
Spectacle makers	1
Ship carpenters	22
Stereotypists	4
Surveyors	8
Stewards	83
Saddlers	176
Stone masons	428
Stone cutters	229
Stone polishers	2
Stone molder	1
Stone quarriers	15
Students	162
Sextons	41
Servants	294
Street commissioners	2
Stocking makers	5
Saddletree "	7
Speculators	2
Stock makers	2
Saw millers	2
Slaters	2
Scissors grinders	2
Saw filer	1
Scene painter	1
Stucco workers	2
Straw bonnet dealer	1
Secretary Gas Co.	1
Steel plate printers	2
Steamboat captains	11
Superintend't water works	2
Square makers	4
Secretary Ins. Co.	1
Stove dealer	1
Shopkeepers	35
Stencil cutter	1
Smelter	1
Surgeon	1
Sail maker	1
Sailors	4
Sugar refiners	2
Stage drivers	5
Surgical inst. makers	2
Salve maker	1
Spice & coffee grinders	6
Silk manufacturer	1
Sergeant-at-arms	2
Spirit gas makers	2
Spindle maker	1
Shoe blacks	6
Stamp cutters	2
Sheet iron workers	11
TOBACCONISTS	219
Tailors	1676
Type founders	23
Tinners	197
Turners	143
Teachers	146
Teamsters	141
Tanners and curriers	298
Trunk makers	49
Township trustees	4
Theatre managers	3
Theatrical performers	42
Tiler	1
Tollgate keepers	2
Telegraphers	7
Tin-plate workers	7
Thieves	42
Translators	2
Type case maker	1
UPHOLSTERERS	45
Undertakers	14
Umbrella makers	7
VARNISHERS	32
Varnish makers	3
Vinegar "	4
Vermicelli "	2
WHITEWASHERS	45
Whip sawyer	1
Wire workers	19
Watchmen	23
Watch makers	40
Wagon "	93
Wig "	5
Whisky "	4
Wood sawyers	22
" dealer	1
Weavers	54
Waiters	74
Whitesmiths	3
White lead manuf'rs.	6
Wheelwrights	14
Wool dressers	7
" picker	1
Wagoners	29
Wharf masters	2
Wood type cutters	4
Wine manufacturers	2

III. EDUCATION.

Public Instruction in the United States, is divided generally into three kinds: that of Schools,—so called—that of Academies, or more recently called High Schools; and lastly, that of Colleges, or when Professional Education is added, Universities. The objects of these three classes of institutions is to convey three different kinds or gradations of education, according to the time and means which the pupils or students have to spare. The Primary Schools, whether public or private, simply teach the *elements* of knowledge, such as reading, writing, grammar, arithmetic, and geography. The object of Academies or High Schools, is to give some knowledge of higher studies; such as mathematics, history, or the classics. The object of Colleges is to afford, what is termed, a thorough classical education, being a course of instruction in the Sciences, the Classics,—Philosophy, and Belles Lettres. To this course, is generally added a supplementary one—in Law, Medicine, and Theology—open to volunteer students for professional life. When a college has classes in these subjects, it is termed a University; an institution in which it is presumed, that instruction is given in all branches of human knowledge. In addition to these means of instruction, there are in all large cities, societies and rooms established for popular lectures, or popular reading; such as Lyceums, Mechanics' Institutes, and Mercantile Libraries. The means of education, whether public or private, are thus *diffused* in the United States, through all classes of people; and there are none, who cannot, if they choose, find access to useful instruction, in almost any department of knowledge.

Before Cincinnati had attained half its present magnitude, and before it had reached middle age in an individual, all these modes of education had been established in the midst of its population, and were in successful and prosperous operation. Her schools have been visited by gentlemen of the highest intelligence, both in Europe and America, and thought not inferior to the same class of institutions in the most civilized states. That the reader may understand clearly the means and system of Education adopted in Cincinnati, the following brief review of its Schools, Colleges, and Institutions of education is given:

I. PRIMARY SCHOOLS.—Of these, there are in Cincinnati, three different kinds, viz.: 1. The Public or City Schools: 2. The Parochial, or Church Schools: and 3. The Private, or Individual Schools.

The PUBLIC SCHOOLS of Cincinnati arose out of a *general principle*, adopted in the first legislation—not only for the State of Ohio; but for the north-western territory. In the ordinance of 1787—for the north-western territory—Article 3, of the COMPACT between the original States and the people and States in said territory; it is declared, that

"Religion, morality, and knowledge being necessary to good government and the happiness of mankind, schools and the means of education *shall forever be encouraged*."

This positive compact and injunction has been carried out practically, both in the legislation of Ohio, and of Congress. The latter has reserved *one thirty-sixth part* of all the public lands for the support of Education in the States in which the public lands lie; and to this munificent grant, has added endowments for numerous universities, of which two, thus endowed, are in Ohio; those of Miami and Athens.

The system of Public Schools, thus founded in the original compact of Government, and sustained by liberal grants of public property, was carried into effect by the Legislature of Ohio, in 1824, and established in Cincinnati, 1830–31. In these "COLLEGES OF THE PEOPLE,"* as they are termed, the children of the masses of the people, of all conditions, are educated. There they acquire in the short time most of them can spare for education, those simple elements of knowledge, which are most useful in common life. The majority of children who enter these schools, probably acquire little other knowledge than that of reading, writing, and arithmetic; but the instruction afforded by the schools is not confined to these elementary branches. On the contrary, the studies of the elder and higher classes exhibit ample proof, that a wide range of study and acquisition is included in the scheme of Public Education. To this may be added, that these Public Schools are literally FREE; those

* Remarks of E. D. Mansfield; reported in the transactions of the College of Teachers.

attending them having all the advantages which the best course of elementary instruction can confer, without price, charge, or special tax.

To describe accurately, the system of Public Education in Cincinnati, we shall arrange the facts under the following heads, viz.: Funds, Organization, Buildings, Teachers, Course of Study, Statistics.

I. OF FUNDS.

The Funds by which the Public Schools of Cincinnati are sustained, are derived from two sources: *first,* the city's portion of the State School Fund; and *secondly,* by a direct tax on the property of the city in proportion to the wants of the schools. The State has granted $200,000 per annum, heretofore, to the Public Schools—and it is probable will increase that sum in future—in addition to the tax, which the several school districts pay, or the other funds they have. Cincinnati has her portion of this general fund; then, she taxes herself, to the additional amount required, for the support of the schools. In the last few years, the city has paid seven-eighths of the whole. Of the city school tax, about one-fourth or one-third, is called the Building Fund, and is permanently appropriated to the repair, furnishing, and erection of buildings. The total amount of school revenue in Cincinnati, for the fiscal year 1848–9, was $65,103; of which, $7204 was derived from the State School Fund.

II. ORGANIZATION.

The Public Schools of Cincinnati are managed and controlled by three distinct sets of officers, each of which has distinct duties, and all of which result in a very simple and easily controlled system. These are the Board of Trustees; the Board of Examiners, and the Corps of Teachers. These are entirely separate bodies, but are harmonious and efficient in the school government of the great body of youth committed to their care.

1. The Board of trustees are elected by the people at the annual municipal elections, two for each ward, and have charge exclusively of what may be termed the business arrangements of the schools. Their duties are to make the necessary appropriations of money; to furnish, repair, and arrange the buildings; to appoint teachers and make rules for their government, with all such powers as are incidental to the immediate government of the schools. 2. The Board of Examiners are appointed by the city council, are seven in

number, and their duties are to *examine* the teachers, in respect to their qualifications and their pupils, whenever it seems to them proper. Without their certificate no teacher can be appointed. To perform this duty with due regard to the various capacities of the teachers, the Board of Examiners have divided their certificates into: first, that he is qualified, as *male principal;* second, that he is qualified as *male assistant;* third, that she is qualified as *female principal;* and, fourth, that she is qualified as *female assistant.* These classes of certificates are a sufficient division for the different merits of those who are examined, and are found in practice greatly to stimulate the ambition of the teachers. The Board of Examiners have heretofore exercised great discrimination in the performance of this part of their duties, and none have received their first class certificate who have not in fact been very superior teachers. 3. *The corps of teachers.*—This body, one hundred and twenty-five, performs its duties of instruction and government, under, and in conformity to rules prescribed by the trustees; so also the kinds and order of books taught in the schools are prescribed by the trustees.

III. BUILDINGS.

The school buildings of the Public Schools are thirteen in number, constructed on a uniform plan, and conveniently arranged for the objects in view. They are capable of accommodating—including both day and night schools—full eight hundred pupils each. In addition, there are two other buildings used for the purposes of Public Instruction: one is used for the Central School, and the other is the Orphan Asylum, where pupils are under the care of the Common School Instructors.

IV. CORPS OF TEACHERS.

The Public Teachers now number about *one hundred and thirty-eight,* being more than double the number employed in 1840, and thus indicating very clearly, the progress of the Public Schools, in numbers and property. Each of the school districts, occupying a School Building, has a Male Principal and a Female Principal, with such number of assistants for each, as may be necessary to the proper instruction of the pupils attending in that district. The number of teachers in each district varies from seven to fifteen ; thus the 1st district has *ten* Teachers, and the 10th district has *fifteen.*

A difference is made in the age, qualifications, and salary of teachers, in proportion to the age and standing of the classes they are required to teach. For small children, young girls are frequently employed; while for the higher classes of boys, men of intelligence and reputation are required.

The QUALIFICATIONS of the Teachers are generally amply sufficient for all the instructions they are required to give. The examination for a Male Principal, is, in spelling and definitions; reading, writing; English grammar, including composition; geography; United States history; mental arithmetic, written arithmetic; natural history, elements of natural philosophy; American history; elements of algebra; the Constitution of the United States; the Constitution of the State of Ohio; the elements of geometry; plane trigonometry, mensuration, and surveying.

The examination in all these studies, beyond, and higher than those of geography and English grammar, has been introduced within the last ten years; illustrating the fact, that the schools have advanced not merely in numbers, but in the standard of education.

V. THE COURSE OF STUDIES.

Some idea of the course of studies pursued in the Public Schools, may be gathered from the subjects above enumerated, upon which the principal teachers are examined. In fact, the schools contain all varieties of mind, at all ages, between four and twenty-one years; and, therefore, require instruction from the very simplest elements, up to the higher branches of science. It has never been *intended* by the trustees of Public Schools in Cincinnati, to *limit* the amount of knowledge to be acquired in the schools. As there are, however, but few of the pupils who can spare the time required for a study of general science, the trustees have provided for those who need such studies, and are willing to pursue them, a Central School, of which we shall speak separately. The general course of studies, as arranged by the Board of Trustees, is divided into *nine sections*, adapted to the ages and standing of so many classes of scholars.

The BIBLE, without note or comment, is read in all the schools, and by all classes capable of reading.

The *Ninth*, or lowest section, is taught the alphabet on cards, spelling, and the primer.

The *Eighth*, the same,—First Reader and oral arithmetic.

The *Seventh*,—Second Reader; outline geography; mental arithmetic.

The *Sixth*,—Second Reader; oral defining; outline geography, and elements of drawing.

The *Fifth*,—Third Reader; written arithmetic; local geography; elements of drawing.

The *Fourth*,—The same; geography of the Western Continent; penmanship.

The *Third*,—Fourth Reader; arithmetic; history; geography; grammar; music; linear drawing.

The *Second*,—Arithmetic; algebra; grammar; geography, and analysis of language.

The *First*,—Algebra; grammar; history; composition; declamation; music; drawing.

It will be seen, from this course of studies in the Public Schools, that without even entering the Central Schools, pupils who remain a sufficient length of time, may acquire a very good common education, practical and useful.

STATISTICS.

The following figures will show what proportion of the youth of Cincinnati are taught in Public Schools, and what proportion of teachers are allowed them. They are taken from the 20th annual report, published in 1850.

White youth enumerated, between 4 and 21	35,004
Colored youth	1069
Number of pupils enrolled in the year	12,240
Number in daily attendance	5557
Number of teachers	138
Number of pupils in daily attendance on each teacher.	40

In 1840, the number enrolled was	5121
" " in attendance, about	4000
" " of teachers	64
" " of pupils to a teacher	62

It seems that the number of teachers employed in *proportion* to the pupils, is much increased; so that, in fact, much better instruction is given. It is found that very few children are in the schools, beyond twelve years of age; but as that number is continually changing, so that, for example, in the eight years in which those who are under twelve, and above four, are passing beyond twelve, there are about ten or twelve thousand others passing into their places,—it may fairly be presumed, that, at least, *two-thirds* of all the youth of Cincinnati,—say 35,000—within the school age, receive some instruction in the Public Schools. If, to these, we add those taught in parochial and private schools, it is probable, that at least, nineteen-twentieths of the youth of Cincinnati receive some elementary education.

COST OF PUBLIC INSTRUCTION.

Total expenditure in the years 1848–9	$67,884
Average cost of each teacher	492
Average cost of each pupil	550

In the above, is included the expenses of buildings as well as schools they being necessary to the school establishment.

I. CENTRAL SCHOOL.

Two or three years since, the trustees established a Central School, for those youth who have time to pursue a higher course of studies than can be afforded by the common schools. In this school, mathematics, natural philosophy, astronomy, natural history; the ancient languages, the science of government, and moral science are taught. In fine, it is a college of high order, and of very superior instruction. The youth of the common schools have thus a FREE COLLEGE, without cost, and open to all who possess talent and merit. This institution has one great advantage over ordinary colleges; for it receives only the *best talent* from the whole mass of youth in the common schools.

We conclude this notice of the Public Schools, by stating the general fact, that the Public Schools of Cincinnati now furnish as good and complete a course of American education, as can be obtained anywhere, except in the purely professional studies.

II. PAROCHIAL SCHOOLS.

The Catholic Schools are the only ones which are strictly parochial, although there are schools under the special care of the Methodists, and perhaps of other denominations. The following are the statistics of the Catholic Parochial Schools, as stated on the authority of this society.

The number of children attending the Catholic Parochial Schools, is 4494, as appears by the following list:—

1.	St. Aloysius Orphan Asylum	100
2.	St. Peter's Orphan Asylum	162
3.	Schools of the Nuns of Notre Dame	647
4.	Schools of the Jesuits	600
5.	Cathedral School	400
6.	Christ School, Fulton	60
7.	St. Philomena's School	300
8.	Holy Trinity School	310
9.	St. Michael's School	75
10.	St. Joseph's School	275
11.	St Mary's School	500
12.	St. Paul's School	275
13.	St. John's School	790
		4494

All these children are taught by 48 teachers, giving thus 93 2-3 children to each teacher, and the entire annual cost of these schools is $13,000.

III. ACADEMIES AND PRIVATE SCHOOLS.

Schools of this class are all private, except the Central, described above. Of these, there are a great number and variety. The following are a few of the most conspicuous.

I.—*The Catholic High Schools:*

1. YOUNG LADIES' LITERARY INSTITUTE AND BOARDING-SCHOOL, Sixth Street. This school is under the charge of the Sisters of Notre Dame, and its pupils are enumerated in the Catholic Schools above. (3)

2.—URSULINE ACADEMY, Cincinnati.

The boys' Catholic Schools are included, either in St. Xavier College, or the Parochial Schools.

II.—*Private Academies.*

WESLEYAN FEMALE COLLEGE, Vine street:—

Teachers	15	
College department	77	pupils.
Preparatory and primary	360	"

This institution is, in regard to both numbers and course of instruction, of a high grade of American female education.

Cincinnati Female Seminary:

Teachers 5
Pupils 100

This also is an institution of high rank.

Herron's Seminary for Boys:

Teachers 11
Pupils 242

St. John's College.—Dr. Colton.—This institution is chartered as a college, but has not, we believe, yet formed college classes. It has a large number of pupils in course of classical education.

Lyman Harding's Seminary for Girls.
Mrs. Lhoyd's " "
E. S. Brooks' Classical School for Boys.
R. & H. H. Young's " "

The whole number of Private Academies and Schools in Cincinnati, probably amount to *fifty*, and number at least, *two thousand five hundred* pupils.

IV. COLLEGES.

There are in Cincinnati, *three* colleges, properly so called:

1. The Cincinnati College.—This is the oldest collegiate institution in the city; but its instructions are now entirely suspended, except the Law School. It was twice in academic operation for many years, but has been twice suspended, and its fine building is now occupied only for mercantile and municipal purposes. The Young Men's Mercantile Library Association occupy rooms in one part; the Chamber of Commerce in another, and the City Council in another. As the property of the institution is quite large, it is supposed that it will, before many years, be applied to its legitimate purposes.

2. Woodward College.—This institution was founded by the liberal bequest of the late William Woodward. It is amply endowed, and gives instruction in a regular course of college studies. The catalogue enumerates:

Teachers 5
Pupils 161

3. St. Xavier College.—This is a regular college, under the charge of the Roman Catholics. It has a large and valuable library and ample buildings and accommodations.

V. MEDICAL COLLEGES.

There are in Cincinnati, *four* Medical Colleges, corresponding to four different kinds of medical education. There are:

1. Ohio Medical College.
2. Eclectic Medical College.
3. Physo-Medical College.
4. College of Dental Surgery.

The first is the school of the regular medical practitioners. The second is that of what is called the Eclectic School of Medicine. The third is that of the Botanic School; and the fourth is a College for the instruction of those who intend practicing Dentistry. The whole number of medical students in the city during the winter is probably *four hundred and fifty*.

VI. LAW SCHOOL.

There is but one Law School in the city; the Law department of Cincinnati College, and generally numbers about *thirty* students. There are, however, many more law students in private offices, preparing for the practice of the Law.

VII. MERCANTILE SCHOOLS.

Not to refer to a number of schools here, some in high repute, in which penmanship is made a preparatory exercise for mercantile employment, there are several schools, three of which are incorporated mercantile colleges, in which book-keeping in all its various branches, is systematically taught, together with mercantile law, or so much of the law as ordinarily bears upon commercial pursuits: not less than 250 pupils are at an average receiving education in this line.

VIII. THEOLOGICAL SCHOOLS.

There are *five* regularly established Theological Schools. These are:

1. Lane Seminary (Presbyterian, New).
2. Presbyterian Theological Seminary (Old).
3. Seminary of St. Francis Xavier (Catholic).
4. Roman Catholic Theological Seminary.
5. Baptist Theological Seminary.

Neither of the last three have formed classes yet; but all have secured a large amount of property, which places them on a secure foundation. The whole number of Theological students (Presbyterian and Catholic), now in the city, probably does not exceed *sixty*.

IX. GENERAL VIEW OF EDUCATION IN CINCINNATI.

The previous review of various kinds of institutions for education in this city, exhibits the general fact, that Cincinnati is provided with the means of education in all the branches of human knowledge. If the circle of instruction were confined to the Public Schools alone, ascending from the Primary classes to those of the Central School, it is found to embrace nearly all the substantial and useful parts of a public education. If we go beyond these, to the numerous Academies and Colleges, we find the whole round of science, of languages, of history, and many of the accomplishments taught by competent and enlightened instructors. Indeed, we do not know that even the oldest, and richest cities of our country afford, in their schools of education, a wider range of knowledge, although the conveniences, libraries, and number of teachers are greater.

The following table of the results furnished above, will exhibit a general view of the number of institutions, teachers, and pupils in Cincinnati:

	SCHOOLS.	TEACHERS.	PUPILS.
Public Schools*	19	138	12,240
Parochial Schools	13	48	4494
Private Schools	50	100	2500
Colleges	3	15	403
Medical Colleges	4	20	450
Mercantile Colleges	4	12	250
Law School	1	3	30
Theological Schools	5	7	60
Colored Schools†	3	9	360
Totals.	102	357	20,737

This table exhibits the fact, that there are *twenty thousand* youth, of different ages, instructed *annually* in more or less branches of

* The whole number *enrolled* during a year, are here enumerated; for all who are enrolled, have received more or less instruction.

† The Colored Schools are separated from the others. The total number of colored youth returned, is 1069; between the ages of 4 and 21.

useful knowledge in this city. This is about *one-half* of all who are of suitable age for education; and when we take into view, that this period contains sixteen years, can we doubt, that in one form or other, nearly all the youth of the city are brought within the aids of education.

FAIRMOUNT THEOLOGICAL SEMINARY.

The Fairmount Theological Seminary was established by, and will be under the control of, the Western Baptist Education Society; a society organized by a Baptist convention, held in Cincinnati, Nov. 1834, and incorporated by the Ohio Legislature, March 1835. Its aims were to embrace within the sphere of its operations and influence the whole Mississippi Valley, and to increase the number, and to improve the qualifications of the Christian ministry. Its object, as declared by the constitution, was "the education of those who give evidence to the churches of which they are members, that God designed them for the ministry;" and its first effort, to provide an institution for this purpose, resulted in the establishment of what is now the Western Baptist Theological Institute, located in Covington, Ky. The assumption of the exclusive control of the institute by Kentucky, in 1848, and the insuperable difficulties that appeared to forbid the hope of the co-operation of the north-west and the south-west, in an enterprise of this character, together with the large extent of country and the numerous body of churches that would otherwise be unprovided for, determined the society at its annual meeting, June 1848, to enter upon measures preliminary to the establishment of a new seminary for the north-western States. Early in the ensuing year, an offer was made to the society by the Fairmount Land Company, on certain conditions, of thirty acres of land, estimated to be worth $35,000, as the site, and for the use of the proposed seminary. A large convention of delegates and individuals, chiefly from Ohio and Indiana, held in Cincinnati, Oct. 1849, recommended the establishment of the seminary on the offered site at Fairmount, and the raising by voluntary subscriptions and donations, in addition to the thirty acres of land granted by the said company, of the sum of $50,000, as an endowment, and for the purpose of erecting suitable buildings. The society is now engaged in carrying their propositions into effect.

The site is on the principal elevation of Fairmount, about a quarter of a mile west of the point at which the northern boundary of the city intersects Mill creek, and nearly two miles north-west of the Cincinnati court-house. It is a spot of great natural beauty, commanding a full view of the Mill creek valley, from the Ohio river to Cumminsville; of the entire city of Cincinnati, as it spreads out toward the south-east; and of the elevated lands environing the city for many miles around. The principal seminary edifice, now (May 1851), in process of erection, is of brick, 112 feet in length; 50 feet in breadth, and four stories high above the basement. It will contain a chapel, library, lecture-rooms, dormitories, rooms for study, &c. This seminary, called into being by the voice, and relying, as it does, on the combined strength of the Baptist denomination in Ohio, Indiana, and adjoining States in the north-west, cannot fail of eminent success.

LANE SEMINARY.

This is a Theological institution, connected by its charter with the Presbyterian Church, and since the division of that church in 1838, under the patronage of that branch of it known as the New School. It is well endowed, having beside its buildings and library, which cost about $50,000, a considerable permanent fund safely invested, and one hundred and eleven acres of land adjoining the city, sixty acres of which were donated by Rev. James Kemper and sons.

The buildings are a seminary edifice, four stories high; one hundred feet in length, and containing eighty-four rooms for students: a boarding-house; a chapel, seventy-five feet by fifty-five, containing a room for public worship, fifty-five feet by fifty; a library room, capable of receiving thirty thousand volumes; three lecture rooms, and a reading-room. The name was given in honor of Ebenezer Lane, Esq., of Oxford, who, with his brother Andrew, made the first considerable donation in money. The institution went into operation in 1833. Nearly four hundred students have been connected with it, most of whom are in the ministry, of different denominations, throughout the United States and in foreign lands. The privileges of the institution are open to all members of Christian Churches, who have pursued studies equivalent to the common college course, and desire to prepare to preach the Gospel. The course of study occupies three years, having but one term in each year, which opens on the third Wednesday of September, and closes at the anniversary, which is on the second Tuesday of June.

Library and *Reading Room.*—The library contains ten thousand volumes, carefully selected. It is the intention of the Board to appropriate five hundred dollars per annum for its increase. The reading room furnishes for the use of the students, the leading literary and theological periodicals of this and foreign lands, and about twenty newspapers.

Expenses.—There is no charge for tuition. The annual term bill for room rent, use of the library, and incidental expenses is ten dollars; board, $1.25 per week.

BOARD OF TRUSTEES.

Nathaniel Wright, Esq.	*President.*
John H. Groesbeck, Esq.	*1st Vice President.*
Henry Starr, Esq.	*2d do. do.*
Robert Boal, Esq.	*3d do. do.*
Rev. Samuel W. Fisher	*Corresponding Secretary.*
Rev. Thornton A. Mills	*Recording Secretary.*
Gabriel Tichenor, Esq.	*Treasurer.*
Rev. Benjamin Graves	Reading, O.
Robert Wallace	Covington, Ky.
William Schillinger	Cincinnati.
John Baker	"
Augustus Moore	"
John Melindy	"
Daniel Corwin	"
Ezekiel Ross	"
Rev T. J. Biggs, D. D.	"
Henry Van Bergen	"
Edward D. Mansfield, Esq.	"
Rev. John H. Hall, D. D.	Dayton.
Rev. Harvey Curtis	Chicago, Illinois
Rev. Henry L. Hitchcock	Columbus, O.

FACULTY.

Rev. Lyman Beecher, D. D., *President,* and Emeritus Professor of Theology

Rev. D. H. Allen, D. D., Professor of Theology.

Rev. George E. Day, A. M., Professor of Biblical Literature, and Lecturer on Church History.

Rev. J. B. Condit, D. D., Professor of Sacred Rhetoric and Pastoral Theology, and Lecturer on Church Polity.

D. H. Allen, *Superintendent,* Cincinnati.

CINCINNATI THEOLOGICAL SEMINARY, OLD SCHOOL PRESBYTERIAN.

This Seminary was organized, May 1850, by the appointment as Professor of Church Polity and Ecclesiastical History, of James Hoge, D.D.; and as Professor of Didactic and Polemic Theology, of N. L. Rice, D. D.

It is designed to afford students in Theology, who are preparing for the Christian ministry in the west, a sound and practical education in the largest sense. It has had twelve students during the session of 1850–51, and will doubtless receive large accessions as soon as its operations become familiarly known to the churches which it represents.

A third Professor—that of Oriental and Biblical Literature, and an assistant Teacher of the Greek and Hebrew languages, will, it is expected, be added to the seminary at the ensuing session.

The students have access, free of expense, to the extensive and valuable library and reading-rooms of the Young Men's Mercantile Library Association.

The session opens annually on the first Monday of September.

If the progress of this institution shall correspond with its commencement, it will become one of the most flourishing in the U. S.

One feature peculiar to this theological seminary is novel, no buildings being contemplated to be erected, either as lodging-rooms to the students, or lecture-rooms for the professors. The professors who all hold pastoral charges, will lecture and hear recitations in their own church lecture-rooms; and the students will be boarded in the community at large.

This will enable them to acquire that knowledge of human nature which is one great requisite to their future usefulness, and still preserve them within the pure safeguards and salutary restraints of the family circle.

St. Xavier Seminary is an edifice recently erected upon the hill west of Cincinnati, and commands one of the best views of the city. The edifice is completed, but the classes of students have not been organized as yet.

Law School:

The Law School of the Cincinnati College was founded in 1833 by John C. Wright, Edward King, and Timothy Walker. In 1835, it was made a department of the college. The number of students each year, has ranged from 17 to 34. The present faculty consists of Charles P. James, late Judge of the Superior Court of Cincinnati; M. H. Tilden, late President Judge of the 13th Judicial Circuit of Ohic, and M. E. Curwen of the Cincinnati Bar. The course embraces a period of eight months; from the 23d of September to the 1st of June. A certificate from the institution, entitles the holder to admission to the bar in Ohio, without the usual examination.

Students can have access, for the purpose of reference, to several thousand volumes of law books, sufficient for all practical purposes, free of charge.

CINCINNATI MERCANTILE COLLEGE, south-east corner of Walnut and Fifth Streets; R. S. Bacon, Principal.

This is an academy chartered by the Ohio Legislature in 1851, in which the pupils are taught book-keeping, penmanship, the principles of commercial law, and are thus prepared to engage as accountants, in mercantile or general business.

The system under which these students are instructed, is both analytic and synthetic. It is the taking in pieces, as a study, a complicated but exact machine, to contemplate and learn the relations of the several parts to each other, and to the entire machine, and the putting it together to make it operate accurately, and without impediment.

This school enrolls 130 pupils. E. F. Burk, T. T. Ingalls, Assistants; H. Snow, lecturer on Commercial Law.

ST. XAVIER COLLEGE—Sycamore, between Fifth and Sixth Streets.

This is an incorporated institution, belonging to the Roman Catholics, with extensive library, museum, and philosophical and chemical apparatus.

There are from fifteen to twenty teachers engaged in the instruction of two hundred and forty-two scholars; of these scholars, one hundred and four are boarders, principally from distant places. The officers and teachers of the college are:—

TRUSTEES.

Most Rev. DR. PURCELL.................................*President.*
Rev. J. DE BLIECK.................................*Vice President.*
J. D. JOHNSTON.................................*Secretary.*
Rev. F. SANTOIS.................................*Treasurer*
" E. PURCELL.
" D. KENNY.
" C. H. DRISCOL.

FACULTY.

Rev. J. DE BLIECK, *President;* Professor of Natural Law and Spanish Literature.

Rev. XAV. WHIPPERN, *Vice President;* Prefect of Studies, and Professor of Mental and Moral Philosophy.

Rev. J. ASHWANDEN, Professor of Hebrew and Sacred Scripture.

F. P. GARESCHE, Professor of Mathematics and Natural Philosophy.

J. D. Johnston, Professor of Rhetoric and Belles Lettres

J. E. Keller, Professor of Ancient Languages.

B. Masselis, Professor of French Literature.

H. Schmidt, Professor of German Literature.

F. Boudreau, Professor of Chemistry.

Rev. J. De Leeuw, *Chaplain.*

ASSISTANT PROFESSORS.

Joseph Caredda; F. Stuntebeck; D. Shepperd; L. Heylen; J. M'Mahon.

Wesleyan Female College, Vine, bet. Sixth and Seventh Streets.

This institution has been in successful operation more than eight years past. The fact that it has 437 pupils, in a city so well supplied with public schools as this, is testimony to its merits, that renders any other notice superfluous.

The officers and trustees of the college are:—

BOARD OF TRUSTEES.

Rev. Bishop T. A. Morris, D. D.................*President of the Board.*

John Reeves, Esq.............................*First Vice President.*

Rev. William Herr............................*Second* "

Eden B. Reeder...............................*Treasurer.*

William Wood.................................*Secretary.*

Wm. Wood,	John Dubois,
John Whetstone,	Henry Price,
John Elstner,	Joseph Herron,
Harvey De Camp,	Richard Ashcraft,
Hon. Henry E. Spencer,	Burton Hazen,
William Woodruff,	John W. Dunham, M. D.,
Moses Brooks,	Rev. J. A. Reeder,
Rev. J. P. Kilbreth,	Thomas Fox,
Rev. B. P. Aydelott, D. D.,	James T. Williams,
John Horton,	Abram Inglis,
John F. Forbus,	George Allen.

BOARD OF INSTRUCTION.

Rev. P. B. Wilber, M. A., President and Professor of Mental Science.

Mrs. Mary C. Wilber, Governess and Teacher of Physiology.

Rev. John Miley, M. A. Professor of Ancient Languages and Moral Science.

Edward S. Lippitt, A. B., Professor of Mathematics and Natural Sciences, and Teacher of Linear and Perspective Drawing and Painting.

Misses Mary A. De Forrest; Emilie K. Tompkins; Charlotte Davis; Electa V. Mitchell; Rachel L. Bodley; Amanda A. Hodgman; Susan C. Conner, Teachers of Classes.

James W. Bowers, Professor of Penmanship.

H. Augustus Pond, Professor of Vocal and Instrumental Music.

Edward Thomas, Professor of the Guitar.

Miss Louisa Fingland, Instructress in Vocal and Instrumental Music.

" Cornelia E. Doisy, Instructress in French.

" Charlotte Cadwell, Instructress in German

Woodward College and High School:—

BOARD OF TRUSTEES.

Samuel Lewis, Esq.................................... *President.*
W. Y. Gholson, Esq.................................... *Secretary.*
Oliver Lovell.
Elam P. Langdon.
Daniel Vanmatre, Esq.

Dr. Joseph Ray........... *Treasurer.*

FACULTY.

Rev. Thomas J. Biggs, D. D., *President*, and Professor of Intellectual and Moral Science and Greek Literature.

Joseph Ray, M. D., Professor of Mathematics, Natural Philosophy, and Chemistry.

Charles E. Matthews, A. M., Adjunct Professor of Mathematics.

William G. W. Lewis, A. M., Adjunct Professor of Languages.

D. Molony, A. M., Professor of Modern Languages.

Secretary of the Faculty...........Charles E. Matthews.

The Classes in the course of study in the Preparatory Department, are divided among the Adjunct Professors of Mathematics and Languages and the Professor of Modern Languages.

Herron's Seminary, on Seventh Street, between Walnut and Vine Street has been in existence for several years, with increasing reputation and widening influence. It has a suitable and extensive library; philosophical and chemical apparatus; a cabinet and various other illustrative aids for lecturing and teaching.

The Teachers are:—

Joseph Herron, A. M., *Principal*—Instructor in Natural Philosophy, Physiology, Anatomy, Rhetoric, Elocution, and Moral Science.

Rev. Charles Aiken, A. M., Professor of Latin and Greek Languages, and Natural Science.

Rev. Erwin House, A. M., Professor of Mathematics and English Literature.

Paul M. Schuster, Professor of Modern Languages.

Miss Lucy E. Herron, Assistant.

Miss Elizabeth Jones, Assistant.

William Thompson, Instructor in Penmanship.

William A. King, Teacher of Book-keeping.

C. Aiken, Professor of Vocal Music.

Edward S. Lippett, A. B., Lecturer on Chemistry.

The number of pupils is 242. This school has always enjoyed a high character.

Cincinnati Female Seminary—M. Coxe and J. C. Zachos, *Principals.*

This institution was established in this city, in the spring of 1843, by Miss M. Coxe. It steadily increased in strength and numbers until, in 1850, it had one hundred and twenty pupils, and ten teachers in employment.

This institution has maintained, ever since it commenced, a higher tone and more liberal scope in its range of study and mental discipline, than most others. The methods of instruction are chiefly oral, making use of text-books as auxiliaries to an elaborate and well digested system of lectures. Of these, as well as of their text-books, the pupils take notes, and reproduce subjects from time to time in extempore lectures or elaborate compositions. The pupil is required to study, pen in hand, all the time, and thus exhibit tangible evidence of progress.

In this system appropriate facilities are afforded for all characters and capacities. It encourages the timid, stimulates the indolent, and gives full scope to the strong and willing in the same class, and at the same time. It repudiates the common-place routine, with its feeble results, which prevails in ordinary schools, and infuses a new spirit into both teacher and pupils.

The grand principle which pervades this mode of education, is, that the pupils are not so much learning a lesson, as mastering a subject.

R. & H. H. Young's Academy.

This is a High School in a very flourishing condition, which is kept on Plum, between Seventh and Eighth Streets, on the second and third floors of a building erected for the purpose, and of rare adaptation to its objects, as regards ventilation and light. It numbers sixty pupils.

The range of studies in this academy is comprehensive, embracing ancient and modern languages, mathematics, and the more important of the English branches. The Bible is a text-book in daily use, and its precepts and truths are inculcated as the only system of sound morals.

IV. SOCIAL STATISTICS.

DWELLING-HOUSES AND STORES.

The first recorded enumeration of the buildings of Cincinnati, was made in July, 1816, when they were found to number 1070: of stone, 20; of wood, 800; and of brick, 250. Of these, 660 were tenanted by families; 410 public buildings, shops, warehouses, and offices, making up the residue.

In March, 1819, the dwellings and warehouses of the city were again numbered, and found to be:

Of brick and stone, two, three, and four stories	387
Do. do. one story	45
Of wood, two or more stories	615
Do. one story	843
	1890
Of these were dwelling-houses	1003
Shops, warehouses, and public buildings	887

The next enumeration of houses was made by Messrs. Drake and Mansfield, for their publication, "Cincinnati in 1826," toward the close of that year, when there were found 18 stone, 936 brick, and 1541 frame buildings. Of these, 650 were one story, 1682 two stories, and 163 three and four stories in height; making an aggregate of 2495 tenements, being all places of abode or business. In all these statements, every description of out-building is excluded, and no additions to houses previously erected are taken into account.

The following list, transcribed from official reports, furnishes the buildings of 1827 and 1828:

Brick, of one story	8	
" two stories	131	
" three do..	77	
" four do.	1	217
Frame, of one story	29	
" two stories	250	279
		496

From this period, the enumeration of buildings was taken annually, with the following results:

1829	270	1840	406
1830	205	1841	462
1831	250	1842	537
1832	300	1843	621
1833	321	1844	735
1834	300	1845	853
1835	340	1846	980
1836	365	1847	1140
1837	305	1848	1305
1838	334	1849	1454
1839	394	1850	1418
			13,295
Prior to 1827			2495
1827 and 1828			496
		Total buildings in 1850,	16,286

which are distributed among the different wards, as follows:—

	BRICK.	FRAME.	STONE.	TOTAL.
I,	690	486	—	1176
II,	1142	160	1	1303
III,	858	489	—	1347
IV,	771	410	3	1184
V,	602	114	4	720
VI,	985	729	1	1715
VII,	790	645	3	1438
VIII,	1056	1024	2	2082
IX,	883	763	4	1650
X,	685	683	2	1370
XI,	419	562	3	984
XII,	479	821	17	1317
	9360	6886	40	16,286

Of the buildings put up in 1850, 939 were of brick; 5 of stone, and 464 were frames.

Of these last, only 50 were put up in the central wards.

The following table points out at a glance our progress in buildings.

Dwellings, shops, public buildings, warehouses, and offices in

1815	1819	1826	1832	1838	1844	1850
1070	1890	2495	4016	5981	9136	16,286

This statement shows that Cincinnati has been increasing for the past twenty-five years, at an average rate, which doubles its buildings every nine years. At the same time, the private dwellings and public buildings, in value, convenience, and style of finish, and the warehouses in the space they occupy in the ground, as well as in their increased number of stories, if we survey those erected during the last five years, surpass their predecessors in a far greater ratio.

The buildings constructed in New York during the last ten years, are officially stated at 16,409. Those of Cincinnati, for the same period of time, number 9505. In view of the relative population of these cities, the progress of improvement in Cincinnati, is three times that of the great atlantic metropolis.

It may be also remarked, that, though there appears a slight falling off in the buildings of 1850, from those of 1849, there have been ten per cent. more bricks laid here in 1850, than in 1849; and nearly twenty per cent. more than in any year previous. This is owing to the greater number of churches, extensive warehouses and business offices on a large scale, which have entered into the erections of 1850.

It is worthy of notice, also, that while in 1815 the brick buildings were but 22 per cent. of the whole, they now form three-fifths, or 60 per cent. of all the buildings in Cincinnati.

There is no city in the world of equal or greater size to ours, in which so large a share of the community are property holders.

The number of individuals, in Cincinnati, who own the houses they occupy, is 5360, who, therefore, constitute more than one-third of the voters. This important fact, is at once the cause and the consequence of the progress and prosperity of Cincinnati.

The hope and prospect of securing a permanent home, is a most important stimulus to industry and frugality, as its possession is to the maintenance of family happiness and the culture of public spirit, and the tendency here is constantly to the division, rather than to the accumulation of city estates.

PERIODICALS.

1. CINCINNATI Gazette and Liberty Hall—daily, tri-weekly, and weekly. Proprietors and publishers, Wright, Ferris, & Co. Editors, J. C. Wright, L. C. Turner, and C. J. Wright.

2. Chronicle and Atlas—daily and weekly. Foster & Corwine, publishers and proprietors.

3. Enquirer—daily and weekly. Faran & Robinson, editors, publishers, and proprietors.

4. Times—daily and weekly. Calvin W. Starbuck, proprietor and publisher; James D. Taylor, editor.

5. Commercial—daily and weekly. J. W. S. Browne & Co., publishers; L. G. Curtiss, editor.

6. Nonpareil—daily and weekly. C. S. Abbott, editor; Abbott & Co., proprietors, printers, and publishers.

7. Volksblatt—daily and weekly. S. Molitor, publisher, proprietor, and editor.

8. Republikaner—daily and weekly. Schmidt & Storch, proprietors and publishers; Emil Klauprech, editor.

9. Volksfreund—daily. Jos. A. Hemann, publisher and editor; Wright, Ferris, & Co., printers.

10. Democratische Tageblatt—daily and weekly. Henry Rœdter, editor and publisher.

These are all dailies, tri-weeklies, and weekly reissues of dailies, in folio, devoted to politics and the publication of current news. The Gazette, Chronicle and Atlas and Republikaner are Whig, as the Enquirer, Volksblatt, and Tageblatt, are Democratic in politics. The Times, Commercial and Nonpareil claim to be neutral. The last is professedly the champion of the working classes. Four of this entire list, are, as may be inferred from their titles, in the German language.

Of the weeklies, properly so called, there are the

11. Western Christian Advocate. M. Simpson, D. D., editor; Revs. Leroy Swormstedt and J. H. Power, publishers.—Episcopal Methodist.

12. Presbyterian of the West.—N. L. Rice, D. D., editor; John D. Thorpe, proprietor and publisher.—Old School Presbyterian.

13. Central Christian Herald.—Rev. Thornton A. Mills, editor, proprietor, and publisher.—New School Presbyterian.

14. Journal and Messenger.—Rev. J. L. Batchelder, editor and proprietor.—Baptist.

15. Catholic Telegraph.—Rev. Edward Purcell, editor; James McCormick, proprietor and publisher.—Roman Catholic.

16. Star in the West.—Rev. J. A. Gurley, editor, proprietor, and publisher.—Universalist. All these weeklies are religious papers, and all folios except the Telegraph, which is a quarto.

17. Western Fountain.—Gen. S. F. Cary, editor; William Mitchell, publisher and proprietor.—Temperance Cause.

There are four weeklies published in German:

18. Wahrheits freund.—Rev. P. Krœger, editor; J. A. Hemann, publisher.—Roman Catholic.

19. Christliche Apologete.—Rev. Wm. Nast, editor; Revs. L. Swormstedt and J. H. Power, publishers.—Methodist.

20. Protestantische Zeitblætter.—Revs. Suhr, Krœll, Gœbel and Grassow, editors; Mrs. Stahl, publisher.—Rationalist.

21. Hochwæchter.—Fred. Hassaurek, editor; William Wachsmuth, publisher.—Socialist and infidel of the deepest dye.

The first and third of these are quarto; the other two folios.

There are also of weekly issues, the

22. Columbian and Great West.—W. B. Shattuck, editor and proprietor; E. P. Jones, publisher.—Literary and Family.

23. Cist's Advertiser.—Charles Cist, editor, printer, publisher, and proprietor.—Family, Historical, Statistical, and Literary.

24. Wεcli Fɷnetic Advɷcet.—Longley & Brother, publishers and printers.—Advocacy of Phonotypy and Phonography.

25. Price Current.—Richard Smith, editor and publisher.—Commercial. These are all folio sheets.

26. Youths' Friend.—Rev. H. Jewell, editor; Longley & Brother, printers.—Sabbath School and Universalist.

27. Dye's Counterfeit Detector.—John S. Dye, editor and proprietor.—Mercantile.

These are semi-monthlies. Of monthlies, there are the

28. Western Lancet.—Drs. Lawson and Mendenhall, editors; T. Wrightson, printer and publisher.

29. Journal of Homeopathy.—B. Ehrmann, M. D., Adam Miller, M. D., and Geo. Bigler, M. D., editors; Marshall & Langtry, printers.

30. Physo-Medical and Surgical Journal.—E. H. Stockwell, M. D., editor and publisher; Marshall & Langtry, printers.

31. Eclectic Medical Journal.—J. R. Buchanan, M. D., editor; I. Hart & Co, printers.

These four are medical periodicals, and the organs of the several schools.

32. Journal of Man.—J. R. Buchanan, M. D., editor and proprietor.—Phrenological and Anthropological.

33. Western Law Journal.—T. Walker and M. E. Curwen, editors; Wright, Ferris & Co., printers; H. W. Derby & Co., publishers.

34. Goodman's Counterfeit Detector.—Chs. Goodman, publisher and proprietor.

35. Bradley's Counterfeit Detector.—T. W. Lord, editor and proprietor; Wright, Ferris, & Co., printers.

36. Golden Rule.—Rev. D. F. Newton, editor.—Disciples' Church Doctrines.

37. United Presbyterian and Evangelical Guardian.—J. Claybaugh, D. D., and Rev. J. Prestley, editors.

38. Pulpit of the A. R. Presbyterian Church.—Rev. Jas. Prestley, editor.

These two last are from the press of J. A. & U. P. James, and advocate Associate Reformed Presbyterian principles.

39. Ladies' Repository and Gatherings of the West.—Rev. B. F. Tefft, editor; Revs. L. Swormstedt and J. W. Power, publishers. Religious and Literary.

40. Masonic Review.—Rev. C. Moore, editor; J. Ernst, publisher.

41. Templars' Magazine.—J. Wadsworth, M. D., editor; Marshall & Langtry, printers.—Temperance Cause.

42. Western Horticultural Review.—J. A. Warder, M. D., editor; Morgan & Overend, printers.—Horticultural.

These are all octavos, and in magazine form. There are in sheets, octavo, quarto, and folio monthlies, as follows:—

43. Magazin fuer Nord Amerika.—M. Gross, publisher.—Agricultural.

44. Ohio Teacher.—J. Rainey, editor and proprietor; Wright, Ferris, & Co., printers.

45. School Friend and Ohio School Journal.—W. B. Smith & Co., publishers; Dr. A. D. Lord, H. W. Barney, and C. Knowles, editors.

The two last, as their names import, are Educational.

46. Young Reaper.—H. S. Washburn, editor; D. Anderson, publisher.—Baptist Sabbath School.

W. Anderson Sc.

B. F. Tefft.

47. Sunday School Advocate.—Methodist.

48. Williams' Western Pathfinder.—C. S. Williams, publisher; T. Wrightson, printer.—General Advertising sheet.

49. Crisis.—Rev. W. H. Brisbane, editor; Wright, Ferris, & Co., printers.—Abolitionist.

50. Illustrated Western World.—D. C. Hitchcock, proprietor.

51. Oncken's Western Scenery.—Professor William Wells, editor; O. Oncken, proprietor.

These two last are pictorials.

52. Dental Register.—J. Taylor, D. D. S., editor; J. D. Thorpe, publisher.

53. Chain of Sacred Wonders.—Rev. S. A. Latta, editor; Morgan & Overend, printers. Scenes and Incidents of the Bible.

The two last are quarterly magazines.

In addition to these publications, the Congress-Halle, the only full report, in the German language, of the debates and speeches in Congress, published in the United States, and the Familien Bibliothek, a reprint of current German light literature, both issued from the press of Henry Rœdter, make their monthly appearance.

CHURCHES AND RELIGIOUS SOCIETIES.

Roman Catholic.—1. St. Peter's Cathedral, south-west corner of Plum and Eighth Streets. Most Rev. J. B. Purcell, D. D.; Very Rev. E. T. Collins and Edward Purcell; Revs. James F. Wood and David Whelan, officiate in the services of the Cathedral.

2. St. Francis Xavier, Sycamore, west side, between Sixth and Seventh Streets. Revs. Charles Driscoll, D. Kenny and Florian Sautois, priests.

3. St. Patrick's, north-east corner Third and Mill Streets. Revs. R. G. Lawrence and James Cahill, priests.

4. St. Michael's, Mill creek, west side. Rev. Michael Deselaers, priest.

5. Christ Church, Fulton. Rev. Timothy Farrell, priest.

6. St. Paul's, Lebanon road, east of Broadway. Very Rev. Jos. Ferneding, and Rev. Peter Krœger, priests.

7. Holy Trinity, south side Fifth, between Smith and Park Sts. Revs. William Schonat and J. H. Ridder, priests.

8. St. Philomena's, north side Congress, between Pike and Butler Streets. Revs. B. Hengehold and F. X. Weiniger, priests.

9. St. Mary's, south-east corner Jackson and Thirteenth Streets. Revs. Clement Hammer and J. B. Eckmann, priests.

10. St. Joseph's, south-east corner Linn and Laurel Streets. Revs. J. H. Luers and Andrew Stephan, priests.

11. St. John Baptist, corner of New and Green Streets. Revs. William Unterthiener, Edward Etschmann and Sigismond Koch, priests.

The last six are German Congregations.

12. Chapel Sœurs Notre Dame, Sixth, between Broadway and Sycamore. Rev. J. B. Smedt, chaplain.

13. Chapel Sisters of Charity, Third, between Plum and Western Row. Officiating priests, from the Cathedral and St. Xavier's.

Cincinnati has been for several years an Episcopate of the Roman Catholic Church. It has recently become an Arch Diocese, the late Bishop, Dr. Purcell, having been invested with the office of Archbishop. His suffragan sees, are Detroit, Cleveland, Louisville, and Vincennes.

14. Protestant Episcopal Churches.—Christ Church, north side Fourth Street, between Sycamore and Broadway. Rev. John T. Brooke, D. D., rector; Rev. Alfred Blake, assistant minister.

15. St. Paul's, south side Fourth, between Main and Walnut Streets. Rev. Geo. D. Gillespie, rector.

16. Trinity, corner Pendleton and Liberty Streets. Rev. Richard Gray, rector.

17. St. John's, south-east corner Plum and Seventh Streets. Rev. William R. Nicholson, rector.

18. St. Luke's, corner Wade and Western Row. Rev. George Thompson, rector.

Right Rev. Charles P. M'Ilvaine, Bishop of the diocese of Ohio, resides at Clifton, one of the suburbs of Cincinnati.

19. Presbyterian Old School.—First Church, corner Main and Fourth Streets. Saml. R. Wilson, pastor.

20. Fifth Church, south-east corner Seventh and Elm Streets. Rev. William Hamilton, pastor.

21. Seventh Church, west side of Broadway, between Fourth and Fifth Streets. A. T. M'Gill, D. D., pastor.

22. Central Church, south side Fifth, between Plum and Western Row. N. L. Rice, D. D., pastor.

23. Welsh Presbyterian Church. Rev. Hugh E. Reese, pastor.

24. PRESBYTERIAN NEW SCHOOL.—Second Church, south side Fourth, between Race and Vine Streets. Rev. Samuel W. Fisher, pastor.

25. Third Church, south-west corner of Fourth and John Streets. Rev. J. B. Townsend, pastor.

26. Eighth Church, north side Seventh, between Linn and Baymiller. Rev. John M. Boal, pastor.

27. Tabernacle Church, south-west corner of Clark and John Streets. Rev. D. D. Gregory, pastor.

28. First German Presbyterian Church, north-east corner of Franklin and Sycamore Streets. Rev. Martin Schaad, pastor.

29. Cumberland Presbyterian, north-east corner of Linn and Barr Streets. Rev. F. G. Black, pastor.

30. REFORMED PRESBYTERIAN.—Church of the Covenanters, south side Kemble, between John and Fulton Streets. Rev. William Wilson, pastor.

31. George Street Church, south side of George, between Race and Elm Street. Rev. Thomas Flavel, pastor.

32. Associate Reformed Presbyterian, south side Sixth, between Race and Elm. Rev. James Prestley, pastor.

33. Associate Presbyterian, north-east corner of Elm and Ninth Streets. Rev. R. H. Pollock, pastor.

34. First Orthodox Congregationalist, north side Seventh, between Western Row and John. Willis Lord, D. D., pastor.

35. Second Orthodox Congregationalist, east side Vine, between Eighth and Ninth Streets. Rev. Charles B. Boynton, pastor.

36. Third Orthodox Congregationalist, south side Clinton between Cutter and Linn Streets. Rev. Benjamin Franklin, pastor.

37. Welsh Congregational Church, west side Lawrence, between Symmes and Fourth Streets. Rev. James Davis, pastor.

38. First Baptist Church, north side Catharine, between Fulton and Cutter Streets. Rev. D. Shepardson, pastor.

39. Ninth St. Baptist Church, south side Ninth, between Vine and Race. Rev. E. G. Robinson, pastor.

40. Freeman St. Baptist Church. Rev. D. Bryant, pastor.

41. High St. Baptist Church, east of city water-works' reservoir. Pastorship vacant.

42. Welsh Baptist Church, north side and upper end of Harrison Street. Pastorship vacant.

43. Baker St. Baptist Church, south side Baker Street. Rev. Henry Adams, pastor.

44. Third Street Baptist Church, south side Third, between Race and Elm Streets. Rev. Wallace Shelton, pastor.

The last two are congregations of colored people.

45. DISCIPLES' CHURCHES.—Corner of Walnut and Eighth Streets. Rev. David S. Burnet, pastor.

46. North side Clinton, between Western Row and John Streets. Rev. Benjamin Franklin, pastor.

47. North side Sixth, between Smith and Mound. Pastorship vacant.

48. Fulton. Rev. William Crippen, pastor.

49. Colored, north side Harrison Street. Rev. Aaron Wallace, pastor.

METHODIST EPISCOPAL CHURCHES, East Cincinnati district. Jos. M. Trimble, presiding elder.

50. Wesley Chapel, north side Fifth Street, between Sycamore and Broadway. Rev. John T. Mitchell, preacher in charge.

51. Ninth Street, north side, between Race and Elm Streets. Rev. George C. Crum, preacher in charge; Rev. W. H. Raper, superintendent.

52. Asbury, south side Webster, between Main and Sycamore Streets. Rev William Simmons, preacher in charge.

53. New Street—colored—east of Broadway, and East Cincinnati Mission. Rev. Samuel D. Clayton, preacher in charge.

54. Bethel, south side Front, between Pike and Butler Streets. Rev. William Langarl, preacher in charge.

55. M'Kendree, Fulton. Rev. Ansel Brooks, preacher in charge.

West Cincinnati District. William I. Ellsworth, presiding elder.

56. Morris Chapel, west side Western Row. Rev. John Miley, preacher in charge.

57. Christie Chapel, north side Catharine, between Fulton and Cutter Streets. Rev. G. W. Walker, preacher in charge.

58. Park Street Chapel, south-east corner Park and Longworth Streets. Rev. William Young, preacher in charge.

59. York Street Chapel, south-west corner Piatt and York Streets and West Cincinnati Mission. Rev. Joseph Gassner, preacher in charge.

60. Salem Chapel, corner Elm and Findlay Streets. Rev. Wm. J. Quarry, preacher in charge.

61. First M. E. Chapel, east side Race, between Thirteenth and Fourteenth Streets. Rev. Jacob Frey, preacher in charge.

62. Second M. E. Chapel, south side Everett, between Linn and John Streets. Rev. George Danker, preacher in charge.

63. Third M. E. Chapel, Buckeye, head of Main Street. Rev. William Ahrens, preacher in charge.

The last three are German Churches.

Right Rev. Thomas A. Morris, one of the Bishops of the M. E. Church, resides in Cincinnati.

64. Welsh Calvinistic Methodist, west side College Street. Rev. Edward Jones, pastor.

65. First Wesleyan Church, North Street. Rev. R. Robinson, pastor.

66. Methodist—colored—Sixth Street, east of Broadway. Rev. L. Gross, pastor.

67. Methodist Episcopal, South.—Soule Chapel, west side Sycamore, between Fifth and Sixth Streets. Rev. Richard Deering, preacher in charge.

68. Union Chapel, north side Seventh, between Plum and Western Row. Rev. C. Moore, preacher in charge.

These last five societies are separated from the regular M. E. Church, on various accounts. The first on the list does not fully accord with it either in discipline or doctrine.

The first Wesleyan Church is Anti-Slavery.

The Colored Society on Sixth Street, are Independents.

Soule Chapel is connected with the M. E. Church South; and Union is a pewed chapel, from which fact, the Ohio Conference refuses to recognize it as one of their societies.

69. Methodist Protestant Church, south side Sixth, between Race and Vine. Rev. Josiah Varden, pastor.

70. Second Methodist Protestant Church, east side Elm, between Liberty and Fifteenth Streets. Rev. Simon P. Kezerta, pastor.

71. George Street Church, north side George, between Cutter and Linn Streets. Rev. Joseph A. Waterman, pastor.

72. United Brethren in Christ, south-west corner of Richmond and Fulton Streets. Rev. William B. Witt, preacher to the English, and Rev. William Longstreet, to the German Congregation.

73. Lutheran United Evangelical, north side Sixth, between Walnut and Vine Streets. Rev. Augustus Krœll, pastor.

74. United Evangelical, corner of Thirteenth and Walnut Streets. Rev. Frederick Hofzimmer, pastor.

75. United Evangelical, east side Walnut, between Allison and Liberty Streets. Rev. Frederic Grassow, pastor.

76. United Evangelical, corner of Race and Fifteenth Streets. Rev. Frederic Gœbel.

77. United Evangelical, Storrs, on Delhi road. Rev. Frederic Eisenloh.

78. Lutheran, west side Walnut, between Eighth and Ninth Streets. Rev. Henry W. Suhr.

These are all Rationalist Churches.

79. Lutheran, east side Race, between Fifteenth and Liberty Streets. Rev. J. A. Wiechmann. Puseyite.

80. United Evangelical, east side Elm, between Twelfth and Thirteenth Streets. Rev. Maurice Raschig, pastor.

81. German Reformed, north side Betts, between John and Cutter Streets. Rev. Hermann Rust, pastor.

82. German Reformed, and French Protestant Church, north side Webster, between Main and Sycamore Streets. Rev. Hermann Bokum, missionary.

83. Lutheran, west side Bremen, between Fifteenth and Liberty Streets. Rev. Frederic Schiedt, pastor.

84. English Lutheran, east side Elm, between Ninth and Court Streets. Rev. Wm. H. Harrison, pastor.

85. Friends, south side Fifth, between Western Row and John. Two congregations: one Orthodox, and one Hicksite; and two houses of worship, one brick, the other frame.

86. New Jerusalem, north side Longworth, between Race and Elm. Rev. J. P. Stuart, preacher.

87. First Congregational Society, corner Race and Fourth Streets. Rev. A. A. Livermore, minister. Unitarian.

88. First Christian Church, south-west corner Fourth and Stone. Rev. Nicholas Somerbell, preacher. Unitarian Baptist.

89. First Universalist Society, south-west corner Walnut and Baker Streets. Rev. Henry Jewell, preacher.

90. Second Universalist Society, south-west corner Sixth and Mound Streets. Rev. C. A. Bradley, preacher.

91. Second Advent Church, south side Seventh, between Mound and Cutter.

JEWS' SYNAGOGUES:—

Holy Congregation, Children of Israel.—Broadway Synagogue, corner Sixth and Broadway. Philip Heidelbach, Parnas, or President; Rev. Hart Judah, reader. Founded in 1820. Members and families, residents, ... 910

Members and families residing in the vicinity, . . . 135

Holy Congregation, Children of Jeshurun—Lodge St. Synagogue, between Fifth and Sixth Streets. Abraham Aub, Parnas; Rev. H. A. Henry, reader and lecturer. Founded in 1845. Members and families, residents, . . 803

Members and families residing in the vicinity, . . . 240

Holy Congregation in Brotherly Love—Race Street Synagogue, between Fourteenth and Fifteenth Streets. Charles Kahn, Parnas. Founded in 1847. Members and families, residents, ... 320

Members and families residing in the vicinity, . . . 82

Holy Congregation, Gate of Heaven—Vine Street, between Fourth and Fifth. Founded in 1850. Members and families, residents, ... 186

Members and families residing in the vicinity, . . . 40

Strangers, not belonging to either of the congregations, residing in the city, ... 630

Recapitulation.—Residents in the city, ... 2849

Residing in the vicinity, ... 497

3346

We have here the population of the Jews of Cincinnati, but no other religious society keeps a full register of its members, so that the number of each can only be a subject of estimate. The following table, which is taken from the registers of the Roman Catholic churches here, affords an inference of the numbers of their members:

	MARRIAGES.	BAPTISMS.	DEATHS.
1846	699	1676	994
1847	725	1829	1041
1848	959	2674	1431
1849	1154	3069	4018
1850	1173	3397	2742

1849 and 1850, were cholera years, which account for the disproportion of deaths during those periods. This table indicates the proportion of Roman Catholics to the community, as 35 to 65, and justifies as a fair estimate,

Jews	3	per cent.
Roman Catholics	35	"
Protestants	62	"

V. PUBLIC AUTHORITIES.

COURTS OF JUDICATURE.

Beside the administration of township magistrates residing in Cincinnati, and of the Mayor, who derives his authority under the city charter, there are four courts held here: the Supreme Court of Ohio, the Court of Common Pleas, the Superior Court, and the Commercial Court of Cincinnati.

1. The Supreme Court of Ohio holds its session here, in the month of March, annually. The constitution and laws of this State have conferred upon the Supreme Court, original jurisdiction, concurrent with that of the Common Pleas Court, in all civil cases at law where the cause or matter in dispute exceeds one thousand dollars; and appellate jurisdiction from the Court of Common Pleas, the Superior Court, and the Commercial Court of Cincinnati, in all cases in which these courts have original jurisdiction. This court has also original jurisdiction, concurrent with that of the Court of Common Pleas, of all offenses, the punishment whereof is capital. It is also invested with authority to issue all writs which may be necessary to enforce the due administration of justice, and for the exercise of its jurisdiction, agreeably to the usages and principles of law.

2. The Court of Common Pleas for Hamilton County holds three sessions annually for the transaction of civil business,—four for the trial of criminal causes. This court has original jurisdiction in all civil cases, both in law and equity, where the sum or matter in dispute exceeds the jurisdiction of justices of the peace. It has also *exclusive* cognizance of all crimes, offenses, and misdemeanors, the punishment whereof is not capital, and concurrent jurisdiction with the Supreme Court of all crimes, the punishment whereof is capital. It has exclusive jurisdiction likewise, of all matters of a probate and testamentary nature—though the new constitution formed by the Convention, but subject to the adoption or rejection of the people in the month of June ensuing, among other changes in the judicial system, directs the establishment of a new and distinct court, to which the sole jurisdiction of probate matters shall be confided. The Court of Common Pleas, upon appeal from the decisions of the

ENGRAVED BY F.E. JONES, FROM A DAGUERREOTYPE

S. P. Chase

UNITED STATES SENATOR FROM OHIO.

county commissioners, supervises the public economy of the county. It revises the proceedings of justices of the peace in civil matters upon certiorari and appeal, determines all contested elections of sheriffs and other county officers, grants licenses, fixes the rates of ferriage, and appoints inspectors of meat, flour, &c.

3. The Superior Court was established in 1838, for the purpose of facilitating the dispatch of business on the civil docket of the Court of Common Pleas. It has concurrent jurisdiction with the Court of Common Pleas, in all civil causes at common law and in chancery, wherein the last mentioned court has original jurisdiction. The three sessions of this court commence in January, June, and October.

4. The Commercial Court of Cincinnati was established in 1848, and for the same purpose as that for which the Superior Court was organized, viz.: to expedite the administration of justice in civil causes. It has concurrent original jurisdiction with the Court of Common Pleas of all civil cases at law, founded on matter of contract, whether written or parol, expressed or implied. This court holds three terms in a year, commencing on the first Mondays in January, May, and October.

5. The Mayor, in his judicial capacity, has *exclusive* authority in all causes for the violation of city ordinances, beside possessing such criminal jurisdiction and powers as are vested in Justices of the Peace.

6. Justices of the Peace.—Of these, there are seven in the city. They are conservators of the peace; their jurisdiction in civil cases, is, in general, limited to the townships in which they are elected and reside; and under certain restrictions and limitations they have cognizance in all cases where the matter in dispute does not exceed one hundred dollars. Their jurisdiction, however, in criminal matters, and in the administering of oaths, the issuing of subpœnas for witnesses in causes pending before them, &c., is coextensive with the county in which they reside. Justices have no jurisdiction in actions of assault, and assault and battery, or in actions of ejectment, replevin, slander, verbal or written; or in actions on contracts for real estate, or in which the title to lands and tenements may be drawn into question.

Supreme Court.—Peter Hitchcock, Rufus P. Spalding, William B. Caldwell and Rufus P. Ranney, Judges. Isaac G. Burnet, Clerk; S. G. Burnet, Deputy.

Court of Common Pleas.—R. B. Warden, President Judge; John A. Wiseman, Robert Moore, and James Saffin, Associate Judges; E. C. Roll, Clerk; J. M. McMaster, and W. W. Warden, Deputies.

Superior Court.—George Hoadly, junr., Judge; Daniel Gano, Clerk; John G. Jones, Deputy.

Commercial Court of Cincinnati.—Thomas M. Key, Judge; E. P. Cranch, Clerk.

Master Commissioners in Chancery.—A. H. McGuffey, A. Paddack, A. H. Lewis, L. Mosher, S. Matthews, J. H. Jones, A. Todd.

Justices of the Peace.—Ebenezer Harrison, Elias H. Pugh, David T. Snelbaker, John W. Reilly, Jacob H. Getzendanner, F. W. Rowekamp, and Peter Bell.

LEGISLATIVE AND EXECUTIVE DEPARTMENTS.

The fiscal and prudential concerns of the city, with the conduct, direction and government of its affairs, devolve on the mayor, and a board of trustees of three members from each ward, usually known by the name of the City Council.

The Mayor is elected biennially, on the first Monday in April. It is made his duty by the charter, to cause the laws and ordinances of the city to be duly executed and enforced, to inspect the conduct of the subordinate officers of the city, and to bring to punishment all negligence, carelessness and violations of duty. He is the keeper of the public seal of the city, issues all licenses, commissions and permits, under the authority of the city council, has power to administer oaths, take and certify depositions, and to certify the proof and acknowledgment of deeds and other legal instruments. An appeal lies from his decisions to the court of common pleas for the county of Hamilton.

The trustees, composing the city council, are elected annually on the first Monday of April. They must be freeholders, and residents of the city three years previous to the election. They determine the rules of their own proceedings, and it is made their duty to keep a journal thereof, open to the inspection of every citizen. They are required to take an oath of office, administered by the mayor, and to elect from their own body a president, who is to preside over its meetings, and, when necessary, act as its representative; and a recorder, whose duty it is to keep in his custody the laws and ordinances of the city. They elect from the qualified voters, a city clerk, whose duty it is to keep a journal of their proceedings. They are empowered to appoint all collectors, assessors, surveyors, inspectors, street-commissioners, health-officers, weighers of hay, measurers of wood, lime and coal, &c. They have the control and management of all the real and personal estate of the city, but are expressly prohibited from banking, and restricted in borrowing, for city purposes, to an amount of not more than five thousand dollars in any current year. They have power to establish a board of health, to organize a city watch, establish and regulate markets, wharves and fire-companies, and to license and regulate public shows. They are authorized to abate nuisances, to appropriate ground for new streets or alleys, to open, straighten, widen or repair streets, to license and regulate wagons, drays, &c., and to levy and collect taxes for city purposes. It is made the duty of the council, annually to publish for the information of the citizens, a particular statement of the receipts and expenditure of the public moneys. For their services the members receive one dollar per day, which is restricted to the actual meetings of the board.

A city treasurer, and marshal, a wharf and three market masters, are elected biennially by the qualified voters of the city, on the first Monday in April.

MAYOR—Mark P. Taylor.—MARSHAL.—James L. Ruffin.

CITY COUNCIL.—TRUSTEES.

First Ward.—Wm. B. Cassilly, E. Underwood, M. B. Coombs.
Second.—William Bromwell, John Whetstone, Jona. Spinning.
Third.—Wm. J. Shultz, Ferguson Clements, Henry A. Gott.
Fourth.—A. W. Anderson, John R. Johnston, J. M. Blundell.
Fifth.—Chas. Anderson, Edward Woodruff, Saml. B. Findlay.
Sixth.—Wm. H. Malone, George Graham. R. B. Moore.
Seventh.—R. C. Hazelwood, J. H. Rothert, J. B. Anderson.
Eighth.—P. C. Bonte, Wm. T. Barkalow, William Hand.
Ninth.—John B. Warren, C. H. Vonseggern, Herman Klein.
Tenth.—Jacob Diehl, And. Giffin, J. A. Stolz.
Eleventh.—Charles Snyder, Benj. T. Dale, John Maholm.
Twelfth.—Michl. Gœpper, F. J. Eichenlaub, D. S. Judd.
Thirteenth.—J. W. Piatt, Benj. Loder, jr., John Ryan.
Fourteenth.—Joseph Ross, Chs. F. Wilstach, Geo. W. Runyan.

Fifteenth.—Wm. P. Stratton, John H. Layman, Benj. V. Enos.

Sixteenth.—Geo. W. Skaats, George George, William Sargent.

City Clerk.—William G. Williams.

City Treasurer.—James Johnston.

City Civil Engineer.—A. W. Gilbert.

City Surveyor.—Wm. G. Halpin.

Port Wardens.—Joseph Pierce, Charles Ross.

Wharf Master.—John W. Reily.

Market Masters.—Stephen Jones, Henry Lowrey, Wm. Moody.

Township Officers.—William Crossman, John Hudson, John Hauck, Trustees; John Minshall, Clerk.

VI. MONETARY.

BANKS AND BANKERS.

INCORPORATED.

Ohio Life Insurance and Trust Company, south-west corner Main and Third Streets; Charles Stetson, President; William Greene, Secretary; G. S. Coe, Cashier; S. P. Bishop, Assistant Cashier; Charles Stetson, Jacob Burnet, John C. Wright, Samuel Fosdick, D. B. Lawler, Timothy Walker, S. C. Parkhurst, A. M. Taylor, W. W. Scarborough, George Luckey, W. G. Breese, Cincinnati, D. Kilgore, Samuel Forrer, S. F. Vinton, in the State, Moses Taylor, Robert Bayard, New York, J. B. Hosmer, Ct., Trustees.

Commercial Bank, 132 Main Street; Jacob Strader, President; James Hall, Cashier; Rufus King, Solicitor; Jacob Strader, James Hall, John McCormick, Rufus King, and David P. Strader, Directors.

Franklin Branch Bank, north side Third, between Main and Walnut Streets; J. H. Groesbeck, President; T. M. Jackson, Cashier; W. S. Groesbeck, Solicitor; J. H. Groesbeck, J. C. Culbertson, John B. Groesbeck, T. M. Jackson, John Kilgour, Directors.

Lafayette Bank, north side Third, between Main and Walnut Streets; George Carlisle, President; W. G. W. Gano, Cashier; G. Carlisle, E. S. Haines, S. Wiggins, Moses Brooks, G. K. Shoenberger, F. Lawson, R. W. Lee, S. S. L'Hommedieu, P. Wilson, Directors.

Mechanics' and Traders' Branch Bank, 100 Main Street; T.

W. Bakewell, President; Stanhope S. Rowe, Cashier; T. W. Bakewell, D. A. James, John H. James, Samuel L'Hommedieu, and F. Eckstein, jr., Directors.

City Bank, south side Third, between Walnut and Vine Streets; E. M. Gregory, President; J. P. Reznor, Cashier; E. M. Gregory, L. D. Ingalsbe, J. P. Reznor, William Burnet, Thomas Heaton, J. K. Glenn, William S. Scarborough, Directors.

These banks discount daily.

PRIVATE BANKING

From the limited amount of banking capital, heretofore allotted to Cincinnati by the Ohio Legislature, the business of Private Banking has become an interesting feature in the growing commercial operations of our city. Among the most important Private Banking institutions of Cincinnati, may be named,

Ellis & Morton,

Corner of Third and Walnut Streets.

This Banking House has a large list of customers among the merchants of our city. Persons who keep accounts at this bank, are allowed six per cent. interest per annum on their accounts, and are charged at the rate of twelve, for discounts—thus if they do not borrow more money in the aggregate, in the course of the season, than they have to their credit, the cost is less to them than though they borrowed at six per cent., and obtained nothing upon their balance.

This house does not vary their rate of discount—it remains invariably the same, whether money be plenty or scarce; but they do not buy paper of transient parties, confining themselves at all times, to those keeping accounts with the establishment.

The sales by the firm, of exchanges on the eastern cities for the season past, were upward of ten millions of dollars—their average deposit account during that period, was about eight hundred thousand dollars—they draw bills and make collections on the principal cities, east, west, and south. Their bills discounted, range from five hundred thousand to eight hundred thousand dollars, according to the season of the year and demands for money.

This Banking House pays a tax on capital used in business, to the amount of seventy thousand dollars, and holds real estate and other assets of the value of about eighty thousand dollars. It was established in April, 1838, and was about the first to introduce the general system of allowing interest on current accounts.

T. S. Goodman & Co.,

Main Street, just above Third.

This is an old firm, that does a business similar to that of Ellis & Morton. Their list of depositors, however, does not include so large a portion of the active mercantile men of our city, but embraces many who have retired from business, whose accounts are probably more valuable to the banker on that account.

George Milne & Co.,

Third Street, between Main and Walnut.

This House deals very extensively in exchanges, domestic and sterling, and in time bills on N. Orleans and the eastern cities.

They allow interest on deposits only, when there is a special agreement to that effect.

Citizens' Bank—W. Smead & Co.,

Main, between Third and Fourth Streets.

As this is the oldest of the Private Banks, so it is one of the most extensive in its operations. Its annual discounts are between five and six million dollars. On the 18th April last, when this sheet went to press, the deposits were $749,274, 7 cents; discounted, $965,277, 57 cents, and assets $1,046,248, 58 cents, mostly of paper at short dates. The rate of discount varies with the ease or tightness of the money market. Six per cent. interest is allowed on deposits.

B. F. Sanford & Co.,

Corner of Fourth and Walnut Streets.

This is a new Banking House, composed of the old and well-known firm of Sanford & Park. Its business is rapidly increasing, their policy of taking *time* deposits and allowing eight and ten per cent. interest on the same, having attracted public attention, and secured to it a large list of valuable depositors. Special deposits for twelve months, draw ten per cent. interest; or eight per cent. for six months.

Langdon & Hatch,

Corner of Main and Court Streets.

This Banking Office is also doing a good business. It enjoys the local advantage of being a convenient place of deposit for a large number of up-town customers; discounts business notes, buys and sells city orders, and makes collections generally. Interest allowed on money deposited.

S. O. Almy's Bank,

Third Street, near Walnut.

This is also a new private Bank, conducted by Dr. S. O. Almy, a well-known and distinguished physician, and enjoying a good reputation for integrity of character, business capacity, and courteous manners. He receives both current and special deposits, and confines his discounts to local paper.

Western Bank—Scott & M'Kenzie,

North-west corner Western Row and Fifth Streets.

Discount notes, allow interest on deposits, deal in exchanges, make collections, and do a general banking business.

The location of this bank, in an important section of Cincinnati, with the reputation of its proprietors for integrity and capacity, will insure a heavy business to this establishment, which has just commenced operations.

FIRE, MARINE, AND LIFE INSURANCE.

Cincinnati Equitable Insurance Co.—Incorporated 1827.

Griffin Taylor, President, J. K. Smith, Secretary and Treasurer.

Griffin Taylor, Elam P. Langdon, S. S. Smith, Joseph Jones, John Baker, John Kilgour, George Crawford, George Carlisle, John Whetstone, H. H. Goodman, R. R. Springer, Charles Andress, Directors.

Cincinnati Insurance Co.—Incorporated 1829.

Office, 4 Front, between Main and Sycamore Streets.

John Young, President; George W. Williams, Secretary.

John Young, Henry Lewis, T. S. Dugan, M. B. Ross, Thomas Sherlock, W. McL. White, Ebenezer Nye, Clement Dietrich, James P. Jack, Morgan Ewing, Wm. Laycock, George M'Cullough, C. G. Wayne, J. M. Dickson, Alexander McKenzie, Directors.

Firemen's Insurance Co. of Cincinnati.—Incorporated 1832.

Office, corner of Main and Front Streets.

J. Lawrence, President; L. Clason, Secretary.

WASHINGTON INSURANCE CO.—Incorporated 1836.

Office, 73 Main Street.

William Goodman, President; E. Henry Carter, Secretary.

Wm. Goodman, Calvin Fletcher, Lowell Fletcher, S. S. Smith, Charles Fisher, Henry Emerson, Robert Cohoon, John T. Martin, R. A. Little, S. C. Parkhurst, Jos. C. Butler, Wm. H. Comstock, Geo. T. Stedman, R. J. Latimer, D. W. Corwin, Jos. S. Bates, Henry Hanna, Gardner Phipps, J. M. Niles, Wm. Hooper, Henry Marks, Directors.

MERCHANTS' AND MANUFACTURERS' MUTUAL INSURANCE CO. OF CINCINNATI.

Office, 11 Front Street, between Main and Sycamore, up stairs.

A. M. Searles, President; B. B. Whiteman, Secretary.

This Company insures buildings, and property in the same, against risk of fire. Also, property of all kinds against the hazards of inland and ocean navigation.

CITY INSURANCE CO.

Office, 8 Front Street, between Main and Sycamore.

E. B. Reeder, President; N. Gregory, Secretary.

E. B. Reeder, J. C. Thorp, J. P. Kilbreth, William Burnet, J. M. Blair, E. S. Haines, George Carlisle, J. H. Raper, H. L. Hoffman, Directors.

EAGLE INSURANCE CO. OF CINCINNATI.

Office, 9 Front Street, between Main and Sycamore.

Insures property of all descriptions against loss or damage by fire; also, against the perils of the sea, or inland navigation.

Isaac C. Copelen, President; James B. Stockton, Secretary; J. B. Lawder, Surveyor.

Isaac C. Copelen, Samuel H. Taft, Richard Conkling, William Wood, S. W. Reeder, Henry Kessler, George W. Townley, Directors.

OHIO LIFE INSURANCE AND TRUST CO.

Capital, $2,000,000.

This company insures lives, grants and purchases annuities, and makes other contracts involving the use of money and the duration of life. Allows interest on deposits for a term not less than two months. On deposits intended for accumulation, such rate of interest as may be agreed upon.

Charles Stetson, President; William Greene, Secretary.

Charles Stetson, Jacob Burnet, John C. Wright, Samuel Fosdick, D. B. Lawler, Timothy Walker, S. C. Parkhurst, A. M. Taylor, W. W. Scarborough, George Luckey, W. G. Breese, Cincinnati, D. Kilgore, Samuel Forrer, S. F. Vinton, in the State, Moses Taylor, Robert Bayard, New York, J. B. Hosmer, Ct., Trustees.

Ohio Life Insurance Co.—Joint and Mutual.

Authorized Capital, $200,000; $100,000 paid in and secured.

Office, Reeder's buildings, Third Street, second door east of City Bank.

E. S. Haines, President; J. W. Donohue, Vice-President; S. W. Reeder, Secretary; W. Richards, M. D., Consulting Physician.

William Burnet, E. S. Haines, S. Robert, J. W. Donohue, H. H. Goodman, J. N. Ridgway, J. M. Blair, William Person, Eden B. Reeder, Wm. Aug. Goodman, Directors.

Applicants will be examined by either of the following physicians:—M. B. Wright, M. D., S. A. Latta, M. D., Tom. O. Edwards, M. D., J. S. Unzicker, M. D., J. F. White, M. D., D. Judkins, M. D. George Fries, M. D., John Davis, M. D., and B. S. Lawson, M. D.

This company will insure lives on either the joint stock or mutual plans. Persons insuring in the mutual department, can settle one-half the premium by giving their individual note, and insurances in the joint stock department may pay quarterly, semi-annually, or annually. The rates are lower than those charged by most companies, and as low as entire safety to the insured will warrant.

Jefferson Life Insurance Co. of Cincinnati.

Capital, $100,000.

Office, Bromwell's building, Fourth Street, between Walnut and Vine.

H. H. Goodman, President; W. W. Cones, Vice-President; L. Benton, Secretary. H. H. Goodman, W. W. Cones, Wm. Burnet, Wm. McCammon, Samuel B. Keys, George Carlisle, A. G. Burt, Chas. Conahan, E. Gest, Chas. Goodman, H. B. Payne, Cleveland, O., D. W. Deshler, Columbus, O., Directors.

Hon. J. Burnet, T. S. Goodman, S. Wiggins, Board of Finance.

David Judkins, M. D., P. G. Fore, M. D., Medical Examiners.

The peculiar advantages of this company, are, that it conducts its business on the *joint stock* and mutual plan. It has a capital sufficient to guard against all contingencies—the directors are well known. The rates of premium are reduced thirty-three and one-third, in the joint stock insurance, being equivalent to a dividend in advance of that amount, on the mutual plan. Notes of the persons insuring, are taken for *one-half* of the premium, where the insurance is for life, and an annual declaration of profits to the insured. The establishment of this company will enable the citizens of the west to retain at home, thousands and tens of thousands of dollars, now paid annually to foreign companies for premiums on Life Insurance, which will be invested under the advice of the above mentioned finance committee, whose character and standing is a guarantee of its judicious application.

Ohio Live Stock Insurance Co.

Charter granted 20th March, 1850.

Capital $100,000, with privilege of increasing to 200,000.

Office, Reeder's buildings, Third Street, between Walnut and Vine.

In the same house occupied by the City Fire and Marine Insurance Co., where all applications for insurance may be made.

William Burnet, President; S. W. Reeder, Secretary; Capt. J. S. Ross, surgeon and inspector; residence, Seventh Street, between Plum and Western Row.

This company is now prepared to insure horses, mules, cattle, and sheep, against death or damage, either by fire, water, accident or disease of any or all kinds. All losses paid promptly within thirty days after proof of loss.

William Burnet, William Person, E. S. Haines, H. H. Goodman, S. Robert, Directors.

Ohio Mutual Insurance Co.

Capital Stock, $300,000.

Office, second story, 9 *Front Street, between Main and Sycamore.*

This old and well known company insures property of all descriptions, against loss or damage by Fire.

Geo. W. Copelen, Secretary; John M. Wood, Surveyor.

I. C. Copelen, H. Brachmann, H. Kessler, Directors.

References.—Hon. Geo. P. Torrence, Hon. H. E. Spencer, Gen. A. Mohr, Most Rev. J. B. Purcell, N. C. McLean, G. M. Herancourt, Samuel Cloon, F. Fortmann.

Fraternal Mutual Life Insurance Company

Office, No. 79 *West Third Street.*

J. L. Vattier, Pres't; J. W. Messick, Vice-Pres't. R. Conkling, I. P. Williams, S. Peel, Rich'd Bates, W. M. Cameron, Hon. R. Moore, Smith Betts, Robt. Cameron, J. Evans, H. S. Applegate, Directors.

C. Moore, Secretary; A. H. Baker, M. D., Medical Adviser.

E. K. Chamberlin, M. D., C. L. Avery, M. D., J. S. Unzeiker, M. D., John A. Murray, Examining Physicians.

New York Life Insurance Co.

Morris Franklin, President; Pliny Freeman, Actuary.

I. S. Dodge, M. D., B. L. Hill, and James Hunt, M. D., Medical Examiners.

This company is on the purely mutual plan, and each person insured participates in the profits of the company

Phœnix Insurance Co. of St. Louis.

Capital, $150,000.

Office, 15 *Front Street, over Messrs. Shoenberger's Iron Store.*

John B. Camden, President; W. H. Pritchart, Secretary.

American Mutual Insurance Co.

Capital $100,000.

George Warnick, President; Alden T. Mallery, Secretary.

As agent of the above companies, the undersigned insures cargoes of steamboats, flatboats, canal boats, and vessels navigating the seas and lakes; also buildings, goods, furniture, machinery and other property against loss or damage by fire, on reasonable terms.

A. S. Chew, Agent.—*Office,* 15 *Front Street, east of Main.*

Mutual Life Insurance Co. of New York,

35 *Wall Street.*

Joseph B. Collins, President; Isaac Abbatt, Secretary; Charles Gill, Actuary.

A million of dollars securely invested in bonds and mortgages on real estate in this city and Brooklyn, and stocks of the State and City of New York and United States Government.

All the profits are divided among the insured.

The company declared a dividend of profits of fifty-two per cent., on all existing policies, on the 31st of January, 1848.

Persons may effect insurance on their own lives and the lives of others.

A married woman can insure the life of her husband, the benefits of which are secured by law for the exclusive use of herself or children.

Clergymen, and all others dependent upon salaries or their daily earnings, are specially invited to avail themselves of a resource whereby their surviving families may be secured from the evils of penury.

Annuities granted on favorable terms.

COLUMBUS INSURANCE CO.

Capital $300,000.

Demas Adams, President; D. Alexander, Secretary.

FRANKLIN FIRE INSURANCE CO. OF PHILADELPHIA.

Capital $400,000.

Office, 3 Front Street, east of Main.

The undersigned having been appointed agent for the above companies, is prepared to insure on lives and property and effects of every description, against loss or damage by fire, the perils of marine navigation, and the hazards of inland transportation.

Terms reasonable, and losses promptly and reasonably adjusted. John Reeves, Agent.

DELAWARE MUTUAL SAFETY INSURANCE CO. OF PHILADELPHIA.

Office, Front Street, between Main and Sycamore.

Wm. Martin, President; Thomas C. Hand, Vice-President; Jos. W. Cowan, Secretary; B. Urner, Agent.

Joseph H. Seal, Robert Burton, Henry Lawrence, William Folwell, James G. Hand, John Garret, Davis B. Stacy, William Hay, Spencer McIlvain, Samuel Edwards, Dr. R. M. Huston, George Serrill, Edmund Souder, John R. Penrose, Edward Darlington, John S. Newlin, Theophilus Paulding, Hugh Craig, Charles Kelly, Dr. S. Thomas, John C. Davis, Isaac R. Davis, H. Jones Brooke, J. G. Johnson, John Sellers, jun., Directors.

This company does business upon the mutual insurance principle, combined with a joint stock capital. The assured are protected from loss at ordinary rates of premium; are free from liability for the losses of the corporation, can vote at all elections, and are eligible as directors.

The profits remain in the corporation as additional security to the assured, and are funded and represented by script, bearing interest. The capital and accumulated profits amounted to over $340,000, in Nov., 1849. Fire, marine, and inland transportation risks taken at current rates of premium.

Washington Life Insurance Co. of Cincinnati, Ohio.

Capital, $150,000.

Office, Third Street, next door east of the City Bank, Reeder's Buildings.

JOINT-STOCK AND MUTUAL.

Board of Directors.—E. M. Gregory, Hon. John McLean, Hon. C. Morris, James K. Glenn, S. F. Cary, L. G. Bingham, John Elstner, J. O. Shoup, G. Y. Root, E. P. Coe, Chas, Goodman, G. L. Weed, Henry Van Bergen, D. F. Worcester, James Dunlap, J. P. Kilbreth, W. S. Scarborough, J. P. Reznor, L. D. Ingalsbee, R. B. Hayes, A. Morrell, Thomas Heaton, J. F. Forbus, G. McCullough.

Board of Finance.—George L. Weed, James K. Glenn, W. A. Goodman.

Officers.—E. M. Gregory, President; Hon. C. Morris, Vice-President; George L. Weed, Treasurer; S. F. Cary, Secretary and General Agent; C. Benton, Assistant Secretary and Actuary.

The Washington Life Insurance Company of Cincinnati, Ohio, are authorized by their charter to grant or purchase annuities, and make all contracts pertaining to life risks.

It has a capital of $150,000, paid in and well secured. The joint-stock and mutual rates are as low as those of any other company. When the premium amounts to $40 or upward, the assured may pay one-half in cash and the other in a premium note, if insured in the mutual department. Premiums may be paid annually, semi-annually, or quarterly.

All the advantages which can be secured by life insurance in any office in this country, may be had in this company. The capital is large and well secured, and the character of those who compose the board is a guarantee that the affairs of the company will be judiciously managed, and the interests of the assured protected.

In addition to the usual modes of insurance, this company have made arrangements to insure those who do not use intoxicating drinks, at rates corresponding to the diminished risk, and lower than any other company in this country.

The joint-stock, mutual, and temperance rates, and all other matters pertaining to the business of the company, may be ascertained by reference to their printed pamphlets, or by application at their office.

Penn Mutual Life Insurance Co. of Philadelphia.

Office, 16 Front Street.

Guarantee Capital and accumulated fund over $220,000.

Charter perpetual.

All the profits divided among the policy holders every year.

Daniel L. Miller, President; William M. Clark, Vice-President; John W. Hornor, Secretary.—B. Urner, Agent.

New England Mutual Life Insurance Co.

Office, 16 Front Street.

Established in Boston in 1843.

Guarantee Capital and accumulated fund amount now to over $360,000.

William Phillips, President; Benj. F. Stevens, Secretary; Benj. Urner, Agent.

Dayton Insurance Co.—Fire and Marine.

Office, 53 Third street, west of Walnut, over Almy's Bank.

Daniel Beckel, President; J. F. Dodds, Secretary.

Directors.—Daniel Beckel, L. F. Claflin, D. A. Haines, Joseph Clegg, John Harries, A. Speice, H. M. Brown.

James S. Chew, Agent.

The Utica Insurance Co. of Utica, N. Y.

Capital, $150,000.

Henry R. Hart, President; John S. Hunt, Secretary.

Issues policies on hulls and cargoes of steamboats, cargoes of flat-boats, and buildings and contents of all kinds.

James S. Chew, Agent. Office, 53 West Third street.

Firemen's and Mechanics' Insurance Co., Madison, Ind.

Office, 21 Main, west side, between Front and Columbia Streets, Cin.

Capital $150,000.

David White, President; Thomas L. Paine, Secretary.

David White, C. S. Lodge, N. O. Williams, D. Blackmore, jun., N. McKee Dunn, Samuel M. Strader, Washington Thomas, Matthew Kemberly, Hiram K. Wells, Directors.

Insure steamboats and their cargoes, flatboats, marine and inland insurance, buildings, merchandise, and property generally, as low as any other office.

M. L. Neville, Secretary; Wm. B. Cassilly, Agent.

CHARTER OAK LIFE INSURANCE CO. OF HARTFORD, CONN.—
Joint Stock and Mutual.

$200,000 Capital, securely invested under the sanction and approval of the Comptroller of public accounts of the State of Connecticut.

Gideon Welles, President; Wm. T. Lee, Vice-President; Saml. Coit, Secretary.

Gideon Welles, William T. Lee, Calvin Day, Tertius Wadsworth, Erastus Smith, Thomas Belknap, James G. Bolles, Chas. Seymour, jun., John A. Butler, L. F. Robinson, Directors.

George Beach, President Phœnix Bank; D. F. Robinson, President Hartford Bank; Hon. Isaac Toucey, late Attorney-General, U. S.

This company presents unusual advantages to insurers, from the following considerations:

1st. The capital being $200,000, is larger than that of any company incorporated by the Legislature of Connecticut, and is all pledged for the payment of losses.

2d. It is all invested in securities of the highest character, which are not only approved by the board of directors, but by the comptroller of public accounts of the State of Connecticut.

3d. Conducting its business on the joint stock and mutual plan, it combines all the benefits and privileges of two distinct companies, with only the expenses of one.

4th. It insures lives at the lowest rates, which can afford permanency to the company and safety to the insured.

5th. Its charter is perpetual.

Agency at Cincinnati, Henry E. Spencer,—36 *Fourth, east of Walnut Street, at Willis & Burt's real estate Office.*

O. M. Langdon, M. D., Medical Examiner.

INSURANCE COMPANY OF LEXINGTON, KY.
Capital $300,000.

COLUMBIAN INSURANCE CO. OF BOSTON, MASS.
Capital $200,000.

MUTUAL BENEFIT LIFE INSURANCE CO. OF NEWARK, N. J.
Surplus, $1,082,618.

BRITISH COMMERCIAL LIFE INSURANCE CO. OF LONDON, ENG.
Capital, $3,400,000.

John W. Hartwell, } Hartwell & Hall, Agents.
A. Mitchell Hall, }

19 *Front, near Sycamore Street.*

NATIONAL LOAN FUND LIFE INSURANCE CO. OF LONDON AND NEW YORK.

Capital, $2,000,000.

Office, 26 West Front Street.

Liggett & Hall, Agents.

UNION MUTUAL LIFE INSURANCE CO.—Incorporated 1848.

Directors' office, 68 State Street, Boston.—Original and accumulated Capital, $200,000, constantly increasing.

Office, Reeder's building, Third Street, over City Bank.

This company is a purely mutual one, and *all its profits* are divided among the holders of its life policies.

Its funds are all invested by a Board of Finance, composed of the best financiers in the country.

Board of Finance.—Franklin Haven, President of Merchants' Bank, Boston; Thomas Thacher, merchant, Boston; Reuel Williams, President of Kennebec Railroad.

E. K. Chamberlain, M. D., Consulting Physician; J. F. White, M. D., Medical Examiner; Baker & Groocock, Agents.

This office sustains the highest reputation at home.

CINCINNATI AGENCY OF THE LAFAYETTE INSURANCE CO.

Capital, $200,000.—Stockholders individually liable.

Godlove S. Orth, President; A. M. Crane, Secretary.

References in Cincinnati.—J. C. Butler & Co., Kuhn, Rindskoff & Co., W. H. Thompson, Esq., P. Outcalt & Co., Scott & Sullivan, A. J. Mead & Co.

This company effects Fire and Marine Insurance on as favorable terms as any other responsible company.

Applications received, and losses promptly adjusted, by Joseph J. Davis, Agent.

CONNECTICUT MUTUAL LIFE INSURANCE CO., OF HARTFORD.

John L. Vattier, Examining Physician; Landon C. Rives, M. D., Tom O. Edwards, M. D., E. Kendrick, M. D., A. H. Baker, M. D., S. O. Almy, M. D., Consulting Physicians.

Agent in Cincinnati, Joseph J. Davis, *Reeder's building,* 53 *Third Street, between Walnut and Vine.*

Insurance Co. of Madison, Ind.

Office of the Cincinnati agency, north-west corner of Walnut and Columbia Streets.

A. W. Pitcher, President; E. G. Whitney, Secretary.

Samuel F. Covington, Agent.

This company was incorporated by an act of the Indiana Legislature, approved January 26, 1831. It is empowered to insure all kinds of property against hazards of every description; and also to insure the lives of individuals. The capital stock is one hundred thousand dollars, and is all paid in.

The principal office and business of the company is at Madison, Indiana, where it is also engaged in the business of banking. The stock is generally owned by citizens of Madison, and its business and management have been such as render it one of the safest institutions in the west.

Ætna Insurance Co., of Hartford Conn.

Annuity Fund, $150,000.

The leading idea of the system adopted by this company is, to ascertain precisely what it is worth to insure a given amount upon a life for a certain time, and to charge precisely that sum and no more; it is attended with none of those vexatious contingencies which are inseparable from the mutual system. It has nothing to do with script, dividends or bonuses, the declaration of which, upon true and equitable principles, is attended with so much difficulty and perplexity; it is perfectly simple, as well as uniform and equal in all its operations.

Risks taken in all the different methods ever adopted by any of the English or American companies, at its agency, 1 and 2 Reeder's Building, 57 Third street, between Walnut and Vine.

Thomas K. Brace, President; E. A. Bulkley, Vice-President; S. L. Loomis, Secretary; J. W. Seymour, Actuary; C. L. Avery, M. D., Medical Examiner. E. D. Dickerman, Agent.

References in Cincinnati.—Willis Lord, D. D., James Calhoun, Harrison & Eaton, James Carter.

Hudson River Fire Insurance Co. of Waterford, New York.

Capital $300,000, all paid in and secured.

Risks taken, and losses promptly adjusted, by E. D. Dickerman, Agent.

VII. WATER AND ARTIFICIAL LIGHT.

CITY WATER WORKS.

E. Hinman, Superintendent.
Theodore R. Scowden, Engineer.
J. R. Baldridge, Secretary.
Charles Balance, and Charles Munroe, Collectors.

TRUSTEES.

J. C. Hall, N. W. Thomas, and Wm. McCammon.

The first settlers of Cincinnati drank from the spring in the hill-side, along and below the present line of Third street, and did their washing in the Ohio river.

As the population increased, individuals, for their greater private convenience, sank wells. Still a large portion of the inhabitants obtained their supply from the river, and there are many still living who associate "toting" water by *hoop* and *buckets* with their reminiscences of a washing day.

The summer of 1802 was very dry, and most of the springs failed. Among the rest, the one which supplied "Deacon Wade's" tan-yard. Without water the business could not go on—not a dray in the settlement.—What was to be done? An inventive genius, James McMahan, came to their relief; with an ax and auger repaired to the adjoining fields, cut a couple of saplings, pinned cross-pieces, and upon them secured a cask. To this "drag," by aid of a yoke, or wooden collar, he geared his *bull*, and with this *fixin'* the water was furnished, and the business of the yard kept in operation.

In 1806, when the citizens numbered seventeen hundred, the first move for supplying them with water was made by William, better known as "Bill" Gibson, rigging a cask upon wheels, and undertaking the furnishing of water as a part of his business. The facility this water-cart afforded, was as great a desideratum, and as marked an epoch in the history of the progress of the comforts of the town, as any subsequent improvement for furnishing the city with water.

In 1817, Jesse Reeder built a tank on the bank of the river, near Ludlow street. By means of elevators, worked by horse power, he lifted the water into this tank, and thence sold it to the water carts.

In 1816, the Town Council of Cincinnati granted the "Cincinnati Woolen Manufacturing Company the exclusive privilege of laying pipe in the streets, lanes, and alleys of the town, for the purpose of supplying the citizens thereof with water," conditioned, "That on or before the 4th day of July, 1819, the pipe should be laid, and water conveyed to that part of the town lying south of Third street, commonly called the "Bottom," and to that part of the town called the "Hill," so that it may be delivered three feet above the first floor of James Ferguson's kitchen, in said town, on or before the 2d day of July, 1823."

In 1818, the Woolen Manufacturing Company, with the assent of the Town Council, transferred all their right, interest and privilege of supplying the inhabitants of the town of Cincinnati with water, to S. W. Davies; and the legislature granted said Davies, and his associates, an Act of Incorporation by the name of the "Cincinnati Water Company," with the privilege of creating a capital not exceeding $75,000. Mr. Davies purchased the property now occupied by the Engine House and Reservoir, and commenced preparing for furnishing the city with water.

A reservoir 40 by 30, and 6 feet deep, bottom and sides planked, was excavated on the hill side, a little south and west of the present site. Two frame buildings were erected on the bank, one on the north, and the other on the south of Front street. A lifting-pump, placed in the building south of Front street, lifted the water from the river into a tank in the building on the north of Front street. From this tank the water was forced up the hill, into the reservoir. The pipes, pumps and machinery were of wood, and worked by horse power.

In 1820, there being at the time no improvements between Broadway and the reservoir, the wooden pipes leading into the town were laid along the hill side, through Martin Baum's orchard, down to Deer creek; on the west side of the Creek, through what at the time was Baum's fields, now Longworth's garden, and other lots to Broadway; thence along Fifth street to Sycamore, and down Sycamore to Lower Market. Here the first fire-plug,—a wooden pent-stock—was placed, and from it the first water lifted by machinery from the Ohio river, and passed through pipes for the use of the citizens, flowed on the 3d day of July, 1821.

In 1824, Mr. Davies purchased the engine and boiler of the steamboat Vesta; and Mr. Joseph Dickinson, after having repaired, and fitted the engine up in the frame building south of Front street, attached by means of crank and lever, two lifting-pumps, of 6-inch cylinder, and two force-pumps of 7-inch cylinder and 4-foot stroke. With these the water was lifted from the river into a tank in the same building, and forced, from this tank, up the hill, 400 feet through 5-inch iron pipe, and 350 feet of gum wood pipe, into the reservoir. The trees for these pipes were cut in Deacon Wade's "woods," near the corner of Western Row and Everett streets.

In 1827, Mr. Davies sold his interest in the water works to Messrs. Ware, Foote, Greene and others, when in accordance with the act of incorporation a company organization took place. At this time, there were about 17,000 feet of wooden pipe, five hundred and thirty hydrants, and less than 5,000 dollars income.

In 1828, the engine was repaired, and the entire pumping apparatus remodeled by Anthony Harkness. After this, the water was thrown through a 12-inch iron pipe into a new stone reservoir, 100 feet by 50, and 12 feet deep. This reservoir was enlarged, from time to time, until its dimensions equaled 350 feet in length by 50 feet in width, and 12 feet deep, containing 1,200,000 gallons of water. This reservoir, having served its day, has now to give way to make room for a new one enlarged to meet the present demand.

In 1833, Mr. Harkness made and put up a new engine and pumping apparatus, which is now in use.

In 1839, the water works were purchased of the Company by the City. They consisted, at that time, of the ground on which the engine house is erected, being 300 feet on Front street, running to the river—176 feet of ground fronting on the north side of Front street, running to Congress street—a piece of ground bounding 500 feet on High street, and 350 feet on Morton street, including the reservoir—1885 feet of 10-inch iron pipe, 7914 feet of 8-inch, 10,634 of 4-inch iron pipe, and 117,421 feet of wooden pipe—with 2639 hydrants, and an income of $31,777.

In 1844, the City Council contracted with Messrs. Yeatman & Shield for new engines and pumps, which were put in operation in 1846.

In 1846, the management of the water works was placed, by an act of the Legislature, in charge of three Trustees, to be elected by the people.

The following account of the pumping power connected with the works, at this time, is from the report of the engineer, Theo. R. Scowden, to the Trustees.

"The engine built by Mr. Anthony Harkness is high pressure, slide valves, and is constructed, in its application of power to the pumps, on the principle of direct action.

"The steam cylinder is 25 inches diameter, and works eight feet stroke of piston; the pump barrel is 17 inches diameter, working same stroke of piston as the cylinder, and the centres of bores exactly in the direction of plumb line. Although antiquated in appearance, the simple and durable arrangement admirably adapts it to the pumping of water; operating with much ease and regularity of motion, and capable of forcing into the reservoir 1,500,000 gallons of water each 12 hours.

"The steam engine and pump built by Messrs. Yeatman & Shield were constructed from a design by Mr. Shield, and put in operation in March, 1847. The steam engines are connected at right angles by an arrangement in the main cranks. The steam cylinders are 22 inches bore and 10 feet stroke of piston, and form their connection with the main cranks by means of wrought iron pitmans. The pumps are each 14 inches diameter of bore, and 10 feet stroke of piston. Attached to the pumps are two air vessels, 5 feet diameter and 10 feet long; the pumps throw about 1,800,000 gallons of water into the reservoir each 12 hours."

The engine and pump built by Messrs. A. Harkness & Son, and completed in February, 1851, were from designs furnished by Mr. Scowden, engineer of the water works. "This is a vertical, direct acting, condensing engine, having a cylinder of 45 inches diameter and 8 feet stroke of piston, with double acting vertical forcing-pump, the barrel 18 inches diameter, and 8 feet of stroke of piston; the air vessel attached is 10 feet long and 4 feet diameter.

"For quantity and quality of material, faithful workmanship, and high finish, it is eminently superior, possessing every essential of excellence to give it a high rank as a specimen of American mechanism; likely to give satisfactory results, when thorough trial and experience shall have fully established its practical usefulness."

This machinery is capable of throwing 1,750,000 gallons of water into the reservoir each 12 hours.

The efficient pumping power of the works at this time, is equal to 5,000,000 gallons of water each 12 hours. The average daily consumption of water in the city, is about 2,300,000 gallons, equal to a consumption of coal, daily, of 185 bushels.

The walls of the new reservoir now in progress of construction are of common limestone. The entire length will be 368 feet, width 135 feet, and depth 23 feet; calculated to retain water to the height of 20 feet, and holding 5,000,000 gallons of water.

The water was let into the east division of the new reservoir, last December, and since that time the city has been supplied from that source.

At this time there are connected with the works, rather more than 45 miles of pipe, and 5700 hydrants, producing an income, for the year ending 15th December, 1850, of $72,500.

The cost of the water works, including the sum of $300,000 paid to the old water company, amounts to $796,000. The city bonds have been issued, at different times, to the amount of $680,000 ; the balance, $116,000, has been furnished from the surplus income, after paying the interest on the loans, repairs, and all other ordinary expenses of conducting the works.

CINCINNATI GAS WORKS.

This, which is now a joint-stock company, was originally the private enterprise of J. F. Conover and J. H. Caldwell, to whom the City Council, by ordinance, dated 16th June, 1841, gave the exclusive privilege of supplying the citizens and lighting the city with gas for 25 years, when the city has the right to purchase the works at an equitable valuation, made by disinterested persons, mutually chosen. These individuals subsequently obtained a charter, granted by the Legislature, under the name and style of "The Cincinnati Gas Light and Coke Company," with a capital of $100,000 ; to which company they subsequently transferred their interest, retaining a large majority of the stock, under the sanction and approval of the City Council.

The Works are on Front, between Smith and Park streets, and inclose about one and a third acre of ground. There are between eighteen and twenty miles of pipe laid, and 500 lamps erected throughout the city. Nearly three miles of pipe are annually added to the existing improvements. W. S. Caldwell, President.

VIII. SCIENCE AND LITERATURE.

OBSERVATORY.

The site on which the Cincinnati Observatory is erected is one of great beauty. The building crowns a hill which rises some 500 feet above the low water of the Ohio river, and commands a view of wonderful variety. On the east are seen in the distance the hills of Kentucky, the river coming in from the north-east; the towns of Fulton and Jamestown, with their manufactories and ship-yards;—toward the north and north east, extends the same range of high grounds, on the most southern spur of which the observatory is erected. The nearest of these are now highly cultivated, and are covered with luxuriant vineyards, and orchards of choice fruit. The village of Mount Auburn presents an elegant appearance, especially when lighted by the first rays of the morning sun. Looking west from the summit of the Observatory, the entire city of Cincinnati is spread out before the beholder, as upon a map. There is scarcely a building in the whole city which may not be distinguished from this elevated position. The river is followed by the eye toward the south-west, its continuity occasionally broken by the interposition of high hills;—on the south and south-west, are seen the Kentucky cities of Newport and Covington, separated by the Licking river, whose rich valley indents the country for more than twenty miles.

Such is the character of the position selected for the erection of the first great Astronomical Observatory ever erected by the *people*. Four acres were presented on the summit of this hill, to the Astronomical Society, by N. Longworth; this lot of ground to be forever exclusively devoted to the uses of the Astronomical Observatory. From so elevated a position, there is, of course, an uninterrupted horizon; so that the moment an object ascends above that line, it may be brought within the sweep of the telescope. The height of the observatory above the river and above the plane on which the city is built, frees the observers from the annoyance of smoke, heated atmosphere, and fogs, which would be most serious obstacles on a lower level.

The Observatory building is constructed in such manner as to accommodate the family of the Director, as well as for scientific uses, and for the instruments. The main building, erected of stone, quarried from the hill, presents a front of 80 feet, and rises two stories and a half high on the wings, and three in the centre. The front is ornamented by a Grecian Doric portico, from whose roof there is a beautiful look out on the surrounding country. This portico, in connection with the main building and the transit building, in the rear or on the east side, constitutes a structure whose ground-plan is in the shape of a cross: when viewed from any point north or south, from which the parts of the entire structure may be taken in, the edifice presents an appearance of massiveness and solidity which harmonizes admirably with the known uses to which it is applied.

Through the centre of the main building, and founded on the natural rock, rises a pier of grouted masonry eight feet square, entirely insulated from the floors through which it passes, to furnish a permanent and immovable basis for the great equatorial telescope, the chief instrument of the Observatory. This magnificent telescope, one of the largest and most perfect in the world, was made at the Frauenhofer Institute, Munich, by Messrs. Mertz & Mahler, so distinguished for the perfection of their optical instruments.

The focal length is about 17½ feet; the diameter of the object glass, twelve inches; bearing magnifying powers varying from 100 times up to 1400 times. Clock-work is attached to the ponderous mass of the telescope and all its machinery and circles, by which its mass, weighing some 2500 lbs., is moved with such admirable accuracy, that an object under examination may be followed by the telescope at the will of the observer. This stupendous instrument, mounted on a stone pedestal of great strength and graceful figure, rises, when directed to the zenith, some 20 feet above the floor of the room in which it is located.

This room is surmounted by a roof of peculiar structure, and so arranged that a portion of the vertical wall and the roof, strongly framed together and mounted on wheels on a railway track, may, by a single person, be rolled either north or south, when the entire heavens falls within the sweep of the telescope. It is truly wonderful to behold the admirable manner in which this huge instrument is balanced and counterpoised, until the astronomer handles it with as much facility as if it were divested of gravity or were afloat on some liquid surface.

ENGRAVED BY F. E. JONES FROM A DAGUERREOTYPE

Yours truly

O. M. Mitchel

One story lower, and in the transit-room, is mounted the transit telescope, the property of the U. S. Coast Survey, and furnished to the Observatory by the present Superintendent, Dr. A. D. Bache. Connected with this instrument, is an admirable sidereal clock, by Molyneux, of London, and presented to the Observatory by Wilson McGrew of our city. Here also is found the new machinery invented and constructed by the present Director of the Observatory, Professor O. M. Mitchel: it consists of two instruments of entirely different construction, the one intended to record the observations of right ascension; the other, observations of difference in declination or of N. P. Distance.

It would be quite impossible, in the compass of this notice, to give any just idea of this wonderfully delicate apparatus. By means of the electro-magnet, the clock is made to record its own beats, with surprising beauty, on a disc revolving with uniform velocity on a vertical axis. This disc, covered with paper or metal, receives a minute dot, struck into it by a stylus, driven by a magnet, whose operating electric circuit is closed at each alternate beat, by a delicate vibrating wire attached to the pendulum of the clock by an actual *spider's web;* thus, at each alternate vibration of the pendulum, the circuit is closed, and the second is entered, magnetically, on the revolving disc. At the close of each revolution, the disc moves itself forward about the tenth of an inch, without check or interference with the uniformity of its angular motion, and a new circumference of time dots, commences to be recorded. On the time scale thus perpetually forming, the observer can enter, magnetically, by the touch of a key, the observed instant of transit of any star or other object across the meridian wires of his telescope.

These entries are subsequently read from the disc, even down to the *thousandth of one second of time.*

This apparatus has now been in use for nearly two years, and has furnished observations of accuracy never before reached by any previous instruments. The rapidity, facility, and accuracy attainable by these observations are truly admirable. Results have made it manifest, that the errors, from all sources, were only to be found among the *hundredths* of one second of time. The inventor hopes to banish the errors from this region even, and drive them to the thousandth of a second.

The declination apparatus is also entirely new, and seems to possess astonishing power. It releases the observer from the necessity of reading any circles or other means of identifying his instrumental positions, and enables him, at a single transit, to record as many as *ten* observations for declination—even among the swiftly moving bodies of the equator. This gives an advantage, all other things being equal, of ten to one over the old methods of observing. This instrument has been in use about a year, and is yet incomplete in some of its refined details, but has produced remarkable results, and gives the highest promise, when mechanically complete in all its parts.

Such are the appliances for work in the Cincinnati Observatory. There is no endowment, and the present director has no salary or other compensation, and no assistance out of his own immediate family. The great telescope has been principally employed in the measure of the newly discovered and previously discovered double and multiple stars, and in figuring remarkable clusters and nebulæ.

The other apparatus and transit instrument are employed in redetermining the places of the N. A. standard stars, and other kindred observations.

It is only to be regretted that an enterprise, so nobly conceived, and so well carried out, could not now be permanently endowed, that its instruments might be worked day and night to their utmost capacity.

THE CINCINNATI HORTICULTURAL SOCIETY.

THIS flourishing and useful society was formed in 1843, as the following extracts from its publications will show:

The first meeting with reference to the formation of the Cincinnati Horticultural Society, was held at the house of Robert Buchanan, on the evening of the 17th February, 1843. The following persons were present:—Robert Buchanan, A. H. Ernst, M. Flagg, S. C. Parkhurst, J. B. Russell, H. Probasco, V. C. Marshall, John Locke, George Graham and Thomas Winter. A. H. Ernst was called to the chair, and J. B. Russell appointed Secretary.

On motion, J. B. Russell, M. Flagg, and R. Buchanan, were appointed a committee to prepare a constitution and by-laws of the Society. At a subsequent meeting, they made a report, which was accepted; and the following persons were elected officers for that year:

Robert Buchanan, President; Melzer Flagg, 1st Vice-President; Andrew H. Ernst, 2d Vice-President; L. G. Bingham, 3d Vice-President; S. C. Parkhurst, Treasurer; John B. Russell, Corresponding Secretary; J. G. Anthony, Recording Secretary.

Elisha Brigham, George Graham, George W. Neff, Jacob Hoffner, Thomas Winter, William Smith, John Sayers,—Council.

STANDING COMMITTEES.

On the characters of Fruits and their Synonyms.—A. H. Ernst, M. Flagg, Wm. Smith, John Sayers, Stephen Mosher.

On Flowers.—R. Buchanan, John Sayers, Jacob Hoffner, Gabriel Sleath, S. S. Jackson.

On Vegetables.—G. W. Neff, J. B. Russell, E. B. Reeder, Chas. W. Elliot, John Frazer.

On Entomology, as connected with insect depredations on Fruit and Shade Trees.—John P. Foote, J. A. Warder, R. Buchanan, Charles Cheney, Charles W. Elliot, E. J. Hooper, M. Flagg, Daniel Gano, William Price, John G. Anthony, George Graham, James H. Perkins, Dr. N. B. Shaler.

During the spring, summer and autumn of 1843, the society held meetings nearly every Saturday, in the lower room, on Third Street, between Walnut and Vine, formerly occupied as the Post Office. The number of its members increased very fast, and a great interest in its objects was created. A correspondence was opened with distinguished horticulturists in different parts of the Union; new fruits were thus brought to light, and seeds and scions of superior varieties were exchanged and disseminated. The exhibitions of flowers in the spring, and of fruits, vegetables, and American wine in the autumn, were crowded with visitors, and a great impulse thus given to the culture of fruits and flowers.

From this humble beginning, it has prospered beyond the fondest anticipations of its most ardent friends, and now, in the eighth year, numbers near seven hundred members. Its receipts for the past year were over $1900, and expenditures near $1800; about $1200 being paid out in premiums for fruits and flowers, and horticultural designs and decorations.

That the society has been productive of much good, there can be no doubt; the great improvement in our fruit and flower market, which we notice every year, is the strongest evidence of its utility, while the growing taste for the beautiful and innocent pursuits of horticulture, gives pleasing occupation and a delightful hobby, to the leisure hours of many an amateur in our city and vicinity, affording at the same time, an extensive and liberal market for the nurseryman and florist.

The semi-annual exhibitions of this society, particularly the autumnal, have been rich and varied, and highly creditable to our infant western institutions. Gentlemen from the east have acknowledged that our exhibitions compare favorably with the best of those across the mountains, and in many fruits, even excel them.

Strong efforts are now being made to erect a horticultural hall, upon an enlarged scale, and in a style which shall be a credit to the society and an ornament to the city; and from the liberal encouragement already met with, the object will, no doubt, be accomplished. Long may our citizens continue to cultivate a taste for these useful and ennobling pursuits, so eminently calculated to mend the manners and improve the heart.

The officers of the society for the present year, are:—

A. H. Ernst, President; William Resor, M. S. Wade, N. B. Shaler, Vice-Presidents; John A. Warder, Recording Secretary; George Graham, Corresponding Secretary; William Resor, Treasurer.

Executive Council.—John P. Foote, M. McWilliams, Wm. Orange, S. S. Jackson, G. Sleath, Jos. Longworth, and S. Mosher.

STANDING COMMITTEES FOR THE YEAR.

Fruits.—M. McWilliams, M. S. Wade, S. M. Carter, Wm. Orange, John G. Anthony.

Flowers.—N. B. Shaler, James Hall, Robert Neale, Chas. Patton, Thomas Salter.

Vegetables.—John P. Foote, A. Worthington, Robert M. Moore, George Graham, Henry Ives.

Library.—John P. Foote, John A. Warder, John G. Anthony.

MEDICAL COLLEGE OF OHIO.

This Institution was first chartered, and placed in the hands of a Board of Trustees, in 1819, and went fully into operation in 1825.

The State furnished the means by which a spacious edifice was erected. It contains large lecture rooms and an amphitheatre, together with apartments for the library, as well as private rooms for the professors, and apartments well fitted up for pursuing, privately, the study of anatomy. The library contains upward of two thousand volumes, of well-selected standard works, purchased by the State, and for the use of the students of the college. The cabinet belonging to the Anatomical department is supplied with all the materials necessary for acquiring a minute and thorough knowledge of the human frame. These consist of detached bones, of wired and natural skeletons, and of dried preparations, to exhibit the muscles, blood-vessels, nerves, lymphatics, etc., etc. In addition, are very accurate wooden models of the small bones, and representations in wax, of the soft and more delicate structures.

The cabinet of Comparative Anatomy, is supposed to be supplied more extensively, and with rarer specimens, than any other in the Union. Beside perfect skeletons of foreign and American animals, birds, etc., there is an immense number of detached crania, from the elephant and hippopotamus to the minute orders.

The cabinet belonging to the Surgical department has been formed at great expense, by the labor of more than thirty-five years. It contains a large number of very rare specimens, among which are sections of the thigh-bones, that establish as fact, what European surgeons have long denied, viz : the possibility, by proper treatment, of a re-union, after a fracture, of the neck of these bones. There are near five hundred specimens of diseased bones alone.

Of the department of Chemistry, it seems hardly necessary that we should speak. The known industry and extraordinary enthusiasm, in every department of the physical sciences, of the gentleman who fills the chemical chair, are the strongest guarantees, that for the most full and efficient performance of the peculiar duties allotted to him, nothing that was necessary has been left unprovided. Many of his instruments are the result of his own powers of invention ; but the most important were selected by himself, in Europe, and purchased at great cost.

Belonging to the chair of *Materia Medica,* is a large collection of indigenous plants, their extracts and other medicinal preparations, together with all the foreign articles used in practice ; and the various topics embraced in the department of *Obstetrics* and diseases of women and children, are elucidated, in part, by numerous and exceedingly interesting wax casts, most of which were obtained in Paris, of some of the best French artists.

The students have the advantage of access to the Commercial

Hospital, where they witness the medical and surgical treatment of the patients by members of the faculty. This is an invaluable privilege, and affords the students great facilities for acquiring a correct knowledge of diseases and their treatment. There are in the hospital, annually, 3000 patients; and during the two winters usually devoted to attendance upon lectures, as great a variety of diseases is presented to the student, as generally falls under the observation of a physician during a lifetime of practice. But what is of first importance to the western student, is the fact, that through the facilities afforded by the connection spoken of, he can acquire a perfect knowledge of those diseases which he will be called upon to treat, on his first introduction into practice. A further advantage of this connection, also, is that students have the opportunity of witnessing operations, by one, long and successfully acquainted with the practical use of the knife.

In the prosecution of *Practical Anatomy*, also, every facility is afforded them that can be obtained at similar institutions of the country.

At no period during its entire history have the prospects of the school been more encouraging. The utmost harmony prevails in the faculty, and the present class is as large as any which has ever attended, with one exception. There are, at present, one hundred and eighty-six students.

Board of Trustees.—John P. Foote, President; J. L. Vattier, M.D., Secretary; A. N. Riddle, Treasurer; William Mount, M. D., Jacob Strader, E. C. Roll, E. B. Reeder, G. W. Holmes, Miles Greenwood, Flamen Ball, B. F. Tefft, D. D.

Faculty.—H. W. Baxley, M. D., Professor of Anatomy.

John Locke, M. D., Professor of Chemistry and Pharmacy.

L. M. Lawson, M. D., Professor of Physiology and Pathology.

T. O. Edwards, M. D., Professor of Materia Medica and Therapeutics, and Medical Jurisprudence.

R. D. Mussey, M. D., Professor of Surgery.

Landon C. Rives, M. D., Professor of Obstetrics and the Diseases of women and children.

John Bell, M. D., Professor of Theory and Practice of Medicine.

John Davis, M. D., Demonstrator of Anatomy.

L. M. Lawson, M. D., Dean.

ECLECTIC MEDICAL INSTITUTE

Chartered in 1845.

Z. Freeman, M. D., Professor of Anatomy.

Jos. R. Buchanan, M. D., Physiology and Institutes of Medicine.

Lorenzo E. Jones, M. D., Materia Medica and Therapeutics.

R. S. Newton, M. D., Surgery.

Benjamin L. Hill, M. D., Obstetrics.

I. Gibson Jones, M. D., Theory and Practice of Medicine.

J. Milton Sanders, Chemistry and Pharmacy.

This institution had enrolled upon its list of students, for the session of 1850–51, one hundred and ninety names.

PHYSO-MEDICAL COLLEGE.

Corner of Fifth and Western Row.

Chartered 1850.

Faculty.—	E. H. Stockwell,	M. D.,	Professor of	Anatomy.
"	J. A. Powers,	"	"	Surgery.
"	E. Morgan Parritt,	"	"	Chemistry.
"	Joseph Brown,	"	"	Materia Medica.
"	R. C. Carter,	"	"	Obstetrics.
"	H. F. Johnson,	"	"	Practice of Med.

THE OHIO COLLEGE OF DENTAL SURGERY.

Chartered in 1845.

Board of Trustees.—B. P. Aydelotte, D. D., President; Israel Dodge, M. D., Secretary; Robert Buchanan, Esq., Calvin Fletcher, Esq., William Johnston, Cincinnati, G. S. P. Hempstead, M. D., Portsmouth, Samuel Martin, M. D., Xenia, James P. Hildreth, M. D., Marietta, Ohio.

This Institution has matriculated seventy students, and conferred degrees on forty of them. The Faculty stands:

James Taylor, M. D., D.D.S., Prof. Principles and Practice of Dental Surgery.

George Mendenhall, M. D., Prof. Pathology and Therapeutics.

Thomas Wood, M. D., Prof. Anatomy and Physiology; John Allen, D. D. S., Prof. Operative Mechanical Dentistry; G. L. Van Emon, A.M., D. D. S., Lecturer on Dental Chemistry and Demonstrator of Operative and Mechanical Dentistry.

OHIO MECHANICS' INSTITUTE.

Incorporated 1829.

THIS spacious and well proportioned edifice is at the intersection of Sixth and Vine Streets, and owes its construction to the public spirit of Miles Greenwood and a few other whole-souled mechanics, who have contributed liberally of their time, personal labors, and pecuniary contributions, to erect this highly creditable temple to the mechanic arts. Within its walls the various mechanics' fairs are annually held. Scientific knowledge is taught here by lectures, illustrated by extensive philosophical and electrical apparatus, and mineralogical cabinet; and impressed on the minds of the members by the use of a copious and valuable library, of more than five thousand volumes; and reading-room periodicals of more than forty, of first class pubiic, scientific and philosophical journals of the day.

There are twelve hundred members—five hundred of whom use the library. Of these last, more than three hundred are minors.

Courses of lectures weekly, have been held hitherto, throughout the winter months. These will be hereafter extended to three lectures in each week, during that season.

The edifice is four stories high, and Gothic in its style. Dimensions, 90 feet on Vine, by 75 on Sixth; main entrance on Sixth. The walls are of brick, 85 feet high from the ground floor to top of cornice. The door and window sills are of cast iron, as are also the columns supporting the fronts. The exterior walls are finished with stucco imitation of stone, in the most durable manner. The entire height to the top of the roof is 100 feet, in the centre of which, is a cupola or lookout; and, as the building is situated on the most elevated point of land between the canal and river, from it will be afforded one of the finest views of the city, Covington and Newport, to be had elsewhere, except from the hills themselves.

The interior arrangements are also very complete. The lower part on Vine is occupied as stores, and the corner on Sixth, with its two fronts on Vine and Sixth, as fitted out by W. B. Chapman, is one of the best furnished and arranged drug-stores in Cincinnati. The large room next west of the main entrance, is devoted to the exclusive use of mechanics, as a show room for manufactured articles of home fabrication, embracing every department of the mechanic arts. Here, for a slight rental, the artisan can deposit for inspection or sale, such of the creations of his genius as he desires to bring before the community, both for his own and their benefit.

The second story is occupied as a library, reading and class rooms, exclusively by the Institute.

The third story contains the Institute hall, 90 by 65 feet, with convenient anterooms attached.

The fourth story, halls for the I. O. of O. F.

The building is warmed with hot air, and lighted with gas. Estimated cost $50,000.

Officers.—M. Greenwood, President; R. C. Philips, Vice-President; Wm. G. Neilson, Recording Secretary; W. B. Chapman, Corresponding Secretary; L. T. Wells, Treasurer; Jos. B. Ladd, Librarian.

YOUNG MEN'S MERCANTILE LIBRARY ASSOCIATION.

Officers for 1851.—Joseph C. Butler, President; James Lupton, Vice President; Robert L. Fabian, Corresponding Secretary; H. D. Huntington, Recording Secretary; William H. Neff, Treasurer. Charles R. Fosdick, B. P. Hinman, F. W. Ridgely, L. A. Ostram, Samuel Robbins, Directors; Charles E. Cist, Librarian, George W. Frazer, Assistant Librarian.

Library and reading-rooms in the Cincinnati College, on Walnut street; open every day, Sundays excepted, from eight o'clock in the morning until ten in the evening.

This association was first organized by the election of officers and the adoption of a constitution and by-laws, April 18, 1835.

At the commencement of the present year, the number of members, was sixteen hundred and twenty-three. Two hundred and thirty-four names have been since added to the list. Of this number, one hundred and sixty-five are active, and sixty-nine, honorary.

During the year, twelve hundred and ninety-two volumes have been added to the library; eleven hundred and fifty-nine by purchase, one hundred and thirty-three by donation, together with thirty-two volumes of bound periodicals and magazines; making the total number of volumes now in the library, eleven thousand and ninety-six, embracing the standard works in the various departments of literature, science, and art, and a copious selection from current literature of those works that are attractive, and interesting, and

10

beneficial in their tendency, and will be read by the great majority of readers, while graver works remain upon the shelves.

The Reading Room constitutes one of the most attractive features of the association. Here are regularly received fifteen Quarterly, one Bi-Monthly, thirty-two Monthly, and two Weekly magazines; and the list of newspapers extends to ninety-one, embracing those from every part of our own country, and the most interesting from foreign lands.

Lectures, on various popular subjects, by gentlemen of distinguished reputation from all parts of the United States, are delivered weekly, throughout the winter, and form an interesting feature of this Institution.

The Library and Reading Rooms are much frequented by strangers; of whom there are always great numbers visiting Cincinnati.

The current expenses, as well as the constant additions made to the library shelves and reading desks, are amply met by the contributions of the members, and revenue from lectures; which last year amounted to $5,113 12 cents; an amount highly creditable to the Institution and its supporters.

There are few objects in the city which so forcibly impress strangers in general as this Library, and the Reading Rooms, its adjuncts.

APPRENTICES' LIBRARY.

This Institution was founded, February 8, 1821, and was established by public contributions of books and money. It contains two thousand two hundred volumes of interesting works of history, travels, voyages, arts and sciences, philosophy, chemistry, classics, religion and morality; and in fact, nearly every work which is of an instructive nature to youth. About four hundred volumes are taken out weekly.

It is governed by a Board of Directors, who are appointed annually, by the contributors to the library; if they neglect to do so at the time specified, the city council make the appointment.

IX. THE FINE ARTS.

The Fine Arts appear to seek geographical localities. Many of the cities of the old world give evidence of this; and the sphere of the beautiful in one branch has so harmonized with that of others, so great has been the affinity in the different classes of the ennobling arts, that, in order to enjoy the genial influences of association, they have rendered some of these old, and otherwise worn-out capitals of the European states, the magnets, which to this day, attract to them all those who are in love with the beautiful, from all parts of the civilized world. The fame and character of Florence, is made up in the eye and heart of thousands, who will never see the beautiful things in her rich galleries; of the knowledge, that she has given to the world, and still retains within her borders, unnumbered and glorious evidences, that she had a real and fostering love of the grand, the beautiful and sublime in art and poesy. This is her character; and she has obtained it, by a long course of faithful and truth-loving appreciation of those, who, by their genius, talents and labor, were rendering her, hundreds of years gone by, almost the centre of the artistic world, at the present day. Is it not worth something to have the reflection of genius cast upon a city by her own sons? Is it not a living light that cannot be destroyed, whatever may betide in after time?

Cincinnati has sent from her young bosom, some names, which now have an existence in the world of art, that can never perish. These names, with those of her *savans*, more than any and all her other citizens, have rendered her known in Europe. She is looked upon, by those whose esteem is precious as jewels, as the artistic and scientific city of our great Republic; as the centre of the most cultivated and art-loving, and, consequently, the most refined people on our Continent. Now, for so young a nation, and still younger city, this is a high position: it should be the wish of all that it may be sustained with honor to ourselves, and justice toward those, who are the immediate cause of our reflected greatness. Our love for these great pursuits, should be manifested, so palpably springing from a proper source, that it would be no discredit in our assuming a fair share of the honor of our public position. We should aid those who are aiding us. Heretofore we have enjoyed the honor arising from the exertions, the genius, and taste of our artists, without giving them that sympathy and substantial encouragement, that just appreciation of their laborious efforts, which should make this, the home of their gratitude and affections. This it has not been. Can we point to anything as *our* share in the mutual labor of giving our city the honorable place she now holds? The answer is an expressive silence. It should be our pleasure, as it is our duty, in these efforts at elevation of the public taste, to establish an Academy of Design, which should be open to all classes of artisans. There should be sections of artists in painting and sculpture, architecture, ornamental marble and stone workers, carvers in wood and metal, gold and silversmiths, cabinet makers; and indeed, as many other occupations as choose to unite themselves in separate sections, for the purpose of mutual instruction, in the art of Design. Collections of paintings and models, sculptures, carvings, engravings, engraved gems, original drawings, plaster casts, from the best antique statues, as well as modern, bronzes, and a well-selected library upon the Fine Arts, should be some of the attractions to draw students from all parts of our common country here, to be instructed and elevated in their different walks; thus as from a common centre radiating a just and classical taste to all around us, both in form and color. We should cultivate a study of truth in art, by a just, fearless, and honest criticism upon our own works, which should supersede the newspaper puffs of the present day, that are destitute of all correct knowledge of art or of modesty; and have ruined many of those artists whose success they were meant to promote.

That an Academy of Design, properly endowed, can be established, none can doubt, when they remember how easily the large sum of nearly $25,000 was raised for the benefit of the present Arts Union, and the still more liberal purchase of the Peale Paintings, and the establishment of the Picture Gallery, of which it is to form the nucleus. An Academy of Design, with its different sections, would be a source of instruction, the effects of which would be seen in all our houses as well as in their exterior; in all our cemeteries, and in all our public buildings; each one being a monument itself of the liberality, good taste, and good sense, of its founders. Then could we say, with just pride, that our city had seconded, with a beautiful spirit, the high and ennobling aims, the rich taste, and unclouded genius of her artists. A mirror of strength and talent would be visible on all sides; and in the future, might be discerned, the lofty place occupied by the Queen of the West among the cultivated and enlightened cities of the world.

ARTS UNION HALL.

This fine saloon, with its attendant offices, occupies the fourth story of the building at the corner of Sycamore and Fourth Streets; to which it has given its own name. This hall is 71 by 33 feet, on the floor, and 24 feet to the skylight above. It is not quite as long as the exhibition room of the New York Arts Union, but is wider and higher, and therefore of equal extent. It will serve to display three hundred pictures of average size. As many as three hundred pictures, of various sizes, have been exhibited here at one time. A picture has been recently ordered by the directors, of Mrs. Lily Martin Spencer, at 250 dollars; and a statue or other subject, in marble, to Hiram Powers, with a carte blanche as to design, and the price to be set by himself at from $3000 to $5000 dollars.

PICTURE GALLERY.

William Wiswell, a public-spirited citizen of ours, has recently fitted up a picture gallery, to which visitors are not only admitted without charge, but afforded the opportunity of seeing it during any period of daylight, which may suit their convenience—the entrance door standing open all the time.

A valuable collection of three hundred portraits, fancy and historical pieces, embracing the works of Kellogg, Beard, Rothermel, Heade, and other well-known artists, is there placed, under the safeguard of the community, to whose sense of honor and justice, the proprietor has appealed; and up to this period, with well justified confidence.

The gem of this gallery is Powers' recently executed bust of Gen. Jackson; one of his highest achievements in this line.

ARTISTS.

Cincinnati has been, for many years, extensively and favorably known as the birthplace, if not the home of a school of artists, who may be found in various parts of Europe, to say nothing of those in great numbers, whose talent has found exercise in the various great cities of our own republic. The following list gives their names; the date at which they commenced their course; their present residence, with names of persons in whose parlors their pictures, statues, &c., may be found.

The first class consists of those whose career commences generally at an early date, such as,

Edwin B. Smith, 1815.—Portraits and historical pieces; D. Churchill, J. H. Cromwell.

A. W. Corwine, 1821.—Portraits; Capt. J. Pierce, P. S. Symmes, N. Guilford, Timothy Walker, &c.

Joseph Mason, 1822.—Portraits; George Selves, Mrs. Mason, D. Churchill.

Joseph Kyle, 1823.—New York City. Portraits, and fancy pieces; S. Stibbs, M. Burt. His paintings are mostly in New York, where he has resided for many years.

Samuel M. Lee, 1826.—Landscapes; P. S. Symmes, Joseph Graham, D. B. Lawler, J. G. Worthington, T. H. Yeatman, J. S. Armstrong, &c. His best works are at Louisville, Kentucky.

Alonzo Douglass, 1828.—Cincinnati. Portraits; Andrew Burt, James Douglass.

C. Harding, 1828.—Portraits; S. S. L'Hommedieu, Philip Young.

Tuttle, 1830, was a pupil of West.—Portraits; J. H. Cromwell, T. H. Yeatman, Jacob Burnet.

Daniel Steele, 1830.

John J. Tucker, 1834.—Portraits; Dr. Shotwell and George Selves.

Sidney S. Lyon, 1836.—Louisville. Portraits and landscapes; M. M. Carll, Mark P. Taylor, Jonathan Lyon.

Those to whose names no residence is affixed, are known or believed to be no longer in life. Of those who are known to survive, Douglass and Lyon have engaged in other pursuits.

This list has been confined to portrait and landscape painters—it might, however, include Shubael Clevenger, modeler and sculptor, who commenced in 1836, and died in 1844, on his way home from Italy; and Augustus Rostaing, who executed cameo likenesses and fancy heads in shell, in 1835, and left this country subsequently, for Paris, France, where he now resides. Also Thomas Campbell, a miniature painter, who commenced here in 1840, and has since deceased. Clevenger has left busts which may be seen in the parlors of N. Longworth, William Greene, and Judge Burnet. Rostaing's Cameos; N. Longworth, J. C. Hall; and Campbell's miniatures—Wm. Yorke, J. H. Beard, J. D. Jones, J. P. Broadwell, and A. Baldwin.

Artists living, and in practice—Portrait and Composition Painters—Miner K. Kellogg, 1828.—New York. Portraits, compositions, and fancy pieces; Charles S. Kellogg, N. Longworth, Wm. Manser, Reuben R. Springer, S. I. Kellogg. He has a copy of Stuart's portrait of Washington, and original portraits of Presidents Van Buren and Polk, at Wiswell's gallery of paintings on Fourth Street, and an original portrait of General Jackson at the Masonic Hall. He has painted another copy of Stuart's Washington, for the Legislature of New Jersey,—of Chief Justice Taney, for the Baltimore bar; and General Scott for the New York city authorities. He has also executed the only portrait of General Worth extant. Among his compositions, are the Circassian, a female figure, for James Robb of New Orleans; and what is probably his best work in this line, the Greek captive, ordered by Riggs, of the firm of Corcoran & Riggs, Washington city. A few years since, Kellogg, on a visit to Constantinople, made a full length portrait of Redschid Pacha, Prime Vizier of the Sultan of Turkey; on which occasion, and as a mark of that minister's gratification, Kellogg received from him a superb gold cup, profusely set with diamonds.

J. H. Beard, 1830.—Cincinnati. Portraits, fancy heads and groups; Charles Stetson, R. R. Springer, S. S. L'Hommedieu, J. S. Armstrong, Griffin Taylor, S. E. Foote, G. K. Shoenberger, and W. R. Morris. Beard's portraits are in most of our principal cities. He has painted full length portraits of Charles Hammond and General Harrison, and a three-quarter length, of Gen. Taylor, on orders from public institutions.

His compositions are "The Emigrants," "Poor Relations," "Last of the Red Men," Last Victim of the Deluge;" and more recently, "the Squatters." This last is to be sent to England, as a picture of back woods life in America, in some of its aspects.

John Frankenstein, 1831.—Springfield, Ohio. Portraits, historical subjects, sculptures, and landscapes; Jos. Pierce, Aaron Bowen, W. P. Resor, J Rowan, Bardstown, Kentucky, W. H. Seward, Peter A. Porter, and John C. Spencer, New York State; Professor Frost and Matthew T. Miller, Philadelphia; Thomas Thompson, Boston, and L. Derbyshire, Toronto, Canada. Among his composition and historical pieces, are: The Holy Family—Indian in contemplation—Madonna—The Butt—Day Dreams—The Bud—Isaiah and the Infant Saviour—Christ mocked in the Prætorium. Most of these are owned in our eastern cities and in Canada.

E. Hall Martin, 1831.—California. Portraits and marine pieces; Wm. M. Ward, Wm. Noble, John Martin, B. Kirby, E. J. Miller.

W. H. Powell, 1833.—Paris, France. Portraits, fancy and historical pieces; N. Longworth, Larz Anderson, N. C. McLean, Wm. M. Hubbell, Mrs. Powell, Dr. Smith. "Salvator Rosa among the Brigands," was his first historical piece, and painted in 1823. This was followed by "Columbus before the Council at Salamanca," which being exhibited at Washington City, in 1847, obtained him the appointment, by Congress, to paint an historical piece, to fill the last vacant panel in the Rotunda of the Capitol. This distinction was conferred on him by the unanimous vote of the Senate, and a vote of 195 to 34 in the House of Representatives, over more than sixty artists, who were his competitors. On this painting, now nearly completed, he has been engaged during the last four years; the subject is "De Soto discovering the Mississippi." He has also on hand, "The Burial of De Soto," and a full length portrait of "Lamartine;" which last is a commission from the Maryland Historical Society. Powell has painted two fine portraits of J. Q. Adams, the larger of which he presented to the Cincinnati Observatory. He has also painted "The Signing of the Constitution, of the Pilgrims on board the Mayflower," and "The Calabrian Peasant Girl;" "The Italian Shepherd Boy," and "The Roman Cattle Drover;" the last three of small size.

Thomas B. Reed, is a poet as well as a painter, and of high order of merit in either line, 1836.—Florence. Portraits, landscapes, and historical pieces; E. B. Reeder, W. R. Morton, I. G. Burnet, J. J. Wright, Dr. Drake, George Selves, E. Wiswell. Among his compositions are "Love's First Whisper," and "Milton Dictating Paradise Lost to his Daughters," and "Loves of the Zephyrs," a fine ideal.

W. P. Brannan, 1837.—California. Portraits, landscapes, and fancy pieces. A. Donogh, Mrs. J. P. Campbell, S. Burdsal, D. G. A. Davenport, R. Adams, George Cullum, Dr. S. O. Almy, S. S. Smith, Wm. Piatt, S. M. Hart.

A. Baldwin, 1838.—Cincinnati. landscapes and marine pieces;

Andrew J. Burt, S. S. Smith, R. W. Lee, E. Dexter, S. Stokes, J. B. Russell.

T. W. Whittridge, 1838.—Dusseldorf. Landscapes; R. R. Springer, A. W. Bullock, W. G. Breese, H. Probasco, Miss L. M. Hartwell, W. A. Collard, D. B. Lawler, F. C. Yeatman, James Lupton, Chas. Anderson, Lewis Stagg, S. B. Palmer.

John Cranch, 1839.—New York. Portraits and fancy pieces; E. J. Miller, Mrs. A. Wood, E. Dexter, J. Longworth J. W. Coleman, Dr. L. C. Rives, J. P. Foote, D. K. Este, jr.

G. N. Frankenstein, 1840.—Springfield, Ohio. Landscape and portraits; Griffin Taylor, George Selves, Dr. Locke, C. D. Dana, W. S. Sampson, J. D. Park, B. F. Sandford, W. B. Wood, Donn Piatt, Charles E. Cist, J. F. Taylor, J. H. Coleman, D. B. Pierson, J. T. Hinsdale, R. S. Bacon, Cincinnati. Thomas H. Shreve, Ben Cassidy, Professor Noble Butler, and Rev. J. Craik, Louisville, P. A. Porter, G. W. Holley, Niagara Falls, N. Y., Professor Frost, Philadelphia, Abbott Lawrence, Charles Francis Adams, George Ticknor, and Dr. S. A. Bemis, Boston, Mass., S. Derbyshire, S. Keefer, Toronto, and George Desbarats, Montreal, Canada.

It is characteristic of G. N. Frankenstein, that his landscapes, even in the minutest details, are strictly from Nature. His landscapes are never fancy pieces, or copies from other artists.

Charles Soule, 1841.—Cincinnati. Portraits, fruit pieces, &c.; J. D. Jones, D. K. Este, jr., Charles Anderson, N. Wright, Judge Burnet, Larz Anderson, N. Longworth. He has painted a full length portrait of Josiah Lawrence, for the Merchants' Exchange; indeed, his portraits, like those of Beard, are hard to be numbered; like Beard too, he is the favorite painter of portraits.

William L. Sonntag, 1842.—Cincinnati. Landscapes; A. S. Winslow Charles Stetson, Thomas Faris, J. T. Foote, Adam N. Riddle, N. G. Pendleton, Barton White, Chs. L. Strong, William Wilshire, E. S. Brooks, E. B. Reeder, Henry Howe, J. N. Ridgway; many of Sonntag's best pieces, are in our Atlantic Cities.

Lilly Martin Spencer.—New York. Fancy and historical pieces; W. Gregory, T. Faris, Arts Union, N. C. McLean, Mrs. J. P. Campbell, W. G. Breese, A. M. Taylor. Her compositions are generally subjects taken from Shakspeare, such as "Lear and his Daughters," "Ophelia," "Romeo and Juliet."

J. R. Johnston, 1842.—Cincinnati. Sculpture, portraits, landscapes, and historical pieces; J. J. Faran, G. W. Johnston, T. Faris,

J. D. Jones, Michael Jones, Cullum & Jackson, William Kent, Frank's Museum. Two of his historical pieces, "The Starved Rock," a legend of Illinois river, and the "Mouth of Bad Axe river," are owned by J. W. S. Browne.

J. Insco Williams, 1842.—Cincinnati. Portraits, historical pieces; his "Panorama of the Bible," recently destroyed by fire, has been greatly admired at the east.

C. R. Edwards, 1842.—Cincinnati. Portraits and landscapes; Dr. Gatchell, Dr. Garretson, Dr. Owens, Thomas String, J. H. Coleman.

Jacob Cox, 1843.—Indianapolis. Landscapes, fancy pieces, and portraits; Miles Greenwood, W. S. Groesbeck, T. Faris, Gardner Phipps, F. Lawson, D. B. Lawler, P. C. Bonte, J. J. O'Leary.

R. S. Duncanson, 1843.—Cincinnati. Fruit, fancy and historical paintings, and landscapes; James Foster, W. H. Brisbane, S. S. Smith, Thomas Faris, Dr. Newton, J. H. Oliver, Calvin T. Starbuck, J. Blackford, N. Longworth, Charles Stetson. His historical pieces, are, "Shylock and Jessica," "Trial of Shakspeare," "Ruins of Carthage," "Battle-ground of the River Raisin," "Western Hunters' Encampment."

William Walcutt, 1844.—New York. Portraits and historical pieces; William Dennison, J. Kelsey. His "Battle of Monmouth," with most of his portraits, are in New York.

B. M. McConkey, 1844.—Dusseldorf. Landscapes; Wm. Wiswell, George T. Jones, J. Kebler, W. S. Johnston, William Goodman, Jas. Ruffin, Gardner Phipps, F. Simon, Charles G. Springer, James M. Trimble, T. J. Strait, Victor Williams, B. Urner.

H. W. Grœnland, 1844.—Cincinnati. Marine pieces and landscapes; Broadway Exchange, Judge Burnet, Wulkop and Meyenn.

J. C. Wolfe, 1845.—Cincinnati. Landscapes, portraits and historical pieces; Jos. Burgoyne, Professor Ray, O. Oncken, J. T. Walbridge, James Foster, Elisha Hotchkiss, Timothy Kirby, J. Mills, H. S. Hendrickson, F. G. Cary, S. F. Cary, and Female Academy at Mount Healthy. His "Joseph and Potiphar's Wife," is at the St. Charles Exchange; his other historical or rather allegorical pictures, are Bunyan's "Pilgrim's Progress," and Milton's "Paradise Lost."

J. O. Eaton, 1846.—Cincinnati. Portraits, landscapes, and historical pieces; D. P. Strader, G. H. Brown, J. M. Wade, John Shillito, J. F. Torrence, Charles Stetson, R. L. Fabian, Dr. Judkins,

J. K. Wilson, M. P. Cassilly, D. T. Woodrow, M. J. Louderback, Dr. Caldwell, at Studio. His "Christ Disputing with the Doctors," is at W. S. Sampson's.

D. B. Walcutt, 1846.—Cincinnati. Portraits; John Simpkinson, J. M. Blair, Edgar Conkling, William Wood, Richard Conkling, John Elstner, Thomas Sharp, William H. Crisp, G. R. Baker, Charles H. Wolff.

A. H. Hummell, 1847.—Waynesville. Portraits and fancy pieces; George C. Davis, Mrs. A. Parker, W. F. Barker, Maysville, Ky. O. F. Thompson.

C. J. Hulse, 1847.—Cincinnati. Landscapes and fancy pieces; S. G. Burnet, Dr. Muscroft, E. D. Norris, Franklin Ernst, Charles Spinning, J. C. Buerckle, L. G. Curtiss, Collard Martin.

Jesse Hulse, 1847.—Cincinnati. Landscapes and fancy pieces; S. G. Burnet, F. Ernst, E. C. Hawkins, Dr. Muscroft, Dr. J. F. Johnston, Dr. Murphy, W. S. Merrill.

C. S. Spinning, 1847.—Cincinnati. Landscapes; J. F. Meline, J. W. Hartwell, Dr. Knowlton, Dayton, J. N. McFarland, Tiffin, Ohio.

George W. Phillips, 1848.—Cincinnati. Portraits and landscapes; E. M. Gregory, E. Carll, J. H. Brandt, G. Bown, Studio.

George W. White, 1848.—Cincinnati. Portrait fancy pieces, and landscapes; J. P. Broadwell, C. S. Burdsal, and E. C. Hawkins, P. M'Carty, Thomas Faris.

P. McCreight, 1849.—Cincinnati. Landscapes; William Hiatt, Mrs. J. E. Reeder, R. L. Fabian, Henry Marks, J. W. Phillips.

Miss S. Gengembre, 1849.—Portraits and fancy pieces; W. Wiswell, Arts Union, William Goodman, Gardner Phipps, Edgar Conkling.

Edward Cridland, 1850.—Cincinnati. Portraits; Arts Union.

Jacob H. Sloop, 1850.—Cincinnati. Marine views; T. Faris, John R. Johnston.

Ralph Butts, 1851.—Cincinnati. Landscape and portraits.

A. P. Bonte, 1851.—Cincinnati. Landscapes.

In gathering these facts and dates, a general visit was paid to the professional studios in Cincinnati, and the gratifying admission was everywhere made by the artists, that they had employment ample in its extent, and remunerative in its character; some of them acknowledging, that more commissions were offered than they could possibly undertake to execute. This state of things impresses the hope that Cincinnati will soon become, in the Fine Arts, the mother that takes care of her children, rather than as heretofore, the mother that turns them out to shift for themselves.

Miniature Painters—F. V. Peticolas, 1825.—Clermont County, O.

Thomas Dawson, 1825.—Cincinnati.

J. O. Gorman, 1831.—Frankfort, Kentucky.

William Miller, 1847.—Cincinnati. Jacob Hoffner, W. H. Mussey, M. D., Nathaniel Wright, N. P. Iglehart, Wm. Willis, Saml. R. Bates, Mrs. G. H. Bates, M. S. Rogers, Israel Wilson, G. K. Shoenberger, S. E. Foote.

Modelers and Sculptors—Hiram Powers, 1828.—Florence, Italy. Busts and statuary; J. P. Foote, N. Longworth, Judge Burnet, W. Lytle, William C. Preston, S. C. His bust of Jackson is in Wiswell's gallery. Powers has executed other busts, which may be seen in the eastern cities. His Fisher Boy, Proserpine, Calhoun, Eve, America and California, stamp him as the sculptor of the age, if not of all ages past and to come.

H. K. Brown, 1833.—Brooklyn. Busts; D. Corwin and others.

John S. Whetstone, 1837.—Cincinnati. Busts; Western Museum; John Whetstone.

C. C. Brackett, 1838.—Boston. Busts; Henry Ives and others.

John King, 1838.—Boston. Busts and Cameos; M. L. Neville and others.

N. F. Baker, 1841.—Cincinnati. Busts and statues; John Baker, Professor Mitchel, J. P. Foote, Dr. Worcester. Baker's statue of Egeria is in the Arts Union, and his Cincinnatus is in the college.

T. D. Jones, 1842.—New York. Busts; Henry Clay, Lewis Cass, Thomas Corwin, Mrs. Gen. Taylor.

Of the miniature painters, Peticolas, and Whetstone of the sculptors, have left their employments for other pursuits; and Baker has abandoned his professional implements, it is hoped, only to resume them in due time.

X. TRANSPORTATION AND TRAVEL.

NATURAL AND ARTIFICIAL ROUTES.

RIVERS, ROADS, CANALS, AND RAILROADS.

In the valley of the Ohio, there is no place so central, in relation to its population and resources, as Cincinnati. This centrality has a great and permanent influence on its destiny. It makes it convenient and cheap for a multitude of people to visit it as a mart of commerce and as a depository of the arts. It tends to make it a common depôt of all the things connected with either business or pleasure; because it is central, it must also become the *focus*, or meeting place of a great net-work of internal communications—radiating from, to, and through this common centre, to every part of the country. Accordingly, we find, that, in fact, no city of the Union, even the oldest, has such a various and vast system of artificial communications either actually finished, now constructing, or planned with the strongest probability of success, as this central city. To exhibit this fact clearly, we will first state certain elements which relate to this natural CENTRALITY.

1. The Ohio river is 959 miles in length—from Pittsburgh to the Mississippi. From Pittsburgh to Cincinnati, is 458 miles; and from Cincinnati to the mouth of the Ohio, is 501 miles; so that Cincinnati is very nearly in the actual *centre* of the valley.

2. From Maumee bay to Knoxville, on the Tennessee river, is about 400 miles, in a direct line; and Cincinnati is very nearly on the line, and exactly half way; so that to the whole country, which lies between the Lakes and Tennessee river, Cincinnati is just central.

3. If we take the distance between Cincinnati and Nashville, on the Cumberland river, as a radius, and Cincinnati as the centre, the circle described will include Ohio, Indiana, Kentucky, western Virginia, and western Pennsylvania; a country embracing 150,000 square miles, and capable of sustaining comfortably and happily, thirty millions of people, and which now contains nearly five millions. To this entire country Cincinnati is central by nature,

and central by commerce; for her actual trade extends to every portion of it.

4. If we draw a *straight line* from Baltimore, on tide water, to St. Louis, on the Mississippi, Cincinnati will be on that line; at least, it varies so little from it, that the variation is of no practical importance. On this line, Cincinnati is *three* hundred miles from St. Louis, and *four* hundred from Baltimore; so that it is again central, in the great line of locomotion between the seaboard and the western bank of the Mississippi.

5. If this straight line be extended to the Pacific Ocean, it will touch near San Francisco; so that Cincinnati is on the great line of central communication between the Atlantic and Pacific Oceans.

Advantages equal to these, in relation to internal commerce and migration on the American continent, are not possessed by any other point east of the Mississippi.

In improving this position by artificial communications, the first step was to make ROADS into the valley of the Miamis; after that, the State CANALS were made; one of which, connects Cincinnati with Maumee; and by the junction with the Wabash canal, connects her also with the interior of Indiana, down to the mouth of the Wabash, at Evansville. Next come RAILROADS; and within the last five years, the progress of Cincinnati in Railways, either finished, constructing, or chartered and commenced, with the strongest probability of success, is fully equal to that in any other city whatever, in the same period of time. The principal statistics, in relation to these important highways, are given below, under separate heads.

I. MACADAMIZED ROADS.

Until about 1835, the roads around Cincinnati, were of that primitive character, which are peculiar to all new countries. Many of them led over the tops of the highest hills, without any reference to grades, while all were what are now called *mud* roads. The invention of McAdam seemed to come, as a special remedy for such highways, and a great relief to a people suffering under such evils. It was not, however, until Cincinnati had attained thirty thousand inhabitants, that the macadamized roads were adopted here; since that time, every road of any importance, leading from the city, has been macadamized, generally, by chartered companies, and in some instances, by the county commissioners. The following are the principal macadamized roads leading from Cincinnati.

NAME.	DIRECTION.	MILES.	REMARKS.
1. Goshen, Wilmington, Washington, and Circleville turnpike	..E. N. E...	100	
2. Montgomery, Rochr., Clarksville, and Wilmington	..N. E......	50	
3. Chillicothe & Hillsborough.	.. "		15 miles only finished.
4. Batavia turnpike	..E.	21	
5. Lebanon, Xenia, and Springfield	..N.	72	
6. Lebanon, Centerville, and Dayton	..N. W.....	21	..Continuation of No. 5.
7. Great Miami turnpike to Dayton, through Monroe and Franklin	..N.	38	
8. Cincinnati and Hamilton...	..N. W.....	21	
9. Hamilton and Eaton.......	..N.	30	..Continuation of No. 8.
10. Colerain, Hamilton, and Oxford	..N. W....	37	
11. Cincinnati, Carthage, and Hamilton	.. "	25	
12. Dayton and Springfield....	..N.	24	..Continuation of 6 & 7.
13. The Harrison turnpike....	..W........	20	
14. The Covington and Williamstown, Ky	..S.	36	
Total, fourteen macadamized roads,......		514 miles.	

These roads proceed directly from Cincinnati, but many of them are continued, by their connection with other roads, until they extend through the State. Thus the Dayton and Springfield roads, by their connection with the National road at Springfield, go through the State to Wheeling, and over the mountains to Baltimore.

II. CANALS.

The canal system of Ohio, commenced in 1824, was not fully completed until 1842. Since then, the rapid introduction of Railroads, and the complete demonstration of their success, for the purposes of speedy communication, have arrested the progress of canals. Those, however, which terminate at Cincinnati, have been of great and undoubted utility to the commerce of the city. Immense amounts of freight are transmitted upon them, especially of the heavy products of the country. The canals which connect directly with Cincinnati, are as follows:—

1. Miami canal and Extension	N.	290 miles.	
2. Whitewater canal	N. W.	70 "	
3. Wabash and Erie	S. W.	200 "	...Continuation of 1.
Total Canals		560 "	

The MIAMI CANAL commences at Cincinnati, and follows the great Miami valley, until it passes the summit, at St. Mary's, and enters the Maumee valley, terminating at Toledo.

The WABASH CANAL is wholly in Indiana, but joins the Miami canal at Junction, in the valley of Maumee, and pursues the Wabash valley to Terre-Haute, and will be finished to Evansville, at the mouth of the Wabash. A boat may now pass from Cincinnati to Terre-Haute; and soon may pass to Evansville—more than *six hundred miles* of canal navigation!

III. RAILROADS.

Railways are rapidly taking the place of other means of locomotion, for the purposes of travel, and of rapid transit for light goods, and even for the transportation of such heavy articles as coal and iron. Their effects upon the economy of society, and their social influences generally, are very remarkable. They are making a great and extraordinary revolution in the means of intercourse. Cincinnati is, by its centrality, before mentioned, admirably adapted for the adoption and successful employment of this new element of commercial power. On every side, toward every point, radiating lines from Cincinnati will penetrate the most fertile regions of America. They will connect the lakes with the rivers; they will bind ocean to ocean; they will bear the burdens of enormous harvests; develop the treasures of the disemboweled earth, and carry bread to laboring millions. It was not until 1835, however, ten years after the success of the Liverpool railway, that it was seriously proposed to make a railway from Cincinnati. The one proposed, was the Little Miami railroad; which, after many years of hard struggles, was completed to Springfield, 84 miles. In 1836, the Charleston railway was chartered from Cincinnati, through Kentucky, Tennessee, N. Carolina, Georgia, and S. Carolina, to Charleston. The project, as a *whole,* failed, in consequence of the great burdens laid on the charter as *conditions,* by the State of Kentucky. It has, nevertheless, been *in progress* toward completion ever since; until it is now, on the southern side, more than half completed. From Charleston, South

ENGRAVED BY F. E. JONES FROM A DAGUERREOTYPE

Jacob Strader

Carolina, and Savannah, Georgia, an entire line of railroad is completed to Chattanooga on the Tennessee river, Tennessee; a distance of 447 miles from Charleston, and 433 miles from Savannah. From Chattanooga a railway is in rapid construction to Nashville and another to Knoxville. From both these points, it is quite certain there will be railroads, at no distant day, to Cincinnati; thus completing the original plan of 1836. The railway from Covington to Lexington, now constructing, will be part of the great line.

From Cincinnati, north to the Lakes, the lines which connect the Ohio river with the Lakes, are already finished; these also make a continuation of the great Southern line. The entire line from Charleston and Savannah to Cleveland and Sandusky, through Cincinnati, will be about *thirteen hundred miles* in length.

The great *East and West Line* will be formed, by the *Ohio and Mississippi Railroad*, the *Cincinnati and Belpré*, and the *Baltimore and Ohio*, extending from Baltimore, on tidewater, to St. Louis, on the Mississippi.

Radiating lines to other points of the compass are already in process of construction. Of these there are *three* different lines begun, or chartered, through Indianapolis to the north-west. *One* up the Great Miami to Dayton, there connecting with lines to Indiana, to Sandusky, and to Cleveland. Another line will lead north-east through Wilmington, Ohio, Washington, Circleville and Lancaster, until it joins the Central Line at Zanesville. Other projects have been spoken of, and many charters have been granted for lateral lines of railway, connecting those which radiate directly from Cincinnati, with those which proceed from the Atlantic. When the whole are completed, of which there is strong probability, Cincinnati will have about *four thousand miles of railway*, which are on lines directly leading from, or to, this city. The vast influence of these mighty streams of internal communication, centring here, cannot be anticipated. When connected with the productions of the inexhaustible soil which they traverse, and with the great population already here, the joint influence of such potent causes, will probably create an extent of commerce, and a growth of civic power and wealth, of which we have, at present, only a faint conception.

In the following table are included only those lines, which lead *directly* through Cincinnati, and which are either finished, constructing, or, to which subscriptions have been partially made.

Names and Localities.	Length.	Finished.	Constructing.	Partly provided for.
Little Miami.	84	84		
Mad River.	134	134		
Xenia and Columbus	54	54		
Cincinnati, Columbus and Cleveland	149	149		
Cincinnati, Hamilton and Dayton	60		60	
Dayton and Springfield	25	25		
Hamilton and Eaton	40		40	
Findley Branch *a*	16	16		
Western *b*	45		35	10
Cincinnati and Hillsborough	37		37	
Cincinnati and Belpré *c*	130		34	96
Cincinnati, Circleville and Zanesville *d*	121			121
Lawrenceburg and Indianapolis *e*	85		85	
Ohio and Mississippi *f*	325			325
Covington and Lexington *g*	96		61	35
Indianapolis and Lafayette *h*	51		61	
Indianapolis and Terre-haute *i*	270		70	
Pacific Railway *j*	369			369
North Western *k*	80			80
Baltimore and Ohio	280	177	103	
21 Lines of Railway	2,261	639	586	1,006

The *principle* upon which the above table is constructed includes all the lines,—which are continuations—of those lines, which proceed *directly* from Cincinnati. On the other hand, it excludes all the lines, which are merely *lateral* to those leading from Cincinnati. Thus, it includes the *Baltimore and Ohio* Railroad; but excludes the *Indiana and Bellefontaine* Road, which is lateral to the Mad River Line at Bellefontaine.

On this principle we have the following great lines, viz:

Baltimore and Ohio Line	280	miles.
North-Western Railway to the Ohio	80	"
Cincinnati and Belpré	130	"
Cincinnati and Hillsborough	37	"
Little Miami	22	"
Ohio and Mississippi	325	"
Pacific, to Mouth of Kanzas	369	"
From Baltimore to the Kanzas	1,243	"

In the same manner, the line from Charleston, South Carolina, through Cincinnati to Cleveland, will make about 1,100 miles, in length, of which 700 are actually completed, and 140 more in course of construction; yet, as there is a link, between Lexington, Kentucky, and Knoxville, or Nashville, Tennessee, unprovided for, no notice is taken of it, above, except so far as Lexington.

If the Southern Line, to Charleston and Savannah,—with some continuous lines in the north-west had been included, in the above table,—the *aggregate* would have been, as stated above,—*four thousand miles* of direct railway, from Cincinnati; all which there is the strongest reason to believe, will be completed, in a very few years.

The following notes on the above table, will explain the *connections* of the several posts.

a. The *Findley Branch*, connects the Mad River Railroad with Findley, the county seat of Hancock county.

b. The *Western* Railway, connects Dayton with Greenville, the county seat of Darke county, and thence to the Indiana Line, in the direction of Winchester, Indiana.

c. The *Belpré and Cincinnati*, is to unite the *Baltimore and Ohio* Railroad, at, or near, Parkersburg, Virginia, with Cincinnati.

d. The *Cincinnati, Circleville, and Zanesville* Line is intended to *connect Cincinnati*, joining the *Little Miami*, at the mouth of Todd's Fork, with the *Ohio Central*, at Zanesville.

e. The *Lawrenceburg and Indianapolis*, will be connected with Cincinnati, by the *Ohio and Mississippi*, at Lawrenceburg. At Indianapolis, it connects with the *Lafayette*, making, in all, 166 miles from Cincinnati to Lafayette.

f. The *Ohio and Mississippi*, will connect Cincinnati and St. Louis.

g. The *Covington and Lexington* passes up the Licking to Paris.

h. The *Indianapolis and Lafayette* will be continued north-westerly to Chicago.

i. The *Indianapolis and Terre-haute* will pass on west through Illinois.

j. The *Pacific Railway* connects St. Louis with the mouth of the Kanzas river, and is a continuation of the *Ohio and Mississippi.*

k. The *North-Western Railroad* has been chartered by the State of Virginia, to connect the *Baltimore and Ohio*, at the Three Forks of Tygart's river, with the *Cincinnati and Belpré;* thus making a continuous line to Cincinnati.

All these railroads, it will thus be perceived, have a direct bearing upon the commercial interests of Cincinnati, and will contribute to swell the aggregate of its general business.

The following table presents the aggregate results of roads, canals, and railroads, finished, or undertaken, through Cincinnati.

Works.	Finished.	In progress.	Undertaken.
14 Mc Adam Roads	514 miles		
3 Canals	560 "		
21 Railways	639 "	586	1,006
38 Works.	1,713	586	1,006

Cincinnati has, therefore, *seventeen hundred* miles of railways, canals, and macadamized roads *finished,* nearly *six hundred* in *progress,* and *one thousand* undertaken, on lines radiating from itself. If to these be added other lines, continuous to these, which have a probability of early completion, the whole will make *five thousand miles* of artificial highway, soon to be completed.

CINCINNATI, HAMILTON, AND DAYTON RAILROAD COMPANY.

Office, north-west corner Vine and Fourth Streets.

PRESIDENT.—S. S. L'Hommedieu.

Directors.—J. C. Wright, Samuel Fosdick, E. B. Reeder, William Burnet, A. M. Taylor, Cincinnati; John Woods, Hamilton; Alex. Grimes, Dayton; Jos. B. Varnum, New York.

Secretary.—Isaac Shoemaker; Treasurer—Ohio Life Insurance and Trust Company; Chief Engineer—R. M. Shoemaker.

OHIO AND MISSISSIPPI RAILROAD COMPANY.

Office, Bromwell's buildings, north-east corner Fourth and Vine Streets. Rooms 5 *and* 6, *second story.*

PRESIDENT.—Abner T. Ellis.

Directors.—Alphonso Taft, John S. G. Burt, Charles W. West, Eden B. Reeder, George W. Cochran, John Baker, Henry Hanna, James C. Hall, David Z. Sedam, Joseph A. James, John Slevin, Cincinnati; Joseph G. Bowman, Illinois; William Burtch, Samuel Wise, William R. McCord, Samuel Judah, Vincennes, Ia.; Thompson Dean, John Cobb, Aurora, Ia.; George W. Lane, Lawrenceburgh, Ia.; Elias Conwell, Ripley Co., Ia.

Secretary.—H. H. Goodman; Treasurer—Henry Hanna; Counselor—Alphonso Taft; Chief Engineer—E. Gest.

LITTLE MIAMI RAILROAD COMPANY.

Office, corner of Congress and Kilgour Streets.

President.—Jacob Strader.

Directors.—Jacob Strader, John Kilgour, Griffin Taylor, R. R. Springer, John H. Groesbeck, Nat. Wright, John Bacon, William McCammon, Abraham Hivling, James Hicks, jun., Larz Anderson, Alphonso Taft.

Secretary.—John Kilgour; Treasurer—Archibald Irwin; Superintendent and Engineer—W. H. Clement.

This is the only railroad, leading from Cincinnati, which is actually in operation. It connects, at Springfield, with the Mad river and Sandusky railroad, and at Xenia, with the railroad *via* Columbus, from Cleveland; thus affording two distinct routes to Lake Erie.

The whole number of passengers carried on this road within the past year, was 144,486, and the amount received from them was $204,589 87. Of these 52,288 are *through passengers*, from Cincinnati to Springfield and from Springfield to Cincinnati, who paid an aggregate sum of not far from $125,000. A portion of these passengers, however, although counted as *through passengers* on this line, did not travel beyond the limits of this road, and are therefore, for the purposes of this calculation, to be added to the list of way-passengers. The receipts therefore, from passengers passing *through*, to or from the lake and the eastern lines of travel, did not in fact greatly exceed $100,000, or one-half the aggregate amount received from passengers.

Of the earnings of the road for the transportation of freight, the greater portion belongs to the class of *way-freight*. The table annexed to the Superintendent's report, showing the "principal articles of freight transported," exhibits very clearly the fact, that by far the greater portion were articles of domestic product and consumption, passing between Cincinnati and the country adjacent to the road. The only exception is comprised under the single head of "merchandise;" and as this item, being 18,295 tons, includes no small amount of way-freight, the whole of the through-freight would not yield, for the past year, over $35,000; and the account would then stand as follows:

Way-freight	$157,607 38
Way-passengers	102,294 93
	$259,602 31

Through-freight	$35,000 00
Through-passengers	102,294 93
	$137,294 93

The whole receipts for 1850, would be:

For way-freight and passengers	$259,902 31
For through-freight and passengers.	137,294 93
Carrying the mail	8,500 00
	$405,697 24

It is well understood, that the property of railroads depends, to a great extent, on the magnitude of its way-freight and travel, in comparison with its through travel and freight; because, while the last class is liable to be diverted from it by competitive lines, the first class may be said to be inseparably connected with it. In this aspect of the subject, the comparison thus made of the character of its freight and travel, is a highly favorable feature in the business of the Little Miami Railroad Company.

The cars and machinery of this company have been all made at Cincinnati.

SANDUSKY ROUTE.

P. W. STRADER, Agent.

From Cincinnati to Sandusky, Buffalo, Boston, New York, &c.,

Via Little Miami, Mad River, and Lake Erie railroads to Sandusky, Steamboat line to Buffalo, and thence via railroad to Albany, and steamer to New York.—Also Steamboat line—on and after opening of New York and Erie Railroad—to Dunkirk, and thence to New York.

LITTLE MIAMI RAILROAD.

Two daily trains at five o'clock and twenty minutes A. M., and two o'clock and thirty minutes P. M.

Connecting train at two o'clock and thirty minutes P. M., to Sandusky, Buffalo, New York, Boston, &c.

Passengers by two o'clock and thirty minutes P. M. train—Saturdays excepted—arrive at Sandusky next morning at six o'clock, and leave by regular line Steamer at seven o'clock A. M. for Buffalo, connecting at Buffalo with morning express train for Albany, and evening steamer for New York. Also, on and after opening of New York and Erie Railroad, connecting at Dunkirk with morning express train, and arriving at New York same evening.

Passengers by five o'clock and twenty minutes A. M. train—Sundays excepted—sleep at Sandusky, and take regular line Steamer next morning.

Saturday afternoon train at two o'clock and thirty minutes, to Springfield only.

The Sunday two o'clock and thirty minutes P. M. train.—Through train—

connects Monday morning, with steamer Alabama, for Buffalo, &c.; and with steamer Arrow, for Detroit, &c.

The following staunch and splendid passenger steamers, form the line from Sandusky to Buffalo, and—on and after the opening of New York and Erie Railroad—Dunkirk:

ALABAMA,	Capt. Pease,	leaves Sandusky,	Mondays and Thursdays.
SARATOGA,	Capt. Nickerson,	" "	Tuesdays and Thursdays.
EMPIRE,	Capt. H. Squier,	" "	Wednesdays and Saturdays.

No extra charge for meals or state-rooms, on the boats forming this line.

DETROIT.

Through in twenty-four hours, connecting daily—Sundays excepted—with steamer Arrow, Capt. Atwood, for Detroit, at 8 o'clock A. M.—connecting at Detroit, with all points on the Upper Lakes.

This route connects, at Buffalo, with Niagara Falls and Ontario route, to Toronto, Oswego, Montreal, Quebec, &c. At Albany, with Boston, &c. At New York, with Philadelphia, Baltimore, &c.

Fare from Cincinnati to Buffalo, $8 80; to Detroit, $8 00; to Sandusky, $6 50; to Springfield, $2 50; Buffalo to New York—if tickets are procured at Buffalo—$7 50.

For all information and through tickets apply at Office, east side of Broadway, first door north of Front Street.

TABLE OF DISTANCES.

Cincinnati to

Columbia	4½	Waynesville	6	Bellevue	14
Plainville	5	Spring Valley	7	Sandusky City	15
Milford	4½	Xenia	7	Huron	10
Germany	1½	Yellow Springs	7	Black River	20
Indian Ripple	1½	Springfield	12	Cleveland	27
Loveland's	6	Urbana	14	Grand River	30
Foster's	4	Bellefontaine	18	Ashtabula	30
Deerfield	5	Kenton	24	Conneaut	14
Morrow	5	Carey	24	Erie	30
Fort Ancient	4	Tiffin	16	Dunkirk	46
Freeport	4	Republic	9	Buffalo	46
					484

Buffalo to

Cheetawaga	5	Pittsford	8	Camillus	18
Lancaster	5	Canandaigua	21	Syracuse	8
Alden	10	Vienna	14	Chittenango	14
Darien	5	Geneva	9	Canastota	7
Attica	6	Waterloo	8	Oneida Depot	6
Batavia	10	Seneca Falls	3	Rome	12
Churchville	18	Cayuga Bridge	5	Oriskana	7
Rochester	14	Auburn	10	Whitesborough	4

Utica	3	St. Johnsville	10	Amsterdam	11
Herkimer	14	Palatine Bridge	9	Schenectady	9
Little Falls	7	Fonda	13	ALBANY	16
					325

Albany to New York....................150
Albany to Boston....................200

CLEVELAND ROUTE.

P. W. STRADER, Agent.

Spring, Summer, and Fall arrangement—from Cincinnati to New York in 48 hours;

Via Little Miami, Xenia and Columbus, Columbus and Cleveland railroads to Cleveland; steamboat line from Cleveland to Buffalo, and thence via railroad to Albany and steamer to New York.

LITTLE MIAMI RAILROAD.

Two daily trains at 5 o'clock and 20 A. M., and 2 o'clock and 30 minutes P. M. *Express train at 5 o'clock and 20 minutes, A. M., to Cleveland, Buffalo, New York, &c.*

BUFFALO.

Passengers by express train leave Cincinnati, Sundays excepted, at five o'clock and 20 minutes, A. M., leave Columbus at 11 o'clock 30 minutes, A. M., and arrive at Cleveland at 6 o'clock P. M., connecting with regular line steamer for Buffalo—connecting at Buffalo with express train for Albany; at Albany with evening steamer to New York; making 48 hours from Cincinnati to New York.

Passengers sleep first night on one of the following steamers. Sleep second night on steamer on North river; making the trip from Cincinnati to New York without loss of sleep.

Passengers by 2 o'clock and 30 minutes P. M. train,—daily train—sleep at Columbus, and resume next morning, Sunday mornings excepted.

The following staunch and splendid low pressure passenger steamers form a line from Cleveland to Buffalo.

EMPIRE STATE, Capt. Hazard—BUCKEYE STATE, Capt. Stanard.

N.B. Steamer QUEEN CITY, Captain Titus, takes the place of BUCKEYE STATE, for the present.

No extra charge for meals or state-rooms on the boats forming this line.

The roads of this route are new, and laid throughout with heavy T rail; and no exertion will be spared to secure the safety, speed and comfort of travelers.

DUNKIRK.

On and after the opening of the New York and Erie Railroad, a regular line of steamers will be put on from Cleveland, connecting with the morning express train at Dunkirk, and arriving at New York same evening.

DETROIT.

Steamers leave Cleveland daily for Detroit, connecting at Detroit with all points on the Upper Lakes.

This route connects at Buffalo, with Niagara Falls and Ontario route to New Toronto, Oswego, Montreal, Quebec, &c. At Albany, with Boston, &c. At New York, with Philadelphia, Baltimore, &c.

Fare from Cincinnati to Buffalo, $10,00 ; to Cleveland, $7,50 ; to Columbus, $3,50 ; to Xenia, $1,90 ; Buffalo to New York, if the tickets are procured at Buffalo, $7,50.

For all information and through tickets, apply at the Office, East side of Broadway, first door North of Front street, Cincinnati.

TABLE OF DISTANCES.

CINCINNATI TO

Columbia	4½	Waynesville	6	Cardington	13
Plainville	5	Spring Valley	7	Gilead	3
Milford	4½	Xenia	7	Galion	15
Germany	1½	Cedarville	8	Shelby	12½
Indian Ripple	1½	South Charleston	11	Greenwich	12½
Loveland's	6	London	11	New London	7
Foster's	4	West Jefferson	10	Wellington	11
Deerfield	5	Columbus	14	Grafton	11
Morrow	5	Worthington	9	Olmsted	10
Fort Ancient	4	Berlin	11	Cleveland	15
Freeport	4	Delaware	5	BUFFALO	200
					454

BUFFALO TO

Cheetawaga	5	Geneva	9	Oriskana	7
Lancaster	5	Waterloo	8	Whitesborough	4
Alden	10	Seneca Falls	3	Utica	4
Darien	5	Cayuga Bridge	5	Herkimer	14
Attica	6	Auburn	10	Little Falls	7
Batavia	10	Camillus	18	St. Johnsville	10
Churchville	18	Syracuse	8	Palatine Bridge	9
Rochester	14	Chittenango	14	Fonda	13
Pittsford	8	Canastota	7	Amsterdam	11
Canandaigua	21	Oneida Depot	6	Schenectady	9
Vienna	14	Rome	12	ALBANY	16
					325

Albany to New York	150
Albany to Boston	200

MIAMI CANAL.

The amount of tolls for 1850, collected on this canal, was $315,103 60 cents, leaving, as net proceeds, after deducting cost of repairs, superintendence, &c., the sum of $192,645 38 cents; being $64,‾88 86 cents over the proceeds of 1849.

There arrived in 1850, at Cincinnati, by this canal, 117,655 tons of merchandise, and were cleared during the same period 42,784 tons. There arrived at Toledo in 1850, 122,580 tons, and were cleared 61,390. The increase during the past, over the preceding year, was, at Cincinnati, arrivals, 13,047 tons; clearances 6,568 tons. At Toledo, arrivals, 18,016; clearances, 31,180 tons. The increase of business has been greater at the upper than at the lower end of the canal, both in arrivals and clearances, owing to the extent in which the Little Miami Railroad shares business at this point; but, as will be seen, our railroad facilities have not, thus far, reduced, nor are they ever expected to reduce, materially, or even relatively, the canal business of Cincinnati and vicinity.

CINCINNATI AND WHITEWATER CANAL.

Incorporated, April, 1837.—Charter perpetual.

Length, 25 miles from Harrison to Cincinnati;—connects at Harrison with the Whitewater Valley Canal;—crosses the Dry Fork of Whitewater—the Miami river and Mill creek; the two former through wooden aqueducts; the latter over a free-stone arch;—feeder dam at Harrison, supplied from Whitewater river;—canal passes through the hills dividing the Miami and Ohio rivers by a tunnel 1900 feet long; and comes *up* the bank of the river to the city. Cost of construction and right of way $800,000: the State of Ohio subscribed to the capital stock, $150,000; the City of Cincinnati, $400,000; individuals, about $90,000; the balance of money necessary to complete the work was raised on certificates and bonds, issued by the Company. Boats first passed to the city November, 1843. The great flood in the Whitewater river, in December, 1846, swept away the feeder-dam, and about a mile of the canal at Harrison. The Company repaired the damage during the summer and fall of 1847. In the fall of the same year, another flood swept away the entire canal at Harrison, which determined the company to re-locate on higher ground, which was done in 1848; since which, no accident of any importance has occurred; and it is believed the work is now as permanent as any similar work in the country.—Owing to the interruptions to the business of the canal by these accidents, the revenue has not yet been sufficient to make the repairs, but the increased business, in the last year, leads to the belief, that, though from heavy cost, compared to the *length* of the canal, not much interest will be realized to the stockholders, the city will be exceedingly benefited by the trade from the Whitewater Valley.

Of the receipts of the canal in the month of January, 1851, the collectors' books show

Barrels of flour	19,522	Pounds of bulk pork	1,131,218
" " lard	2,780	Bushels of wheat	7,841
Kegs "	2,765	" " corn	14,177
Casks of hams	76	" " barley	2,284
Hogs	376	" " oats	884
Barrels of pork	504	" " flax-seed	100

Lumber, 92,380 feet, beside wood, stone, shipstuff, bran, bedsteads, &c., &c.

Officers.—William McCammon, President; Larz Anderson, Alex. Webb, John B. Warren, Thomas H. Yeatman, Harvey Calvert, and C. W. West.—Directors; P. Outcalt, Treasurer; C. W. West, Secretary.

Agents—Robe and Higbee, 107, Broad street, New York; C. W. Godard, 98, Pier, Albany, New York; M. Merrick & Co., Oswego, New York; Field & King, Toledo, Ohio.

WESTERN LINE.

Griffith's Western Line, connected with Regular Daily Line of Steamers from Toledo to Buffalo. Also,

We have a Regular line of First-rate Canal boats, to all points on the Wabash Canal.

James Wilson & Co., Commission and Forwarding merchants, Canal and Court streets, between Main and Walnut, Cincinnati, Ohio.

AMERICAN TRANSPORTATION LINE.

James F. Torrence, Commission and Forwarding Merchant, Canal street, between Walnut and Vine streets, Cincinnati, Ohio.

Agent for the American Transportation Company,—through, without transhipment at Albany or Troy. Cargoes Insured.

Two Boats Daily from New York and Buffalo.

REFERENCES.

M. M. Caleb, Hiram Joy, C. V. Clark, 101, Broad street, New York; L. E. Evans, Albany; Niles & Wheeler, Buffalo; Brown & King, Toledo.

MIAMI, WABASH, AND ERIE LINE.

B. & D. Eggleston, Proprietors of a first-rate line of canal boats, on the Miami, Wabash, and Erie Canal, receipt for property to all points on the Lakes and all the eastern cities, and advance on the same, when required. Dealers in New York salt, Lake fish, and produce generally.

JULIUS HULL,

Forwarding and Commission Merchant,

Office, north side Canal, between Main and Sycamore Streets,

Is the proprietor of a line of boats from Cincinnati to Terrehaute, Ia.

Runs eight boats to Wabash canal.

Also, as Agent for New York and Ohio Line, ships goods and produce daily, to New York, Boston, Canada, by way of Toledo, Buffalo, and Oswego.

Runs ten boats in this line; employs seven persons and four horses to each boat; three clerks, and one warehouseman.

Has shipped during the past season, four thousand eight hundred tons goods, to Indiana by canal, and to Toledo, on Lake Erie.

XI. NECROLOGICAL.

THE CEMETERY OF SPRING GROVE.

THIS "rural city of the dead," is situated in the beautiful valley of Mill creek, four miles north of Cincinnati, near what was known, in the pioneer era of this country, as Ludlow's Station. It contains 220 acres, 207 being north of the Hamilton turnpike, and inclosed with a hedge of osage orange, and platted and laid off into sections and lots, for the purposes of sepulture; and thirteen acres south of the road, and bounded by Mill creek, are used for the convenience of the workmen employed about the premises.

The cemetery is laid out in good taste, in the landscape style, and the principal avenues, which are of the liberal width of twenty feet, made to conform to the undulating and picturesque features of the grounds. A more beautiful spot for the purpose, could scarcely have been selected. The original plan was drawn by John Notman of Philadelphia, and afterward altered, in many of the details, by Howard Daniels and the trustees, to harmonize better with the diversified aspect of its rural scenery.

The survey was commenced by Dr. John Locke, upon the system of triangulations, adopted in the United States coast survey; in which he had been for some time engaged; a most accurate and complete method. It was continued by Thomas Earnshaw, assisted by his sons, until his death, in August last.

From a recent report of the trustees, the grounds and improvements, up to the 1st of October last, had cost $54,000, and the improvements by individuals on their own lots, amounted to about as much more. Over fifteen miles of avenues had been opened and graded. The number of lot owners exceeds one thousand.

The following extracts, from a publication of the trustees, will more fully explain the origin and objects of this noble institution; commenced with the purest motives for the public good, without the slightest view to individual gain, but with a sincere wish to confer a benefit on the citizens of Cincinnati, that would endure for ages.

To secure the interesting and salutary associations connected with a rural cemetery, and prevent the evils inseparably connected with burial-grounds within the confines of a city, had long engaged the attention of many of our citizens; some of whom having repeatedly examined the grounds in our vicinity, and fixed upon a proper site called together a few of our prominent citizens, known to be interested in the object, and communicated the result of their explorations. At this meeting, a committee of seven was appointed, to select a suitable site for a cemetery. Of this committee, only four are now living. It was composed of William Neff, R. Buchanan, S. C. Parkhurst, Melzer Flagg, A. H. Ernst, T. H. Minor, David Loring.

This committee proceeded immediately to the discharge of the duty assigned it, and after a careful examination of the ground around our city, reported, at an adjourned meeting, held on the 20th of April, 1844, in favor of purchasing the Garrard Farm, containing about 166 acres, situated in Mill creek township, about four miles from the city. This ground presents every variety of landscape, very beautifully diversified with hill and dale, forest, lawn, and running brook, while the soil is admirably adapted to the purposes of sepulture. It is sufficient in extent to accommodate a great population for many generations, and remote enough from the city not to be disturbed by its extension.

At an adjourned meeting, held on the 27th of April, it was agreed to buy the ground recommended by the committee, and to obtain the necessary funds by subscriptions of $100 each; the payment of which should entitle each subscriber to an area of the ground equal to 50 feet square. So apparent was the necessity of providing a secure place of interment, that the amount necessary to buy the grounds was readily obtained. This gratifying intelligence was communicated to a meeting of the subscribers on the 11th of May, and the proprietors of the ground were directed to be notified that the Association would be prepared to pay for it as soon as the title could be made.

In the autumn of 1844, a committee of eminent legal men was appointed to draft a charter, which was submitted to a meeting on the 25th of October. It was examined, discussed, and amended, at several subsequent meetings, and finally adopted on the 1st Dec., 1844, and John C. Wright, Jacob Burnet, and Timothy Walker, appointed a committee to present it to the Legislature. The Act of Incorporation was immediately procured, the prominent features of which, are as follows:

Every lot-holder is a member, and entitled to a vote.

The corporation is authorized to hold land exempt from execution, and any appropriation to public use, for the sole purpose of a cemetery, not exceeding 300 acres, 167 of which, such as shall be designated by the directors, shall be exempt from taxation.

All receipts, whether from the sale of lots, or otherwise, shall be applied exclusively to laying out, preserving, protecting, and embellishing the cemetery, and the avenues leading thereto.

The original conveyance of lots from the corporation to individuals, shall be evidenced by a certificate under the seal of the corporation, which shall vest in the proprietor, his heirs and assigns, a right in fee simple to such lot, exempt from execution, attachment, taxation, or any other claim or lien, or process whatever, for the sole purpose of interment, under the regulations of the corporation, and said certificate shall have the same force and effect as a deed, duly executed in other cases.

The first meeting of the lot-holders, for the election of directors, in accordance with the provisions of the charter, was held on the 8th February, 1845, when the following persons were elected:

R. Buchanan, William Neff, A. H. Ernst, R. G. Mitchell, D. Loring, N. Wright, J. C. Culbertson, Charles Stetson, Griffin Taylor.

The directors met and organized on the 11th February, 1845, by electing R. Buchanan, President; S. C. Parkhurst, Secretary, and Griffin Taylor, Treasurer.

The board immediately made arrangements for obtaining a survey and plot of the grounds; but as full possession of them could not then be obtained, only the leading avenues were marked out and graded.

On the 5th June, 1845, the lot-holders met and determined their right of choice in the selection of lots.

On the 28th August, the grounds were dedicated with appropriate religious ceremonies, and an address was delivered by the Hon. John McLean.

In the spring of 1847, an opportunity occurred of buying 40 acres north of the cemetery grounds, the diversified character of which, made it a very desirable addition to the cemetery; and as the possession of it would allow of a much better disposition of the avenues than could otherwise be made for the proper development of the original grounds, the funds necessary to buy the tract were readily supplied by the liberality of our citizens; and on the 10th April, 1847, the purchase was fully completed; and the cemetery now comprises an area of 206 acres, all of which is inclosed; and within the inclosure, the whole grounds are surrounded by a hedge of the osage orange.

No labor or expense has been spared by the directors in having the survey carefully and properly made; and when finished, they believe it will be found more accurate and complete than that of the grounds of any other cemetery in the world. Thus, they fondly hope, has been commenced an enterprise, which will be an honor to our city and our age—one which, while it secures a place of repose sacred to the dead, shall purify and refine the living who may resort to it, to linger over the objects of their love, where none of the dreary and revolting associations, connected with a city grave-yard, can ever exist.

Officers.—R. Buchanan, President; E. J. Handy, Secretary; D. H. Horne, Treasurer.

Directors.—R. Buchanan, William Neff, A. H. Ernst, S. C. Parkhurst, Griffin Taylor, James Pullan, Daniel H. Horne, Charles Stetson, William Resor.

Office, Arts-Union building, corner of Sycamore and Fourth Streets.

COMPARATIVE MORTALITY TABLE.

The proportion of deaths to population, in the cities and large towns of the old and new world, is as follows:

EUROPEAN CITIES.		AMERICAN CITIES AND TOWNS.	
Glasgow and Manchester....	1 to 44	Newark, N. J.............	1 to 53
Geneva..................	1 " 43	Natchez..................	1 " 48
London..................	1 " 38	New Haven...............	1 " 48
St. Petersburg............	1 " 37	Charlestown, Mass..........	1 " 48
Birmingham..............	1 " 36	Cambridge	1 " 47
Leghorn.................	1 " 35	Philadelphia..............	1 " 45
Berlin..................	1 " 34	Baltimore................	1 " 45
Lyons, Leeds, Paris, and Sheffield...............	1 " 32	Boston	1 " 44
Bristol..................	1 " 31	Charleston................	1 " 40
Nice and Palermo.........	1 " 31	Cincinnati................	1 " 40
Manchester and Madrid.....	1 " 29	Dayton..................	1 " 40
Liverpool................	1 " 28	Pittsburgh................	1 " 39
Naples	1 " 28	New York................	1 " 38
Brussels.................	1 " 26	Providence, R. I...........	1 " 36
Rome	1 " 25	St. Louis.................	1 " 35
		New Orleans..............	1 " 20

The cities which are lowest on these lists, are rendered so to a great extent, by the influx of foreigners, who—especially emigrants from Ireland—reach this country in circumstances of great destitution, and in many cases, suffering under ship and typhus fever; the effects of unwholesome food, protracted confinement and defective ventilation on board passenger vessels.

XII. PUBLIC INSTITUTIONS, ETC.

COMMERCIAL HOSPITAL AND LUNATIC ASYLUM OF OHIO,

Incorporated January 21, 1821,

Is located on a four acre lot, in the north-western part of Cincinnati, with a view to retirement, and to derive advantages from a pure atmosphere, and free ventilation. It is a brick structure, three stories high, exclusive of the basement, and is large enough to accommodate, at one time, nearly four hundred and fifty persons. Three thousand and sixty were admitted during the past year.

A portion of the building is appropriated as a poorhouse—there are separate apartments for the insane, at this date, numbering ninety individuals—on the second and third stories are the medical and surgical male wards, the female and lying-in wards, and the operating and clinical lecture-room.

The patients of this institution consist of several classes of persons, whose expenses are defrayed from different sources.

Those boatmen who have regularly paid their hospital clearance, according to the commercial regulations of the United States, are maintained at the expense of government.

Others, who have no certificates, testifying as above, are supported out of a portion of the auction duties, collected in Cincinnati.

The poor of Cincinnati township, and transient paupers, also receive support from the treasury of said township. Beside these, patients from other portions of Ohio are received, and charged two dollars per week, for board and medical attendance.

The hospital is intrusted to the trustees of Cincinnati township for its management, except the medical department. Everything appertaining to this, is by law under the direction of the faculty of the Ohio Medical College. As a compensation for the services of the latter, they are permitted to introduce the students of the college to witness the treatment of diseases, the performance of operations, and to receive clinical instruction in the hospital.

CINCINNATI ORPHAN ASYLUM.

Elm, near Thirteenth Street.

THIS has been built up by contributions from the citizens from time to time. It is a well-planned and proportioned building, which has cost about $18,000, and presents a handsome appearance, its interior arrangements being highly convenient. The dimensions are 64 by 54 feet.

Including the basement, it consists of four stories, which contain spacious sleeping apartments, bath-houses, a separate department for infants, where they are provided with proper nurses, and the sustenance suited to their age; a library, and a well organized school, in which the children are not only taught the common branches of education, but receive that moral and religious training, which prepares them to become useful members of society: at the same time, in the ample grounds surrounding the house, they are enabled to take such exercise as is necessary to promote their health.

The laws of the institution appear formed with a careful regard to the future well-being of the orphans.

No child is permitted to be taken out of the asylum, until it has remained there at least one year, so that vicious habits may be corrected, before they mingle with society. The strictest scrutiny is made into the character of individuals who apply for children, and they are placed only in those situations, where, it is believed, the same attention will be given to train their minds to virtue as in the asylum. Stipulations are made as to the amount of education they shall receive, and with regard to their future prospects in life. When a child leaves the institution, a manager is appointed as its guardian, to whom, in case of grievance, it may apply for redress, and look for protection.

An average number of sixty children have annually been supported in the asylum, so that upward of three hundred children have been, from time to time, maintained and educated, under its protecting roof. Sixty-seven orphans and destitute children are now enjoying the benefits which this institution affords.

ST. PETER'S ORPHAN ASYLUM.

UNDER THE CARE OF EIGHT SISTERS OF CHARITY.

Corner of Third and Plum Streets.

INMATES one hundred and forty-five females.

ST. ALOYSIUS' ORPHAN HOME.

UNDER THE CARE OF THE SOCIETY OF THAT NAME.

South side of Fourth Street, west of Western Row.

INSTITUTED for boys, of which there are one hundred within its walls.

The value of systematic efforts in benevolence, is here clearly shown in the fact, that these asylums are supported by the contributions of sixteen hundred members of the Roman Catholic Church, in monthly payments of twenty-five cents each.

GERMAN PROTESTANT ORPHAN ASYLUM.

Chartered 1849.

LEWIS WEITZEL, President; Adam Hornung, Corresponding Secretary; Jacob Menzel, Recording Secretary; John N. Siebern, Treasurer.

Frederic Reisz, Jacob Hust, F. H. Lilie, Simon Fieber, Henry Weichers, Dietrich Meyer, Henry Stegner,—Trustees.

This institution is just about going into operation, and it is expected, will accommodate one hundred and fifty orphans.

The lot on which the asylum has been built, is 484 by 360 feet, and comprehends four acres. The asylum is built on the skirts of Mount Auburn, and is 54 by 48 feet. It is three stories in height—the basement being six feet above the ground, the first and second stories, twelve feet, and the third, fifteen feet high. It will be finished in a few days, and ample resources are provided for its support.

There is an Asylum for Colored Orphans, on Ninth, between Elm and Plum streets, capable of accommodating sixty or seventy children; the children being put out to various employments, as soon as they become capable of usefulness; there are, therefore, rarely more than twelve or fifteen inmates dwelling at one time in this asylum.

THE WIDOWS' HOME.

An impulse was given, by a few public spirited individuals, during the inclemency of the winter of 1850, to the claims of aged, infirm and indigent females on the sympathy and support of the community. An effort had been already made which secured $1500 toward a building lot, on which to erect the necessary edifice suited for an asylum for individuals of this class. But the enterprise languished under the weight of responsibility to carry it through, when Wesley Smead, the banker, making a thirty days' business of the project, by personal application to all classes, succeeded in obtaining contributions for the erection of "The Widows' Home and Asylum for aged and indigent Females," to the amount of $16,000. Messrs. Burnet, Reader, Shillito and M'Lean, generously presented the institution with a lot on Mount Auburn, two hundred feet square, worth $4000 more; and a spacious building, with a neat and elegant Grecian front, is now rapidly in progress. This edifice will be one hundred and thirty by fifty feet, three stories high, in the main building, and two stories on the two wings.

Mr. Smead's own liberal contribution of $6000, together with the $1500 already alluded to, as invested at ten per cent., will form an endowment for the support of the institution, when in operation. In addition to this, there are already four hundred annual subscribers, at three dollars each—a number which will greatly enlarge, so soon as the house shall receive its inmates—and the act of incorporation, by the State Legislature, directs an annual appropriation of $500 by the township of Cincinnati. The Widows' Home, when finished, is capable of accommodating comfortably one hundred individuals; and its projectors and patrons entertain no doubt that the necessary funds for its support, beyond the resources already pointed out, can be raised in the city without any difficulty.

HOUSE OF REFUGE.

Established April 25th, 1850,—went into operation September 1st, 1850.

The grounds connected with the House of Refuge are pleasantly situated between the Colerain Turnpike and the Miami Canal, about three-quarters of a mile north of the present corporation line. They were purchased from Joseph R. Riddle, for the sum of $7896.

There are 430,000 feet, nearly ten acres, in the whole tract;

260,000 of which are inclosed with a wall seventeen feet high, and averaging two and a half feet thick. The remaining 170,000 feet, lying between the turnpike and the walls, will be ornamented with trees, shrubbery, &c., and used as pleasure grounds.

The dimensions of the buildings are as follows, viz: The front, facing the road, is two hundred and seventy-six feet long, fifty-seven and a half feet wide, and four stories high above the basement. The centre building is eighty-four and two-thirds feet long. The three lower stories are appropriated for the use of Directors, Superintendent, Matron, and others, in charge of the Institution. The fourth story is to be used as an Infirmary.

Joined to the main building are the two wings, each ninety-five and two-thirds feet long, in which are one hundred and eight dormitories for boys, and seventy-two for girls.

The buildings are of limestone, obtained from the adjacent hills. The coping to the walls, caps and sills to windows, &c., are of Dayton stone.

The front is ornamented with a beautiful portico, of marble, obtained fourteen miles below Madison, on the Ohio river.

In the rear of the centre building, and connected with it by a gallery twenty-five feet long, is a back building one hundred and fourteen feet long, fifty-six feet wide, and two stories high. The second story contains two school rooms, each fifty feet by twenty-five, and a chapel fifty-eight by fifty-two. The lower story is designed for dining-rooms for the boys and girls, kitchen, store-rooms, &c.

Still in the rear is a one story building, forty feet long, used as a boys' bathing-room, and room for washing clothes.

There are in all over two hundred and fifty rooms, including the dormitories. All the rooms are to be warmed by steam. There is to be a boiler outside the boys' bathing room, of sufficient capacity to do all the cooking, washing, heating water, and also to generate steam to warm the whole building completely throughout.

A large drain passes under ground from the Canal to Mill creek, by which all the filth and offal is carried away from the premises.

Large cisterns, receiving water from the slated roofs, will afford an abundant supply of wholesome water for the whole establishment.

The rooms are lighted with gas manufactured on the premises.

The entire cost of the buildings and fixtures is about $150,000.

Competent judges, after surveying the premises, pronounce them to be the best constructed and most convenient of the kind in the United States.

There are about ninety inmates of this establishment, at present.

Officers.—Thomas J. Biggs, D. D., Chairman; Miles Greenwood, Treasurer; Rufus Hubbard, Superintendent; Ann Carter, Matron; Morris B. Fifield, Steward; William Leuthstrom, Secretary.

Directors.—Thomas J. Biggs, D. D., William Neff, Elam P. Langdon, William McCammon, Charles Thomas, Miles Greenwood, Hudson B. Curtis, Alphonso Taft, and Wm. Burnet.

POOR HOUSE AND FARM.

The city has purchased a farm, in the vicinity of Carthage, on which paupers, who are now depending on the public for support, will be employed, in earning their own means of subsistence. On this suitable buildings are in process of construction, and will be made ready for occupation in the course of the current year. The farm consists of 164$\frac{47}{100}$ acres, and cost $16,500. The building is expected to cost $120,000. Much benefit will doubtless result to Cincinnati from this institution, if it should accomplish nothing more than to rid the community of idlers and street beggars, which are yearly, in enlarging numbers, coming in from other parts of the country, and from foreign lands.

CINCINNATI RELIEF UNION.

This admirable institution owes its existence, as well as much of its efficient organization and success, to the late Rev. James H. Perkins, whose whole life was spent in promoting the welfare of his fellow-beings, by relieving suffering wherever it fell under his notice, and searching out objects of beneficence, as opportunity served. His sudden and regretted death is a great loss to his associates in this labor of love.

The present officers are, Rev. A. Blake, President; G. Taylor, Treasurer; Dr. A. L. Bushnell, General Agent.

The general objects the Relief Union have in view, may be briefly comprehended under the following heads:—

1st. The *temporary relief*, of those who are actually needy, and who have none to help them but the hand of charity.

2d. The prevention of *street-begging*, from house to house, and the detection of impostors.

3d. To act, as a voluntary agent, for the poor and the stranger—by obtaining for them employment, and raising up for them friends.

4th. By a faithful and continued effort, to bring the young under proper and healthful moral influences—by obtaining homes for the homeless, and instruction and employment for the ignorant and idle.

Many other objects might be mentioned, but it is believed that all may be included in these.

Temporary relief has been given to more than five hundred families, embracing between two and three thousand individuals. The amount given, and the time of its continuance, has varied according to circumstances.

This has been done, after personal visitation and investigation, by donations of money, provisions, clothing, shoes, beds, bedding, fuel, medicines, and nurses.

As will be seen by reference to the Treasurer's report, two thousand one hundred and thirteen dollars and seventy-eight cents have been *received*, and one thousand nine hundred and thirteen dollars and seventy-seven cents paid out to the members of the board of control, for expenditure in their respective wards. The above sum, only embraces a part of what has been expended by the society, as donations of clothing, provisions, &c., do not pass through the treasurer's hands, but are given out in the different wards, under the direction of the superintendents and visitors. The whole amount expended by the society during the year, including clothing, food, fuel, &c., will probably more than double that reported by the treasurer ; and this sum, will not include a large amount given indirectly through the influence of the Relief Union, by individuals and families, who are thus made acquainted with needy and worthy cases.

There are two or three houses of employment, for the relief of women seeking work, such as that of the Daughters of Temperance and Female House of Industry, which are the means of obviating much suffering during the inclement period of winter.

HOTEL FOR INVALIDS,

AND ORTHOPŒDIC INSTITUTION.

Corner of Broadway and Franklin Streets.

It is the object of this institution to provide for transient persons sick in our city, and such of our citizens as have not families to administer to them, when afflicted, the constant and efficient attention of well-regulated hospitals, with the comfort and quiet of the best conducted boarding-houses. In every city of considerable population within the United States, the want of such provision has been most painfully felt. Hotels or boarding-houses are objected to, either because of charges too heavy to be long borne, or the want of such nurses as can be trusted; and to the public hospitals there is attached a prejudice, however unjustly, so strong, that many risk their lives rather than enter them. These difficulties, it is hoped, will be avoided so far as possible, by keeping the best nurses, and by making the rates of the establishment so low, that its advantages may be within reach of almost every class of the community.

The institution is spacious, and delightfully situated; is superintended by J. A. Denis; has the constant presence of a competent house physician, and will be subject in all its arrangements, to the directions of the medical attendants.

Every variety of disease will be admitted into the house, except those that are *contagious.*

Beside their uniting in the attendance to the sick of the house generally, they will give *special attention* to all the operations and diseases of the eye and ear, and diseases of females. Diseases of the skin, chest, and urinary organs, as well as the operations of lithotomy, lithotrity, club foot, wry neck, curvatures of the spine, and other deformities. The house is furnished with warm, cold, shower, salt, iodine, sulphurous, and other medicated baths.

Applications for admission may be made to the superintendent, at the house, or to the medical attendants at their residences.

Charles L. Avery, M. D., south side of Seventh street, between Vine and Race. John L. Vattier, M. D., west side of Vine street, between Ninth and Court. E. K. Chamberlain, M. D., Sixth street, opposite U. S. Hotel. John F. White, M. D., south side Fourth street, between Race and Elm.

TRACT DEPOSITORY,

AND AGENCY OF THE AMERICAN TRACT SOCIETY.

This depository and agency, under the superintendence of Seely Wood, as agent of the society, is located in the Melodeon building, 163 Walnut Street.

This City was selected, ten years since, as a central point for the supervision of colportage in the west and south-west, and for the reshipment of books to colporteurs, of whom it employs more than one hundred English and German in this State, and in Indiana, Kentucky, Tennessee, North Alabama, Mississippi, and Arkansas, whose supplies are shipped by boats running on the Ohio, Muskingum, Kanawha, Kentucky, Green, Wabash, Cumberland, Tennessee, Mississippi, and Arkansas rivers, and the canals and railroads centering here.

The depository is furnished with a complete assortment of the society's publications, consisting of more than 1200 different books, tracts, and children's tracts, in English, German, French, Spanish, Portuguese, Italian, Dutch, Danish, Swedish, and Welsh; which in point of execution, are the most beautiful specimens of typography the country affords. These publications are furnished not only to colporteurs, but to individuals and to the trade generally, on the same terms as at the society's house in New York; the purchasers thereby saving five per cent. in freight and exchange.

This agency distributes more than $40,000 worth of publications annually, of which, $6000 worth are disposed of gratuitously, among the destitute native and foreign population, by colporteurs.

American B. C. Foreign Missions.—Missionary rooms, 28 west Fourth Street.

Rev. H. A. Tracy, District Secretary; Dr. Geo. L. Weed, Receiving Agent.

Publications.— Missionary Herald, Journal of Missions, and Youth's Day Spring.

American and Foreign Christian Union.—Office, 28 west Fourth Street.

Rev. Samuel Day, District Secretary.

American Sunday School Union.—Book Depository, 28 west Fourth Street.

Rev. B. W. Chidlaw, General Agent; G. L. Weed, Depositary.

Cincinnati Young Men's Bible Society.— Office, 28 west Fourth Street. G. L. Weed, Depositary

BENEVOLENT SOCIETIES.

Cincinnati Colonization Society. Ohio Anti-Slavery Society. Caledonian Society. Scots' Benevolent Society. St. George's Society. Cincinnati Typographical Association. Hibernian Benevolent Society.

TEMPERANCE SOCIETIES.

CADETS OF TEMPERANCE.

Washington Section, No. 1, meets Monday evenings, at Foster Hall. Queen City Section, No. 2, meets Friday evenings, at Foster Hall. Cincinnati Section, No. 3, meets Monday evenings, at Losantiville Hall.

DAUGHTERS OF TEMPERANCE.

Washington Union, No. 1, meets every Thursday afternoon, in Foster Hall. Olive Branch Union, No. 2, meets every Tuesday afternoon, at Foster Hall. Queen City Union, No. 3, meets every Monday afternoon, at Foster Hall. Bethel Union, No. 4, meets every Tuesday afternoon, at Bethel Chapel, on Front St. Friendship Union, No. 6, meets every Wednesday afternoon, at Foster Hall. Cary Union, No. 8, meets every Saturday afternoon.

SONS OF TEMPERANCE.

Ohio Division, No. 1, meets every Monday evening, at Foster Hall, south-east corner Fifth and Walnut Streets. Cincinnati Division, No. 2, meets every Thursday evening, at Foster Hall. Queen City Division, No. 3, meets every Friday evening, at Foster Hall. Fulton Division, No. 8, meets every Wednesday evening at their hall in the basement story of the McKendree Chapel, Fulton. Lafayette Division, No. 18, meets every Tuesday evening, at Temple Hall. Jefferson Division, No. 24, meets every Friday evening, in the Hall of the Eastern Fire Co., No. 6, adjoining the 3d District School-House, Front Street. Union Division, No. 30, meets every Monday evening, at Foster Hall. Star Division, No. 50, meets Monday evenings; Hall, corner Clinton and Cutter. Third Ward Division, No. 55, meets on Thursday evening, in Bethel Chapel, east of Front Street.

TEMPLES OF HONOR.

Grand Temple of Honor of the State of Ohio, meets semi-annually in the months of May and November; annual session in May. Cincinnati Temple of Honor, No. 1, meets every Friday evening, at Temple Hall. Washington Temple of Honor, No. 2, meets every Thursday evening, at Temple Hall. Ohio Temple of Honor, No. 7, meets every Wednesday evening, at Temple Hall. Union Temple of Honor, No. 9, meets every Thursday evening, at Hall, corner of

Western Row and Wade. Losantiville Temple of Honor, No. 10, meets every Tuesday evening, in Losantiville Hall. Mechanics' Temple of Honor, No. 17, meets every Friday evening, in Fulton.

DEGREE TEMPLES.

Aurora Degree Temple, No. 1, meets the first and third Saturday evenings of each month, at Temple Hall. Mt. Sinai Degree Temple, No. 12, meets second Tuesday evening in each month, at Hall, corner of Western Row and Wade Street. Apollo Degree Temple, No. 6, meets in Fulton.

MASONIC.

Cincinnati Encampment, No. 3, meets second Monday in each month. Cincinnati Council, No. 1, meets 3d Monday in each month. Cincinnati Chapter, No. 2, meets 1st Monday in each month. Mc Millan Chapter, No. 19, meets last Tuesday in each month. N. C. Harmony Lodge, No. 2, meets 1st Wednesday in each month. Miami Lodge, No. 46, meets 1st Tuesday in each month. Lafayette Lodge, No. 81, meets 1st Thursday in each month. Cincinnati Lodge, No. 133, meets last Thursday in each month. McMillan Lodge, No. 141, meets last Wednesday in each month. Cynthia Lodge, No. 155, meets 1st Friday in each month.

The Masonic Hall.—This fine edifice stands at the north-east corner of Walnut and Third streets, occupying a front of one hundred and fifteen feet on its southern, and sixty-six feet on its western exposure, and is eighty feet high from the pavement to the top of the angle buttress. It was erected at an expense of thirty thousand dollars, and its appropriate furniture and decorations, cost five thousand more. It is in the castellated style of the Gothic architecture of the Elizabethan era. The lower story is partitioned into five store rooms, and a spacious banking hall and offices occupied by Ellis & Morton for banking purposes.

The front is divided by buttresses, two feet face, and eight inches projection. These buttresses run above the battlements, the tops of which are finished with openings in the ancient castle style. The windows to the principal hall are sixteen feet high, and are divided by a heavy centre mullion and cross rail, making four parts in each. Each window is surmounted by a hood of fine cut stone. The windows of the third story are nearly of the same size, order, and finish.

At each end of the building on the south front, two of the buttresses are elevated a few feet above the centre, and returned on the west front the same distance. Each angle of the west front, is made to correspond with each angle of the south front. The centre of the west front is gabled ; in the centre of which is a shield, with an inscription bearing the name of the building and date of its erection, together with the era of masonry. An iron balcony surrounds the building, on a level with the floor of the main hall in the second story. This is designed for public assemblies, and is one of the most spacious in Cincinnati, being fifty-one by one hundred and twelve feet, fronting west, and twenty-three feet high, with an orchestra on the east end. The ceiling and cornice of this hall are finished in the richest style.

The third story is designed as a hall, for the use of the several lodges of the city, together with the chapter, council, and encampment, and is eighty by fifty-one on the floor, and twenty feet in height. There are various passages, antechambers, and committee rooms, which fill up the residue of this story. The chapter room proper, is fifty-one by twenty-eight feet. The finish of these rooms, especially the ceilings and cornices, are truly elaborate. The exterior of the edifice is rough-cast, and the roof slate.

The furniture of the chapter room is of mahogany, with Gothic open panel work, on a rich crimson satin ground. That of the Masonic Hall is of bronzed work of the same character, excepting that the satin is of mazarine blue. The carpets are of ingrain, of the best quality of Mosaic work pattern, with tesselated borders. Seven splendid Gothic chandeliers ornament the various halls—these are lighted with gas.

ODD FELLOWS.

THE Hall of the Independent Order of Odd Fellows is at the north-west corner of Third and Walnut.

Grand Lodge of Ohio, meets in Cincinnati on the 1st Wednesday in January and July. Grand Encampment of Ohio, meets on the 1st Saturday, after 3d Wednesday in July, October, January and April. Ohio Lodge, No. 1, meets Monday evening, at Odd Fellows' Hall. Washington Lodge, No. 2, meets Tuesday evening, at Odd Fellows' Hall. Cincinnati Lodge, No. 3, meets Wednesday evening, at Odd Fellows' Hall. Franklin Lodge, No. 4, meets on Thursday evening, at Odd Fellows' Hall. Wm. Penn Lodge, No. 56, meets Tuesday evening, at their Hall, corner of Eighth and Western Row. Fidelity Lodge, No. 71, meets on Monday evening, north-west corner of Western Row and Wade. Magnolia Lodge, No. 83, meets on Monday evening at Magnolia Hall. Eagle Lodge, No. 100, meets Wednesday evening at Odd Fellows' Hall. German Lodge, No. 113, meets on Thursday evening on Court street, between Main and Walnut. Metropolitan, No. 142, meets on Tuesday, at Odd Fellows' Hall. Mohawk, 150, meets Tuesday, at Richardson Hall, near Mohawk bridge. Woodward, No. 149, meets Tuesday, at the Hall on Court street.

ENCAMPMENTS.

Wildey, No. 1, meets at Odd Fellows' Hall 1st and 3d Fridays. Washington, No. 9, meets on Western Row, 28th, 1st and 3d Thursdays. Cincinnati, No. 22, meets at Magnolia Hall, 2d, and 4th Fridays. Mahketawah, No. 32, meets at Odd Fellows' Hall, 2d, and 4th Friday. Hesperian, No. —, meets between Western Row and Wade street. Schiller, No. 42, meets Monday evening, north side of Court, between Main and Walnut.

PUBLIC HALLS.

Within a few years past, spacious and commodious buildings have been erected as public halls, for concerts, lecture and society rooms, and public offices. Among these, alphabetically, may be noticed as of special importance:

Apollo Hall.—North-west corner of Walnut and Fifth streets. A range of stores on the ground floor; Wood's Museum, Gundry's Commercial College, Hawkins' Daguerrean Gallery, and various private offices, on the upper stories. The building is five stories in height, and eighty-three by one hundred feet in its front. J. P. Broadwell, proprietor.

Bromwell's Building.—North-east corner of Vine and Fourth street. Height, four stories, and fifty, by fifty feet on the ground. A range of stores below; offices of the Ohio and Mississippi Railroad, daguerrean rooms, and various private offices on second and third stories. Hall on the fourth story, the entire size of the building. Dayton marble fronts; Jacob Bromwell, proprietor, J. O. Sawyer, architect.

Centre Hall, is a building at the intersection of Western Row and Fifth street. It has a large saloon for public meetings and various rooms, including a banking-house at the corner, on the first floor; and office rooms throughout the building. J. L. Scott, proprietor.

CINCINNATI COLLEGE.—This is a modern edifice, of the Grecian Doric order, with pilaster fronts, and facade of Dayton marble. It is of three stories, exclusive of an attic, the whole being one hundred and forty feet by one hundred in depth, and sixty in height, and has cost forty thousand dollars.

It is on the east side of Walnut, between Fourth and Fifth streets. The ground story, in front, is divided into eight spacious rooms for stores. In the rear of these are three spacious halls, occupied as a hall for meetings of the City Council, and for city public offices of various descriptions. The front range, on the second floor, is designed for the accommodation of the Young Men's Library Association and Reading rooms, and as a Merchants' Exchange. The Exchange is forty-five by fifty-nine feet; the reading and library rooms, each, forty-five by twenty-nine feet. There is also a room fourteen by sixteen feet for the use of the directors. In the rear of these is the great Hall of the building for public meetings of the citizens, which is one hundred and thirty-six feet long, by fifty feet broad, and thirty-one high.

The various study and recitation rooms appropriate to the college itself, are in the third story, and occupy a space of forty-five feet by one hundred and thirty-six feet, being the whole length of the building.

The attic is subdivided into a spacious gallery, a room for chemical and philosophical apparatus, and the lecture-room of the law school connected with the college. Fourteen large offices occupy the entire range in the rear.

The whole is thoroughly lighted by gas, and properly ventilated with suitable passages and openings, and an ample amount of daylight secured in the rear, for the benefit of the rooms and offices which face in that direction.

The entire building is roofed in the most substantial manner; finished with projecting stone cornice, and surmounted with a cupola, modeled on a design taken from the Tower of the Winds, at Athens.

One million of bricks, beside a large quantity of building and ornamental stone, have been employed in the construction of this edifice.

COURT-STREET HALL.—North side Court, between Main and Walnut streets. This building is occupied, on the second and third floors, with the office of the sheriff of Hamilton County, and the clerks' offices of the courts. In the fourth story are held the sessions of the Court of Common Pleas, the Commercial, and the Superior Courts of Hamilton County. J. Wilson & Co., proprietors.

THE MELODEON.—This is one among the most prominent and elegant buildings in Cincinnati. It is situated on the north-west corner of Fourth and Walnut streets, and covers an area of sixty-nine feet by one hundred. The lower story is divided into eight stores, with basement rooms, several of which, have tesselated marble floors, and are otherwise handsomely fitted up. The corner store of this building, is occupied as a Dentist's and Daguerreotypist's depôt, at which place these professions are furnished with every variety of business stock and tools. Adjoining this, and fronting on both streets, is a Music Publishing establishment, on a most extensive scale. Next, fronting on Fourth street, is a Drug and Apothecary store, fitted up with exquisite taste; and adjoining this, the Universalist Book depôt, and publication office, fronting on Walnut street. One store is occupied as the American Tract Depository, and another as Jennings' Patent Phosgene Gas and Lamp establishment. The second story is divided into eight well finished single and double rooms, with marble floor on the landing of the main entrance. The principal part of this story is occupied as Bartlett's Commercial College, and Faris's Daguerrean Gallery, the remainder as dressing rooms, janitor's rooms, proprietor's office, etc. The third story is a Public Hall, which covers nearly the whole area of the building, being about one hundred feet in length, sixty in width, and twenty-five in height. It is fitted up and finished in the most elegant style, with stuccoed frieze, cornice and ceiling, and in architectural beauty, is probably equal to any hall in the country. This building was erected by Lewis Williams, of Philadelphia, in 1846, and has been much admired for its beauty and simplicity of architecture.

There are other buildings, more or less of public character, which are dismissed without special notices, as being collections of business offices, mostly; many of these are of great extent and importance, however, in this respect. One of these may be referred to as an example. This is

REEDER'S BUILDING—Between Walnut and Vine Sts., fronts sixty feet on Third, and seventy-six feet on Pearl street, being two hundred and twenty feet in depth. It is six stories high on Third, and four stories on Pearl street. Not less than 1,250,000 bricks have been laid into these walls. This makes it the largest brick building, with partitions, in Cincinnati. It comprehends one hundred and twelve rooms, for stores, offices, and sleeping chambers; all well lighted, ventilated, and amply supplied with water, and protected by water-tanks—in every story, kept full, at all times—from fires that may originate within its walls. All its other arrangements and business appliances are perfect.

The Third street front is faced with free-stone and protected, by revolving iron window-shutters, alike from fraud and violence.

HOTELS

Burnet House, north-west corner of Third and Vine streets. This is undoubtedly the most spacious, and probably the best, hotel, in its interior and domestic arrangements, of any in the world. It is of recent construction, and put up by a joint-stock company, who have leased it for a term of years, to A. B. Coleman, its present proprietor. The building, including the terrace, is two hundred and twelve feet on Third street, and two hundred and ten feet to its rear on Burnet street. Its style of architecture is the Bracketed Italian. It is six stories in height, with a dome forty-two feet in diameter, which is one hundred feet above the basement floor. The observatory commands a fine view of the city, and more particularly of the river Ohio and the Kentucky scenery beyond, being one hundred and forty-two feet above the level of the street on which it fronts. The entire house contains three hundred and forty rooms, all properly lighted and ventilated. The Burnet House is central to the river and canal; and when the railroad communications, in progress here, shall be completed, will be so to all the traveling public landings and depôts.

Gibson House—D. V. Bennett, proprietor. This is located on the west side of Walnut, between Fourth and Fifth streets, and is seventy feet front by two hundred feet deep. It is convenient to the mercantile and general business region of the city, and is immediately adjacent to the College buildings, which are occupied by the Chamber of Commerce, the Merchants' Exchange, and the Young Men's Library Association. In this building, also, the City Council holds its sessions and keeps the various city offices. The Gibson

House comprehends one hundred and twenty-three chambers and parlors, and can seat two hundred and fifty guests at the public table. The dining-room is one hundred, by thirty feet, with an elevation of twenty feet to the ceiling. The house is heated, and the cooking and washing done, entirely by steam. A corridor, extending the entire length of the rear building, affords entrances to each series of chambers, adding also to the light and ventilation of the various rooms. The main staircase is spiral, of great beauty, convenience and safety, a dome and skylight gracefully crowning the entire ascent. The construction of the Gibson House affords peculiar advantage to travelers in whose case order and quiet repose are desirable. From the nature of the building, which possesses but one entry on a floor, and one staircase to the entire house, and that of a character which does not reverberate sound, there need not be, and there is not, more disturbance during sleeping hours than in an ordinary private house.

Dennison House.—One of the oldest, as well as the most popular of our hotels, is the Dennison House.

This has always been one of our most important public houses; and being in the centre of the wholesale dry-goods and hardware trade—contiguous to the principal market-houses—to the Merchants' Exchange and Library Rooms, as well as to the Post-office, it has always been a favorite house with a large share of country merchants, from Kentucky, Ohio, Indiana and Virginia, and persons on business from other quarters. It has recently undergone an extensive rebuilding, and entire re-modeling, inside, as well as in its external appearance, enlarging itself to double its former front, and greatly increasing its depth.

As the result of these improvements and additions, it is now one of the most spacious of our city hotels, presenting an imposing front of ninety-four feet extent, with a depth of one hundred feet. It is five stories high, besides the usual basement.

The building is well lighted and admirably ventilated; with a fine parlor and drawing-room for ladies, and one hundred and four lodging apartments of ample size. The *facade* of the hotel is ornamented with two porticoes, and galleries pass round each side of the area, in the rear, of every story of the house.

This Hotel was established in 1824, by William Dennison, Sen., who has since connected his son, E. B. Dennison, in the enterprise.

Walnut Street House—At the corner of Walnut and Gano

streets, is a new and very commodious edifice, kept by J. W. Sweney. It covers ten thousand square feet of ground; is five stories high, exclusive of the basement, and comprehends one hundred and eighty-three rooms, all of convenient size and arrangement, and many of them spacious and elegant.

The floors of the business rooms are covered with ornamented cast iron plates, tesselated into squares. The residue of the house is carpeted throughout.

The dining-room is one of the finest to be seen in Cincinnati—if not anywhere. It is 90 feet by 40 feet, with a height of 20 feet; the ceiling enriched with elegantly rich frescos. The entire furniture in this house, in its various departments, cost over twenty-five thousand dollars.

A magnificent view, for miles, in all directions, is afforded by the observatory, at the summit of this building.

Pearl Street House—Kept by W. H. Henrie. This is one of our oldest hotels. It is about to be re-modeled, if not re-built, by extending its Walnut street front, north, to the corner of Third street, and thence east one hundred feet. This improvement and enlargement, will render it as spacious as any hotel in Cincinnati. The proprietor, Henry Brachmann, is just setting out for Europe, and as soon as he returns, these changes will, doubtless, take effect.

The Pearl Street House is contiguous to the wholesale stores, to the public landing of Cincinnati, and central to the depôts of the various railroad lines to this city. It has always shared largely in the hotel business of Cincinnati.

Woodruff House—P. E. & G. P. Tuttle, proprietors, Sycamore street, between Third and Fourth. This is a newly erected edifice, which has a west front on Hammond street, as well as its principal front on Sycamore street. Each front is fifty feet, and its entire depth two hundred. The lot on which it stands, contains ten thousand square feet. It is five stories high, exclusive of the basement, and measures, from the side-walk to the top in front, seventy feet. The building contains rooms, equal to one hundred and thirty of the size usual in hotels. This house is located in the most populous and business portion of the city, a short distance from the Ohio river, at the centre of the public landing, and convenient to the railroad depôts, Post-office and Canal, and within one square of Main street.

The roof of the building affords a pleasant promenade, as well as a fine view of the river and surrounding country.

UNITED STATES HOTEL—A. Wetherbee, proprietor, corner of Walnut and Sixth streets. It fronts 130 feet on Sixth street, and 40 feet on Walnut street, and contains one hundred and fifty chambers. This house has always been popular and prosperous.

HENRIE HOUSE—L. Mount, proprietor, north side of Third street, between Main and Sycamore. The Third street front, is 96 feet—depth, 100 feet, with a front on Hammond street. It has nearly one hundred rooms. This is one of our long established houses, and enjoys a high reputation.

WAVERLEY HOUSE—R. H. Hendrickson, proprietor. This hotel is well adapted, from its vicinity to Main and Court streets, to the reception and accommodation of travelers who have business with the county offices, and the courts of justice, of Hamilton county, which are in session nearly all the time. It enjoys the best share of the travel, from the interior of Ohio and Indiana, and, in the winter season, of Kentucky also.

The building is 51 feet on Main street, by 200 feet deep, and contains one hundred rooms, of various sizes, but all convenient.

BATH HOUSES.

SEVERAL of the Hotels—the Burnet, Woodruff, and Gibson Houses, among others—have bathing rooms for the use of the public, on a scale commensurate with their other appointments. Beside these, there are several public bath houses, of which two may be selected to advantage. These are:

1. The Metropolitan Bath House, No. 137 Sycamore street, Jackson & Ophof, proprietors. These consist of an arcade of 130 feet in length, divided into twenty-six rooms, thirteen on a side, and eight by ten feet in size. Twenty of these are for gentlemen, and six, including dressing-room, for ladies. These have separate entrances. The ceiling is vaulted, and lighted by a series of sky-lights. A hall of 7½ feet separates the two suites of bathing rooms. Warm, cold and shower baths at all hours. In the rear is a plunge bath, 14 by 18 feet, and 5 feet deep.

2. Bath House, corner of Third and Masonic Alley. This is the well-known establishment of W. W. Watson—now occupied by Watson & Barnett, his successors. It is in the most central part of the city, well ventilated, and lighted with gas. Shower, hot and cold baths, at the pleasure of the visitor, at all hours.

FIRE DEPARTMENT.

THERE are eighteen companies of Firemen belonging to the Fire Department, as follows:

No. 1. Washington,
2. Relief,
3. Independence,
4. Franklin,
5. Invincible,
6. Eastern,
7. Northern,
8. Marion,

No. 9. Union,
Independent, No. 1.
Independent, " 2.
Independent Western,
Eagle,
Mohawk,
Brighton,

Each of these companies is provided with Fire and Suction Engines and Hose Reel; so that every company possesses the full apparatus to extinguish fires, without depending on the aid of other independent companies, to furnish any part of the apparatus on the ground. There are thus forty-five carriages, of the best construction and materials, dispersed all over the city, and as many always in attendance as can work to advantage.

There are beside, two hook and ladder companies, and one company of fire guards, to render appropriate services, as they may be required. There are eighteen hundred members of these various companies, a large share of whom, are young men, and in unmarried life.

There are eighty-three public cisterns, and seventy-nine fireplugs, employed for the extinguishment of fires exclusively.

FOREIGN CONSULATES.

James F. Meline, Consular Agent of the French Republic.—Office, No. 99 West Third Street.

C. F. Adae, Consul of the Kingdoms of Württemberg, Bavaria, Hanover, and the Grand Duchy of Oldenburg.—Office, No. 16 West Front Street.

ENGRAVED BY F. E. JONES FROM A DAGUERREOTYPE.

George W. Neff

XIII. MANUFACTURES AND INDUSTRIAL PRODUCTS.

Manufactures, being the great source of the prosperity of Cincinnati, and the great element of its progress, should, therefore, naturally occupy a large share of this volume. In this article it is designed to exhibit these features—the share which raw material bears to the final product; the number of hands employed; and the value of the products. An opportunity is thus afforded, by a scrutiny of the details, to determine the accuracy of the aggregates they make, and the justice of the deductions to which they point.

Agricultural Machines. A. C. Brown, 37 Walnut street.—These consist of harvesters and mowing-machines, grain and grain thrashing machines, and horse powers, for one, two, four and six horses; portable French burr-stone mills; stock mills, for grinding corn and cobs together, and other grain for feeding purposes; corn-shellers, to shell twenty to fifty bushels per hour; straw-cutters, tanning mills, clover hullers, corn planters, cultivators, drilling machines, wool carding machines, and machine cards. Steam power; employs thirty hands, and manufactures, yearly, to the value of thirty-six thousand dollars. Raw materials—22 per cent. of the value of product.

Alcohol and Spirits of Wine.—These are articles, which, although usually considered the same, are materially different. Alcohol is whisky, distilled to its highest grade of proof, and is employed in the mechanic arts, as the basis of essences and medical tinctures, and as a solvent in various manufacturing operations.

Neutral Spirit, is the same article in point of strength, but divested, in its manufacture, of all empyreumatic odor and taste. It forms the basis of domestic brandies, gins, &c. When abundant harvests in the west are likely to depress the price of corn, the same motive which prompts the farmer to put his crop into pork, by the feeding of it to hogs, suggests, also, the manufacture into whisky; in both cases, a bulky and heavy product, being converted into an article of greater value and profit, because more convenient for transportation to market. The same principle, carried out, induces the shipment of whisky, in the form of alcohol, which, condensing two barrels into one, saves one-half the expense of transportation, to various distant markets.

There are six manufactories here of these articles — all large. Such is the simplicity and efficiency of the apparatus employed, that twelve men suffice for the manufacture of an entire product of 35,750 barrels; equal, at 40 gallons to the barrel, to 1,430,000 gallons, and of the value of seventeen dollars per barrel; value of product six hundred and eight thousand and two hundred and sixty dollars—of raw material 80 per cent.

These results are day-light operations, of twelve hours. When the stills are run day and night, as is sometimes the case, the product is, of course, double; in fact more, because no time is lost in rekindling fires and reheating the stills.

The largest operators in this line, are Lowell Fletcher & Co., south-east corner of Vine and Front streets, and S. S. Boyle, Second street, between Sycamore and Broadway. Their capacity of manufacture is nearly equal. Fletcher & Co., confine their products to alcohol and neutral spirits. Boyle, in addition to these, manufactures domestic liquors on a very extensive scale. The manufacture of alcohol and neutral spirits, at these laboratories, is more than 8,000 barrels, or 320,000 gallons, annually, for each establishment.

The labor saving genius of the age is remarkably illustrated in these laboratories. The space occupied by the apparatus, at each, does not exceed twenty feet square, in which narrow limits, with stills of 1400 gallons capacity, such an immense quantity of alcohol and pure spirits, is the annual product. Nothing can surpass their simple and efficient arrangements, and the adaptedness to its purpose, of the apparatus already referred to.

Animal Charcoal. One factory.—Employs twelve hands, and produces to the value of twenty-five thousand dollars; value of raw materials 10 per cent.

Apple Butter, &c. Three establishments.—Nine hands; value of product, five thousand dollars; raw material consumed, 50 per cent.

Architects and Draughtsmen.—Fifteen principals and assistants; product twenty-two thousand dollars — labor entirely. Walter & Wilson; office at the Mechanics' Institute, and J. O. Sawyer, Bromwell's building, corner Fourth and Vine Streets, are skillful and judicious architects, to whose designs and superintendence our city owes many of its best buildings.

Artificial Flowers. Three manufactories.—Forty hands, principally females; value of product, fourteen thousand two hundred dollars; of raw materials, 40 per cent.

Awnings, Tents, Bags, &c. Seven factories.—Sixty-six hands; value of product, forty-five thousand dollars; raw materials 50 per cent.

Bagging Factories.—Of these, there are two, the Fulton and the Globe mills—steam power. They employ two hundred and thirty-eight hands, one half of which are females; product, bagging for cotton bales, to the value of two hundred and seventy thousand dollars; raw material, hemp, is of a value of 60 per cent. to the product. The market for this is entirely in the southern states.

Bakers.—There are one hundred and forty bakeries; which employ four hundred and forty-five hands, and manufacture to the value of six hundred and thirty thousand seven hundred and sixty-two dollars in bread, biscuit, &c.; raw material 60 per cent.

Samuel Cloon, 15 Sycamore, west side, between Front and Second streets,—steam power—manufactures yearly to the value of eighty-five thousand dollars, principally hard baked bread for exportation; has sixteen hands.

John Bailie, Front, above Ludlow street, has nineteen hands, and turns out, annually, a product in value, of thirty-six thousand seven hundred and fifty dollars, principally of biscuit and pilot bread, which are exported to far distant climes.

Thomas W. King, of the late firm of King & Heffner, stated to me that some years ago, being then a supercargo of an East Indiaman, and at Canton, China, he made one of a party at the American consul's, where everything procurable that could remind them of their native country, made a part of the entertainment; among other things produced, was a tin can of water crackers, which being unpacked, were handed round to the guests. King, carelessly crushing one in his hand, glanced at the stamp, and saw, J. Bailie, Cincinnati. A thousand memories of his old home—he was a native of Ohio, and long a resident of the city—rushed to his heart and filled his eyes. Those who recollect the emotion displayed by Capt. Cook, the great circumnavigator, on discovering the stamp, LONDON, on a pewter spoon which fell into his hands, while thousands of miles from home, may appreciate his feelings.

C. H. Bennett, wholesale and retail bakery, south side Court, east of Vine street—fifteen hands; makes bread, biscuit, and cakes; the first principally, to the annual value of twenty-three thousand four hundred and fifty dollars.

Alfred Burnett, 76, and 164, west Fifth street, manufactures wedding cakes, principally; employs nine hands; consumes annually, seventy-five thousand eggs, twenty-four thousand pounds sugar, and fifteen thousand pounds butter, in this article. Mr. Burnett has sold, of wedding cake, to the value of thirteen hundred dollars, in twelve days.

Band and Hat-boxes and Cases for Ladies' Shoes, &c. Six factories—Sixty hands; value of product, thirty-six thousand dollars per annum; raw material, 50 per cent.

Baskets, Cradles, Wagons, and other willow-ware. Seven shops, with thirty hands, manufacture a product of eighteen thousand dollars; raw material, 35 per cent.

The finer qualities of baskets, as well as the willow wagons, cradles and chairs are made from a variety called the Italian or white willow, which is cultivated for this purpose in the vicinity of the city. The willow sprouts are cut off, so as to leave a stump or head, which grows thicker yearly, but is not suffered to form a regular top, the new sprouts being taken off in the spring as fast as they become large enough for use. There are many small patches in this vicinity, amounting, in the aggregate, to several acres, cultivated to much profit for this purpose. The common baskets sold in our market are made of the common or swamp willow, which grows spontaneously on the banks, or in the water-courses of our creeks and rivulets.

Bell and Brassfounders.—There are two bell founders who are also brassfounders and finishers; and ten brassfounders who do not connect bell founding with their business. The entire value of the products made in these twelve founderies is, bells—eighty-five thousand dollars; raw material 67 per cent. Brass castings finished, one hundred and twenty-four thousand five hundred dollars; raw material 35 per cent.; total product, two hundred and nine thousand five hundred, and an average of 45 per cent., cost of materials.

G. W. Coffin & Co., of the Buckeye Foundery, Second street, near Broadway, have made during the past season, four hundred and forty-seven bells of all sizes, from a dinner alarm to the largest class of church bells, which have weighed four thousand and ninety-five pounds. The aggregate weight of these bells was forty thousand and seventy-six pounds. This is the only bell foundery in the United

States, in which bells are constructed upon purely scientific principles, and made to conform rigidly to the laws of acoustics.

An ingenious invention, on the principle of a set of keys—original with Mr. Coffin, has been introduced in playing upon chimes of bells, made in his establishment. By this, the connection of which with the bells, is out of sight, musical pieces are played as on a piano or any other keyed instrument. Obviously, this is a great improvement on the old and awkward mode of ringing by ropes.

The "Buckeye" is the largest bell foundery in the United States; indeed, the only one that approaches it in magnitude, is Meneely's, in Troy, New York.

One or two incidents to bell casting, which are connected with this foundery, may not be out of place. A large bell made here, was put up on the Fulton bagging factory, and during the conflagration of that building, in 1843, was *consumed*, or at least, so far destroyed, that not a vestige of it could be found. The only reasonable conjecture respecting its fate is, that as the cupola, with the roof below, were burnt before the rest of the building, the bell, in melting, spread out upon the sheeting and remaining roof, among the ashes, into particles so minute as to be absolutely lost.

It is a debatable point whether the addition of silver to the metal usually prepared for bells, improves the sound; and one still more disputed, whether that precious ingredient ever actually composed a part, at least any great part, in the composition of bells. One of the bells cast here, was for the Roman Catholic church at Mobile. This was a large one, and the old bell, which had been cracked, made a part of the new one. The old one had been cast at Toledo, in Spain, and one-eighth part of its weight was made up of one thousand four hundred and seventy Spanish dollars. Mr. Coffin considers it one of the finest toned ones he had ever cast.

Samuel Cummings, Front street, east of Pike, makes every variety of brass work, for land and steamboat engines, city and steamboat fire engines, of any pattern or size. Hydraulic machines—such as water rams, fire plugs, and stop valves for water works, of all kinds. Plumbers', brewers', and distillers' brasses, well, and soda pumps. Makes four fire engines annually; fourteen hands.

Kirkup, Potts & Co., Pearl street, west of Walnut—and Front street, east of Deer creek bridge; manufacture all kinds of copper, brass, zinc, and anti-friction castings; steam, liquor, soda and water cocks and valves of all descriptions, hose, salt-well and other joints, spelter solder, copper rivets, &c. They employ twelve hands.

R. T. Thorburn & Co., Front, west of Walnut street, make bells and brass faucets of every description; brass bannister and bar railing for steamboats and hotels; fountain cocks, and generator work; hose and salt-well joints; oil globes; cylinder and gauge cocks; steamboat-table castors; copper rivets; also plated faucets for tea-urns and water-coolers. Employ eight hands, and make nine thousand dollars worth of work.

Bellows.—Three factories supply this market with blacksmiths' bellows, for home and foreign demand; eight hands are thus employed; the value of product, is eighteen thousand dollars; of raw material, 75 per cent.

Blacking Paste.—Three factories: one of them on a large scale; sixteen hands; value of product, twenty-four thousand dollars; raw material, 50 per cent.

Butler & Brother, 215 Main street, make blacking extensively. The boxes for the blacking, are all made by machinery. Of these, they use yearly to the extent of eight hundred and sixty-four thousand, in putting up six thousand gross of blacking.

Blacksmithing. Eighty-two shops—Two hundred and twenty-three hands; value of product two hundred and thirty-five thousand three hundred and ninety-five dollars; of raw material, 50 per cent.

Blinds, Venetian. Six shops.—twenty-seven hands; value of product, forty thousand dollars; raw material, 70 per cent.

H. Read, 147 Sycamore street, employs eight hands, as an average; and sells annually, to the value of ten thousand dollars. These blinds, even to the tassels and binding, are all made in Cincinnati.

Block, Spar, and Pump makers. Five shops.—Eighteen hands; products, twenty-one thousand dollars; value of raw material, 40 per cent.

Boilers for Steam-Engines.—There are ten boiler yards, employing ninety-seven hands. The product for 1850, is seven hundred and thirty-five boilers; three hundred and forty-nine thousand dollars in value, inclusive of repairing operations; raw material, 70 per cent.

In 1840, four yards, with ninety hands, made but one hundred and sixty thousand dollars worth of work.

Washington McLean, on Congress, east of Ludlow street, employs sixteen hands; and manufactures boilers to the value of fifty-two thousand dollars.

Bonnet bleaching and pressing. Ten shops.—Thirty-three hands; product twenty-two thousand dollars; raw material, 5 per cent.

Book-binding. Fifteen binderies, with one hundred and thirty-six hands. Of these, some are connected with printing offices or book publishers, whose work they finish—others, with booksellers and stationers in the blank-book, pamphlet, or job line—others, again, work principally or entirely on job-work. Of these binderies, again, some are branches of publishing houses, and some of printing offices; which makes it difficult to present accurate statistics of binding business operations. The amount of binding for publishers, is, therefore, not included in this article, as it will be embraced in the value of books published, in a subsequent paragraph.

The value of products in these establishments, exclusive of what is done for publishers, is one hundred and twenty-two thousand dollars; raw material, 35 per cent.

James T. Morgan & Co., book-binders, 111 Main street, bind for a number of publishing houses; employ thirty-eight binders and folders, and execute work to the value of thirty thousand dollars annually. Their binding, of which "Cincinnati in 1851," is a specimen, will compare favorably with the highest order of work, in this line, done for the New York and Boston publishers.

J. F. Desilver, blank-book bindery. Among those who have spared neither efforts nor expense, to supersede the dependence of Cincinnati on the eastern cities, for the finer class of blank-books, is this establishment. Books of accounts or of records, may be had here, in a style unsurpassed elsewhere. Spring backs and raised bands, which as well as the ends and fronts, are of prime Russia leather, confine the pages as firmly as if on clamps; so that whether laid open or shut, the edges are kept mathematically exact, and the book is rendered strong enough, to resist the strain to which such heavy books are exposed by constant use. The ends, fronts, and backs are finished with gold filleting of the richest style. The paper, cream or blue laid, of superb texture, and made of the finest linen materials.

Boots and Shoes.—Of these, there are every variety made in Cincinnati; fine and coarse work for foreign markets, and custom work for home consumption. The purchases of our own citizens alone, annually, reach four hundred and fifty thousand pairs of boots and shoes; worth more than one million two hundred and fifty thousand dollars. Two-thirds of these at least, are made here, wholesale, or at custom shops. There are three hundred and seventy-four boot and shoemakers, with seventeen hundred and sixty hands; and a product of eleven hundred and eighty-two thousand six hundred and fifty dollars; value of raw materials, 40 per cent., as an average.

Filley & Chapin, corner of Pearl and Main streets. Every day is adding to the variety, as well as to the extent, of our manufacturing operations. When the statistics in this line, of the census of 1840, for Cincinnati were taken, although the value of the leather annually manufactured in the place, was three hundred and thirty-five thousand dollars, yet, at that period, the entire consumption of leather here, was by custom-work boot and shoemakers, and the amount of raw material beyond that demand, was exported east, whence it came back, to a great extent, worked up into the cheaper qualities of ready-made boots and shoes.

Within the last three years, a beginning and successful progress has been made in changing this course of things, by Filley & Chapin, C. W. Williams, M. A. Westcott, and other business houses, who have entered the field, as wholesale boot and shoe manufacturers; and there is no doubt, that in the course of ten years or less, not a pair of boots or shoes will be brought here, of New England manufacture; and a high probability exists, that within a few years more, we shall be supplying the very markets in which we now purchase.

A brief statement of the business of Filley & Chapin, will illustrate the subject. Their manufacturing operations are carried on in the upper stories of the Clayton building, on Second and Sycamore streets. Here they occupy eight rooms, of a space equal to *fourteen thousand and eighty* square feet. Their operations are in fine and coarse shoes and boots, principally the last. The leather, with the exception of a small portion of hemlock tanned sole, is all made in this city. They work up yearly, ten thousand sides sole leather, twenty thousand sides upper leather, No. 1, and 2, in equal quantities; twenty thousand sheep-skins, and two thousand five hundred calf-skins: of value—sole leather, twenty thousand dollars; upper leather, thirty thousand dollars; sheep and calf-skins, each five thousand dollars. This, with five thousand pounds boot nails, six hundred bushels shoe pegs, and other trimmings, run up their annual supply of raw material, to a value of sixty-seven thousand five hundred dollars. As nine-tenths of these materials are manufactured in Cincinnati, these details exhibit the manner and extent to which this, as every other new branch of business embarked in here, aids existing manufacturing operations, or contributes to the establishment of new ones.

Messrs. Filley & Chapin, employ two hundred hands in the various branches of their business, principally journeymen, although the stitching and binding is done by women. It is pleasant to notice, that one beneficial result of this enterprise has been to find employment for the poor and the destitute. A case occurred here, recently, where a woman with three boys, earned in this business, three dollars a-week, and each of the boys, three more; and another, in which an elderly man, who was out of employment when he came to Cincinnati, is now earning, with three or four children, twenty dollars per week. These are evidences, that employment for our poor, is of more efficiency, as well as less burthensome to the community, than the periodical efforts made to relieve distress in the community, after it is rendered apparent.

This firm manufactures, weekly, at the rate of one hundred and forty cases, or seven thousand five hundred cases of boots annually; what falls short of this, is made up in shoes. Sixty thousand dollars is paid out yearly to the hands, and not less than one thousand living beings are fed by earnings in this establishment alone.

Every description of boots and shoes, as has been ascertained at this factory, can be made as cheap here as at the eastward, and the finer kinds much cheaper.

The only inducement to purchase in eastern markets that remains, is the long credit of four and eight months given there, which tempts new beginners of limited capital to submit to the higher rate of cost, which carriage and exchange—at least ten per cent.—to say nothing of traveling expenses, imposes on our dealers who lay in at the east.

This is so well understood by capitalists here, that heavy dealers, who can afford to buy for cash, make their purchases principally of this firm. As an example, the heaviest shoe and boot merchant in Louisville, himself owner of a boot and shoe factory, in Grafton, Mass., deals largely with Messrs. Filley & Chapin, and has a standing order on their books to the value of eleven thousand dollars, in deliveries of one hundred and forty dollars per day, or in that proportion weekly. The country merchant can buy always to better advantage in the west, also, not merely in the saving of traveling expenses and freight or carriage, but in the certainty of getting his goods almost at his door at a day's notice, and of individuals within reach, of responsibility for the wares they manufacture.

Thomas Sharkey, a journeyman in Filley & Chapin's employ, has frequently made six pairs of these boots per day of eight hours, and has more than once made twelve pairs at a sitting of fifteen hours in each instance, and will make a pair of boots at any time, in the presence of any one curious to witness the performance, in one hour, or even less.

These are feats which cannot be paralleled or even approached in New England, the head-quarters of the boot and shoe manufactures.

Another class of boot and shoemakers consists of those who measure for customers, beside keeping a supply on hand, of the same quality, for those who require to be supplied on short notice, or without notice at all. A proper representative of this class, is Eshelby, No. 16 West Sixth street, a man, who has acquired considerable celebrity in business. He employs, on an average, thirty hands, manufactures as many pairs of women's and children's shoes as of men's, and all of the finest quality of materials. He makes to the value of thirty thousand dollars annually.

Eshelby makes one article that deserves special notice; this is a substantial calf-skin boot, tanned with the hair on, which is turned inside, and is designed for winter wear, especially of persons whose business exposes them to travel through the snow or water—surveyors and railroad parties, for example.

Yet another class exists. There are persons in large numbers in cities, who rarely, or never bespeak their boots and shoes, but purchase at the period of want, and many of them at its last moment. They expect, however, to get an article equal to the best, both in neatness and service.

C. M. Williams, Fifth, east of Walnut, supplies this line of customers, and on the most extensive scale. He employs from seventy-five to one hundred and twenty-five hands, all upon fine work of men's dress boots, congress boots, and fine shoes, and ladies' gaiter boots, buskins and slippers. These are of every suitable material, calf-skins, morocco, lasting, and patent leather of the best material and finish. He makes what is termed seamless gaiter boots for ladies, which are so constructed, that there is no strain whatever upon the boot except at the corded side, which being gored with elastic cloth, accommodates itself to the pressure. As these gaiters adjust themselves to the shape and fullness of the ankle, they are equally neat and durable. Mr. Williams sells yearly to the value of sixty-seven thousand dollars, and like all city manufacturers, for cash only.

Every article here is sold under guarantee of its quality, both of work and materials, and the extent of the sales enables Mr. Williams to supply his customers at as low rates as they might otherwise pay for an article inferior to his.

There are great advantages, in manufacturing, over purchasing at the eastward for this market. The latter course requires keeping large stocks on hand, part of which lies over and deteriorates in various ways, by lying on the shelves; the sizes put up in assorting the cases do not run out equally; the extreme small and extreme large lying on hand.

The seller here is held responsible for the quality and durability of an article for which after his purchases reach home, he finds no corresponding responsibility. On the other hand, by manufacturing for himself, he can use up his stock as closely as he chooses; he can take off or put on hands according to his convenience or interest, and fill up the demand with the exact kind or size he happens to want;—and his journeyman is just as responsible to him for faithful work, as he is to his customers.

M. A. Westcott, No. 42, and 197, and 199, Walnut street, is in the same line of business, substantially, as Mr. Williams; and much of the statement just made will apply also to his business. He employs one hundred hands in various capacities, and manufactures to the value of forty-five thousand seven hundred dollars.

E. G. Webster & Co., corner of Fifth and Lodge street, and opposite Fifth street Market-house, is at the head of yet another class. He employs one hundred hands, who make, annually, sixty thousand pairs of ladies', misses', and children's shoes. They use French and Philadelphia calf-skins, colored roans, patent and enameled leather, morocco, French and English kids, drillings, and shoe-duck, lastings, French sateens and Italian cloths. This list of materials, exhibits the variety of the stock they keep on hand, all of their own manufacture. They manufacture gentlemen's dress boots, also, although theirs is principally a ladies' shoe-store.

They are also extensive wholesale dealers in eastern boots and shoes, and keep constantly for sale the various materials already specified, as well as other trimmings.

There is lastly, a class who make ladies' shoes to measure, in all cases: such as Todd, Fifth street, who employs twenty hands, and makes ten thousand dollars value of ladies' and misses' shoes. These are all of the finest quality of work and materials.

Brand, Stamp, and Venetian Blind Chisel makers. Six shops—Sixteen hands; thirteen thousand five hundred dollars, product; raw material, 10 per cent.

Breweries.—Of these, there are twenty-one in Cincinnati, which employ one hundred and seventy-two hands. These make respectively, per annum, of half barrels beer or ale:

25,000	13,040	6220
25,000	12,500	6220
25,000	12,500	6220
25,000	12,500	5240
16,900	10,400	4160
16,900	8,320	2780
13,540	7,480	2080
		257,000

Of this, there are:

Beer	205,000	at $2	$410,000
Ale	52,000	" 3	156,000
			$566,000

Of this product, 75 per cent. is raw material.

Bricks. Sixty brick makers.—Employ three hundred and sixty-seven hands; value of product, two hundred and seven thousand dollars; raw material, clay and wood, 40 per cent.

Bricklayers and Plasterers. Two hundred and eight master workmen.—Eight hundred and seventy-six hands; labor value, four hundred and eight thousand, six hundred and fifty dollars; raw material, 5 per cent.

Bristle and Curled Hair dressers. Four establishments.—One hundred and four hands; product, forty-eight thousand eight hundred dollars; raw material, 5 per cent.

Britannia Ware.—Two factories, which employ thirty-two hands, and make a product of thirty-eight thousand six hundred and ninety dollars in value; raw material, 45 per cent.

Sellew & Co., 208 Main street, manufacture Britannia coffee and tea-sets, pitchers, cups, lamps, candlesticks, castors, tumblers, candle-molds, etc. This establishment is of long existence, and is constantly enlarging its business, as well as improving the quality of its wares, which find a market throughout the entire west and southwest. The firm employs twenty-two hands, and manufactures thirty thousand dollars in value.

Brushes. Of these, there are fifteen factories, all small, except one or two—ninety hands; annual product, sixty thousand five hundred dollars; raw material, 40 per cent.

Sleeper & Mintzer, 163 Main street, are making brushes to considerable extent, and in infinite variety. They manufacture not only most durable and convenient articles for housekeepers, but many descriptions of goods finished to a degree, that might gratify even the fastidiousness of a Parisian exquisite. They employ thirty-six hands.

Buckets, Tubs, &c.—There is but one of these factories here, that of N. C. McLean, which is on an extensive scale. One thousand to twelve hundred buckets, and one hundred and fifty tubs are turned out every day at these works. These are all made by machinery, and finished, including painting, in the best style; annual product, eighty-four thousand two hundred dollars; raw materials, 48 per cent.

The logs, which are brought from the head waters of the Allegheny river, are floated to the factory, by the agency of the Miami canal, at whose termination it is built. There they are sawed into stave lengths and bottom pieces, split into blocks of suitable size, and fed to a cylinder saw, which cuts them into staves of the proper thickness and curve. They are then put into the drying-house, jointed, hooped and sandpapered, to smooth the inner and outer surface; eared and handled, and lastly, painted in the usual variety of colors. There are four large drying-houses, and eight of smaller size, through which the entire stock of material is passed, being kiln-dried or steamed, to the necessary point of thorough seasoning for use. It is hardly possible to name a single feature, in the comparison of these buckets with the old-fashioned article they supersede, in which they have not the advantage.

These buckets come into market in competition with an article made at Beaver, Penn., which they must finally supersede to a great extent, if not totally, for the following reasons:

1. The Beaver bucket is made with ears projecting above the edge, which are thereby unduly exposed to being broken off. The ears of these are made differently, and can be set below the edge of the bucket.

2. The Beaver buckets are coated with paint mixed with glue, dissolved in water. These are painted in oil colors.

3. Lastly, all purchasers prefer buying an article made on the spot, as they can avail themselves thereby, of a direct responsibility in the seller, if the article they buy prove inferior to the warranty. Every business man understands the advantage of this.

Burr Millstone makers. Four factories.—Nineteen hands; value of product, twenty-four thousand dollars; raw material, 65 per cent.

James Bradford & Co., 65 Walnut street, manufacture yearly, seventy-five pairs burr millstones.

The burrs, of which the millstones are composed, are imported from France, in cubes of about twelve inches average. We have the same material in our own west, but it is not hard enough for service. The burrs are cemented with plaster of Paris, which is received from Nova Scotia and the Lake Erie region; and each stone is secured with four bands of iron, which being put on hot, as they shrink in cooling, serve to confine the whole under any amount of strain to which it may be exposed.

Butchers. One hundred and twenty-one.—Occupy five market-houses. This does not include a large number, who slaughter cattle and sell them either by the quarter or entire carcass, outside the markets. There are six hundred butchers, employers and journeymen. The value of pork, beef, mutton, &c., cut up and sold in our markets to families, public houses, steamboats, and sent off to families in the vicinity of Cincinnati, reaches two millions eight hundred and fifty thousand dollars, per annum; raw material, 80 per cent.

Camphine and Spirit Gas. Three factories.—Seven hands; product, seventeen thousand two hundred dollars; raw material, 75 per cent.

Candies and Confectionaries.—Of these, there are twelve shops, with eighty hands; value of product, one hundred and twenty-eight thousand one hundred and twenty dollars; raw materials, 60 per cent.

P. Hall, 52 Main street, employs at an average, twenty-three hands, and makes six to eight hundred pounds candies per day. Large quantities of sirups for soda-water establishments, are also made here, when the weather is favorable. He has worked up fifteen boxes Havana sugar, weekly, into candies and sirups.

Caps—men and boys. Nine factories.—Employ fifty hands; value of product, thirty-nine thousand dollars; raw material, 40 per cent.

Carpenters and Builders. Two hundred and eighty-four shops.—Employ two thousand three hundred and twenty hands; value of product, two million one hundred and sixteen thousand dollars; raw material, 5 per cent.

Cars and Omnibuses—railroad. Four establishments, for making and repairing. Employ one hundred and ten hands; value of product, one hundred and eight thousand four hundred and forty-seven dollars; raw material, 70 per cent.

Carriages, Buggies, etc. Twenty-four factories.—Two hundred and twelve hands; product, two hundred and forty-seven thousand four hundred dollars; raw material, 40 per cent.

J. W. Gosling, corner of Sycamore and Sixth streets, employs forty-five hands; makes buggies, barouches, carriages, etc., to the value of fifty thousand dollars. There is a novelty introduced here, of a carriage step, which by hidden machinery, is so connected with the door, that the opening of the door uncovers and lets down the step, as its shutting restores it to its place and covers it. The step is, therefore, out of sight, except for the brief space during which it is in actual service.

George C. Miller & Sons. This is a long established house, who have recently put up spacious work and sale-rooms, on Seventh, west of Main street. They make every description of fine carriages, buggies, and barouches; employ thirty hands, and manufacture to the value of thirty-seven thousand five hundred dollars.

I. & B. Bruce & Co., 75 Walnut street. This establishment makes every variety of wheeled vehicle, including carriages, buggies, barouches, omnibuses, hose-reels, and light wagons; it employs sixty hands. It does the largest repairing business, in its line, of any shop in Cincinnati. The concern is about to open separate workshops on Elm, below Columbia street.

Carpet weavers. Eighteen shops.—Sixty-five hands; fifty-six thousand dollars, labor product.

Carvers in wood. Three shops.—Seven hands; value of product, seven thousand dollars; raw material, 5 per cent.

A. W. Anderson, Second, west of Race street, makes figure-heads for steamboats and sailing vessels, Ionic, Corinthian, and composite capitals and columns, and patterns for ornamental castings. The full length statue of Jefferson, on the Vine street engine hall, was executed by Mr. Anderson.

Castor Oil. One factory, that of Conkling, Wood & Co.—Employs eight hands, and produces to the value of fifty-five thousand dollars; value of raw material, including barrels, 75 per cent.

Charcoal, pulverized for rectifiers. Three establishments.—Nine hands; value of product, eighteen thousand five hundred dollars; raw material, 50 per cent.

Chemicals. Five laboratories.—Seventy-nine hands; product in value, two hundred and twenty-six thousand dollars; raw material, 40 per cent. Here are made oil vitriol, copperas, alum, prussiate of potash, prussian blue, etc.

J. C. Baum, on Dunlap street, south of Hamilton road, works twenty hands, in the manufacture of prussian blue and prussiate of potash; manufactures to the value of twenty-five thousand dollars.

Cistern builders. Three.—Thirty-six hands; value of product, seventy-five thousand dollars.

Jos. S. Cook has been several years engaged in cistern-building—has built all the public cisterns in Cincinnati—was the first man that ever turned an arch in this line of business, and has never been called upon to repair or alter a cistern built under his charge.

Cloaks and Visites. Two shops.—Six hands; three thousand dollars value; raw material, 65 per cent.

Clothing manufactories.—This is a very extensive business here, which is principally engrossed by the Israelites of Cincinnati. One hundred and eight stores and shops; employ nine hundred and fifty hands at their workshops. More than nine thousand women work at their own houses, for these establishments. Value of product, one million nine hundred and forty-seven thousand five hundred dollars; raw material, 60 per cent.

There are six establishments alone, in the city, which manufacture more than half a million of dollars of clothing. Cincinnati is the great mart for ready-made clothing, for the whole south and west.

Coffee roasting, etc. One establishment, with seventeen hands, and a product of thirty-eight thousand dollars; raw material, 75 per cent.

Combs. One factory.—Employs eighteen hands; value of product, eighteen thousand dollars; raw material 60 per cent.

Composition-roofing. Four establishments.— Eighteen hands; value of roofs, forty thousand dollars; raw material, 50 per cent.

S. M. & C. M. Warren, put on these kind of roofs, very extensively. They first introduced them here, in 1847.

The usual covering hitherto, has been shingles, sheet-tin, slate, and sheet-zinc. The two last very expensive; the others far from durable. *Warren's* composition roofs, in their first cost, are not much higher than shingles, and taking durability into view, are much less expensive.

The composition is a preparation of tar and sand upon paper, which is fastened to the sheeting usually prepared as a basis for shingles. Thick and strong paper is first secured to the boards, and two or three coats of prepared tar are then spread on the surface. Sand or fine gravel forms the final coat or covering.

Such a roof does not leak, even when just made, and a few months serve to render it perfectly dry and indestructible by fire.

The advantages of this roof are:

1st. Its durability. To this no period can be assigned, save that it will last as long as the house it covers.

2d. The beauty it confers upon a roof. The slightest possible declivity serves for such a roof, as the water cannot penetrate it in the slightest degree. The benefit of this light slope, is also a material advantage. Usually, the upper rooms of a house, are of little value, the greater part not being high enough to permit persons to stand upright. With these roofs, the whole of the upper floor can be readily used for ordinary purposes.

3d. Its efficiency. Such a roof becomes so substantial that rain cannot, in the slightest degree, penetrate it.

4th. Its indestructibility by fire has been often tested, and always with success. The workshop of the Messrs. Warren, themselves, took fire not long since, and although the sheeting of the roof was charred through to a coal, the fire could not pass through the roof, and the adjacent buildings were saved thereby from the extension of the fire.

5th. Not least in the advantages, is the perfect foothold it affords in the surface as well as in the slope. These roofs may be walked over in perfect safety, except when covered with sleet.

Coopers. There are sixty-three shops, with seven hundred and ninety-six workmen employed; value of product, three hundred and eighty-seven thousand dollars; raw material, 20 per cent.

One shop alone, works one hundred and fifty hands, and turns out cooperage, annually, to the value of ninety thousand dollars.

Copper, Tin, and Sheet-Iron workers. Forty-two shops.—Two hundred and forty hands; value of products, two hundred and fifty-eight thousand six hundred and forty dollars; raw material, copper-ware, 60 per cent.; tin-ware and sheet-iron-ware, 30 per cent.; average value of raw material, 48 per cent.

Copperplate Printers. Two establishments.-Employ twelve hands; labor product, fifty thousand dollars; raw material, 10 per cent.

E. C. Middleton, Odd Fellows' building, is one of the inventors and patentees of a novel press, which enables the copper-plate printer to execute his work without lifting the plate after it has been placed on the bed. Every artist can appreciate the importance of such improvement.

Cordage, etc. Nine rope-yards.—One hundred and thirty hands; value of product, one hundred and eighty thousand dollars; raw material, 35 per cent.

Cured Beef, Tongues, etc.—There are thirteen establishments, with forty hands, in this line, most of them operating on a small scale, or carrying it on as an adjunct to business of greater magnitude. Of this latter class, is the firm of Stagg & Shays, which does a heavy business in sugar-cured hams, and has this year put up one hundred and fifty thousand pounds dried beef; and cured fifteen thousand beef tongues. The rounds of thirty-one thousand two hundred beef cattle, have been cured here, this season, which, together with that number of tongues, reaches a value of one hundred and thirty-five thousand dollars. Raw material, 65 per cent.

Cutlery—Surgical and Dental Instruments—Tailors' Shears, etc. Four workshops.—Twenty-five hands; value of product forty thousand dollars; raw material, 20 per cent.

W. Z. Rees, Sixth, near Walnut street, is one of the most important of these. He makes surgical instruments of admirable delicacy of construction and finish, and his couching or cataract needles, are preferred in the United States, to those of any others made in this country. Drs. Mussey, Taliaferro, Smith, and others, surgeons, get all their instruments here.

Daguerreotypists.—Thirty-two, with seventy-eight assistants; produce to the value of eighty thousand dollars; raw material, 60 per cent.

Our daguerreian artists stand high everywhere. Reed, the artist, who carried portraits taken by Hawkins and Faris, to Europe, states, in a letter home, that their works were recognized at a glance in Florence, by Frenchmen and others, as American productions, and superior to anything produced on the continent of Europe.

Hawkins, in addition to his daguerreotypes, produces, what he terms, a solograph picture. These are portraits and miniatures which possess the beauty of superior oil paintings, and the exquisite finish of highly-wrought miniatures. Nothing can exceed their truthfulness of likeness and life-like coloring.

They possess the great advantage of not being liable to change: while, on the contrary, like a fine painting, they improve by time.

While these pictures are equal to finished paintings in color, they excel even the daguerreotype, in fidelity.

Dentistry.—There are thirty-six dentists, with forty-four assistants; value of operations, ninety-two thousand dollars; raw material, 65 per cent.

Die sinkers. Three shops.—Five hands; value of product, five thousand dollars; raw material, 10 per cent.

Domestic Liquors—Brandies, Wines, Cordials, etc.—Of these, there are eight extensive establishments, and as many more on a small scale, employing forty-six hands, which manufacture sixty-six thousand barrels of forty gallons, annually, worth at eleven dollars per barrel, seven hundred and twenty-six thousand dollars; raw material, 60 per cent.

Kellogg, Brothers, on Second street, consume sixty barrels whisky, per day; other materials, proportionately. Here may be seen a tub or tun employed in the manufacture of native sweet wine, which is of *fifty thousand gallons capacity*, the staves being three inches thick; the bottom of six inch timber, and bound with nineteen iron wagon-tire hoops, of four and a-half by one quarter inches. It is twelve feet high, and over twenty-five feet diameter. There are five other tubs, which in the aggregate, contain as much as the great mastodon just described, and which, if seen anywhere else, would be considered of enormous capacity; but whose size here, is lost sight of, in the contemplation of the largest one.

This firm supplies brandy, gin, old reserve whisky, sweet wines, cordials, etc., to the south-east and south-west.

Dyers. Fifteen dyeing and scouring establishments.—Twenty-four hands; value of product, twenty-eight thousand dollars; raw material, 25 per cent.

William Teasdale, corner Walnut and Gano street, carries on these various operations, on an extensive scale. He has never failed at the various state exhibitions and mechanics' fairs, to receive premiums and diplomas for superior tints and permanent colors.

Edge-tool makers. Nineteen factories.—Seventy-two hands; value of product, ninety-seven thousand nine hundred dollars; raw material, 35 per cent.

J. F. Fowler & Co., on Lock street, fabricate all kinds of edge tools, pump augers, tanners', fleshers', and lath knives, hatchets, plane bits, carpenters' and coopers' tools, of all descriptions.

James Galbraith, Seventh, west of Main street, makes annually, one thousand two hundred dozen stone hammers, lathing and shingling hatchets and drawing-knives, chopping, broad, and carpenters' axes, of the value of eighteen thousand dollars.

Edge-tool grinding.—A. Cunningham, Lock street, employs eighteen hands. Value of annual labor product, twenty thousand dollars; raw material, 5 per cent.; grinds two thousand four hundred pieces every week. Fancy grinding and polishing, is also done here.

Engravers.—There are eight wood, and six steel and copperplate engraving establishments here; thirty engravers, including assistants; value of labor product, fifty thousand dollars; raw material, 10 per cent.

Fancy job printing. Two establishments.—These are those of Messrs. Schmidt & Storch, Third street, east of Main; and C. Clark & Co., of the Ben Franklin office, on Walnut street. Their ornamental work in bronze or silver and gold, and in tints and colors are executed in a style unsurpassed at other offices, here or elsewhere. The gold lettering of Schmidt & Storch, upon ultramarine paper, is truly magnificent. These are largely employed in wine labels, for our native wine manufacturers. C. Clark & Co., are extensively engaged on fancy steamboat bills, printed also in gold and silver letters. Both these firms execute fine circulars, checks, notes, bills lading, bill-heads, and indeed, every species of letter sheet printing. Twenty-five hands are employed in these job offices; value of product, thirty thousand dollars; raw material, 30 per cent.

Some notion of the extent of Clark & Co.'s operations, may be

No. 148
Main St.
5
FIVE
5
FIVE
Rawdon, Wright, Hatch & Edson
ENGRAVERS
Printers
corner of 4th &
Streets
Cincinnati
July 4th 1851.
ONE
Geo. F. Jones
Agent

formed, by the statement here made, that they employ in their job office, more than *one thousand fonts of type;* and keep employed, seven hand presses, four power presses, two card presses, one tip press, and one embossing press. They occupy more business space, and are provided more extensively with business materials, than any establishment of the kind in the Atlantic cities.

Feed and Flouring mills.—There are fourteen mills here, the more important of which, manufacture wheat flour, and steam-dried corn meal, for foreign markets. They grind oil-cake into meal, and make feed for horses, etc., by grinding up corn in the cob, and oats, and by chopping rye and buckwheat, etc. Value of aggregate product, one million six hundred and ninety thousand dollars; employ sixty-five hands; raw material, 75 per cent.

C. W. West & Co., have two mills, one on the Miami, the other on the Whitewater canal; manufacture three hundred and fifty barrels flour per day. Their flour is of the highest reputation in the markets.

C. S. Bradbury, corner Eighth and Broadway, manufactures one hundred and fifty barrels superfine flour, and one hundred and forty barrels steam dried corn-meal per day. Prepares from wheat and corn, using only the germ of the grain, farina of the finest quality. This is the basis of various delicious culinary preparations, such as puddings, custards, blanc-mange, etc. Five hundred pounds of this article is made at this mill daily. His steam dried corn-meal, is shipped to every part of the globe.

A. Erkenbrecher, Lock street, north of Miami canal, makes and sifts corn-meal for family use, buckwheat flour, chopped feed, and pearl barley. Also, kiln dried corn-meal, for exportation.

Fire-engines, Hydraulic Apparatus, etc.—One very important manufacture which has been established during late years in Cincinnati, is that of fire-engines and other hydraulic apparatus. These are made by D. L. Farnam, on Elm, between Fourth and Fifth streets. Mr. Farnam is the inventor, as well as manufacturer of these hydraulic fire-engines. They are constructed on the novel principle of working horizontally, the firemen being seated in the body of the engine. Those who have handled, in times of fire, engines on the ordinary principle, know what an exhausting process it is to work them with spirit, even for twenty minutes. In the present description of engine, the men exert themselves as if rowing a boat, the motion of the body and the muscles employed, being precisely the

16

same. Eubank, in his celebrated work on hydraulics, appears to have referred to this very kind of engine as a desideratum, in saying, "when a man's strength is applied as in the act of rowing, the effect is nearly one hundred and fifty per cent., more than in moving a pump lever. This is sufficient to induce efforts to supersede the present mode of working the pumps of engines."

In these engines, the firemen sit with one or both feet braced up nearly level with the seat. In this position, a man of ordinary strength can raise a weight of one hundred and fifty pounds, thirty inches, and keep that weight passing up and down that distance, as many times a minute as the usual number of strokes of an engine.

As it has been ascertained that firemen working on side-engines, do not apply on an average over thirty pounds, and on an engine with long levers working across the ends, about fifty pounds, the advantage this engine possesses over its predecessors is manifest. This does not include the greater power of enduring protracted exertion in the position of rowing, which is as five to one against the old fashioned exercise of the arms. Accordingly, it has been found that these engines, with less working power, deliver more water a greater distance, than those on the ordinary principle.

On a recent trial, twenty men forced water up Race street, on an ascent of thirty-five feet, a distance of six hundred and fifty feet, and threw it from the nozzle at the end of the hose, a further distance of one hundred and twenty feet.

Another great advantage these engines possess, is their being one-third to one-half lighter in weight, than those already in use; a difference which enables the first two or three who reach the engine house to start off to a fire at once, as well as lessens the labor of dragging the apparatus the whole distance.

Of these engines, thirty-seven have been already built, and orders are on file, sufficient to keep the concern employed for the ensuing six months.

There is in this establishment, a double acting force-pump, just finished, that has been ordered for a flouring mill at Hamilton, Ohio. Another of the same is making here, for Zanesville, Ohio. These are designed for the protection from fire, of the mills, being worked by the water-wheel, with which they are connected. When wanted for use, sixteen streams of one inch each, can be thrown at once, the volume of water being one foot diameter in capacity. These afford not only protection to the mill or factory which uses them, but may be carried on in pipes through a town or village, and taken from water plugs at various points by an attachment of hose, so as to perform the duty of a fire-engine, without the labor or expense of that apparatus. In this way, at trifling cost, comparatively, any place which has water or steam power employed in manufacture, can protect itself from the ravages of fire.

With the exception of castings in the rough, every part of these hydraulics is made on the premises; thirty-seven hands are employed here. Value of product, sixty-five thousand dollars; raw material, 50 per cent.

This is the only hydraulic apparatus factory, west of Philadelphia.

Flooring-mills.—Beside planing machines, which face boards, as well as shave other lumber, there are fourteen of Woodworth's machines, for planing and tonguing flooring-boards. These supply an aggregate of three hundred and fifty-one thousand two hundred dollars, as a product, and a value of raw material, of 65 per cent. Seventy-two hands.

Florists.—A large amount of plants are disposed of wholesale and retail, in this market. There are fifteen sale gardens, whose annual sales reach one hundred and twenty thousand dollars. Thirty-five hands; raw material, 10 per cent.

J. S. Cook, has recently commenced a sale garden and nursery, on the Madison road, just beyond the Lane Seminary. It is of twenty acres extent, and as every dollar made from it for years, will be invested in further improvement, it will eventually become one of the most charming flower-gardens in the west. As to the nursery, Mr. Cook is determined to have nothing for sale which is not of his own planting, budding, or grafting, as the case may be; and the purchaser can therefore, always rely on obtaining with certainty, the very article he desires to purchase.

Foundery castings.—This is one of our heaviest branches of manufacture, and is carried on in every possible variety, in which iron can be cast, from a butt hinge to a burial case. A number of these founderies, include finishing shops. A few of them, simply supply castings in the rough; others finish their work to the last degree of polish required by the purpose to which it is applied. A share of them confine their products to a single great staple or two of manufacture, and in the case of others, a thousand different articles are the product. It would be impossible, therefore, to reduce these founderies, with their products, to classes; and the aggregate being first stated, the operations of a few of them will be given, as samples of each class.

There are forty-four founderies, one-third of which, are mainly or entirely in the stove trade, which is itself a heavy department of the business, as high as *one thousand stoves* having been manufactured here, in *one day alone.* The value of foundery products, is three millions six hundred and seventy-six thousand five hundred dollars; hands employed, four thousand six hundred and ninety-five; average value of raw material, 22 per cent.

Horton & Macy, Fifth, between Elm and Plum streets, employ sixty hands, and manufacture to the value of seventy-five thousand dollars. These products are, iron-railing castings, in every variety of pattern, for exportation; also, for cemeteries; enameled grates; one-third for home use, two-thirds sold for the supply of other markets. Iron mantles, hat racks, chairs, and settees; value of raw material, 20 per cent.

There are some of the hands in this foundery, who earn twenty dollars weekly.

A. B. Holabird, west Front St., makes steam-engines principally—fifty per year, for the last three years; will this year increase those figures. These are worth one thousand five hundred dollars each. One hundred corn shellers, which sell for one hundred dollars each. Their repairing and small machinery business, fifteen thousand dollars.

A finished engine on the premises, of his own manufacture, and of novel construction, is worth a visit; for finish and ease of working, and general efficiency, it cannot be surpassed.

Reynolds, Kite & Tatum, build steam-engines and boilers, and are brass and iron founders; fitters of wrought iron welded pipe, for steam, gas, etc.; fitters of lard-oil, stearine, star candle and soap apparatus, and steam fixtures for rendering lard, tallow, and oil; make to order, all kinds of tools and machinery; also, tanks for rendering lard, under Wilson's patent. They employ eighty hands; value of product of labor, eighty-five thousand dollars. Their repairing business alone keeps twenty hands occupied.

Niles & Co. The principal business of this establishment, is sugar-mill and steam-engine building, for the south. P. A. Champomier, in his statistics of the sugar crop of Louisiana, for 1850, says:

Since 1846, there have been erected in the State, three hundred and fifty-five engines and sugar-mills, most of them to replace old

Onkens Lithography, Cincinnati, O.

ones, or those previously worked by horse power. Of these engines and mills, the founderies of Cincinnati have furnished two hundred and eighty-one; Pittsburgh, thirty-seven; Richmond, seven; Baltimore, four; Louisville, three; New Orleans, ten; Algiers, La., two; Gretna, La., six; and the Novelty works, New York, five.

It will be seen by this statement, that Cincinnati has built four-fifths of these engines; and so great as well as rapid, has been the absorption of that business to this point, that probably, in two or three years, not a sugar-mill and steam-engine will be built for Louisiana, Texas, and Cuba, but at Cincinnati. This is owing, not only to the superior quality of work and materials here, but to the fact, that we can deliver these articles at New Orleans, at a price 10 per cent. less than they are made in the eastern cities. As an index of the future, all the sugar-mills, etc., of 1851, for the coast, as it is called, and the Cuban market, with the exception of six at New York, have been contracted for at Cincinnati. Niles & Co., will have built by the 1st July, ensuing, which is the close of the business year in this line, seventy sugar-mills and steam-engines, of the value of two hundred and eighty thousand dollars. Their other operations, including repairing, increase this amount to four hundred and ten thousand dollars. They employ two hundred hands; value of raw material, 25 per cent.

The view in these pages, of this foundery, exhibits distinctly and faithfully, its external appearance.

Tunnicliff & Co., east Front, near Butler street, manufacture stoves of every variety, and for every purpose, and to a great extent. They also make grates, hollow-ware, wagon-boxes, charcoal furnaces, sad-irons, stove fronts, sash weights, water gutters and shoots; and, to order, every other description of castings. Employ sixty hands, and manufacture to the value of ninety thousand dollars.

J. H. Burrows & Co. Foundery, Second, west of Elm street, manufacture steam-engines and various descriptions of castings, to the value of thirty thousand dollars. Their principal manufacture, however, is of portable mills, intended for the south and south-west, and especially for sections of country, where water-power is scarce. This is an invention of Mr. Burrows, senior of the concern, and is every year extending its popularity; the firm having made four hundred of these mills, worth sixty thousand dollars, during the past year. This mill merits a special description, as it is an invention, equally simple and ingenious. It proposes to perform in a small compass, with less expense, greater safety and equal efficiency, the work of a merchant mill. If it does not accomplish all this, it is nevertheless, a remarkable improvement.

The mill is a square frame with four stout pillars, on which the mill-stones, which are of burr blocks, cemented as usual, rest. The whole apparatus forming a cube of about four feet. The upper mill-stone is inclosed in a *cast iron case* of suitable weight, which supersedes the usual iron bands, and gives all the power in an equable and steady motion, which is derived in the larger class of mill-stones by extra thickness or height; thus rendering them top-heavy, and producing an inequality of pressure and motion, which is obviated here.

The mill-stones are two to two and a-half inches diameter. Owing to the casing referred to, there is at once the proper degree of pressure, and at the same time, elasticity, which furnishes the perfection of grinding; avoiding, on the one hand, the irregular motion of a top-heavy upper stone, and on the other, the evil of friction and want of spring, which results from the old-fashioned plan, in portable mills, of fastening down the upper mill-stone by screws, to say nothing of the greater liability of getting out of order. These mill-stones can be run with greater velocity, compatibly with safety, than the large ones, the two feet making two hundred and forty, and the two and a-half feet, two hundred revolutions per minute.

The power necessary to drive one of these mills, is not more than that of three horses, or the equivalent water or steam power; with these they will grind fourteen to sixteen bushels per hour, which is as good a performance as a merchant mill; the quality of the flour being superfine, and passing inspection as such, in our markets.

These mills are driven according to the necessity or convenience of the case, and to equal advantage, by either horse, water, or steam power. This is of importance, because the great mass of these mills, go to the west and south-west.

How capricious are all measures of value. In 1790, when the early pioneers ground all their corn by hand, and were obliged to dispense with the luxury of wheat, from inability to reduce it to flour, one of these portable mills would, even at its present low price, have bought all Cincinnati, from the canal, north, and Sycamore street, west.

Two facts, both of which are striking and unimpeachable, attest the quality of flour made in these mills. The "Chapultepec mills" flour, sold by Sprigman & Camp, has no superior, and for family use, few brands equal it in this market. It is all made upon one of these portable mills. Another remarkable incident, is, that the family flour made by C. S. Bradbury, of this city, which carried off the premium for the best barrel of flour, at the recent Ohio State agricultural fair, was also ground upon one of these mills. It carried the prize from a number of competitors, whose flour brands have always stood among the highest in the Miami valley.

Miles Greenwood, Walnut, from Canal to Twelfth street; at this—in addition to the heavy machine and other castings, common to all founderies—are made a great variety of small castings, especially those adapted to the house building business. Of these, many articles are new inventions, superseding, by their convenience and adaptedness to the object, the awkward and imperfect contrivances of the past, and others are improvements which convert the flimsy and rough articles of twenty years ago, into neat, exact, and serviceable substitutes.

Here are made, among other things, which within the lifetime of the present generation, could only be had from England, or until the last five years in the eastern factories, pendant pullies, shutter lifts, shutter screw bolts and fastenings, steamboat shutter catches, sash weights, and side and screw pullies, shutter sliding bolts and turn buckles, butt and parliament hinges, stubbs and plates, spittoons, tea-kettles, and sad-irons.

No judges of builders' hardware can examine these articles without being forcibly impressed with the superiority, not only over the foreign hardware of 1825, but even over most of the manufactured articles at this time at the east. It is in the department of hinges, however, that most important article of builders' use, that the superiority of those made in Cincinnati, is distinctly manifest. The English hinges are unequal in thickness, imperfectly jointed, and too light for service, and are, therefore, apt to give way when exposed to sudden jars or strains. M. Greenwood's hinges, on the contrary, are made substantial, and cast as evenly as if made by machinery.

Nearly every article referred to here, is in some respect or other of superior excellence to those imported from Europe. The tea-kettle lids, and the sad-iron handles, are very neat and appropriate. So with the counter weights, which are finished in superior style, and every weight in the set graduated to the city standard before it leaves the foundery.

The whole west, is now supplied from this city with the various hardware for building and our own consumption, no limited supply, in a city which constructs one thousand five hundred houses annually within its limits and immediate suburbs, is furnished entirely by this establishment.

Nearly all the hinges sold in our hardware stores, are of Cincinnati manufacture, and the few that are brought from abroad are sold to country customers only.

The annual sales of hinges alone, at this establishment, are stated, to be about fifteen thousand dollars, and the show of neatly papered and labeled goods in the warerooms, is worth a visit from all who desire to see our country in fact, as well as in name, independent.

Let us add one fact. In 1808, only forty years since, as clerk to a hardware house in Philadelphia, the writer of this article, filled the spring order in that line, of the principal business house in Cincinnati, doing at that time, at least one-fourth of the hardware business here. On that occasion, he put up eighteen dozen butt hinges, being at the rate of about one hundred and fifty dozen of that article for a year's supply, a quantity which would now not suffice for more than a single day's sales in our market. Such is the west.

A separate department in this establishment, is occupied by the firm of M. Greenwood & Co., in the manufacture of malleable cast iron into an infinite variety of important articles, heretofore the products of wrought iron and hand labor. In this department are made carriage wrenches, staples, pole crabs, nuts, screw wrenches, table hinges, pen racks, tailors' shears, and a variety of other articles. All these, when put to the appropriate tests, prove equal in every respect for service to the correspondent wrought articles. As regards drilling, they seem tougher. Cards of these articles were exhibited at the late mechanics' fair, and excited the general admiration of the visitors.

The tailors' shears are remarkable articles, as may be inferred from the fact, that a pair finished with steel edges, was lately furnished for the English market, and sold for *seventy-five dollars.*

Greenwood employs three hundred and fifty hands, and manufactures annually, a value of three hundred and sixty thousand dollars.

W. C. Davis & Co. Foundery, Hunt street, east of Broadway;

ENGRAVED BY F. E. JONES FROM A DAGUERREOTYPE

Miles Greenwood

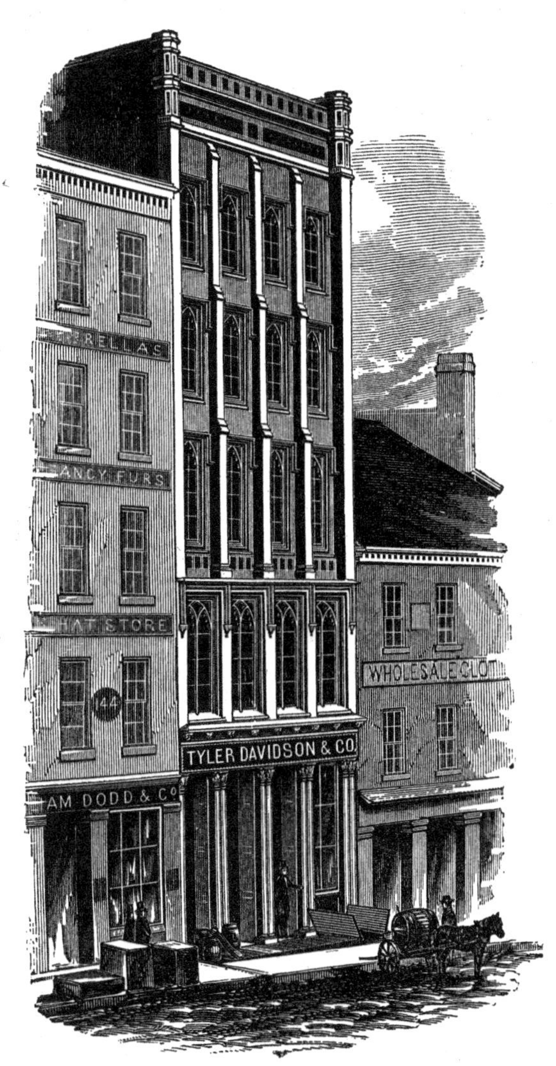

WHOLESALE HARDWARE MERCHANTS,

MAIN STREET, BELOW FOURTH.

sale-rooms, north-east corner Ninth and Main streets. This is principally a stove establishment, in every variety of use and pattern, and on a very extensive scale, employing one hundred and twenty-five hands—two-thirds of whom, are molders. This firm melted, last year, three thousand tons pig-iron, including three hundred tons scraps. Their present operations, are at the rate of four thousand two hundred tons. They also make plain and ornamental grates, sad and dog-irons, mold-boards, cauldrons, potash and sugar-kettles, and a variety of other castings.

Davis & Co., have recently constructed an extensive foundery and warerooms, five stories high, exclusively for the manufacture and fitting up of Fisk's patent metallic burial-cases, a new article, and every way superior to the ordinary cabinet ware coffins, which they must supersede. These cases, in their figure, follow the general outline of the human body in a recumbent position, and consist of an upper and lower metallic shell, which are joined together in a horizontal line in the centre, each part being of about equal depth. The shells have each a narrow flange, which when placed together are bound by screws, and cemented at the point of junction with a substance which becomes as hard as the metal itself. They are thoroughly enameled both inside and out, and thus rendered as entirely air-tight as any case can be constructed. The upper shell is raised-work, and ornamented in the casting, with the appearance of rich folding drapery thrown over the body. A heavy glass plate, oval in its shape, and corresponding in size and position to the human face, affords to the last moment, a view of the lineaments of the deceased, while the air-tight character of the case, cemēnted together as it is, will preserve the body, it is believed, for any period of time. It has been thus far tested for two and a-half years only, the longest period it has been in use, and exhibits in this case, the unchanged and undecomposed features of a child of ten years in their pristine expression and loveliness.

These cases afford great facilities for transporting those who have died at a distance from their surviving friends, to be brought home to family vaults and burying-grounds. The indestructible character of these receptacles, also so greatly facilitates the raising and reinterment elsewhere, when necessary, at any period, however remote, of the relics of departed friends, and so thoroughly divests exhumations of their usually revolting features, as to justify the belief, that these burial-cases will soon become of general and extensive use. These burial-cases are sold wholesale, at from three to twenty dollars, the sizes ranging from twenty-eight inches, to six feet six inches.

W. & R. P. Resor. One of the best specimens for convenience, extent, and adaptedness of all its arrangements to their appropriate purposes, is the Phœnix Foundery, belonging to this firm, at the intersection of Smith street with the river landing. It is a striking example of economy in space, and still more in the labor required to carry on a furnace; accomplishing in these respects, more with the same number of hands, than any other concern of the kind in this vicinity, if not anywhere else.

The establishment bears the title of the Phœnix Foundery, and is designed for the casting of stoves and hollow-ware principally. It is in the form, externally, of an L, occupying a space of eighty-two by one hundred and eighty-eight feet in depth upon the Smith street front, and sixty-six by one hundred and forty-three feet on the river front. Two molding floors, seventy-five by sixty-six, and one hundred and fifty-nine by sixty-six feet, occupy the interior of the foundery. These are intersected with five feet alleys radiating from the cupolas, which are paved with bricks and protected with curb-stones. The grade of those which connect directly with the cupolas, is a descending one; so that the hands take their loads along a gentle descent, and return with the empty ladles by a corresponding ascent. This, and the treading a smooth brick surface, which permits none of the melted iron, when spilled, to become imbedded in the walk, are advantages to both owner and hands, which every one conversant with the business can appreciate. The pig-metal, in lieu of being pitched up on to a platform, as is the usual tedious and laborious process, is wheeled up by an inclined plane, standing along the outside foundery wall, which, after reaching the proper height, crosses to the cupolas by a platform, which stretches over the intermediate space, being supported as in bridge work, by substantial rods, secured by heavy timbers, which form part of the building.

On the Smith street front is a warehouse five stories high, the lower floor being employed for weighing and assorting the various plates, which are raised to the second story, where they are mounted, put together, and distributed to the different warerooms above. All the hoisting, drilling, punching, etc., are carried on by steam.

The two cupolas are situated at the angles of the L, forming a central point to the molding operations. The hot-blast process, similar to that in use at the blast furnaces, is introduced here, and placed above the cupolas, heated by hot air which escapes from them, and which otherwise would be wasted.

The cupolas are lined, and of thirty-six inches diameter. They are of a capacity to melt twenty tons per day.

The pig-iron is also of that fine metal, made in Lawrence and Scioto counties under the hot-blast process, and the result is, that pots and kettles are made here, of such ductility, as to receive indentations by the hammer, without any risk of cracking the article.

This foundery casts door fronts, also, to considerable extent. It employs seventy hands.

Williams & Adams, Novelty Works, Pearl street, manufacture house fronts, tobacco and cotton presses, iron staircases, balcony and graveyard railings, wagon-boxes, awning posts, iron gutters and stoves, sash weights, cistern tops, gratings, hitching-posts, grate bars, star anchors, vault grates, clock weights, hoisting-wheels, and mill work generally. They employ twenty-three hands.

James Todd & Co., corner of Seventh and Smith streets, build steam-engines; manufacture planing machines, turning lathes, cotton, hay, lard, and tobacco screws, portable corn and flour-mills, thrashing machines and horse-powers, castings of all descriptions; also, various kinds of tools. They employ fifty hands.

A. B. & E. Latta, Buckeye Works, Fifth street, east of Broadway, manufacture all kinds of lathes and machinists' tools. Steam-engines, high and low pressure, stationary, locomotive and marine. Also steam, water, and vacuum gauges, reliable for quality and correctness.

This firm obtained a premium at the last fair of the Ohio Mechanics' Institute, for their improved steam-engines, as unsurpassed for cheapness, durability, and economy of steam and oil; and advice is given here, in the construction of machinery and mechanical operations.

Fringes, Tassels, etc.—Four establishments, mostly on a small scale; value of product, twenty thousand dollars. Forty hands in employment; raw material, 50 per cent.

Peter Ruhl, Fourth, below Walnut street, manufactures fringes, tassels, gimps, cords and fancy trimmings. Coach laces, carriage trimmings, Masonic and Odd Fellows' regalias, and military trimmings, of every description

Furniture.—Under this general head, is usually comprehended various equipments for housekeeping, such as bedsteads, bureaus, tables, stands, wardrobes, desks, bookcases, cribs, sofas, settees, lounges, divans, plain and fancy chairs, ottomans, etc. It would have been desirable to classify these by assigning them to their respective workshops, but in point of fact, these establishments are so various in their fabrics, some confining themselves to one or two prominent articles, others making every possible variety, and others, again, blending the chair business with what is called cabinet ware, that such classification becomes imperfect and unsatisfactory, and fails to exhibit a clear statement of this important department of our manufacturing interest; a general synopsis of the business will, therefore, be given in its aggregate of products, and number of workmen, and the various descriptions illustrated, as in the case of the founderies, by the statistics of particular establishments, as specimens of the various classes that exist.

"Cincinnati, in 1841," exhibited in its table of manufacturing and industrial pursuits, forty-eight cabinet ware factories, with a force of three hundred and eighty-four hands, and a product of three hundred and eighty-four thousand dollars. Of chairs, eleven factories, exhibiting a force of one hundred and twenty-eight hands, and a product of one hundred and thirty-one thousand six hundred dollars. At that date, these branches of furniture were kept distinct, as they are yet to some extent. Since that period, the application of steam power and machinery, to general furniture fabrics, has greatly changed the entire business character of this branch of manufacture, as well as tended to increase its sale.

Two or three popular errors exist, respecting the making of furniture by machinery, which it may be well here to refer to. One of these is, that the ware is not as exact in fit, or reliable for durability, as that made by hand; the reverse of this, is however, the fact. The least exercise of the reflecting powers, must suggest that work performed by machinery must be the more accurate. Another erroneous prejudice is, that the employment of machinery lessens not only the number of persons employed, but reduces their wages and profits. The fact, in reality, is, that the machinery, as a general result, takes the coarsest, hardest, and most unprofitable work out of the journeyman's hands—such as rough planing and ripping—and enables him to make his customary wages, at more pleasant employment. It is true, at the same time, that a great reduction in the price of these articles, is effected by the use of machinery, but this is done by the increase of product, which is both the cause and effect of low prices. But a comparison between past and present wages, will show clearly that the journeyman has been no loser, but in fact, gainer, by the introduction of machinery in the fabrication of furniture.

There are several shops which make up furniture, as a supply for auction sales; but the great bulk, beyond what is wanted for our own citizens, finds its market throughout the entire south and southwest.

The entire product of cabinet ware, chairs, etc., amounts to one million six hundred and sixty thousand dollars, and the business affords employment to one thousand one hundred and fifty-eight hands; value of raw material, 25 per cent.

One of the most remarkable of our manufacturing establishments, is the bedstead factory of Clawson and Mudge, on Second below Vine street.

The building, which is of brick, is five stories in height, and one hundred and ninety by seventy feet, on the ground. The machinery consists of seven planing and two tapering machines, sixteen turning-lathes, six boring, and two tenoning machines, four splitting, and four buff saws, all which, are driven by steam. One hundred and thirty hands are employed in this establishment. A very vivid impression of the power of machinery is given in this case, by the fact, that one hundred and thirty bedsteads are made and finished, as an average, every day, or one bedstead to each workman; while under the hand system of manufacture, a first rate bedstead is more than a week's work for one journeyman. The escape steam is employed not only in warming the building, in winter, but softens the glue, and being taken through a cylinder in which the veneers are steamed, fits them for being fastened to the bedsteads. Three million feet of lumber are annually worked up here into bedsteads, of which, forty thousand are the yearly product, and two hundred and fifty thousand dollars, the aggregate value. The stock of lumber on hand is never less than one million five hundred thousand feet, and of bedsteads a value of fifty thousand dollars. The lumber used here, is seasoned by steam, and air exposure afterward.

These bedsteads are of every variety of pattern and material, and degree of finish and cost; not less than ninety-five varieties being manufactured on the premises. They range from one dollar thirty-seven and a-half cents, to seventy-five dollars in price, at wholesale.

Poplar, sycamore, black walnut, and cherry, are the lumber; and black walnut, mahogany, and rosewood, the veneers employed in the fabrication of these bedsteads.

The headboards of the finer kinds of bedsteads, are not morticed into the post, as usual, but are fastened at the ends by iron hooks, secured to the head posts, and are let down by mortises into the head-rail. This is obviously a very great improvement, and greatly facilitates their being taken to pieces and put together, when necessary. The market for these bedsteads, is throughout the west, south, and south-west. All the principal hotels in Memphis, Nashville, Mobile, and New Orleans, have been furnished with bedsteads from this factory.

This is, probably, the most extensive factory of the kind in the United States, and if so, the most extensive in the world. There is no single manufacturing establishment here, which is better fitted than this to be shown a stranger, for the purpose of impressing on him a sense of the industrial and mechanical energies of Cincinnati.

John K. Coolidge, corner Smith and Front streets. Here are made tables, stands, cribs, lounges, desks, and bookcases, by steam propelled machinery. Forty hands are employed, in this establishment.

S. J. John, cabinet, chair, and sofa wareroom, Third, near Sycamore street. There are no finer articles made in Cincinnati, than his pier and sofa tables, covered with Egyptian marble; dressing bureaus, sociables, and *vis-à-vis,* mahogany wardrobes and canopy bedsteads, among a variety of fine furniture, are sure to catch the visitor's eye, and to open the visitor's purse.

One of the remarkable articles in his line, is an extension table, which draws out to various lengths, and shuts up again, by turning a crank, affording, when opened to its full extent, a platform large enough for the guests at a sizable hotel, and when closed up, taking up no more room than an ordinary circular table. Large numbers are made, and of course, sold, of this article, which is a great convenience everywhere that room is scarce.

E. Rowe, north-west corner Smith and Augusta streets, manufacture bedsteads, patent and common, including trundles, at from two to twenty dollars, wholesale. His workshop is four stories high, and stands eighty by thirty-five feet on the ground. He employs thirty hands, and manufactures to the value of thirty thousand dollars.

Mitchell & Rammelsberg, steam furniture factory, at the corner of John and Second street. Sale and exhibition rooms, Second street, between Main and Sycamore. This, which is one of the heaviest of our furniture establishments, does not, as is generally the case with the others, confine its operations to two or three staple articles, but comprehends in its fabrics almost every description of cabinet ware and chairs. Two-thirds of their business, however, is cabinet ware manufacture. The lot on which this factory stands, is eighty by one hundred and twenty feet. The main building occupies three-fourths of this breadth, and the entire depth. It is six stories high, and filled with workmen and materials to its utmost capacity. Other buildings take up the residue of the premises.

In the manufacture of furniture, the rough work is performed here, by machinery, with great celerity and exactness—the finishing being, as in other furniture shops, executed by competent and skillful workmen. This concern employs, directly and indirectly, two hundred and fifty persons, and manufactures to the value of two hundred and twenty thousand dollars annually.

The various articles made, are cut into lengths and shapes otherwise, by the agency of a series of circular saws. Every process here, from the ripping out and cross-cutting of rough boards, to the finest slitting, progresses with inconceivable rapidity; the saws performing at the rate of from two thousand five hundred to three thousand revolutions in a minute; a speed which renders the teeth of the saw absolutely invisible to the eye.

As many as two hundred pieces of furniture, and the various parts in the same series, prepared and adjusted to fit, as fast as they progress, at a time, are taken from story to story, until on the upper floors, they receive their final dressing and finish, for market.

The sale-rooms referred to, occupy five stories, each floor being thirty-four by ninety feet, and display full stocks of furniture, in every variety of style, pattern, and quality. This is but one of the many cabinet ware establishments in Cincinnati, which supply the south, west, and south-west, with materials for housekeeping of all sorts, on an extensive scale.

Mitchell & Rammelsberg, are about to introduce a bedstead of novel construction, for which they have the exclusive manufacturing right in this market. The improvement made, is by connecting the rail to the post by a dovetail, thus dispensing entirely with screws, and enabling the bedstead to be put up and taken down in less than five minutes; which of course, affords great facilities to the removal of this article from house to house, or room to room, and of readily taking them out in case of fire.

Burley & Lyford, south side Third, east of Sycamore street, manufacture all kinds of ornamental cabinet ware: cottage furniture, chamber sets, enameled or painted in scroll, landscape, and flowers. French, Italian, and Grecian bedsteads, bureaus, sinks, wardrobes, commodes, wash-stands, and toilets, grained to imitate every variety of wood.

Their styles of fabrics are admirably adapted to the equipment of steamboats, as well as for family furniture, of a light and elegant description.

Henry Boyd, Broadway, above Eighth street. This establishment has long enjoyed a distinguished reputation for bedstead work of high finish, fancy style, and excellent quality, although its operations are not confined to that article alone. Boyd works twenty hands.

The peculiarity of Boyd's bedsteads—which are the patent right and left, wood screw, and swelled rail—is the solidity of fit, when put together; which enhances their durability; as well as forms a perfect protection from vermin, which find no harbor at the joints.

John Geyer, Fourth, east of Main street, occupies in his manufacturing and sale of cabinet ware and chairs, a building fifty-six feet front, by one hundred feet deep, and five stories high. He has recently succeeded to A. McAlpin; a well known establishment, in the cabinet making line, on whose business he has engrafted, to a great extent, a fancy style of articles of the richest cast. Among these, are, cottage, Italian, and Minster parlor chairs, reclining and lounging chairs, fancy sofas; black, white, and Egyptian marble centre tables, with oval and lozenge-shaped slabs; fancy dressing bureaus, etagers, corner etagers with closets, papier-maché work-stands and tables, ladies' cabinet and writing desks, Italian marble slab and mahogany work-tables, with fancy basket around the pedestal.

Geyer manufactures furniture and chairs, also, of the staple articles and patterns, and of all descriptions, as regards quality and style.

One of the most commodious, as well as extensive factories in Cincinnati, is that of George W. Coddington, on Vine, between Front and Second streets. Having been built for the express purpose of carrying on the business, nothing can surpass the convenience and efficacy of its machinery and arrangements. The factory is forty-six by ninety feet on the ground, and six stories in height.

The machinery of this establishment is propelled by two steam-engines, each of twenty horse power. These drive four ripping, and seven circular saws, twenty-five cutters, two mortising, three boring, three planing, and twelve turning machines. One of these saws, which is concave, is a Cincinnati invention, of great ingenuity, and singularly well adapted to its purpose; which is to cut out the chair tops in circular form and equal thickness.

This factory has made as many as one hundred and eighty thousand chairs, yearly. These are principally low and medium-priced articles, although cane-seat and rocking-chairs, are made to a considerable extent. The prices range from four dollars twenty-five cents, to twenty-two dollars, and average eight dollars per dozen; just such chairs may be bought here, at five dollars per dozen, as were bought, twelve or fifteen years ago, at sixteen dollars. Such is the economy and power of machinery.

All the painting and gilding to the chairs, is done on the premises. The gilding of the finer qualities, is of the highest style of finish and ornament.

The principal market for these chairs, is in the south and south-west, although they find customers throughout the west and the north-west. In the south they have entirely driven out the eastern article, their quality and price rendering them more acceptable.

There are at times as high as one hundred and eighty hands employed in the factory; and its annual product, in value, one hundred and twenty thousand dollars.

In other articles, reference has been made to the benefit of machinery to the interests of the working-man, in taking the roughest and hardest of the ripping and planing out of his hands, and leaving to him only those delicate operations, which give play to the exercise of skill and judgment. It may be added, on the same subject, that the low prices at which machinery permits articles to be sold, so increases the quantity made, that more hands are now needed in these factories, than found employment under the old order of things, and at an average of better wages than heretofore.

M. L. Duncan & Brother. Factory, Augusta street, between Western row and John; sale-rooms and office, Second, between Vine and Walnut streets. This establishment manufactures wardrobes, breakfast and extension tables, stands, bureaus, cribs, lounges, desks, and bookcases, of mahogany and black walnut. Their market is exclusively the south and west, and their furniture disposed of at wholesale. They employ seventy-five hands, and manufacture to the value of one hundred thousand dollars annually, of which are two thousand wardrobes, worth from ten to forty dollars; three thousand tables, two and a-half to six dollars; five hundred bookcases, ten to twenty dollars; five hundred desks, seven and a-half to twenty dollars. The largest share, of course, at the lower prices.

Henry Clostermann, corner Augusta and John streets, employs seventy hands, and manufactures chairs to the value of sixty thousand dollars, principally cane-seats. Large quantities of black walnut and mahogany, are worked up in this establishment.

Dobell & Hughes. Manufactory, corner of Smith and Augusta streets, make breakfast, dining, circular, centre, card, and end tables, cribs, tin safes, stands, children's bedsteads, etc.

E. B. Dobell. Chair and cabinet factory on Lower Market street, manufactures chairs, bureaus, tables, looking-glasses, mattresses.

Cincinnati steam bureau manufacturing company, D. F. Meader, agent; corner Front and Smith streets, manufactures rosewood, mahogany and walnut dressing and plain bureaus, sideboards, writing desks, inclosed and plain wash and workstands, wardrobes, card-tables, bookcases, tin safes, etc. Employs eighty hands, and manufactures yearly, to the value of ninety thousand dollars.

The buildings in which these articles of furniture are made, are respectively, one hundred and forty-two by forty-five feet, five stories; one hundred by thirty feet, four stories; and fifty by fifteen feet, two stories in height. The work, as far as practicable, is done by machinery driven by a steam-engine of forty horse power.

In the first story are located the engine, a large turning-lathe, the machinery for a scroll saw and for mortising, and the apparatus by which the veneering is done, the glue and cauls for which, are heated by steam. The second story is occupied by three heavy planing machines, and four saws. Here the lumber is dressed, and cut into convenient sizes for use in the third story, where are three smaller circular saws, and where the tenoning, boring, and grooving are all done, which being accomplished, the stuff is elevated by steam to the fourth story, and there put together.

The fifth and sixth stories are divided into finishing rooms, where the bureaus are varnished, and finally prepared for market. From these rooms, seven thousand bureaus are annually taken out, which are sold, on an average, at ten dollars each. In their manufacture, over seven hundred thousand feet of lumber are consumed, with about seven thousand dollars worth of veneering, and at least nine hundred gallons of varnish.

Connected with the manufactory, is a lumber yard, three hundred and eight feet long, by one hundred and eight wide. The amount of lumber, at all times, stacked in this yard, will average one million feet.

Refuse lumber and shavings are all consumed, and the entire rooms are warmed by the escape steam, which is conducted through the building in iron pipes.

Shaw & Rettig, north side Fourth, between Main and Sycamore streets. This establishment confines its operations entirely to fine and fancy furniture of fashionable styles. Here are to be found every variety of carved rosewood, mahogany, and walnut chairs and sofas of antique and gothic patterns, with fancy seating of plush, Louis XIV, and brocatelle. Parlor tables, with lozenge-shaped tops of marbles, of every variety and shade of tint, Egyptian, Italian, etc. Cottage furniture, chamber sets, enameled and painted in scroll, landscapes and flowers. French, Italian, and Grecian bedsteads.

Smith & Hawley. Factory, south-west corner John and Augusta street; salerooms, 64 Sycamore street, north of Lower Market. The manufacture here, is altogether of fine cabinet and upholstery ware, such as fine dressing bureaus, centre and card-tables, sofas, lounges, sociables, divans, ottomans; all varieties and patterns of mahogany, cane, and stuffed hair and plush seated parlor chairs; rocking and easy chairs. Rosewood and mahogany and walnut veneers, are extensively used here, as materials. This firm employs sixty hands, and makes yearly, one thousand two hundred sofas, two thousand five hundred parlor chairs, and one thousand centre and card-tables.

The largest building employed in the manufacture of chairs in this city, or anywhere else, is that of C. D. Johnston, on the south side of Second, between John and Smith streets. His operations have been heretofore confined to a building forty by eighty feet, and six stories high, a space, large as it is, entirely inadequate to that demanded for a first class chair factory in Cincinnati, working on the scale required of late years. He has, therefore, recently made an addition, eighty-six by sixty-eight feet, which affords him a front on Second street of one hundred and twenty-six feet, and an average depth of seventy-four feet. The new building is seven stories high, the additional story affording a favorable opportunity to carry out, from the upper floor of the one, to the roof of the other building, the chairs, as fast as they are ready for drying in the open air. This extensive building fronts on two streets, which affords it thorough ventilation and ample light.

An engine of twenty horse power, drives by steam the various machinery employed on the premises, and the escape steam from the engine is carried, story by story, through seven hundred and sixty feet cast iron pipe into every part of the edifice, during the winter season, so as perfectly to dispense with the use of fire throughout the building. On the same account, steam is taken direct from the boiler to prepare the glue and the cauls for use.

Mr. Johnston's business is entirely wholesale, and extends the whole range of the valleys of the Ohio and Mississippi—that is, the country watered by these rivers and their tributaries. All the important towns or cities in the south and west are extensively his customers. As an illustration of the magnitude of his business, he has a standing order on his books, from the largest furniture sale house in the west, for thirty thousand chairs of the various descriptions made. This is the house of Scarritt & Mason, St Louis. Chairs are made here from the finest mahogany cane, to the ordinary wood seats. The manufacturing value, when the new building is fully occupied, will exceed one hundred and twenty-five thousand dollars yearly. Hands employed, one hundred and sixty, mostly Germans.

In concluding the subject of furniture, it will be appropriate to add that Joseph Walter, who was the first individual in Cincinnati to apply machinery propelled by steam-power, in the manufacture of cabinet ware, has just made arrangements to resume that business on a very extensive scale.

The application of steam to the melting of glue and preparing the cauls for veneering, which originated in his factory, is one of the most important improvements in this line, for several years past.

Gas and Coke.—The Cincinnati Gas and Coke company, employ fifty hands, and manufacture to the value of sixty-five thousand dollars annually; raw material, 60 per cent.

Gas-Fitting. Two establishments.—Twenty-four hands; value of product, forty-five thousand dollars; raw material, 50 per cent.

Goodin & Mahon, Main, above Court street, are extensively engaged in this business.

Gas Burner Caps. This is an ingenious article recently invented here, and calculated so to consume the escaping gas, as to increase the intensity of the light fifty per cent., or if many burners be used, to reduce the expense one-third. D. Andrews, jeweler and silversmith, Fifth, near Race street, is the inventor and patentee.

Gilders. Ten establishments.—Thirty-six hands; amount of product, thirty-nine thousand dollars; raw material, 50 per cent.

Thomas Bown, Fourth, between Main and Sycamore streets, manufactures every description of gilt work for pictures, etc., of fancy and ornamented styles, as well as plain work. Employs ten hands, on a product of twelve thousand dollars.

Glass works.—Two; value of product, forty thousand dollars; employ thirty hands.

The largest of these, that of Gray & Hemingray, is on a scale so much inferior in magnitude to those of Pittsburgh, that the statistics just given, would have concluded this subject, but for the conviction which the writer of this entertains, that Cincinnati will hereafter lead Pittsburgh in cotton fabrics, rolling mill products and glass manufactures, as we already do in everything else. It becomes, therefore, an object of interest and solicitude to examine the details of what it is evident, is the germ here, of a vastly important branch of industrial pursuit, as suggestive of the great future. Sand, pearl-ashes, and lead, are the main constituents of glass. The sand necessary for glass works in Pittsburgh and Cincinnati, is brought from Missouri, and the lead from Illinois, both at less expense to this point, than to Pittsburgh; and the pearl-ash, always rules in price lower here, than in the markets of our sister city.

Nor is this all; the means of living here, are lower than at Pittsburgh, every item but rent, being so much cheaper, as to more than equalize general expenses. In this state of the case, and with the rapidly growing business of this establishment as an encouragement, other glass works must spring up; and as their operations enlarge, a point of purchase in these articles will be created, which must concentrate large sales of glass here, of city product, which have heretofore been made elsewhere.

Gray & Hemingray, make tumblers, decanters, packing-bottles, lamp glasses, apothecary shop furniture, and generally, most articles manufactured in Pittsburgh. A greater variety of perfumery glass is manufactured in these works, than at any in Pittsburgh. All the operations alluded to, are of flint glass, except insulators, which are made for lightning rods and for telegraph lines, here, and at Pittsburgh; which place is entirely supplied from this point.

Glove factories. Three.—Employ thirty-three hands, principally females; value of manufacture, twenty thousand dollars; raw material, 65 per cent.

Glue. Five factories.—Forty hands; value of product twenty-eight thousand dollars.

Forgey, Warren & Co., manufacture glue, curled hair for upholsterers' use, also dress bristles, etc. Employ twenty-two to fifty hands, according to the season; these articles requiring to be made or prepared in the fall or winter, principally. There are twenty thousand pounds glue made, and twenty thousand pounds long curled hair, and two hundred thousand pounds short curled hair, and ten thousand dollars worth of bristles prepared here, for market. The curled hair is purified by chemical processes; the long being put to use in first quality mattresses or in chairs and sofa seats, and the short filled into a more common article.

Gold Leaf and Dentists' Foil.—One factory, that of James Leslie, employs five hands, and makes a product of eleven thousand dollars; raw material, 50 per cent.

The beating of gold leaf affords a striking illustration of the diffusibility, or rather extension, of substances. A piece of gold equal in size to ten grains No. 1 shot, will beat out seven thousand five hundred square inches, and each shot a surface of gold sufficient to cover an extra imperial sheet, as large as the "Cincinnati Enquirer."

Gold Pens. One factory.—Three hands; value of product, thirty-five hundred dollars; value of raw material, 50 per cent.

Grate manufacturers. Two.—Number of hands employed, fifty-two; value of product, forty-five thousand dollars; value of raw material, 20 per cent.

Grinders of Spices, Coffee, Drugs, etc. Six establishments.—Fifty-six hands; value of product, one hundred and forty thousand dollars; raw material, 60 per cent.

Harrison & Eaton, 101 Walnut street, grind pepper, allspice, ginger, cloves, cinnamon, mustard, African cayenne. These are put up in bulk, or in packages for the retail trade. They also grind coffee and rice, and roast coffee and pea-nuts. These are supplied at all times, perfectly fresh and warranted pure.

Ground Drugs and Concentrated Medical Preparations.—Jacob S. Merrell, Steam Drug mills, grinds or powders every species of drugs, to order, and prepares concentrated extracts of vegetable medical articles, such as podophyllin or mandrake, sanguinarin or blood-root, macrotin or black cohosh, leptandrin or black-root extracts.

These extracts are so highly concentrated by chemical processes, that the active principle of an article worth not more than ten or fifteen cents the pound, acquires a value of one dollar per ounce. These preparations are sent out the whole length and breadth of the United States, and even into Canada.

The vegetables whose roots furnish these extracts, are indigenous to the west, abounding especially in Indiana and Missouri. Employs ten hands, and a thirty horse-power engine, and manufactures to the value of thirty thousand dollars, annually; raw material, 30 per cent. This is a rapidly growing establishment, and must become one of extensive operations.

Ground Mustard. Two establishments.—Ten hands; fifteen thousand dollars product; raw material, 40 per cent.

Ground Marble Dust. Two establishments.—Employ four hands; annually grind fifteen hundred barrels for use of mineral water establishments; value of product, thirty-five hundred dollars; raw material, 5 per cent.

Gunsmiths. Six establishments.—Thirty hands; thirty-five thousand dollars, value of product; raw material, 40 per cent.

Eaton & Kittridge, 236 Main street, are engaged in the manufacture of rifles, shot-belts, etc. Employ ten hands. These rifles are of every quality and price. Make and finish two hundred and fifty rifles, and two hundred dozen belts annually. Use black walnut and maple stocks. The business is yet in its infancy; value of product, twelve thousand dollars; of raw material, 50 per cent. This firm are extensive importers of guns, pistols, and sporting apparatus, gun makers' materials, powder, etc. It is the first wholesale house established here, and by far the most extensive in the west.

Hats. Forty factories.—Three hundred and sixty-seven hands; value of product, four hundred and forty-five thousand dollars; raw material, 30 per cent.

There was a period, when, if one of our citizens wanted a fine hat, Platt Evans was commissioned to buy it in New York or Philadelphia; nothing but cheap hats being at that time made here. Dodd, on Main street, was the first to engage in the enterprise of manufacturing hats of a quality which should supersede the hats made in the eastern cities, and now the fine hats for the entire market of the west, are made here by Dodd & Co., L. H. Baker & Co., C. B. Camp, Bates & Whitcher, and Sherwood & Chase.

There are others who make hats, but on a limited scale of operations. There are no low-priced hats made here of late years.

Dodd & Co., employ from twenty to forty hands, according to the season, and manufacture to the value of sixty-seven thousand dollars.

Baker & Co., make silk and fur hats, two hundred and fifty per week. They work twenty hands on an average.

C. B. Camp, employs eighteen hands at an average, and manufactures fine hats to the value of forty thousand dollars.

All those who are largely in this business, also sell the common article made at the east. The sales at our principal hat stores, including those of their own manufacture, range from one hundred thousand to two hundred and fifty thousand dollars each.

Hat-Block Factory.—William H. Carver, south side Pearl, between Vine and Race. Four hands; value of product, four thousand five hundred dollars; of raw material, 10 per cent.

Horse-Shoeing. Twelve shops.—Thirty-five hands; value of product, forty-eight thousand dollars; raw material, 50 per cent.

Hose and Belts, etc. Four factories.—Twenty-six hands; a product in value of ninety-six thousand dollars; value of raw material, 75 per cent.

Cincinnati supplies hose as well as fire-engines, to the principal towns in its vicinity.

Jeffrey Seymour, north side Fifth, between Main and Sycamore streets, manufactures steamboat, fire-engine, factory, and garden hose, to the value of twenty thousand dollars, annually. His hose is all copper or iron riveted, and of the best quality; also makes belts and bands for machinery, elevator belts, etc.

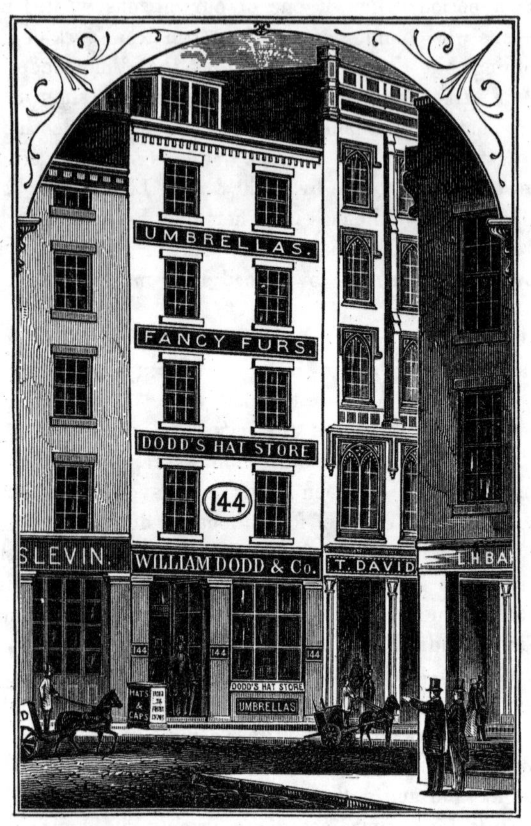

DODD & Co.—HATTERS,

MAIN STREET, BELOW FOURTH.

George E. Minister, 31 Sycamore street, makes hose—garden, steamboat, and fire-engines; also machine belts, fire hats, capes, belts, trumpets, spanners, torches, branch pipes, nozzles, etc. Engines, etc., are also repaired here. Minister makes of these various articles, to the yearly value of twenty-five thousand dollars.

Hot Air Furnaces.—A. Lotze, 219 Walnut street, is extensively engaged in this line. These furnaces have been put up in almost all our churches and public buildings, and to a great extent in private dwellings of the finer class. By the introduction of evaporatory radiators and registers, the air is kept moist, which obviates that dry heat, the presence of which, in public assemblies, is directly indicated by the short tickling cough it provokes. Product of manufacture, sixty thousand dollars per annum; raw material, 60 per cent.; employs twenty hands.

Ice. Ten ice dealers.—Sixty hands; value of product, one hundred and fifty thousand dollars; raw material, 10 per cent.

Milton Shute, in his ice operations, employs thirty men in getting out ice, and thirteen in its delivery to customers. He has three spacious ice-houses at Troy, and three more at Social Hall, on the Miami canal, beside the necessary buildings in which to pack it away here, when ice of sufficient thickness is made in Cincinnati. His sales for 1850, were twenty-one thousand four hundred and twenty-two dollars.

Iron—Bar, Boiler, Plate, Sheet, Hoop, Round, Square, Wire, Nails, etc. Five rolling-mills.—Five hundred and fifty hands; annual manufacture, ten hundred and fifty thousand dollars; raw material, 45 per cent.

Licking Rolling Mill—Morrell, Jordan & Phillips, employ one hundred and twenty hands, and is in steady operation throughout the year, day and night, Sundays excepted; consumes annually, one hundred and seventy-five thousand bushels of coal. The yearly products are, fifteen hundred tons small, round, and square, hoop, etc. One thousand tons large, round, and square, railroad chair iron, etc. One thousand tons fire-bed and sheet-iron. Five hundred tons boiler-iron, heads, etc. Four thousand tons iron, of all descriptions, averaging in value, seventy-five dollars per ton; aggregate, three hundred thousand dollars.

The sheet-iron made here, is annealed on the surface, which renders its appearance almost equal to the Russia sheets.

This establishment consumes annually, over three thousand tons pig-iron, and one thousand tons Tennessee clear blooms. The company has six acres of ground upon which the works stand, requiring room for large improvements, which are now in contemplation. The main building, is one hundred and eighty by one hundred and fifty-five feet, and covered with sheet iron. Three furnaces have been added to these works, within the last year. The actual cost of the entire works, as they now stand, amounts to about eighty thousand dollars.

Globe Iron and Wire Works—Worthington & Co., proprietors, manufacture every description of rolled iron, such as bar, sheet, boiler, and fire-bed, etc. Yearly product, two thousand six hundred tons. Also make railroad chairs, iron rivets, and wire of all sizes. Wire product, three hundred tons; they work from one hundred and ten to one hundred and twenty-five hands, and produce to the value of two hundred and ten thousand dollars.

Newport Iron works, D. Wolff, proprietor. Employ fifty-eight hands, and manufacture sheet, boiler, and fire-bed iron; is now putting up machinery for the manufacture of bar-iron; value of annual product, one hundred and twenty-five thousand dollars.

Iron Safes, Chests, and Vaults.—Three factories, which employ fifty-six hands, and manufacture to the value of ninety-six thousand dollars; raw material, 45 per cent.

Charles Urban, Pearl street, west of Vine, makes the Salamander safe; employs twenty-eight hands, and manufactures annually, one hundred and eighty safes, assorted sizes. They are a thoroughly tested and approved article.

Iron Railing. Five factories.—Seventy-seven hands; value of product, ninety-six thousand dollars; raw material, 25 per cent.

Horton, Leonard & Walton, east side of Elm, between Front and Second streets, make iron railing, bank doors and vaults, and jail safes. These safes are intended for the south, where materials for building jails securely, are scarce. They are made of three-quarter inch by two and a-half inch iron bars, which are put together so as to form a cage. When they get to their destination, walls of hard-burnt brick, and of proper thickness, are built on every side, so as completely to inclose the iron frame. A security is thus afforded the jails at the south, which is hardly possessed even here, in buildings of stone and mortar.

Dorr, Thompson & Magness, corner of Western Row and Betts street, manufacture all kinds plain and fancy railing, for street fronts, burial-grounds, etc.; gratings and balconies, iron stairs, jail doors and vaults. Employ fifteen hands; value of product, twenty-five thousand dollars.

Improved *Filters*.—J. H. Laning, makes these articles, and of approved quality. They render our turbid river water as clear and sparkling as that which gushes from the purest spring. Four hands; product, six thousand dollars.

Japaned Ornamental, and Pressed Tin Ware.—There are four establishments manufacturing these articles, one only of which, that of Geo. D. Winchell, corner of Walnut and Pearl streets, is worthy of notice. A statement of what is here made, would be an extensive catalogue. Every article of Japaned ware, from a child's whistle to a beautifully ornamented water cooler, may be bought here. Among the principal articles, are tea-caddies and chests, knife trays, trunks, lard and lard-oil lamps, candlesticks, etc. All the ware here, is made by small machinery, of which there is on the premises, what has cost three thousand dollars. Winchell works up one thousand two hundred boxes tin-plate, worth twelve thousand dollars, and paints, varnish, and other articles, to the value of three thousand dollars more. He employs thirty-four hands; yearly value of product, fifty-two thousand dollars; raw material, 30 per cent.

The water coolers made here, are a superior article, and excel alike in beauty and usefulness; worth, according to size, from two to twenty dollars each.

Mr. Winchell has twice enlarged his capacity for manufacturing, and expects shortly to put up more extensive buildings, adequate to his enlarging business.

Lever Locks.—Ten factories, most of them on a small scale; sixty hands; value of product, fifty-three thousand dollars; raw material, 40 per cent.

McGregor & Lee, 132 Fifth street, manufacture bank locks, store and house lever locks; also plate hinges and screws, and put up house and hotel bells, with copper tubing to conceal and protect the wires. They employ nineteen hands.

Their combination and detector bank lock, an invention of Mr. McGregor of the firm, is remarkable for its ingenuity.

It not only defies tampering with; twelve tumblers being required to be raised, which no skeleton key can accomplish; but such is the exactness required to imitate the genuine key, that the thickness of a slip of bank paper suffices, when added to the size of its own key, to prevent that key from opening the lock to which it belongs. Its tumbler, also, may be so adjusted to its own key, that any person other than the owner, making use of that key, would have only one chance in favor of opening it, to four hundred and seventy-nine millions one thousand six hundred chances against his doing so. This renders it next to impossible for any person but the owner to open it.

Lightning Rods.—These are made here, by Thomas Phillips, on Sixth, near Walnut street, of superior quality, and on an extensive scale. The whole country, of which Cincinnati is the business centre, purchases these rods, which have stood the test of public opinion for years. There are fifty hands employed, and the value of product is one hundred and fifty thousand dollars; raw material, 50 per cent.

Lithographers.—Four establishments, mostly on a small scale. Twenty-four hands; aggregate value of labor product, twenty thousand dollars; raw material, 30 per cent.

Livery and Sale Stables. Cincinnati is the great horse market of the United States, and during the war with Mexico, horses in greater numbers, as well as finer quality, went from this city, than from all other points. We have here, forty-five livery and sale stables, one only of which, will be referred to in this place, as worthy of a visit by strangers.

Isaac D. Johnson, the proprietor of this establishment, occupies a space of ground averaging seventy feet by upward of three hundred feet. His stables front on Walnut, above Eighth, and reach nearly to Main street. This is a space exceeding twenty-one thousand square feet of ground. The buildings are separated by St. Clair alley, on which they also front. These stables are two stories high, and are doubtless the largest in the west, and probably in the United States. Beside carriages and horses left in his charge, Mr. Johnson keeps not less than seventy-five buggies, carriages, barouches, etc., and one hundred horses for hire; two hundred tons of hay, and twenty thousand bushels grain of various sorts, are consumed here yearly. In winter, the grain, whether whole or in meal, is steamed for feeding use.

One hundred horses, together, cannot readily be found, to compare with these in condition, beauty, and fitness for service; and these stables are well worth a visit from those who are judges of the horse, and delight in examining fine specimens of the race.

Looking-glass and Picture-Frame Factories.—The manufacture of looking-glass and picture frames, is carried on upon a small scale, by hand labor, in five or six shops of the city, but the product is comparatively insignificant. There is, however, an establishment of the kind operating by steam-power here, worthy of a passing notice. This is the factory of E. Blakeslee, on Seventh street, near Broadway, whose saleroom is on Main, between Fifth and Sixth streets.

Mr. B. has only established himself here recently, as a manufacturer, although he has for years had those articles for sale, together with clocks of all sorts. His factory operations, until that period, have been carried on at the east. He keeps four circular saws in motion, and employs eight hands. Had he the necessary room, he could enlarge his operations to twice their present extent; as it is, he finds sale for two thousand five hundred picture-frames weekly. All his frames, of every description, are to order, and the concern is not idle a single day for want of orders. All the mahogany veneers used here, are cut on the premises.

The looking-glass and picture-frame business of Cincinnati, of which Mr. B. does the largest half, is of an annual value of forty-eight thousand dollars, and employs thirty hands. It is yet only in its commencement.

Mr. Blakeslee's marine time-pieces, or patent lever clocks, are a curiosity. These are of various sizes, the case shaped like that of a watch, and adapted accordingly, to steamboat, canal-packet, or railroad car use. They can be carried either horizontally or perpendicularly, being no more affected by the roughest motion, than a pocket watch would be. They are in fact, admirable chronometers.

These are at very reasonable prices, and well worthy of purchase by the captains or owners of our best steamboats; on board which, they would be articles equally of use and ornament.

Machinists.—Most of the machine shops of this city are either appendages to, or are in direct business connection with, founderies, their products, etc., and have, therefore, been already included in the foundery statistics. A few, however, which sustain neither of these relations, may be grouped together, by saying that there are twelve of these last, who employ one hundred and twenty hands, and exhibit a product, in value, of one hundred and thirty thousand dollars.

Burdge & Johnston, south side of Second, between Race and Elm streets, manufacture planing machines, portable mortising, ogee, and tenoning machines, circular saws, shafts, slide and hand lathes, shafting, small engines, tobacco, lard-oil, wine, cider, and bookbinders' screws. They also are manufacturers of Converse & Burdge's patent screw-cutter, for cutting screws on the heads of bed-rails; of which it is sufficient to say, that it is employed to the exclusion of all other machines, at the great bedstead factory of Clawson & Mudge.

Marble working. Seven marble yards and shops.—Employ one hundred and sixty-four hands; value of product, one hundred and ninety thousand dollars; value of material,. 50 per cent.

D. Bolles, whose marble works are on Fourth, west of Walnut street, may be considered the introducer to this city of the modern style of monumental art. His marble works afford admirable specimens of ornamental, carved and sculptured marble in every variety. He employs twenty-five hands.

Lowry & Rule, south-west corner of Broadway and Fifth street, are extensively engaged in marble works. They are also prepared to exhibit a variety of chaste and appropriate designs, as well as executed specimens of monument carving and sculpture. They employ sixty-five hands.

If it should be asserted, as it here is, that tomb and monument work is executed here in a style of greater originality, taste, and excellence than in any of the Atlantic cities, the fact would doubtless be regarded as incredible, not only by eastern people, but by many individuals here who have not had it in their power to compare specimens. But the assertion is susceptible of easy proof. There are enough of eastern monuments in Spring Grove Cemetery to afford the necessary materials for comparison. Works of art—cenotaphs, sarcophagi and obelisks—from the best marble works of New York and Philadelphia, are there. Now let any man for himself, compare the L'Hommedieu or Burrows family monument, by Bolles, with that executed in the same style, by Hargraves of Philadelphia, for John Bailey, and put up in the same cemetery; or the obelisk for William H. Clement, by Lowry & Rule, with that made by R. I. Brown, the first artist in this line, of New York, for Henry Nye; or the sarcophagus for Larz Anderson, from Lowry & Rule's yard, with that executed for G. R. Shoenberger, by the celebrated J. Struthers of Philadelphia: or the splendid Gothic monument by D. Bolles, to the memory of George Iuppenlatz, with any eastern work of corresponding character in any of our cemeteries, and he will feel the utmost surprise, that work of this description should have ever been brought from the east, when it can be so much more skillfully executed here.

Another fact, which is conclusive on the subject. Nathaniel Silsbee, a well known individual, of Salem, Mass., on a recent visit to the west, accidentally saw specimens of mortuary sculpture and ornamental designs at Lowry & Rule's marble saloons, of so high an order of merit, as to induce him to leave an order for a monument to a design exhibited to him here, and to be executed in the style of which he had seen abundant specimens. Mr. Silsbee, after visiting the marble yards of Boston, Philadelphia, and New York for designs, had concluded to order a monument from Italy, when a model, just suited to his views and taste, was offered him in the Far West. The monument, which is of a sufficiently costly character, is to the memory of a group of his children lost in infancy, and is singularly chaste and felicitous. It will be put up in Mount Auburn Cemetery, and stand forever as an acknowledgment of Cincinnati skill and taste.

Masonic and Odd Fellows' Regalia. Four manufacturers.—Eighteen hands; value of product, twenty-one thousand dollars; raw material, 50 per cent.

Mathematical, Optical and Astronomical Instruments. Six workshops, principally on a small scale. J. Foster, Jr., on Walnut street, and Hasert, on Fourth, near Walnut street, execute instruments of a finish and accuracy that cannot be surpassed. Employ twenty-four hands; value of product, forty thousand dollars; raw material, 50 per cent.

Mat maker. One factory.—Three hands; value of product, seven thousand two hundred and forty dollars; raw material, 30 per cent.

Mattresses, Bedding, etc. Ten establishments.—Eighty hands; value of product, ninety-five thousand dollars; raw material, 50 per cent.

William Morehouse, furniture and bedding depôt, 134 Sycamore street, manufactures spring wire mattresses, one of the best articles in that line ever made; this mattress folds up conveniently in sections; lines church pews, and makes all sorts of cushions. Feather beds and mattresses are renovated here.

Millinery.—Miss Mulliner, 106, north side Fifth street, between

Vine and Race streets, fashionable millinery and dress-maker; employs fifteen to twenty-five hands, and makes up annually to the value of twenty thousand dollars; raw material, 50 per cent.

Mineral Water Factories.—The manufacture of soda-water, a very refreshing beverage during the heats of summer, has been carried on in this city for some years quite extensively, and the consumption of it at home and abroad, is increasingly great.

Soda-water is made by impregnating water with carbonic acid gas, in the proportion of five parts in bulk of one, to twelve of the other; the gas in a fountain of any given capacity, being condensed into a volume of one-twelfth its natural space.

It is the expansion of that gas, when discharged, which creates effervescence, and the pungency of the soda-water, when taken at a draught.

The following is the process of manufacture. The gas is generated in a strong leaden vessel by the action of diluted sulphuric acid, on marble dust—carbonate of lime. It is passed into a gasometer, and thence forced by steam-power, acting on air pumps, into a fountain or the bottles, compressing fifty gallons of carbonic acid gas into the space of seven gallons in an inconceivably short space of time. The safety valve on the machine indicates a pressure of eighty-five pounds to the square inch.

There are eight of these factories here, employing sixty-four hands; value of product, one hundred and five thousand dollars. Four-fifths of this value is contributed by labor alone. The operations at one of these factories are propelled by a miniature steam-engine, so small that it might be packed in an ordinary coffin, and yet so powerful, the force being derived from its shortness of stroke and strength of steam, as to be equal to a four-horse power. It is capable of making four hundred and eighty revolutions in a minute.

Mineral Teeth. One factory.—Five hands; value of product, nine thousand dollars; raw material, 20 per cent.

Morocco Leather.—Seven establishments, for tanning and dressing this article. Two hundred thousand sheep skins are annually brought to this market and converted into morocco. Not only does our regular sheep market for food, contribute largely to this supply, but great quantities are rendered here and in the vicinity, for the hide and tallow. Two butchering and rendering establishments alone, tried out this season, sixty thousand sheep. The skins, divested of the wool, are worth twelve and a-half cents each, and the dressed article commands four dollars per dozen; aggregate value of product, sixty-seven thousand dollars; raw material, 30 per cent.

J. H. Ballance, on the Miami canal, near Race street, tans and dresses thirty thousand skins yearly, which are sold here for shoemakers' and saddlers' use. The supply of skins here has increased, since 1840, six-fold. Ballance is also a wool dealer, extensively.

Musical Instruments.—Pianos are made here on a small scale, in two shops, which employ four hands. A value of four thousand five hundred dollars is the product; raw material, 50 per cent.

There is also an organ factory, which employs twelve hands; builds organs to the value of twenty thousand dollars annually. Raw material, 40 per cent. The largest business in this line, is, however, that of making melodeons or melopeans and reed organs. Of these, there are three factories, which employ from forty to fifty hands, and make to the value of sixty-five thousand dollars; raw material, 50 per cent. This is a rapidly increasing business.

Murch & White, workshop on Fifth street, between Main and Sycamore; saleroom, 74 Fourth, near Walnut street. Manufacture the melodeon pianos, with Carhart's patent exhausting bellows. These are sold at from forty-five to five hundred dollars, varying with size, increased capacity, and finish. The melodeon piano, is a new and splendid instrument, one that will supply the place of the piano-forte, better than any instrument ever made; better, for anything slow and plaintive, than the piano. It is intended for parlor, lodge-rooms, churches, and singing societies, and is the cheapest and best parlor instrument extant. Murch & White are the only manufacturers of these instruments west of the mountains, and the only manufacturers who make the double reeded and six octaves. They also manufacture Carhart's improved melodeon, four, four and a-half and five octaves. Their yearly sales here, are to the value of thirty thousand dollars.

Murch & White keep also for sale, Gilbert's boudoir pianos, an article well worthy of inspection by those wanting pianos.

George A. Prince & Co., also manufacture their latest improved melodeons at Buffalo, New York; one of their principal depôts is in this city, which will shortly become the place of its manufacture. Their wareroom is in the same building with that of Murch & White.

As this is a novel instrument, having been only introduced within the last three years, a description of the article may not be out of place here.

The cases are made of rosewood, and are as handsomely finished as any piano-forte. The key-board is precisely the same as the piano or organ, and the tone—which is very beautiful—closely resembles that of the flute stop of the organ—the notes speak the instant the keys are touched, and will admit of the performance of as rapid passages as the piano. The pedal, on the left, is intended for a *swell*, and by which the most beautiful effects can be produced. The pedal directly under the instrument supplies the wind, and works so easily that a child can manage it without any exertion. The bellows—which is something entirely new, and for which a patent was granted in December, 1846—is a reversed or exhaustion bellows; and it is this, in a measure, which produces the peculiar tone. The instrument can be *immediately made portable*, without detaching any part; the bellows receding into the body of the instrument, and the legs folding under and springing to their places, leave the whole in a compact form. Each instrument has a packing-case, secured by lock and key.

The volume of tone is equal to that of a small organ, and by means of the swell, may be increased or diminished, at the pleasure of the performer; it is sufficiently loud for small churches, and is well calculated for a parlor instrument. They have been examined and approved by hundreds of persons; but the best evidence of their merit is their rapid sale. But it is a new instrument—a new invention, and is yet but little known in the musical world; and it is for this reason that the attention of all lovers of music is called to it, under the conviction that there are thousands who would lose no time in securing one, were they aware of the existence of such an instrument, and the *low price at which it can be obtained.*

Music Publishing, etc.—W. C. Peters & Sons, Melodeon building, are publishers of various approved works of instruction, for the piano, guitar, violin, etc., of which they are the authors, or hold the copyrights. They also issue the newest and most popular music; of which their catalogue presents a variety of solos, duetts, trios, and glees, adapted to vocal and instrumental use, marches, quicksteps, etc., to the extent of one thousand six hundred pieces, sixty of which, have been published during the last six months. Of these the paper is of Cincinnati manufacture, and the engraving, printing, etc., is all executed here. The firm supplies eastern publishers, and the business exchange is largely in favor of Cincinnati. Their stock of engraved copper and zinc plates, cost upward of thirty thousand dollars, and they have paid out, during the past year, three thousand dollars for copyrights; also manufacture ruled music paper for copyists. They employ thirty hands; value of product, fifty thousand dollars; raw material, 25 per cent.

This establishment is largely in the piano-forte line of business, having since its first establishment as W. C. Peters, sold one thousand of A. H. Gale & Co.'s pianos, and upward of two thousand of those of Nunns & Clark, of New York.

Nut and Washer Factory.—Edwin Hills, Eighth street, near canal, has just commenced this business with three hands. They make three hundred and fifty to four hundred pounds per week, which at ten cents, the wholesale price, is equal to twenty thousand dollars yearly; raw material, 50 per cent.

Oil—Castor. One factory, that of Conkling, Wood & Co.—Seven hands; value of product, sixty thousand dollars; raw material, 75 per cent.

Oil—Lard and Stearine. Thirty-four factories.—one hundred and twenty hands; value of product, three millions fifteen thousand nine hundred dollars; of this, 65 per cent. is oil, and 35 per cent. stearine; raw material of lard oil, 93 per cent.; of stearine, 87 per cent.

Mitchener & Co., are probably the largest operators in this line in Cincinnati or anywhere else. His annual manufacture of lard oil is one hundred and fifteen thousand one hundred and seventy-five gallons; of stearine, seven hundred and thirteen thousand five hundred and eighty-three pounds; aggregate value, two hundred and one thousand and sixty dollars. It would surprise most persons to learn that this immense business was carried on by six hands in a two story building, ninety by sixteen feet, from which is taken, on the lower story, a space of fourteen by sixteen feet for other purposes than this manufacture.

Thomas Emery, 33 Water, between Main and Walnut streets, manufactures lard-oil, star and adamantine candles. These are of first quality, and the candles actual weight. Mr. E. is among the oldest manufacturers in this line of business.

Oil—Linseed. Three mills.—Employ thirty-eight hands; value of product, two hundred and sixty-three thousand dollars; raw material, 75 per cent.

N. C. McLean, at the intersection of High street and Miami canal, manufactures daily, two hundred and fifty bushels flax-seed; product, five hundred and thirty-one gallons oil, and nine thousand five hundred pounds oil-cake; employs seventeen hands.

Oils— Vitriol, etc.—Eugene Grasselli, manufactures chemicals on a large scale. One thousand five hundred barrels alum and twenty-eight thousand carboys oil vitriol, beside twenty-five or thirty articles on a smaller scale. Employs twenty-four hands, half by day and half by night, the works being in constant operation. His sulphuric acid or oil vitriol, is distilled in platina stills, imported from France, which cost him nine thousand one hundred dollars. A very heavy capital is invested in permanent buildings for his operations. His annual sales are to the extent of one hundred and thirty-five thousand dollars.

Packing-Box makers.—Twelve factories, which employ sixty-five hands, and produce the value of one hundred and twenty thousand dollars; raw material, 45 per cent. Two-fifths of this amount is made in the steam-power factory of J. & J. M. Johnston, who manufacture extensively, also, bathing-tubs and refrigerators.

Painters and Glazers. Seventy-two workshops.—Six hundred and thirty-two hands; labor value of product, three hundred and eighty-five thousand dollars.

Hamilton Cummings, corner of Walnut and Baker streets, executes graining in a style that cannot be surpassed. Fine specimens in that style of painting may be seen at N. Longworth's and Larz Anderson's mansions, on Pike street.

Paper— Writing, Wrapping, Printing, and Book.— Cincinnati having a large book and newspaper publishing business, the manufacture in and for this market is correspondingly extensive. The Miami mills at Hamilton, Becket & Rigdon proprietors; Graham's mills, also, in Butler county, manufacture almost exclusively for use and sale here, together with other mills nearer to the city. Value of product, seventy-five thousand dollars; raw material 45 per cent. Butler & Brother are their agents.

The paper on which this volume is printed, is from the Miami mills, and compares favorably with that of any other market.

E. O. Goodman, Walnut, below Pearl street, is agent for L. F. Claflin & Co., Dayton mills, which make five hundred thousand pounds book and printing, and two hundred and fifty thousand pounds wrapping-paper per year; for Nixon's mills at Clifton, which make five hundred thousand pounds printing and book paper and flat cap, and for other mills in the vicinity, which make two hundred and fifty thousand pounds printing, and two hundred and fifty thousand pounds wrapping paper. These mills make Cincinnati their market. Annual sales of eastern writing paper, thirty thousand dollars.

W. Colville's paper factory, on the Miami canal, is the only establishment of the kind in Cincinnati. Its appointments are ample and complete, and calculated for a mill of the first class. These consist of two rag-engines, carrying three hundred pounds each, propelled by water. In the machine room is a sixty-two inch Foudrinier machine, of the latest pattern and improvements. This machine turns out one thousand two hundred pounds paper every twelve hours of daylight. Hands employed, seven men and seven girls. The water is supplied by two wells in the basement of the mill, which can afford the necessary quantity in the driest season. Two more rag-engines will shortly be added, which are to be steam propelled. This will keep the machine in active employment at night, and double its paper manufacture.

S. Ruffner, manufactures wrapping paper at Lockland, in this county, exclusively for this market. Warehouse, corner of Western Row and Pearl street. He consumes, every day, one thousand pounds rags, and one thousand five hundred pounds straw. Employs nine hands in a daily product of two thousand pounds wrapping paper. The mill is propelled by water-power from the Miami canal, and runs about two hundred and fifty days in the year. Value of product, twenty-one thousand dollars; raw material, 50 per cent.

Patent Medicines. Fourteen factories.—Ninety hands; value of product, six hundred and sixty thousand dollars; raw material, 50 per cent.

Pattern Makers.—Most of our pattern makers are connected with the various iron founderies. There are, however, ten which follow the business on their own account. Thirty hands; value of product, twenty-five thousand five hundred dollars; raw material, 10 per cent.

Perfumery.—There are twelve manufacturers of perfumery, fancy soap, etc., principally, however, on a small scale; employ seventy-five hands on an average, and manufacture to the value of one hundred and twenty thousand dollars; raw material, 40 per cent.

A. E. Wetherill, manufacturer of perfumery, essences, extracts for the handkerchief, cologne waters in every variety, pomades and other hair preparations; soaps and shaving creams, cosmetics and powders. This is the largest, and, in fact, the only establishment in the west that has ever succeeded in competing with eastern manufacturers of perfumery. Sales store in Bromwell's Building, corner Vine and Fourth streets. Laboratory, on Hammond street.

This factory employs as large a number of hands as any in the country, and has not only controlled the market here, but to a great extent, as far south as New Orleans. It has recently entered the New York and Philadelphia markets with its products, where they have found a ready sale.

H. David, manufacturer of fancy soaps and perfumery. Sale store, 203 Main street, west side. Value of annual product twenty-four thousand dollars; employs twelve hands as an average. His sales are principally to the south and south-west.

Mr. David is one of the longest established manufacturers in this line, and has repeatedly taken the premium at the fairs of the Ohio Mechanics' Institute, for the best specimens of fancy soaps and perfumery.

Pickles, Preserves, Sauces, etc. Two establishments.—Twelve hands; value of product, twenty-five thousand dollars; raw material, 40 per cent.

C. T. Hughes, & Co., 1 Hopple's Alley, put up pickles, preserves, sauces, catsups, and hermetically sealed articles, warranted to keep in all climates. Their customers are in every part of the south and south-west.

Planes, etc. Seven factories.—Ninety-six hands; value of product, one hundred and sixty-seven thousand dollars; raw material, 35 per cent.

E. F. Seybold, 207 Main street, is one of our oldest manufacturers in this line. His products are planes, squares, gauges and saws, to the annual value of fifty thousand dollars. His salerooms are depôts also of truss hoops. Coopers' and carpenters' edge tools are also made here, or in the immediate vicinity; of which, are sold to the value of sixty thousand dollars. Fifty hands; raw material, 40 per cent. Sells also, extensively, mechanics' tools of all descriptions.

C. B. Schaefer & Co., salerooms 224 Main street; factory on Miami canal, manufacture planes, squares, gauges, bevels, etc., of all descriptions; value of planes, etc., fifty thousand dollars; twenty-five hands; also edge tools, such as cooper's, carpenter's, wagon makers' coach makers', etc. No finer article of edge tools is made anywhere else.

Planing Machines.—These are made here, by B. Bicknell, as the commencement of an important branch of business. His manufacture is yet on a small scale, employing twelve hands; value of product, thirty thousand dollars; raw material, 25 per cent. Extra knives may be obtained when ordered. Leather or India-rubber bands forwarded to customers.

Platform Scales, etc.—There are six factories in which scales, including platform scales, are made. Thirty-six hands; value of product, sixty thousand dollars.

W. J. Groves, on Second, west of Main street, manufactures platform and counter scales, beams, trucks, skids, and truck-wagons. Hay-scales built and put up to order; employs eight hands, and makes annually, four hundred scales, twenty-two to seventy-five dollars each; average value, forty dollars.

Colville & Stryker. Factory and saleroom, north side Second street, east of Sycamore, manufacture brass and iron scale-beams, platform, and hay scales. On contract with the Secretary of State of Ohio, they have recently made scales and weights of exquisite finish and accuracy; one for each county in the state, and deposited with the respective county auditors, as legal standards of weight.

Plows. Six factories.—Twenty-four hands; value of product, forty-five thousand dollars; raw material, 40 per cent.

Garrett & Cottman, Seventh, west of Main street, manufacture steel mold-boards by machinery, and make annually, one thousand plows of light draft, which scour themselves in all sorts of soils. These average nine dollars in value, each. Large quantities of these mold-boards are sold to plow makers in the country. Three-fourths of the plows are retailed at the factory.

Plumbers. Ten shops.—One hundred and thirty hands; value of product, one hundred and ninety-five thousand dollars; raw material, 40 per cent.

George W. Brooks, Fifth, between Main and Sycamore streets, manufactures pumps, both force and lift, suitable for wells, cisterns, etc. Hydrants, bathing apparatus, water closets, with latest improvements; and lead pipes of all sizes, made and put up; also battering-rams, for carrying water into upper stories. Employs thirty hands, and manufactures annually to the value of forty-five thousand dollars.

P. J. Moore, 223 Fifth street, manufactures hydrants, pumps, bath and water closets, supplies lead pipe of every size, and puts up Douglass' improved hydraulic ram, for forcing water to any required distance or elevation, when a proportionate fall can be applied. Employs ten hands, and manufactures yearly to the value of twelve thousand dollars.

Plug, Bung, and Tree Nail Factory.—Employs eight hands; product, twelve thousand dollars; raw material, 40 per cent.

Potters' Ware. Ten potteries.—Fifty hands; value of product, thirty-six thousand dollars; raw material, 25 per cent.

Pork and Beef Packing, Sugar-Cured Hams, etc. It would have been desirable to divide and classify these several operations, but the mode in which they run into each other, forbids the effort.

Pork is our great staple, and hogs to the number of four hundred and ninety-eight thousand one hundred and sixty, have been cut up in the market in a single year. The yearly average number of hogs put up here, during the last four years, will not, however, exceed three hundred and seventy-five thousand. That of 1850–51, was three hundred and twenty-four thousand five hundred and thirty-nine. The beef business is of increasingly great extent. There are as many as thirty-three pork and beef packers and ham and beef curers on a large scale, beside numerous others, who do business on a smaller one. The number of hands, of course, varies with the various stages in the process of cutting up, pickling and curing. They may be averaged at two thousand four hundred and fifty for the various departments. The value of these products of beef and pork packed and cured here, is five millions seven hundred and sixty thousand dollars; raw material, 90 per cent.

In the city of Covington, on the opposite side of the river Ohio, is the pork and beef house of Milward & Oldershaw. This mammoth establishment incloses an area of nearly two acres. Lofty and well ventilated cellars lie under the whole house—these are used for bulking the meat; and so excellently adapted are they to the purpose, that spoiled meat is comparatively unknown on these premises. The first floor, immediately over the cellars, is used for cutting and packing barrel pork. On a level with this, and of the depth of fifteen feet, are nine water-tight brick cisterns, each capable of containing four hundred barrels pork. In warm weather the pieces of pork are packed down in these, and immediately covered with pickle. By this method, there is but a slight chance of any of

Onken's Lithography, Cin: O.

the meat being pronounced "sour," by the inspectors in the various markets.

The rendering-house is furnished with large kettles, capable of containing three thousand pounds each, while, for those who prefer to have their lard rendered by steam, two of "Wilson's patent iron tanks" are kept in constant work.

The slaughter-house, which will contain four thousand hogs, is on the upper floor, and the hog-pens are on the roof, the hogs being driven up an inclined plane, which may be seen on the north or right hand side of the illustration. The building measures three hundred and sixty feet front, and runs back one hundred and sixty feet. It is doubtless the largest building for the purpose in the United States, and the proprietors assert with truth, that a more commodious or more excellently arranged establishment can nowhere be found. They do a large business on their own account, but their avowed business is pork and beef packing on commission, for the home and foreign markets. Their brand, of all products, stands deservedly high, and eastern operators, intrusting their orders to them, will have them executed to their entire satisfaction. Part of the premises consists of a large singeing establishment, which was erected exclusively for the benefit of our friends on the other side the Atlantic. This establishment cut up and packed, last season, eleven thousand seven hundred and forty-six hogs, and more than three thousand beef cattle for the European markets.

S. Davis, Jr. & Co., beef and pork packers, commission merchants, and curers of extra family hams—"Diamond Brand."

An award of diploma and silver medal was made them by the Ohio State Board of Agriculture, at the fair held October, 1850, "For the best hams exhibited."

Their packing, and warehouses are on the south-west corner Court street and Broadway—occupying ninety-four feet front on Broadway, running to Miami canal, one hundred and fifty feet in depth. They cut and pack annually from fifteen to eighteen thousand hogs, and five to seven hundred head of cattle; pack five thousand barrels pork. The number of hams cured here, in a season, varies from fifty to eighty thousand. A large proportion of these are put up in pickle for the eastern market. In the winter, when cutting and packing meats, they employ thirty to seventy hands. They are dealers, also, extensively in pork and provisions generally.

The pork cutting and packing operations of Cincinnati, are sufficiently known, one department only excepted. This is that of hams and even shoulders of extra quality, put up for family use. And first, of Schooley & Hough's "Queen City" ham establishment.

The extensive buildings occupied for the purpose of curing hams by this firm, are situated on the side of the hill, on the Deer creek road, East Court street. They were erected expressly for the purpose, and consist of a main curing and drying apartment, and three extensive smoke-houses, and commodious apartments for storing and packing during the summer. The main building is built of brick, and is three and a-half stories in height, ninety feet front, running back one hundred and forty feet to the washing department, and separated from it by a heavy brick wall, with doors and windows of iron. Underneath this building is a cellar of the same dimensions, which will contain upward of seventy-five thousand hams at one time, under the process of curing; this cellar is so constructed, that it can be kept throughout the winter at the same temperature, all being under ground with the exception of the front, which constitutes the first story of the building. The first floor above, is divided off, similar to the smoke-houses, and is used for the drying-room, where the hams go through a process preparatory to the smoking. In the third and attic stories are done the canvasing, coloring, decorating, etc., of the hams, which, during the appropriate season, are also hung up here. At the rear of the main brick building, is the washing apartment, connected still farther in the rear with three smoke-houses, which are built separate and apart, having no connection, and at the same time under one roof; they are separated by twelve inch walls, slushed, with fire-walls on the roof. The hanging rooms are distant from the pits where the fires are made, from twelve to fifteen feet; these smoking apparatus are so arranged as to make them absolutely fire proof. Each smoke-house will contain one hundred thousand pounds, giving to the three houses a capacity of three hundred thousand pounds at one time, or equal to twenty-four thousand hams; the only connection that these houses have with the main building is a temporary avenue, running from the second story, closed at the entrance with an iron door.

Schooley & Hough cure from seventy-five to one hundred thousand hams every year, and the well-known care and skill they give to their extra curing and preparing for market, gives character to their brands.

Diplomas and certificates were recently awarded them by the

Ohio State Fair, and Ohio Mechanics' Institute, for the best article exhibited, and there can be no doubt that their sample of hams and shoulders sent to the World's Fair, London, will recommend our city fancy hams, etc., to the English epicures. This firm employs fifty-five to seventy men in their various operations, including canvasers, cutters, inspectors, colorers, and decorators.

Trowbridge & Beatty, cure beef; also hams and shoulders extensively. Their hams and shoulders are sugar-cured. Of the hams thirty thousand; of the shoulders, twenty thousand are annually cured here.

They use up, for covers to these articles, thirty-seven thousand yards cloth. Most of these hams are sold for the supply of the retail market here, these hams being considered among the most juicy in the city. They are shipped, also, to Natchez, Vicksburg, New Orleans, New York, Philadelphia, Baltimore, etc.

On the 20th March last, from seven o'clock A. M. to five P. M., deducting the dinner intermission of forty-five minutes, there were four thousand and thirty one hams papered and covers sowed on, by twelve hands; one of these, a boy of fifteen, sewed six hundred and seven hams as his share. This was the greatest day's work, in this line, ever yet done.

Printing Ink. Two factories.—Employ eight hands, and manufacture a value of fifteen thousand dollars; raw material, 50 per cent.

Geo. S. Stearns, on Liberty street, makes yearly eight thousand dollars of printing ink, which is consumed in western and southern markets.

Printing Presses, etc.—C. Foster & Brother, corner of Smith and Seventh streets, Cincinnati, manufacture power presses, hand, card, seal, standing, embossing, and all other kinds of presses. Brass rule, chases, galleys, composing sticks, cases, etc. They are prepared to fit out an office in twenty-four hours from the time of receiving the order.

This factory works thirty hands, and produces yearly fifty-two thousand dollars; raw material, 30 per cent.

The Cylinder hand press, recently invented, is calculated to print with twice the speed of any other hand press in use, and is designed for both book and newspaper printing. It is managed by one person only, inking the form and throwing off its own sheet by the same operation, and is less liable to get out of order than the ordinary kinds. The price does not exceed that of other hand presses.

This establishment has also just completed a new and improved card press, which for style, durability and cheapness, is not equaled in the United States.

Publishers—Book and Newspaper.—There are three large printing establishments, which issue largely for the periodical press. These are the "Gazette" Office, on Main street, with five power and cylinder presses, and twenty-four hands; Morgan & Overend, on the Miami canal, with nine Adams power presses, which employ thirty-two hands; work off daily five thousand impressions each; and the Methodist Book Concern, with four cylinder and power presses and twenty hands. These print books, newspapers, etc., to order. Beside these, there are the various newspaper publishers, who print at their respective offices.

There are twelve regular publishing houses of booksellers, who issue their publications on the presses first alluded to, principally at Morgan & Overend's establishment.

The value of these book and newspaper publications, is one million two hundred and forty-six thousand five hundred and forty dollars; hands employed, six hundred and fifty-six; raw material, 40 per cent.

H. S. & J. Applegate & Co., booksellers and publishers, 43 Main street. This is a new establishment, which has commenced the publication of books here, during the past year, with great spirit, and on quite an extensive scale. They have issued within that period, one thousand copies Clarke's Commentary, four vols; ten thousand copies Dick's works, two vols.; four thousand copies Plutarch's Lives; three thousand copies Rollin's Ancient History, two vols.; two thousand copies Spectator, two vols. All these are imperial or royal octavo. Also, Histories of Texas, Oregon and California, Christianity, Methodism Explained, Young Ladies' Companion, duodecimos, nine thousand copies; Lyons' Grammar, five thousand copies, and the Parley History series, six thousand copies. To this should be added the Sacred Melodeon and Sabbath Chorister music books, ten thousand copies of each.

The aggregate value of these various works will reach sixty-two thousand five hundred dollars.

W. H. Moore & Co., 118 Main Street, have been publishing school books, during the last eight years, and they are now entering the field as general publishers of standard literature, of which, their recent publications, "Footprints of the Creator," by Hugh Miller, and "The Course of Creation," by J. Anderson, D.D., are the commencement. These have attracted general and favorable notice at the east, as evidences that books can be got up in the west, as regards paper, printing, and binding, in a style not inferior to those in the east, and that miscellaneous literature can be published to advantage in Cincinnati, although a contrary opinion prevails in our Atlantic cities.

W. B. Smith & Co. This is a veteran publishing house, whose operations are principally confined to school books, in which their issues are counted by millions, one million two hundred and fifty thousand copies having been put to press since 1840. They have also published that masterly work, "Drake on the Diseases of the Mississippi Valley," which is sufficient for the fame of its accomplished author, if he should never write anything else. This is an edition of one thousand two hundred and fifty copies, large octavo, of nearly nine hundred pages.

J. F. Desilver, 122 Main street, publishing bookseller, has issued various law and medical books, the most important of which, are "Hope's Pathological Anatomy," Lawson's edition, with two hundred and sixty lithographic illustrations, five hundred copies; Worcester on Cutaneous Diseases, illustrated in similar style. The paper, printing, engraving, coloring and binding will compare advantageously with any eastern publications of the same cast—"Harrison's Therapeutics," two vols. All these are of royal octavo size.

He has also put to press the first four vols. of "Hammond's Ohio Reports," and by the 1st November next, will complete the publication of the whole series, in seven volumes. The remaining three are edited by M. E. Curwen, of the Cincinnati bar, and one of the professors in the Cincinnati law college, who is known to the profession as the author of several works on the Ohio statutes and reports. These publications will bring his issues, during the past twelve months, to more than twenty-seven thousand dollars.

Desilver is agent for the publications of the Philadelphia house of Thomas, Cowperthwaite & Co., the publishers of Mitchell's series of School Geographies, etc.

E. Morgan & Co, 111 Main street. This is one of our oldest, as well as most extensive houses in the publishing line. Within the last twelve months, they have issued from the press twenty thousand, Family Bibles; fifteen thousand, Josephus's Works; five thousand each, Pilgrim's Progress and Hervey's Meditations; ten thousand, Life of Tecumseh; ten thousand, Psalms of David; ten thousand, Talbott's Arithmetic; ten thousand, Walker's School Dictionary; one thousand, Macaulay's History of England, and one hundred thousand, Webster's Spelling Books, with various other publications in smaller editions. Total value, fifty-four thousand dollars.

J. A. & U. P. James, book publishers. This is also a long established publishing house. Within the past year, they have issued Guizot's Gibbon's Rome, two vols, one thousand one hundred and fifty; Library of American History, five hundred; Universal Pictorial Library, one thousand; Library of General Knowledge, three thousand; Dick's Theology, five hundred; Erskine's Works, two hundred and fifty, all imperial octavo. The Gem, one thousand; Burns' Works, five hundred, and of other octavos, two thousand. Among these are Collins' History of Kentucky, Young's History of Mexico, etc. Various duodecimos, to the extent of twenty-two thousand copies. Pamphlet editions, octavo and duodecimo, forty-five thousand vols. Primers, and catechisms, twenty thousand. Almanacs for 1851, ninety-six thousand. One thousand five hundred, quarto Family Bibles, stereotyped, and first edition just issued. Seven thousand James' Traveler's Companion, first edition just out. Beside these, within the last two years, the firm has published fourteen thousand, Hughes' Doniphan's Expedition. Most of the octavos are put into substantial library binding; many of the Poets, etc., in fancy and extra gilt covers.

Not the least in importance in our publishing establishments, although among the last referred to, is the Methodist Book Concern, south-west corner of Main and Eighth streets. There are issued from their presses, of the Western Christian Advocate, twenty-one thousand copies; Ladies Repository, sixteen thousand five hundred; Sunday School Advocate, twenty-five thousand; Christian Apologist—German, three thousand. They keep five steam presses in constant occupation; employ twenty-five hands in the printing-office, and forty-six in the bindery.

Beside these periodicals, they issue various religious publications. Value of books and periodicals published last year, one hundred and twenty-five thousand dollars.

Roofing, Patent Composition.—James McGeorge, office, corner

Fourth and Race street, employs, at an average, twelve hands. This covering is made of stiff, thick paper, stretched in courses upon the sheeting, the entire length of the roof and fastened down at the ends. A coat of boiled tar, mingled with fine gravel, is spread over the entire surface to a sufficient depth, and becomes perfectly hard and impenetrable by heat or rain, as soon as it cools and hardens. Thirty-six thousand dollars value of work, is annually executed in this line; raw material, 30 per cent.

Nearly all our best houses are now covered in this mode, which, taking durability into view, is cheaper than shingling.

Saddlery, Collar and Harness makers.—Of these, are forty shops, which employ two hundred and twenty-two hands, and produce a value of three hundred and forty-six thousand five hundred dollars; raw material, 50 per cent.

Wilson & Hayden, 17 and 19 West Second street, manufacturers of saddlery and coach hardware, carriage trimmings, saddle-trees, hog skins, are engaged in the handling and finishing of saddle and harness leather, which they make to the value of fifty thousand dollars; saddle-trees and saddlery hardware, to the value of forty thousand dollars; raw material, 80 per cent. Their annual sales of saddlery, etc., including those of their own manufacture, extend to two hundred and seventy-five thousand dollars.

E. N. Slocum, 102 Main street, manufactures the finer qualities of saddles, harness and trunks, carpet bags, ladies' satchels, etc. Employs twenty-five hands; value of product, thirty thousand dollars. As high as fifty saddles have been sold here in one day, and harness for two hundred and fifty horses — all stage or carriage harness—during the last six months. Four hundred and fifty-five trunks, ranging in price from eighteen to twenty dollars each, have made a part of their last year's sales. The saddlery here, is equal to any in New York or Philadelphia, and the trunks, a superior article. There have been sold here, bridles of a quality commanding fourteen dollars each. Side saddles worth fifty dollars, and sets of harness for two horses, at two hundred and fifty dollars.

Saddle Trees.—One shop, with five hands; manufactures forty-five hundred dollars; raw material, 50 per cent.

Sail makers. Four shops.—Fifteen hands; a product of nine thousand dollars; raw material, 65 per cent.

Saleratus. Three factories.—Employ six hands. Three hundred tons are annually sold in this market of this article, two-thirds of which is made here; value of product, fifty thousand dollars; raw material, 65 per cent.

H. Emerson, Walnut, below Second street, manufactures two hundred thousand pounds yearly. The article made in his factory does not deliquesce on exposure to the atmosphere. This has been tested by filling a box with saleratus and exposing it to the open air for twelve months.

Sand-Paper. Two factories.—Ten hands; value of product, twelve thousand dollars; raw material, 30 per cent.

Sarsaparilla Cough Candy, etc.—I. Baker, College building, is largely manufacturing these articles. Sales of sarsaparilla, seventy-two thousand dollars, and of candy, twenty thousand dollars annually. Ten hands; raw material, 50 per cent.

Sash, Blind and Door Factories.—Of these, there are twenty-five, all but two of hand operations; value of product, three hundred and twelve thousand dollars; raw material, 25 per cent; employ two hundred and twenty hands.

One of the largest manufacturing buildings in the United States, is the sash, blind and door factory and floor-board planing machine, on Front street, opposite the gas works, of Hinkle & Guild. This edifice occupies a space of two hundred and fifty feet in depth, by sixty feet breadth upon Front street and the river. The building is six stories in height on the river front, and five stories and basement upon the Front street face. The first and second story walls are of stone masonry, two feet thick, and the residue of the building with the partitions of brick, of which as many as eight hundred thousand have been employed to construct the edifice. It was built for a planing-mill and a sash, blind and door factory, and is the largest building in Cincinnati, that carries its length and breadth to such a height. The lot which the building occupies, is one hundred and twenty-two and a-half by three hundred and seventy-five feet, and such is the extent of the operations of this firm, as well as of the manufactured article kept on hands in this new and important business, that they calculate to occupy every available spot upon this vast space.

Persons at a distance, who contemplate building, are supplied by this establishment with their carpenter work, in whole or in part, as they may need, so much cheaper and better prepared for the purpose, as to make it their interest to pay transportation on the finished work to any point in the west and south-west, either by land or water carriage. This will be readily understood, when it is considered that everything here, is made out of materials already seasoned, fitted together with great exactness by machinery, of course at cheaper rates than even the lowest charge for carpenter work by hand can supply it here, and at one-half the price that a carpenter in the country must charge. It would be impossible, in a publication like this, to go into full exemplifications of these facts, but one feature of these operations will suffice as a specimen of the rest. Eight by ten inch window sash are supplied here, at three and a half cents, and ten by twelve at four and a half cents per light. There are very few places, outside of Cincinnati, where a carpenter will make them at less than twice this price—the employer being at the expense of the lumber beside. Every other building article, panel doors, blinds, shutters, door and window frames, weather-boarding, base, shelving for stores, flooring-boards and plank, etc., will exhibit a proportionate saving to the purchaser.

Hinkle & Guild have been several years engaged in this business, at the corner of Smith and Fourth streets, upon a lot supposed by them sufficiently large for their purposes, but the growing conviction in the south and south-west, that they can build to better advantage by buying carpenter work in Cincinnati ready prepared for use, has compelled a removal to a more spacious site, as the only adequate means to do justice to this enlarging business.

Sausages. Twenty-two shops.—One hundred and sixty-six hands; value of product, one hundred and sixty-two thousand dollars; raw material, 40 per cent.

Sawed Lumber, Laths, etc. Fifteen mills.—Two hundred and six hands; manufacture a value of four hundred and eleven thousand dollars; raw material, 30 per cent.

Saws. Two factories.—Employ six hands; value of product, six thousand seven hundred dollars; raw material, 30 per cent.

Turner & Sons, First Premium Saw Manufactory, on Seventh, north side, between Western Row and John street, manufacture saws of every description, warranted, and made of the best material. Circular, mill, and cross-cut saws gummed and hammered, hand, back, or butchers' saws, buckled or bent, restored as good as if new — also, retoothed, set and filed in a workman-like manner. Sheet-steel for sale; also, cut and straightened, and all kinds of carpenters' and other mechanics' tools tempered; all at the shortest notice.

Screw Plates. Two factories.-Ten hands; value of product, eleven thousand five hundred dollars; raw material, 40 per cent.

Sheetings, Cotton Yarn, Candle-Wick, etc. Five factories.—Employ four hundred and ten hands; manufacture to the value of six hundred and thirty-six thousand dollars; raw material, 50 per cent.

Shirts, etc.—Fifteen shops, which employ two hundred and fifty hands, all females; value of product, one hundred and fifty-seven thousand dollars; raw material, 50 per cent.

J. Richardson, shirt and stock factory, 119 Main street. This is of recent establishment, and manufactures the articles alluded to and supplies everything usually kept in a gentleman's furnishing store. Two hundred shirts are made here weekly, and stocks in proportion. A large manufacture for wholesale purposes, will shortly make a part of the business here. The articles made are of a fine class exclusively. Shirts, undershirts and drawers are also made here, of lambs' wool, merino and shakers' flannel, Canton flannel, buckskin and silk fabrics.

Silver and Goldsmiths and Silver Platers. Five establishments.—Fifty hands; value of product, ninety thousand dollars; raw material, 75 per cent.

J. R. Haynes, 40 West Fourth street, manufactures to order all kinds of jewelry and silver ware. Value of product, during the past year, five thousand dollars. He is also a dealer, wholesale and retail, in watches, jewelry, silver ware, pocket cutlery and fancy goods.

Palmer & Owen, 135 Main street, keep three hands engaged in the manufacture of silver ware, on a product yearly, of twelve thousand dollars. Watches, silver ware, jewelry, etc., also sold here.

Soap and Tallow, and Star Candles.—There are thirty-eight of these factories, some making soap principally, some making tallow candles and soap, and others star candles, either alone or in addition to what they produce in soap and tallow candles, or in the last article merely. These employ seven hundred and ten hands; value of product, one million four hundred and seventy-five thousand dollars; raw material, 75 per cent.

Spectacle maker.—John Owen, Third, between Main and Walnut streets, employs four hands, on a product of nine thousand dollars; raw material, 75 per cent.

Spokes. Two factories.—Employ thirty-six hands, and manufacture to the value of seventy thousand five hundred dollars; raw material, 20 per cent.

Curtis & Byrn, spoke and felloe factory, intersection of Park street and the Whitewater canal, manufacture spokes, felloes, hubs, etc. They work up weekly, four thousand feet of ash and hickory, and employ nine hands.

C. G. Shane & Co., Great Western Spoke Manufactory, sale-room, Second street, between Walnut and Vine, turn all sizes and patterns of white oak and hickory spokes out of the best seasoned timber, of which they are making over three thousand six hundred per day. They also turn and keep on hand axe, pick, hammer and hatchet handles.

Their spokes are used in every carriage shop in Cincinnati, and all along the river from Pittsburgh down; and on our canal and railroad routes, which is sufficient to show the estimation in which they are held by our carriage and wagon-makers. The price is such that they will bear transportation to any part of the country, and one trial is all that is necessary to insure their permanent use.

This establishment employs twenty hands, and runs ten lathes.

Stained Glass.—Painting in glass, which is another name for stained glass, is one of the long-lost, but finally recovered arts of antiquity. It is carried, in modern times, however, to a degree of perfection unknown to the ancients. Glass of this description is employed extensively in churches and in the finest class of private dwellings, where it serves admirably to distribute a mellowed light, more grateful to the eye, than that which passes in its full strength through perfectly transparent glass.

Stained glass is prepared by coating one side of the plate with phosphate of lime in a flux of pulverized glass, in cases where it is designed to render the plate semi-opaque or obscure. This gives it the appearance of being ground on one face. Where the various brilliant colors are sought, oxydes of almost all the metals, such as iron, zinc, tin, antimony, cobalt, manganese, lead, silver and gold, are the agents resorted to, silver being the base of the yellow, as gold is of the purple, and cobalt of the blue. The coating, in a liquid state, being brushed over the surface of the plate, and lime sifted over it to prevent the adhesion of the glass, the plates are lodged in a furnace where they are submitted to a degree of heat which blends the coloring matter with the outside of the glass, which is then suffered gradually to cool to its final and permanent temperature.

The white color is imparted by grinding figures upon glass made transparent, and colored on one side in the first instance, the grinding barely penetrating through the colored side.

J. C. Miller, Third street, east of Sycamore, employs five hands, and manufactures to the value of fifteen thousand dollars; raw material, 50 per cent. Miller is preparing illuminated windows for St. John's and the First and Seventh Presbyterian churches of this city, which will illustrate this article. This is the only establishment of this kind in the west.

Stair Building. Three shops.—Eighteen hands; value of labor product, twenty-four thousand dollars.

Starch.—Five factories, which employ forty-two hands, and make a value of ninety-eight thousand dollars; raw material, average, 60 per cent.

Starch has heretofore been made principally from wheat, and a portion of it is still made here from that grain. Of late, Indian corn has been resorted to in the manufacture of starch, and with great success, although the discovery is comparatively recent. Yet it is found to contain almost as great a proportion as wheat. The per centage of starch, in the best varieties of corn, is about sixty per cent.; nitrogenous substances, 15 per cent., with a considerable portion of sugar, and 10 per cent. of oil and gum. All practical men are well aware of the great superiority of corn over every other kind of grain for fattening purposes.

The amount of starch, in sweet corn, is very small, not over 18 or 20 per cent.; but the per centage of sugar is very great. The nitrogenous matter about 20, gum 14, and oil 11 per cent. If it could be made to yield as much per acre as the more hardy kind, it would be the most profitable, because the most nourishing of all the varieties.

Everding & Erkenbrecher, on the Miami canal, manufacture three thousand pounds starch, weekly. For this purpose, they consume one hundred and twenty-five bushels wheat in the same space of time. Their starch bears a high reputation in this market.

Steamboat Building and Repairing.—Seven establishments, which employ five hundred and fifty four hands; value of product, four hundred and eighty-eight thousand dollars; raw material, 30 per cent.

Stencil Cutters. Three shops.—Eight hands; value of labor product, five thousand dollars.

Stereotypers.—Three establishments, which employ sixty hands, and produce to the value of forty-six thousand dollars; raw material, 33 per cent.

Stereotyping is the transfer to solid pages of type, by the intervention of a cast of plaster of Paris, of the contents of pages of movable type set for that purpose. The stereotype page is a thin plate, which is fitted to blocks so as to bring it up to the ordinary type height for printing. The object of stereotyping is to permit small issues at a time, of publications, so that if they should not prove saleable, a large surplus may not be left on hand, or if repeated editions should be needed, that the original type setting will suffice for the repeated issues. In this way, an opportunity is afforded of using up paper and paying for binding, no faster than the demand for the volume. Stereotyping, it will be thus seen, is costlier in the first instance, but cheaper in the entire course of business. All standard works, and most others, are now stereotyped.

This business is rapidly increasing here in extent and importance. C. A. Morgan & Co., Hammond street, between Third and Fourth streets, are extensively employed in this line; they have recently stereotyped, The Footprints of the Creator, The Course of Creation, Service Afloat and Ashore, and the present volume, any of which is a sufficiently favorable sample of their skill and taste. In all the facilities for executing work promptly and accurately, this establishment will compare favorably, with similar establishments in the east.

Stocking Weavers. Four shops.—Twenty-one hands; value of product, thirteen thousand dollars; raw material, 40 per cent.

Stone Cutters. Twenty-two yards.—Employ two hundred and forty-nine hands; value of product, two hundred and twenty-two thousand dollars: raw material, 40 per cent.

The freestone used most extensively in Cincinnati, is that of the Buena Vista quarry, which is preferred for price and quality.

An article like building stone, which constitutes so important a material to the physical improvement of Cincinnati, must always be of interest to the community, which has consumed it to the value of millions of dollars. Various quarries have been opened for the supply of this market, the stone of which has failed to inspire confidence in that compactness of grain which protects it from the action of frost. Other descriptions—Dayton limestone, for example—cost too high in the transportation, sawing and dressing, to render them suitable for general building purposes.

The Buena Vista stone, is substantially the article which has been for a long series of years employed in our best buildings. It has all the requisite qualities of close grain, hardening under exposure to the atmosphere, fineness of surface, and comparative cheapness, which should give it a preference for our best buildings. Stone masons here, agree in stating it to be superior to all other stone for building use.

Stone Masons. Thirty-six builders.—Employ four hundred and twenty-eight hands; value of labor product, three hundred and eight thousand dollars.

Straw Hats and Bonnets. Five factories.—Fifty hands; value of product, sixty thousand dollars; raw material, 60 per cent.

J. Webb, Jr., straw bonnet and hat factory and fashionable millinery establishment, 168 Fifth street, employs fifteen hands, and manufactures to the value of fifteen thousand dollars. Bleaching and pressing bonnets, also, attended to here.

Stucco workers. Two shops.—Fourteen hands; value of labor product, twelve thousand dollars.

J. F. Taylor, manufacturer of stucco and ornamental plaster work, office, corner Vine and Baker streets. Designs and models all kinds of floral work, and every description of ornaments in the stucco line. Employs from twelve to fifteen hands, and executes work yearly, to the value of twelve thousand dollars.

Tailors.—In this statement is not included the manufacturers of ready-made clothing, made here for sales to foreign markets, or for retail sales at home, the details of which, will be found in its proper department. Of those who make to measurement, we have ninety-eight merchant tailors, who employ eight hundred and sixteen hands, exclusive of women, who sew at their own dwellings. These produce to the value of eight hundred and thirty-two thousand dollars. Among our most fashionable tailors are:

S. P. Thomas, south-east corner of Walnut street. He employs fifteen hands, and makes up garments, and sells other articles in his line, to the value of fifty thousand dollars.

Mr. Thomas bears a high reputation in his line, among our city fashionables. Every variety of materials for articles of gentlemen's dresses, is constantly kept here.

W. W. Northrop, 42 west Fourth street. This is a recently fitted up tailor establishment in fashionable style, by Mr. Northrop, formerly associated in business with Platt Evans, on Main street.

Employs, as an average, thirty hands, and fits and finishes in the best style, every article of gentlemen's dress. The manufacturing department is in charge of Mons. Vandokum, recently from Paris. A full and well selected supply of materials for garments, and an assortment, in the furnishing line, to gratify every taste, always to be found upon his stands and counters.

E. M'Elevy, merchant tailor, 1 Broadway, makes custom work principally, of the finest quality. Employs sixty hands; value of yearly product, forty thousand dollars.

M. C. Jennings, is one of our best known artists in this line, who has been engaged in the business for many years on Main, north of Third street, and has recently opened on Fourth street, opposite the First Presbyterian church. He keeps the usual assortment of fancy and staple goods for customers, and fits in the most approved and fashionable style, every article that constitutes gentlemen's dresses.

C. S. Jelleff, west side Western Row, between Eighth and Kemble streets, is in the centre of a rapidly improving region of Cincinnati. He has an abundant stock of best materials for gentlemen's garments on his shelves and counters. His work is of first-rate quality and fit. Youths' clothing also made here, and the usual assortment of fitting and furnishing for gentlemen, kept for sale.

Tanners and Curriers.—This is another of our heavy manufacturing interests, consisting of thirty establishments, which employ three hundred and eighty hands, and manufacture to the value of nine hundred and sixty-five thousand dollars.

Richard Thornton, 9 and 310 Main street, tanner, currier and morocco manufacturer, makes every description of leather, suitable for shoemakers, saddlers, bookbinders, hatters, etc. Has tanned, during the past year, thirty-six thousand skeep skins, five thousand hides, and thirty thousand calf skins. Imports, also, English and French calf skins, roans and skivers.

Tin, Copper and Sheet-Iron workers.—Forty-two shops, which employ two hundred and forty hands, and produce a value of two hundred and fifty-eight thousand six hundred and forty dollars. Raw material, tin and sheet-iron ware, 30 per cent.; copper, 60 per cent.; average value of raw material, 48 per cent.

W. & G. W. Robson, coppersmiths, Front street, between Pike and Butler, manufacture, and have constantly on hand, a large and general assortment in their line, such as copper wash, stew, tea and glue kettles, still and hatters' do.; engine, well, cistern and liquor pumps, lift and force pumps, for wells and distilleries; soda-founts and stands, Patten's generator, for making soda-water, etc. They manufacture brew-kettles, from three hundred to three thousand gallons. Engine and lard steamer work, on the shortest notice.

Robson & Moorhead, tin-plate workers, on Second street, west of Walnut, employ twelve hands, and manufacture tin ware to the value of twelve thousand dollars. They are largely in the bathing-tub, shower-bath, and tin safe line, as well as manufacturing the usual assortment of tin ware. Their business is principally wholesale.

Tobacco, Cigars, etc.—This business comprehends, first, those who in this city and in Covington manufacture tobacco in the wholesale line exclusively. Second, of those who make fine tobacco for regular customers, and third, of various factories, principally on a small scale, in which cigars and snuff are the main articles.

There are sixty-two tobacco manufacturers here. Of these, twenty-eight factories in the wholesale line, employ one thousand one hundred and fifty hands, principally boys; value of product, six hundred and sixty-five thousand dollars. The residue work two hundred and sixty hands, not including boys, and manufacture to the value of two hundred and sixty-six thousand dollars; raw material, 55 per cent.

Carpenter & Ford, 14 Front street, are largely engaged in the manufacture of Virginia, Missouri and Kentucky tobacco. Employ one hundred and fifty hands of both sexes and almost all ages; value of product, one hundred and fifty thousand dollars; raw material, 65 per cent. They operate fifty iron presses, which are supposed to be the largest in the United States. The manufacture of tobacco conduces to the health of the work hands.

Nuilsen & Ficke, 233 Main street, manufacture cigars, at the rate of one hundred and twenty thousand per month, equal to Havana; being made of the best quality of Spanish leaf. Snuff and smoking tobacco of all descriptions. Spanish, Ohio, and Kentucky leaf tobacco, constantly kept for sale. They employ thirty hands, on a product, in value, of twenty-five thousand dollars.

Charles Bodmann, 45 Walnut street, sign of the Indian Queen, manufactures lump tobacco, from five to sixteen plugs to the pound. Scotch rappee, fine scented maccoboy snuffs; best chewing and smoking tobacco, and every description of domestic cigars. Fine cut chewing, of best honeydew and sweet fine cut cavendish papered and on bulk. There are ninety-one hands in his employ, with a product of eighty thousand dollars in value; raw material, 70 cents.

This is an offshoot of the establishment of F. Bodmann, long and favorably known here, for the quality of its snuff, tobacco, and cigars.

Trunks, Valises, Carpet-Bags, etc. This is a manufacture connected with the saddle and harness business, to a great extent, especially the finer qualities, but the principal amount is made in establishments which are devoted exclusively to the business. One of these, which makes low-priced articles principally, manufactures to the value of one hundred and five thousand dollars. Leather trunks are made in Cincinnati of every quality, from two dollars to thirty. The frames, in the low-priced articles, are of wood; of the more costly and permanent, of the best quality of gasket boards; an article more durable than wood, as well as not subject to split, and more flexible as well as lighter than iron, which it has superseded for this purpose.

There are fifteen leather trunk makers, who employ two hundred and seventy-five hands, and manufacture to the value of five hundred and six thousand dollars; raw material, 67 per cent.

Parvin & Johnson, Broadway, between Front and Second streets, manufacture leather trunks, valises, carpet-bags and satchels or traveling bags; employ thirty hands; finish, annually, twelve thousand five hundred trunks, one half of which are low-priced articles; the other half, first-rate or medium quality; average wholesale value of trunks, forty-two thousand dollars; one thousand three hundred valises and carpet-bags, value, three thousand five hundred dollars, and six hundred satchels.

Turners. Thirty shops.—One hundred and forty-three hands; value of product, one hundred and fifty-two thousand dollars; raw material, 20 per cent.

Warner B. Mahone, turner in general, corner of Western Row and Laurel street, executes balustrades of any and every pattern; columns of the several orders of architecture, and mahogany, oak, cherry, walnut and maple banisters. All kinds of turning used by cabinet makers, including nulling of every pattern, furnished at the shortest notice. Shade and map-rollers, turning in ivory, done in a superior style.

Mr. Mahone employs steam power, with seven lathes and ten hands, and turns to order any article, from a column twelve inches diameter and twenty-five feet in length, to an ivory cane head.

Type Founders.—There are two type founderies here, the Cincinnati Type Foundery Co., and the foundery of Guilford & Jones. Type are made of antimony, lead and tin, in certain proportions; the antimony being employed in hardening the lead; and the tin, as a means of amalgamating the other two.

The Cincinnati Type Foundery was chartered by the Ohio legislature, January 12, 1830. It employs one hundred hands, men, girls and boys, and affords an annual product of seventy thousand dollars; raw material, average, 20 per cent. More than seven hundred dollars are paid out weekly, in wages. Every kind of type that can be got at the east, is cast here, and more than two thousand different fonts may be found on the shelves in this establishment.

They have recently cast fancy type by steam, under a pressure of two hundred pounds to the square inch, for the purpose of condensing the metal and thereby hardening its face, with what effect, may be judged by the fact, that an ordinary size of duodecimo page, under this new process, weighs three additional pounds.

Guilford & Jones, 41 Second street, execute type founding in all its branches. They employ twenty-one hands; value of product, thirty thousand dollars.

Undertakers. Fourteen establishments.—Four hands; value of labor product, seventy-six thousand dollars.

Varnish, Copal, etc.—There are two varnish factories in Cincinnati, both on an extensive scale—that of the "Queen City" varnish factory, of which James Calhoun is agent, and the factory of Price and Pfaff. These are both on Walnut street, the one south of Second, and the other north of Pearl street. There is so little difference in the character, as well as the extent of their operations, that one statement will answer for the business statistics of either.

Copal varnish is an article extensively used by cabinet, chair and coachmakers, and although made heretofore, in Cincinnati, as an adjunct to the existing drug and apothecary business, has only for the last few years been commenced as a distinct operation, and on a large scale, commensurate with the wants of the entire west and south-west.

In one of these factories are manufactured of coach, furniture and japan varnishes, as high as eight hundred gallons per day, of which sales have thus far been effected as fast as made. In this factory is consumed daily, twelve hundred pounds gum copal, and shellac—principally the first—one hundred gallons linseed oil, and three hundred and fifty gallons spirits turpentine. The copal is melted at one furnace, while the oil which has already received the driers, is boiling at another, and when brought to precisely the same temperature, they are then mixed in a cooler. These boilers are copper, and of sixty gallons capacity. The cooler is twice that size. When the substances unite in the cooler, so great an amount of latent heat is disengaged, that the most active and laborious stirring is necessary to prevent running over. This is also the case when the turpentine is added, the whole mass foaming, as though placed on raging flames. The materials are thoroughly amalgamated, by being stirred to a point the exact degree of which, constitutes the great art of varnish making, and the varnish, in this stage, is passed through a cloth strainer, to divest it of impurities, into a reservoir, of which there are two in alternate use. These are large block-tin vessels hooped with iron, each of four hundred gallons capacity. In these it stands to cool, after which it is barreled off for market. The coach and furniture varnish are made of gum copal, the japan varnish, of gum shellac. They differ as much in the preparation as in the ingredients.

The first and second qualities of furniture varnish differ in the character of the copal employed. Coach varnish is made of the purest gum, carefully selected, piece by piece.

A large and increasing market is thus furnished for the linseed oil of the west, to the extent in which that ingredient is used in this manufacture.

The cost of transportation east, on our oil, and the return transportation of the varnish, together with the profits of the manufacture, now remains at home, as so much revenue to the west. An additional advantage is also gained to purchasers. They have responsible persons to look to at home, for the integrity of the article, that it is what it professes to be, and are not likely to experience imposition, which the introduction occasionally, of rosin, in an article where the maker's name is not apparent, and the means of redress five hundred miles from home, exposes them to, at times. In addition to this, varnish needs always to be bought on guarantee, since it is impossible to test its quality in any other mode than actual use.

Copal varnish made here, is disposed of not only in our city market, but throughout that extensive circle of country of which Detroit, Cleveland, Pittsburgh, Wheeling, Louisville, Lexington, Nashville, St. Louis and Galena form the edges or prominent points. Our own cabinet, chair and carriage business in Cincinnati, require also a large supply, especially during the spring and fall seasons of business. If, at any time, the manufacture accumulates so as to exceed the demand, it will be an advantage to both buyers and sellers, since varnish, like many other articles, improves by age.

Gum copal is found in the islands of the Indian ocean and on the coast of Africa. An inferior article is brought from South America, also. The best is gathered at Zanzibar, in the dominions of the Imaum or Sultan of Muscat. It is not a concretion gathered from the living tree, as is usually the case with gums, but is obtained in deposits, frequently many feet below the surface of the earth. How it became thus buried, can be a matter of conjecture merely. It is supposed that the accumulation of sand, which covers it, has destroyed the trees while it buried the gum exuding on their surface. It is gathered by the natives, and loaded in bulk in the hold of the vessels, the gum requiring no package, as water makes not the slightest impression on gum copal, which is one of the most insoluble of gums, neither alcohol, turpentine or ether serving to dissolve it. The agency of heat, by melting, alone serves this purpose. Most of this article is imported at Salem, Mass. On its arrival, it is washed from adhering sand, assorted in qualities and boxed for market.

As has been already stated, this description might substantially suffice for either factory, so little difference exists in their business. Four or five hands suffice for each establishment. These factories manufacture to the value of one hundred and thirty-five thousand dollars; raw material, 80 per cent.

Veneers. Two mills.—Twenty hands; value of product, thirty-six thousand dollars; raw material, 40 per cent.

For the benefit of multitudes who purchase the finer qualities of furniture, ignorant that the outside wood is a *veneer* or facing upon some other, which is either cheaper or stronger, or perhaps both, it may not be impertinent to state that most of what they buy is of this description. In this, there is, however, no deception, they being supplied with an article of furniture equally good, if not better, and much cheaper, than if made solid. The veneers brought to this market are mahogany, rose and zebra, of foreign woods, and black walnut and curled maple of domestic growth, much the larger share being of the first class. Already a reduction of 25 per cent. in prices has taken place, and we shall soon supply our own and foreign markets with native woods of unrivaled beauty in surface and figure. Not less than fifty thousand dollars in value of them have been annually sold or used here.

In those revolutions of manufactures which are constantly occurring, Cincinnati is now becoming the head-quarters to the west for the supply of this article.

There are no finer ornamental woods in the world for furniture, than those of American growth, the black walnut, cherry and curled maple, for example. Fashion has heretofore patronized those of foreign countries, on the principle which governs thousands, that nothing is valuable but what is "far sought and dearly bought." But fashion, like all despots, has her caprices, and the rose and zebra and mahogany are evidently declining in favor; and as our native growth of woods appears winning its way into use in England and France, and challenges the admiration of foreigners, it will command a preference, before long, in the domestic as well as the foreign market.

But our American woods are not only equal to any of foreign growth, but the various western articles are superior, for cabinet ware, to the corresponding kinds east of the mountains. This is no doubt owing to the greater rapidity of growth incident to our more fertile soil and milder climate.

As a specimen of the value of western timber for these purposes, it may be stated, that black walnut forks have been sent from St. Louis to the eastern cities, sawed into veneers, and sent back and sold in that shape for twelve and a-half cents per superficial foot. These veneers are so thin that it takes thirty-two to make an inch in thickness, they being not as thick as pasteboards, and the same log which furnishes boards of a given quantity, will saw into veneers fifteen fold. Specimens of black walnut, plain and curled, sawed here and worked up into chair-backs, cabinet furniture, and piano frames, which cannot be surpassed anywhere, may be seen at our various cabinet and chair factories.

The parts of trees adapted to ornamental purposes are the forks or crotches, curls, warts, and other excrescences, which, valuable as they are for this purpose, are fit for nothing else. As these have heretofore been sawed into boards, in which shape they are not one-fifteenth part as productive as in veneers, an inadequate supply only has been furnished the saw mills. But the increased supply created by their multiplication into veneers, will not only provide for our domestic markets, but furnish an extensive sale abroad in Europe, and our Atlantic cities.

Our domestic veneers are now sawed entirely in Cincinnati, and are from black walnut, curled maple, cherry, sugar-tree, oak, ash, and apple; which afford, when sawed up, an infinite variety of curls, dottings, waves, streaks and other fancy figures, some being of the most graceful, and others of the most grotesque appearance. These are furnished at the mill, at a price so low as from one and a-half to four cents, according to description, per superficial foot, and of first rate specimens. They also saw for the owners of the logs, if desired, and as low as at one dollar per one hundred feet. It is easy to conceive the increased demand and use, which this reduction in prices must create. Nor is it less obvious that, hereafter, the entire veneer supply of the west, will be sawed in the west. Independently of its own growth of woods, which, wherever it can be done, will be cut up on the spot, the foreign woods from Hayti, Campeachy, Honduras, and other places can be imported at as little expense into Cincinnati or any other place in the west, of steamboat access, as into any of the Atlantic cities. The freight from New Orleans, which is the butt end of the expense, is only twenty-five cents per cwt., and must become even less as the demand enlarges.

Henry Albro, who was burnt out some months since, on Front street, has recently put up new veneer and saw-mills, for sawing mahogany, on Pearl street, west of Elm. These have been constructed by Ferdinand Walters, who has the reputation of being one of the most ingenious machinists in the United States; and certainly there are many evidences of it on the premises, the machinery being greatly simplified as well as improved, one lever here serving to run the carriage back and forward; while on most of these saw-mills, two, and even three are requisite. Nor must it be supposed, that it requires no more skill or judgment in these than in the ordinary saw mills, for eight or ten years in attending a veneering saw, is preparation little enough for the employment.

The veneering saws are driven with such power and velocity as to make three hundred and fifty revolutions in a minute. Each one has the capacity to cut two thousand feet per day, but such is the severity of its service, that more than half the time is occupied in sharpening it.

One of these buildings is forty-two by twenty-two feet, and runs entirely upon veneering, having two seven feet, one four, and two three and a-half feet veneering saws. The other is designed for sawing black walnut and mahogany boards and plank, and preparing the black walnut crotches for the veneering mill.

Smith W. Horton, Cincinnati mahogany saw-mill, north side Second, between Race and Elm streets, saws to order, scroll work, and chair tops of every material. Walnut and other veneers made to order and for sale; walnut crotches, knots and mottled woods, constantly bought. Employs ten hands, and runs three veneer saws, one each, three, five and a-half and eight feet; manufactures yearly, to the value of thirty thousand dollars. More than one hundred thousand chair tops are sawed here in twelve months.

Vermicelli, Maccaroni, etc. Three factories.—Seven hands; value of product, twenty-one thousand six hundred dollars; raw material, 40 per cent.

Vinegar Factories.—This is a business of comparatively recent establishment. In 1837, there were not one thousand barrels made in Cincinnati; now, there are twenty-six factories, exclusive of those who manufacture vinegar, in connection with, and incident to, other business, as R. Conkling & Co., and Conkling, Wood & Co. The entire vinegar manufacture here, reaches a value of one hundred and sixty-eight thousand seven hundred and fifty dollars, the business employing fifty-nine hands; raw material, 40 per cent.

Many persons suppose that the vinegar made here, is entirely a mineral and unwholesome product. Such, some of it, doubtless is; and the sales of that description to families should be severely reprehended, it being only fit for mechanical and chemical purposes. But there is a great deal of cider vinegar made, Conkling, Wood & Co., having received five hundred barrels from Marietta in a single shipment.

Sparkes & Gogreve, 62 and 64 Broadway, are largely in the vinegar manufacture. Their factory comprehends the second, third and fourth stories of the building. The upper is a loft in which the vinegar undergoes its highest degree of acidification, the summer temperature of it ranging from one hundred and thirty to one hundred and sixty degrees Fahrenheit. Here are from one hundred and fifty to two hundred hogsheads at a time. In the third story is a mixing tub of one thousand five hundred gallons capacity, of which diluted beer, whisky, etc., form the contents; another tub, holding two thousand five hundred gallons, is filled with diluted cider alone. Beside these, the third story contains thirty large vinegar stands of five hundred gallons capacity each. The yearly sales of this house, exceed nine thousand barrels.

Wadding, Glazed Cotton.—Stearns & Foster, employ eleven hands, and manufacture a value of twenty-five thousand dollars; raw material, 60 per cent.

Wagon, Cart, etc., makers. Forty-two shops.—One hundred and thirty-six hands; value of product, one hundred and thirty-two thousand dollars; raw material, 40 per cent.

Wall Paper Stainers. Four factories.—Employ thirty-six hands; manufacture to the value of thirty thousand dollars; raw material, 60 per cent.

Wash-Boards, Zinc. Three factories.—Employ forty hands; value of yearly product, eighty-five thousand dollars; raw material, 50 per cent.

There are more zinc wash-boards made here than in any one state in the Union, or any city in the world.

Orrin Rice, the original patentee of this article, north side Second, between Race and Elm streets, has just recommenced business. Made last year, for six weeks, as many as twelve hundred wash-boards per day, and averaged during the year, more than six hundred per day.

J. B. Holmes, Cincinnati zinc wash-board factory, north side of Seventh, between Sycamore street and Broadway, employs six men and eight boys; value of product, twenty-five thousand dollars annually. Lumber, five thousand; zinc, seven thousand; nails, eight hundred dollars, consumed in the year's business.

Whisky.—This is the great whisky mart of the world. That article is manufactured for the Cincinnati market, for several miles up and down the Ohio—along the lines of the Whitewater and Miami canal—along that of the Little Miami railroad, as far as Milford, and within the city itself, to the extent of one thousand one hundred and forty-five barrels per day. Yearly value of product, two millions eight hundred and fifty-seven thousand nine hundred dollars; raw material, 65 per cent.

White Lead, etc. Four factories.—One hundred and twenty-three hands; value of product, three hundred and eighty-five thousand dollars; raw material, 70 per cent.

Conkling, Wood & Co., Court street, east of Broadway, manufacture white lead, dry and in oil, red lead, litharge, colored paints,

Hawkins Dag.[the] Jewett & Co. Engravers
W. Anderson Sc.

Middleton Printer

Edgar Conkling

(of the firm of Conkling Wood & Co.)

putty, whiting, cider vinegar, etc., to the value of one hundred and twenty-six thousand six hundred dollars. They import their chalk direct from England.

Wig makers. Two shops.—Five hands; value of product, seven thousand five hundred dollars; raw material, 20 per cent.

Window Shades, and Oil Furniture Cloth. Three factories.—Employ forty hands, on a product of fifty thousand dollars; raw material, 50 per cent.

The manufacture of oil-cloth did not exist here in 1834, except such as was afforded in a coarse article printed with wooden blocks. During that year, Sawyer & Brackett commenced manufacturing oil-cloth, printed from copper blocks. Two or three years sufficed so to perfect their operations, that they found an extensive market in the eastern states, in which these goods were awarded premiums at several mechanics' fairs. New designs and metallic blocks were added, until a large amount had been expended in the business. They also manufactured oil-cloth in imitation of mahogany, marble, etc.

In 1847, the manufacture of transparent oil painted window shades, was commenced by Sawyer & Co. The firm has made such improvements, in quality and style of shade, as greatly to reduce the price, and their operations are constantly on the increase. Sawyer & Co. employ fifteen hands, on a product of twenty thousand dollars; raw material, 40 per cent.

Wine.—This is a new and very important business, of which the great feature will be found under the appropriate section, "Culture of the Grape." In the various stages of wine growing and making, not less than five hundred persons are employed; value of product, one hundred and fifty thousand dollars; raw material, 25 per cent.

In addition to wine manufacturers who produce a common article merely, there are eight or ten individuals whose brands have already become known abroad, or who are preparing for the production of superior wines, principally from the Catawba grape. Of these, Longworth is the oldest and best known. But there are others who also make fine wines. Among these are R. Buchanan, Corneau & Son, T. H. Yeatman and G. & P. Bogen, whose wines are already in market, and find purchasers at remunerating prices, as fast as they can be made ready for sale.

Nicholas Longworth has been engaged in the cultivation of the grape thirty years, but has not given it that degree of attention necessary for full success until within a few years past. In a note to the writer of these pages, he says: "I have about one hundred and fifteen acres in grapes. I am now raising, and shall, in future, raise new seedlings extensively, both for wine and for the table, from our best native grapes, and may cross them with foreign grapes. I have within the past few years, grafted more than one hundred and twenty kinds of native grapes, obtained east, west, north, and south, and generally have them to bear the first year. I obtain them by express, and by mail, and private conveyance. We cultivate almost exclusively, the Catawba; we should extensively cultivate the Herbemont and Missouri. The former is our most vigorous grower, is a fine table grape, and makes a heavy wine, resembling, and equal to the Mansinælla. The Missouri, a wine resembling Madeira, and the fruit less subject to rot than other varieties.

Sparkling Catawba has hitherto been a losing business, as all experiments are. This was in part, owing to the small quantity made. The making of champagne wine is often a failure, except in very skillful hands, from want of effervescence. The breakage sometimes is so great, in a single year, as to break up the establishment. This, the French writers tell us. In future, I hope to make up for past losses. The wine house and cellar I built some years since, was too small; the present establishment is forty-four feet by one hundred and thirty-five feet, four and a-half stories high; bottom of cellar, twenty-five feet below the surface, double arches; top, say twelve feet below; basement wine cellar, half below the surface. I have not this season, for want of bottles, bottled as much as I intended; quantity, say seventy-five thousand. I have this season aided Mr. C. Zimmermann with funds to buy up the best Catawba wine, to prepare to fill as dry wine. He is an experienced German wine merchant, and believes he can, from the Catawba, make a dry wine, superior to the best German and French. I have paid for wine enough to put up forty thousand bottles of dry wine, when of a proper age, and expect to increase the quantity yearly. Corneau & Son, are experienced French wine merchants, and will make superior wines, and expect to do a large business. Much depends on the season, and neatness and care in gathering and pressing the grapes, and fermentation, for the quality of the wine, but equally as much on the skill exercised for the next two or three years. Pure wines require great attention and a cool cellar, or they will not keep.

From the Isabella grape a fine ladies' wine may be made. There are but two methods of having good sweet wines. The one by drying the grapes before pressing, the other by adding the best loaf sugar or candy, before fermentation. Where drugs are put in to prevent fermentation the wine is not good. The French sparkling wines are made from a mixture of three varieties of grapes. French writers say the one is to give aroma and flavor, a second, to give strength, a third, to give effervescence. I should believe the reason for the mixture true, if all cost the same price, but that which gives the aroma and flavor, costs three times the price of the others."

Robert Buchanan being written to on the same subject, replies:

"You ask for my experience in grape culture and wine making. It is but small, and acquired only within the past six or seven years. I commenced my vineyard in 1844 by planting about an acre, adding one or two acres annually, until it has grown to six acres, where I intend it shall remain.

"Two hands are sufficient to attend and keep the vineyard in complete order—these cost twelve dollars per month, each, and their board. In the season of the vintage, additional hands have to be employed. The cost of gathering the grapes and making the wine, I estimate at about twenty-five to thirty dollars per acre, of attending the vineyard and keeping it in order annually, sixty to seventy dollars per acre.

"In 1848 I made from one and a half acres then in bearing, five hundred gallons; in 1849, from two and a half acres, nine hundred gallons, and, in 1850, from three and a half acres, one thousand, six hundred and thirty-eight gallons. I have found a ready sale for my wine at one dollar and twenty-five cents per gallon, when prepared for market; say, from one to two years after each vintage.

"My wine cellar is ten feet deep. The wine press is in a cellar adjoining, seven feet deep. The grape vines are planted three by six feet apart in the vineyard. A vineyard, with the proper attention and in a favorable position, should yield an average product of three hundred to four hundred gallons per acre, for a succession of years. Very good years five hundred gallons, and seasons subject to the rot, one hundred to two hundred gallons.

"A bushel of grapes in bunches, will yield three to three and a half gallons of must or juice.

"The loss, by evaporation, lees, etc., in fermenting wines, is about 10 per cent.

"The greatest care should be taken to select for pressing, only the sound and ripe grapes, and cleanliness is as absolutely necessary in making wine, as in making butter. When the grapes are sound and well ripened, no sugar or brandy should be added, these additions are only used in making inferior wines."

Corneau & Son, manufacturers and dealers Catawba and other varieties of American wine, 82 West Fourth street, near Vine. Vineyard and wine presses, four miles beyond Covington; employ five hands in the manufacture of the wine. In 1849, their first vintage, put up three thousand; in 1850, ten thousand bottles Catawba wine. They are preparing to make sparkling Catawba from their next crop, if the season be favorable.

Their vineyard comprehends seven and a-half acres, and contains twenty thousand vines; and they plant additionally every year.

Messrs. Corneau estimate the wine product, as at an average of four hundred gallons to the acre for a series of five years, which must date after the vines commence bearing.

G. & P. Bogen have fifteen acres in grapes, near Carthage, of which ten acres are in bearing condition. They have ten acres elsewhere, in smaller patches—two acres of which, are in the city. Will have the entire twenty-five acres bearing in the course of 1851 and 1852. They have made, in favorable seasons, as high as from five hundred to eight hundred gallons to the acre. Grapes for wine are worth three dollars per bushel, and wine, when newly made, if of good quality, one dollar twenty-five cents per gallon. Of course, it is a more profitable business to bottle it off when fit, as good Catawba commands six dollars per dozen bottles.

In 1848 made one thousand one hundred, in 1849, two thousand one hundred, and in 1850, three thousand three hundred gallons; would have been more but for three hail-storms. In 1850, bought five thousand gallons additionally. Twenty thousand bottles constitute half their present stock; the other half is in casks. They make both still and sparkling Catawba.

One side of their wine cellar, which is sixty feet in length, is filled with casks of wine. Of these, fifteen hold each, from three hundred to four hundred; two, five hundred; two, seven hundred and fifty; two, eight hundred and fifty, and two, one thousand and fifty gallons each.

No pains or expense has been spared, to make the cellar everything which a wine-cellar should be.

Wire working. Five establishments, principally small.—Employ thirty hands on a product of sixty-nine thousand dollars; raw material, 50 per cent.

Wm. Bromwell, wove and worked wire manufactory, Walnut street, three doors below Fifth street market space, makes every description of riddles and screens, for all kinds of grain, seeds, powder and sugar; strainer wires of all numbers, wire for spring-house and cellar windows, hair sieves and strainers of all sizes; safes and sieves, rat and mouse-traps, riddle and screen wire. Employs sixteen hands, on a product of fifty thousand dollars.

Wool Carders. Four factories, principally small.— Thirteen hands; labor value, ten thousand five hundred dollars.

Wrought Nails. Four shops.—Twelve hands; value of product, nine thousand dollars; raw material, 50 per cent.

This chapter of "Cincinnati in 1851," may be appropriately closed, with the following remarks of Horace Greeley, published in the Tribune after his return, in 1850, from Cincinnati. It affords a brief summary, and just estimate of our advantages and prospects as a manufacturing city.

"It requires no keenness of observation to perceive that Cincinnati is destined to become the focus and mart for the grandest circle of manufacturing thrift on this continent. Her delightful climate; her unequaled and ever-increasing facilities for cheap and rapid commercial intercourse with all parts of the country and the world; her enterprising and energetic population; her own elastic and exulting youth; are all elements which predict and insure her electric progress to giant greatness. I doubt if there is another spot on the earth where food, fuel, cotton, timber, iron, can all be concentrated so cheaply—that is, at so moderate a cost of human labor in producing and bringing them together—as here. Such fatness of soil, such a wealth of mineral treasure—coal, iron, salt, and the finest clays for all purposes of use—and all cropping out from the steep, facile banks of placid, though not sluggish navigable rivers. How many Californias could equal, in permanent worth, this valley of the Ohio!"

SYNOPSIS OF MANUFACTURING AND INDUSTRIAL PRODUCTS.

	1841.			1851.		
Factories, Shops, Works, Mills, Yards, etc.	No.	Hds.	Product.	No.	Hds.	Product.
Agricultural machines			$	1	30	$ 36000
Alcohol and spirits, wine distillers				6	12	608260
Animal charcoal factory				1	12	25000
Apple butter makers				3	9	5000
Architects	6	9	17000	10	15	22000
Artificial flower factories				3	40	14200
Awning, tent, bag makers	3	8	12000	7	66	45000
Bagging factories	1	87	78650	2	238	270000
Bakers	52	132	259000	140	445	637662
Band and hat box makers	1	5	9000	6	60	36000
Baskets, cradles, makers	2	5	2800	7	30	18000
Bell and brassfounders	8	62	81000	12	132	209500
Bellows makers	2	6	12600	3	8	18000
Blacking paste makers	2	12	11000	3	16	24000
Blacksmith shops	52	294	311400	82	223	235395
Blinds, venetian, shops				6	27	40000
Block, spar, and pump makers	6	20	26172	5	18	21000
Boiler yards	8	90	106000	10	97	349000
Bonnet bleachers and pressers				10	33	22000
Book binderies	15	102	100700	15	136	122000
Boot and shoemakers	166	652	488000	374	1760	1182650
Brand, stamp, and blind chisel makers	3	7	6800	6	16	13500
Breweries	8	60	126000	21	172	566000
Brick yards	35	175	87500	60	367	207000
Brick masons and Plasterers	108	466	208650	208	876	408650
Bristle and curled hair dressers	2	42	16600	4	104	48800
Britannia ware factories	1	8	12840	2	32	38690
Brush makers	4	15	19000	15	90	60500
Bucket and tub factory				1	90	84200
Burr mill-stone makers	2	15	10500	4	19	24000
Butchers	62	157	1098015	121	600	2850000
Camphine and spirit gas makers	2	7	19000	3	7	17200
Candy and confectionary makers	12	35	54000	12	80	128120
Caps—men's and boys', makers				9	50	39000
Carpenters and builders	160	645	418600	284	2320	2116000
Cars and omnibuses, railroad				4	110	108447
Carriage factories	6	87	127000	24	212	247400
Carpet weavers	7	37	46000	18	65	56000
Carvers in wood				3	7	7000
Castor oil factory				1	8	55000
Charcoal, pulverized				3	9	18500
Chemical laboratories	3	29	68000	5	79	226000
Cistern builders	4	12	21300	3	36	75000
Cloak and visites makers				2	6	3000
Clothing factories	86	813	1223800	108	950	1947500
Coffee roasters				1	17	38000
Comb factory	1	20	18550	1	18	18000
Composition roofers				4	18	40000
Coopers	31	176	167000	63	796	387000
Copper, tin, and sheet-iron workers	32	208	211300	42	240	258000
Copperplate printers	5	8	21000	2	9	50000
Cordage and rope makers	4	18	33600	9	130	180000
Curers of beef, tongues, etc				13	40	135000

Factories, Shops, Works, Mills, Yards, etc.	1841.			1851.		
	No.	Hds.	Product.	No.	Hds.	Product.
Cutlery, surgical and dental instruments—tailors' shears makers	8	13	$ 10700	4	25	$ 40000
Daguerreotypists	1	1	950	32	110	80000
Dentists				36	80	92000
Die sinkers				3	5	5000
Domestic liquor factories				16	46	726000
Dyers and scourers	10	30	15540	15	24	28000
Edge tool makers	8	37	41600	19	72	97900
Edge tool grinders				1	18	20000
Engravers	8	11	23550	14	30	50000
Fancy job printers				2	25	30000
Feed and flouring mills	10	43	816700	14	65	1690000
Fire-engines, hydraulic apparatus builders	2	13	13750	1	37	65000
Flooring mills	6	31	73000	14	72	351200
Florists				15	35	120000
Founderies and engine shops	13	563	668657	44	4695	3676500
Fringes, tassel, etc., makers	1	7	15400	4	40	20000
Furniture factories	59	335	664000	136	1158	1660000
Gas and coke works				1	50	65000
Gas fitters				2	24	45000
Gas burner cap factory				1	3	5000
Gilders				10	36	39000
Glass works, cutters, etc.	1	5	10000	2	30	40000
Glove factories				3	33	20000
Glue do.				5	40	28000
Gold leaf and dentists' foil makers				1	5	11000
Do. pen factory				1	3	3500
Grates, etc., factories				2	52	45000
Ground spice and drug mills				6	56	140000
Ground mustard do.				2	10	15000
Do. marble dust do.	1	15	14000	2	4	3500
Gunsmiths	5	15	16842	6	30	35000
Hatters	25	181	312000	40	367	445000
Hat block factories				1	4	4500
Horse shoers				12	35	48000
Hose, belts, etc., factories	1	2	2109	4	26	96000
Hot air furnace builders				1	20	60000
Ice packers				14	60	150000
Iron, rolling mills	2	148	394000	5	550	1050000
Do. safe, chest, and vault factories	1	12	11400	3	56	96000
Do. railing do.				5	77	96000
Japaned filter maker				1	4	6000
Do. tin ware factory	1	2	2000	1	34	52000
Lever lock do.	5	49	39000	10	60	53000
Lightning rod do.				1	50	150000
Lithographers	1	4	3500	4	24	20000
Looking-glass factories	6	17	26000	7	34	48000
Machinists	4	42	77000	12	120	130000
Marble workers	1	3	10000	5	164	190000
Masonic & Odd Fellows' regalia embroid'r's				4	18	21000
Math., astron., & optical instrument makers	3	16	30000	6	24	40000
Mat maker				1	3	7240
Mattress makers and upholsterers	10	58	84800	10	80	95000
Milliners				60	650	820000
Mineral water factories				8	64	165000

Factories, Shops, Works, Mills, Yards, etc.	1841. No.	1841. Hds.	1841. Product.	1851. No.	1851. Hds.	1851. Product.
Mineral teeth factory			$	1	5	$ 9000
Morocco leather yards				7	76	67000
Musical instrument makers	7	18	25000	6	62	89500
Music publishers				1	30	50000
Nut and washer maker				1	4	20000
Oil, castor factory				1	7	60000
Do. lard and stearine factory	1	4	31000	34	124	3015900
Do. linseed, mills				3	38	263000
Do. vitriol laboratory	2	4	36000	1	24	135000
Packing box and refrigerator factories	8	28	39000	12	65	120000
Painters and Glazers	41	148	78000	72	632	385000
Paper makers				9	120	330000
Patent medicine factories	4	10	68000	14	90	660000
Pattern makers	2	3	3500	14	30	25500
Perfumers				8	45	120000
Pickles, preserves, sauce makers				2	12	25000
Plane, etc., makers	4	34	95000	7	96	167000
Planing machine factory				1	12	30000
Platform scale makers				6	36	60000
Plow makers	6	30	37900	6	24	45000
Plumbers	4	18	48000	16	135	195000
Plug, Bung, etc., factory				1	8	12000
Potters	2	11	12000	14	50	36000
Pork, beef, and ham curers factories				33	2450	5760000
Printing ink factories	1	4	2500	2	8	15000
Do. press factory	2	11	9000	1	30	52000
Publishers				12	656	1246540
Roofers' patent				1	12	36000
Saddlery, harness, and collar makers	22	102	23100	40	222	346500
Saddle tree makers				1	5	4500
Sail Do.				4	15	9000
Saleratus factories				3	6	50000
Sand-paper factories				2	10	12000
Sarsaparilla, cough candy factories				1	10	92000
Sash, blind, and door do.	22	90	71700	25	220	312000
Sausage do.		15	21000	22	166	162000
Saw mills	6	31	73000	15	206	411000
Saw factories				2	6	6700
Screw plate factories				2	12	16500
Sheeting, yarn, and candle wick factories				5	410	636000
Shirt and stock makers	5	75	40000	15	250	157000
Silver and gold workers	8	36	56500	5	50	90000
Soap and candle factories	17	122	322940	38	710	1475000
Spectacle makers				1	4	9000
Spoke factories				2	36	70500
Stainers, glass				1	5	15000
Stair builders				3	18	24000
Starch factories	2	16	45000	5	42	98000
Steamboat builders	5	306	592500	7	554	488000
Stencil cutters				3	8	5000
Stereotypers				3	60	46000
Stocking weavers	2	7	12000	4	21	13000
Stone cutters	6	70	83000	22	249	222000
Stone masons	44	218	101000	36	428	308000
Straw hat and bonnet factories				5	50	60000

Factories, Shops, Works, Mills, Yards, etc.	1841. No.	1841. Hds.	1841. Product.	1851. No.	1851. Hds.	1851. Product.
Stucco workers	2	6	$ 6000	2	14	$ 12000
Tailors	60	295	276000	98	816	832000
Tanners and curriers	21	126	335000	30	380	965000
Tobacco, cigar, and snuff factories	26	358	225000	62	1310	931000
Trunks, carpet-bags, etc., makers				15	275	506000
Turners	12	27	28275	30	143	152000
Type founders	3	85	45400	2	121	100000
Undertakers				14	56	76000
Varnish factories				2	9	135000
Veneer factories				2	20	66000
Vinegar do.	5	11	30500	26	59	168750
Wadding do.				1	11	25000
Wagon makers	21	96	104300	42	136	132000
Wall paper stainers		43	34400	4	36	30000
Wash boards, zinc factories				3	40	85000
White lead do.	3	44	121750	4	123	385000
Wig makers	3	8	6000	2	5	7500
Window shade factories	4	81	73000	3	40	50000
Wine manufacturers				40	500	150000
Wire workers	4	12	13000	5	30	69000
Wool carders	2	18	30000	4	13	10500
Wrought nail makers				4	12	9000
Whisky distilleries	3	37	145000	38	110	2857920

This synopsis affords an opportunity to compare the past and present.

The preceding table of manufactures and industrial pursuits classifies itself, as follows:

Raw Material.	Labor, etc.	Aggregate Product.	Per Cent. Raw Material.	Pr. Ct. Labor.
181100	3440900	3622000	5	95
57400	576600	574000	10	90
184800	739200	924000	20	80
816200	2893800	3710000	22	78
631000	1893000	2524000	25	75
484500	1130500	1615000	30	70
245000	455000	700000	33	67
1801600	2702400	4504000	40	60
681300	832700	1514000	45	55
168000	182000	350000	48	52
3155000	3155000	6310000	50	50
511500	418500	930000	55	45
3135600	2090400	5226000	60	40
2641600	1422400	4064000	65	35
562100	240900	803000	70	30
3957000	1319000	5276000	75	25
2876000	719000	3595000	80	20
7898610	877400	8776000	90	10
29988300	25028700	55017000		

XIV. COMMERCE.

Our wholesale and retail dry goods, grocery, hardware, iron, crockery, glass, etc., trade, may be stated at thirty-six millions annually. One-fourth of this is a home consumption business. The following tables of imports and exports, illustrate this subject. It runs, as may be perceived, from 1845–46 to 1850–51, a period of six successive years. As the business year expires on August 31st, the column for 1850–51 comprehends a period of forty-one weeks only, being to the 18th June.

IMPORTS AT CINCINNATI,

For five years, commencing September 1st, and ending August 31st, each year.

ARTICLES.	'45–'46	'46–'47	'47–'48	'48–'49	'49–'50	'50–'51
Apples, green,.......bbls.	17502	26992	28674	22109	6445	16778
Beef,....................	2420	186	659	348	801	1098
Beef,.............tierces	737	5		27	15	18
Bagging,..........pieces	6805	5561	79228	2094	324	
Barley,.................	90225	79394	165528	87460	137925	108531
Beans,.................	10202	11668	8757	3067	5565	29760
Butter,..............bbls	3339	6345	6625	7721	3674	7237
Butter,...firkins and kegs	6841	7090	6405	7999	7487	10099
Blooms,............tons	42770	2017	2203	9519	2545	2452
Bran, etc.,...........sks	3117	14594	1941	21995	49075	44257
Candles,...........boxes	241	207	133	414	718	697
Corn,............bushels	57245	896258	361315	344810	649227	443746
Corn meal,..............	9289½	56775	29542	5504	3688	4920
Cider,..............bbls	812	3261	2289	4346	453	1029
Cheese,..............cks	808	483	164	281	97	74
Cheese,............boxes	99059	120301	138800	143265	165940	166980
Cotton,............bales	4830	12528	13476	9058	8551	5702
Coffee,..............sks	55468	59337	80242	74961	67170	72719
Codfish,..........drums	220	292	311	515	464	431
Cooperage,........pieces	105915	186186	179946	147352	201711	133497
Eggs,....boxes and bbls	2400	561	4035	4504	2041	6057
Flour,..............bbls	202319	512506	151518	447844	231859	434359
Feathers,............sks	3514	2767	4467	4908	3432	1943
Fish, sund.,.........bbls	14613½	16836	19215	18145	14527	16689
Fish,......kegs and kits	996	2142	725	1059	1290	2413
Fruit, dried,......bushels	2566	82871	27464	38317	11802	40144
Grease,.............bbls	426	482	585	878	1169	770
Glass,.............boxes	13088	18002	20281	33868	34945	33217
Glassware,......packages	11058	17121	15025	19209	25712	24562
Hemp,..bundles and bales	9167	26678	15349	11161	12062	9592
Hides,............. loose	19781	24376	33745	23766	30280	22558
Hides, green,........lbs	5007	7513	10829	22774	14181	24244

ARTICLES.	'45–'46	'46–'47	'47–'48	'48–'49	'49-'50	'50–'51
Hay,..............bales	8092	7049	8036	12751	14452	12269
Herring,..........boxes	2226	1603	4191	2960	3546	3482
Hogs,.............head	....	38774	49847	52176	60902	102391
Hops,.............bales	....	1064	645	238	799	687
Iron and Steel,....pieces	130965	188126	197120	187864	186832	190059
Do. do....bundles	31820	33463	34213	29889	55168	58168
Do. do.......tons	358½	1685	827	1768	2019	1163
Lead,.............pigs	25238	43675	39609	45544	49179	46736
Lard,.............bbls	13898½	21991	37978	28514	34173	36658
Do.,..............kegs	51870	22722	41714	48187	63327	30961
Leather,.........bundles	1904	5069	6579	6975	9620	7832
Lemons,..........boxes	1904	2185	3068	4181	4183	2817
Lime,.............bbls	9212	32016	63364	61278	56482	42507
Liquors,.....hhds and ps	1222½	3369	3115	4476	5802	1465
Merch'ise and sund. pkgs	967868	263944	381537	68582	308523	169050
Do. ....tons	2815	7941	7308	837	4540	2196
Molasses,.........h. bbls	36510	27218	51001	52591	54003	63032
Malt,............bushels	8758	12562	7999	29910	41982	16034
Nails,.............kegs	33207	54918	59983	55893	83073	67040
Oil,....................	3706	5663	6618	7427	5049	5856
Oranges,..boxes and bbls	2863	4137	5007	4317	6819	8702
Oakum,............bales	551	1100	1486	1423	1799	1329
Oats,............bushels	106852	372127	194557	185723	191924	133711
Oil Cake,..........lbs	1647462	2225988	2811793	1767421	27870	194000
Pork and Bacon,....hhds	4089	5476	4420	6178	7564	5878
Do. do. ...tierces	98	124	140	465	2358	980
Do. do. .....bbls	53969	40581	69828	44267	43227	31210
Pork in bulk,........lbs	6037163	8027399	9643063	9249380	325756	14348204
Potatoes,...........bbls	12707	15829	22439	17269	13898	19127
Pig Metal,..........tons	13685½	15868	21145	15612	17211	11482
Pimento and Pepper, bags	1741	3180	3455	1257	2558	1879
Rye............bushels	8582½	41016	24336	22233	23397	91681
Rosin, etc.,..........bbls	2161	5004	11668	3298	12349	10727
Raisins,...........boxes	12021	11990	22796	14927	11936	15388
Rope, Twine, etc........	4341	8002	7806	3950	3061	1923
Rice,.............tierces	3140	1145	2494	3365	3556	4672
Sugar,..............hhds	13710	16649	27153	22685	26760	29917
Do................bbls	4956	7196	11175	7575	13005	14879
Do.............boxes	2184	5117	2928	1847	2467	2721
Seed, flax,..........bbls	20494	25753	32260	22859	15570	12693
Do. grass............	2759	4964	4968	5920	4432	3982
Do. hemp...........	400	290	214	510	314	49
Salt,................sks	13147	56292	65265	76985	110650	37817
Do.,...............bbls	111005	124360	94722	76496	114107	61516
Shot,...............kegs	580	1118	809	818	1447	1239
Tea,.......... packages	4255	5443	2931	7412	9802	5275
Tobacco,...........hhds	5078	6200	4051	3471	2213	2391
Do. ....bales	655	822	1229	1311	887	1571
Do. ..boxes and kegs	6918	9241	14815	12463	17772	14855
Tallow,............bbls	1734	1748	2472	1829	1225	3017
Wines,..bbls and ¾ casks	2621	4006	2252	2663	6874	3069
Do.,....baskets and bxs	1331	1419	2272	2101	4296	2080
Wheat,..........bushels	434486	590809	570813	385388	322699	360516
Wool,..............bales	4471	2960	1943	1686	1277	788
Whisky,............bbls	178336	184639	170436	165419	186678	199248
Yarn, cotton,....packages	4367	9271	6403	5562	3494	4726
Do...............bales	165914	146541	288095	262893	174885	88915

EXPORTS AT CINCINNATI.

For six years, commencing Sept. 1st, and ending August 31st, each year.

ARTICLES.	'45-'46	'46-'47	'47-'48	'48-'49	'49-'50	'50-'51
Apples, green,............bbls	3920	14444	8512	5824	3519	8064
Alcohol,......................	1615	1943	1771	3022	3302	3483
Beef,.........................	8896	10367	14811	12523	7558	18949
Do..................tierces	11301	7970	3615	9332	6625	9028
Beans,.................. bbls	2048	3782	1097	1685	2496	1590
Brooms,................ dozs	1514	5108	3760	3333	7265	7898
Butter,..................bbls	1624	1348	2937	1272	964	2748
Do., ...firkins and kegs	20390	31194	28315	24398	24393	30490
Bran, etc,................sks	....	3842	3761	233	4322	5769
Bagging,.............. pieces	19716	8867	12632	15910	9353	6407
Corn,..................... sks	....	258198	53021	7176	57248	20008
Corn-meal,.............. bbls	1258	88882	19999	3660	1179	1988
Cheese,..................casks	604	1132	30	122	106	25
Do.,.................. boxes	35459	70104	59374	55134	86902	102825
Candles........................	3757	16622	29189	39640	67447	102328
Cattle,.........................	168	872	733	97	30	364
Cotton,..................bales	....	5019	6123	4009	1896	4097
Coffee,.................... sks	....	13037	18587	18909	22030	28002
Cooperage,.............pieces	18388	41121	36924	55617	73637	54588
Eggs,................... bbls	4787	10303	9450	5229	4246	8309
Flour,........................	194700	581920	201011	267420	98908	347471
Feathers,..................sks	29	4000	3736	3824	5380	2828
Fruit, dried,...........bushels	684	16077	5074	8317	1850	14328
Grease,................... bbls	370	694	4268	6922	7597	3600
Grass seed,....................	642	3967	2431	2387	2528	2611
Horses,..................head	654	2026	1268	378	468	581
Hay,.....................bales	....	327	94	1040	564	588
Hemp,.........................	....	8733	5659	2198	1164	1881
Hides,.................pounds	....	164930	60880	73029	62865	29180
Do.,......................No	....	12444	9024	7731	11225	10301
Iron,...................pieces	2937	68905	127193	43025	54075	78937
Do.,.............. bundles	....	9339	17351	7081	36245	34898
Do.,.....................tons	1238	5646	6916	6270	5767	7187
Lard,.................... bbls	22747	49878	81679	37521	39192	28900
Do.,. ....kegs	135008	150828	208696	130509	170167	65638
Lard Oil,.................bbls	1650	6199	8277	9550	16984	22330
Linseed Oil,..................	455	6032	3878	3020	4879	799
Molasses,.....................	....	9046	18332	17750	25878	21538
Oil-Cake,.............. tons	2792	5246	4897	3274	743	873
Oats,..................... sks	17944	140067	41675	212	5023	11708
Potatoes,.................bbls	14956	34130	15687	7073	5283	15889
Pork and Bacon,..........hhds	15287	31538	37162	39470	23529	27309
Do.,...............tierces	3874	7894	8862	10930	22477	18849
Do.,.................. bbls	29302	137218	196186	186192	193581	119858
Do.,........in bulk, pounds	404426	3478850	759188	924256	2310699	4742405
Rope, etc.,...........packages	13037	8723	5556	4369	3151	4574
Soap,....................boxes	2708	10080	11095	11303	17443	15510
Sheep,...................head	100	726	1400	522		460
Sugar,................... hhds	....	4998	11559	8443	9650	10250
Salt,..................... bbls	....	65346	39656	39960	29509	26659
Do.,.................... sks	....	4416	5057	5403	8301	5301

ARTICLES.	'45-'46	'46-47'	'47-'48	'48-'49	'49-'50	'50-'51
Seed, flax,...............bbls	138	291	2785	808	333	368
Sundry merchandise,..packages	23603	224957	341363	210049	615641	329397
Do., Do. ....tons	2106	18179	16849	21466	11109	9725
Do. liquors,...........bbls	358	7193	9364	10913	11798	15580
Do. manufactures,.....pieces	7975	22251	42412	94934	56810	22103
Do. produce,....... packages	1085	17879	28822	17609	10327	13858
Starch,................boxes	2499	5820	8177	7904	9491	11856
Tallow,......................	3452	4543	5682	4975	4311	5883
Tobacco,......kegs and boxes	1473	9718	9352	7497	6904	13957
Do. ....hhds	3803	6011	3812	3309	4847	1620
Do. ....bales	....	275	123	126	77	134
Vinegar,.................bbls	204	3814	2753	1288	2404	2650
Whisky,......................	133220	183928	186509	136911	179540	188873
Wool,...................bales	....	8452	2298	1109	2156	2024
Do.......................bs	....	36710	7037	10230	16841	
White Lead,.............kegs	....	....	....	....	40294	37619
Castings,..............pieces	....	....	....	....	54399	27921
Do. ....tons	....	....	....	....	2385	935
Pork,...................boxes	....	....	....	....	13448	2956

The commission business of Cincinnati is a heavy one, although there are not materials within reach to compute its aggregate. One house, that of Wann & McBirney, Reeder's building, 57 West Third street, may, however, be given as a sample.

Their shipments of produce to Great Britain, from October 1, 1850, to July 1, 1851, sums up $540,000
Advances on Consignments to the eastern and southern markets, and sales here, for same period 362,170

$ 902,170

This, it will be seen, is a nine months business simply, and in the ratio of twelve hundred thousand dollars, annually.

WANN & McBIRNEY,

Are agents for the Philadelphia and Liverpool steamship, "Lafayette," and for McHenry's Philadelphia and Liverpool packets, sailing every month.

Make advances on consignments of produce, to their friends at Liverpool, London, Dublin, Belfast, and all the eastern and southern markets.

Draw sterling bills of exchange, for £1, and upward, payable on demand, which will be cashed without discount, at any of the bankers in the United Kingdom.

XV. MISCELLANEOUS.

CULTURE OF THE GRAPE.

THIS is already an important branch of horticulture in the valley of the Ohio, and rapidly on the increase.

The time will come when our beautiful river may, not inaptly, be termed the "Rhine of America."

The greatest number of vineyards in this valley are in the neighborhood of Cincinnati; and the "vine-clad hills" of the picturesque vicinity around us are among the most pleasing and attractive objects to strangers. Within a circle of twenty miles, we number more than three hundred vineyards, containing, in the aggregate, about nine hundred acres, one half of which are now in bearing. The product, last year, was estimated at one hundred and twenty thousand gallons of wine. This will, of course, be doubled when all come into bearing, within one to three years. New vineyards are annually planted, and additions made to the old ones; so that it may be fair to infer, that within six or eight years the number of vineyards will be doubled. The business is as yet but in its infancy, but its profits will justify such efforts and experiments as must eventually lead to the most complete success. It has been fully and satisfactorily demonstrated, that from our native *Catawba grape*, excellent wines can be made, rivaling the better qualities of the Rhenish wines, and more suited to the American palate. They are fast growing into public favor, and in due time, will displace—to a considerable extent—their foreign rivals.

The culture of the grape, for making wine, has been attempted in various parts of the United States, for the last fifty years—at Philadelphia, New York, Lexington, Ky., Vevay, Ia., and in North and South Carclina—but nowhere, else has it succeeded so well as in the vicinity of this city; and here only satisfactorily within the last ten years. Much of our present success is owing to the various experiments, and the indomitable perseverance of Mr. N. Longworth, to whose zeal and liberal expenditure in various experiments, both with foreign and native grapes, for the last twenty-five years, the wine-growers are greatly indebted.

But few publications have been made, in the West, on the subject of grape culture, except occasional articles in the newspapers, by Mr. Longworth and others. In 1826, a small book was published by John James Dufour, of Vevay—in 1845, a pamphlet by C. A. Schumann—and in 1850, a short treatise on grape culture, with a copious appendix, by R. Buchanan. Nothing in this way can be perfect, for the business itself is but a new one, and every year's experience adds to our knowledge of the subject.

The most favorable region for the grape is supposed to be the valley of the Ohio, from Marietta to the mouth of the river, and extending twenty to thirty miles wide on each side. Further north is thought to be too cold, and further south more subject to the "rot."

As before stated, the principal vineyards of the West are in *our own vicinity*, say about nine hundred acres—near *Ripley*, fifty miles above, are some seventy-five acres—near *Vevay*, eighty miles below, thirty or forty—around *Charlestown*, Ia., one hundred miles below us, are over two hundred acres—at *Belleville*, Ill., a few vineyards have been recently established, and at *Hermann*, a flourishing German settlement, about fifty miles above St. Louis, on the Missouri river, a number of fine vineyards have been started—in all, probably, forty or fifty acres, from which samples of excellent wine have been sent to this city.

Near *Lexington*, *Maysville*, and *Louisville*, Kentucky, a few vineyards have recently been planted, which are said to be in a flourishing condition. In *Berks* county, Pa., the *Catawba* and *Isabella* grape are said to succeed well on the slate lands—many vineyards have been established, and some excellent wines made.

In *North* and *South Carolina* and *Georgia*, the culture of the grape has been pursued for many years past, and in some sections with considerable success. The "*Scuppernong*" is the favorite grape, from which, with the addition of sugar, a pleasant sweet wine is made.

It is therefore evident, that in a country like ours, of vast extent, of great diversity of soil and climate, abounding in native grapes, and settled by an intelligent and enterprising population, the making of our own wines is no longer problematical, but will soon be established on a sure and permanent basis, as one of the great branches of home productions.

SUBURBS.

With the growth of Cincinnati, increasing the value of ground, and diminishing in the same degree, space for occupation and improvement within its limits, has sprung up, a species of necessity, to add in all directions, suburbs to the city. Under this influence, subdivisions which either are adjacent to Cincinnati, or in the progress of improvement, are expected to become so, have been made of farms and out-lots of ground, which have readily found purchasers among those whose occupations permit a residence at greater or less distance from their business. Omnibuses, stages, and railroad cars, bringing them into Cincinnati, in a briefer space, than a walk from the extremities of the city would require.

There is yet another class of persons, whose business can be carried on as conveniently and more cheaply, at a still greater distance. They make up work and manufactures of various kinds, which they need not bring in oftener, perhaps, than at the close of each week. Obviously, the cost of traveling and transportation is of no importance, compared with the advantage of cheap rents and ample space to breathe in, which the country and country towns yield to residents. To accommodate this latter class, the laying off towns at points contiguous, or otherwise of ready access to Cincinnati, has been extensively done. Among these is Industry, ten miles west, which will communicate with this city, by canal, the river Ohio, and the Ohio and Mississippi railroad, which makes it a point in the route. The site is well chosen, and a foundery and other improvements, have been recently made. It is already a thriving place.

Caledonia, near the mouth of the Little Miami, is another favorable location, being on the Ohio, as well as of easy access from the city, otherwise. There is a foundery erected here, also, which like that at Industry, is on the principle of associative mutual labor. Caledonia has been but recently laid out.

Camden, at the intersection of the Little Miami railroad, with the river of that name, is a village, also, lately laid out. It is a beautiful spot.

These are given as specimens of other towns, at various distances, and in various directions, designed to afford cheap lots for those who desire homes of their own, and whose pursuits in life, allow them to live outside of the great city which supplies a market to the business avails of their industry.

There is another class of citizens, whose business is in Cincinnati, but who propose to reside outside its corporate limits, either to escape the heavy taxation, which city improvements impose, or in the expectation that the increasing facilities of railroads will enable them to reach their workshops, stores, or other places of employment, at as early an hour as necessary.

Covington, in Kentucky, which is only separated from us by the river, which is usually crossed in a few minutes, and with little delay, is one of these points. The inducements to reside here, held out to our citizens, have swelled the population of that city, from two thousand and twenty-six in 1840, to twelve thousand; its present number of inhabitants. Newport, under the same impulse, has increased during the same period, from one thousand and sixteen, to six thousand and twenty-six souls.

If, as is expected, a bridge shall be built across the Ohio at this point, these cities must increase, even beyond their present rapid ratio of progress.

Another adjacency is the territory lying on both sides of Mill creek, on our west. The largest share of this is in fact within our city limits, but being subject to inundation from high-water in the Ohio river, which spreads Mill creek, at times, over a large part of its surface, it becomes necessary, by embankment or otherwise, to obviate this check on its progress. Measures are about being resorted to, for this purpose, and "Mahkatewa," the aboriginal name of the stream which traverses it, must, eventually, become one of the most important sections of the city.

Farther north, is Fairmount, a north-western suburb immediately adjoining our corporate limits. It rises from the west side of Mill creek, in a gentle slope, and embraces some of the most charming knobs, or hills, within view of the city. The whole place is distinguished for beauty of scenery and landscape. Commanding a full view of Cincinnati and the circumjacent vicinage of twenty miles diameter; it embraces the valley of Mill creek to Spring grove cemetery; the Farmers' College, and a wide sweep of country chequered with villas, vineyards, gardens and groves. It is unsurpassed for healthfulness, removed from the smoke and dust of the city, enjoying pure air and wholesome water.

About one hundred and fifty acres have been platted with large and small lots, to suit purchasers; and extensive sales have already been made. Many of the purchasers, being shrewd and wealthy citizens of Cincinnati. The Western Baptist Educational Society, have located their seminary at this place, and the Cincinnati, Hamilton and Dayton Railroad, passes directly through it. The Western Railroad to St. Louis, also, will enter the city through Fairmount.

In the northern section of Cincinnati, east of Freeman street, lies a well located property, belonging to George Hatch, which is selling out at private sale only. He proposes to protect those who are willing to secure desirable lots for residences, from coffee-house neighbors and other business nuisances, by controlling, in his sales, the character of the buildings and improvements.

Following the outer edge of the city to the north-east is Mount Auburn, in contiguity to which are Burnet and Reeder's subdivision, and the property upon Prospect Hill, of Drs. W. & P M. These offer great inducements for those who desire dwellings removed from the dirt, tumult, and impure air of the crowded city, on which the last looks down from a commanding height. This site was originally abrupt and broken hill grounds, but the taste and industry of the proprietor, is carrying out a system of grading, filling and paving in connection with other improvements, which must render this part of Prospect Hill, eventually, one of the most desirable spots in the immediate vicinity of Cincinnati for residences. These lots are sold at a specified rate, the principal of which may lie for several years, six per cent. interest on the purchase-money being paid annually: the proprietor grades and paves all streets, &c., at his own expense.

The Burnet and Reeder property is a suburb also, which will be probably occupied with residences only. It embraces elevated ground of irregular surface, but which, when its grades shall be completed, will possess no more slope than sufficient properly to drain it. Pure air and water are the characteristics of this locality, which must become as densely populated as is desirable for private residences.

BIOGRAPHY.—S. P. CHASE.

The subject of this sketch, was born in Cornish, N. H., on the 13th of January, 1808. He is a lineal descendant of Capt. Aquila Chase, one of the original settlers in Newburyport, from whom have sprung a numerous progeny, now scattered over the United States.

At the age of ten years, Mr. Chase was deprived, by death, of a father's care, and shortly afterward, he was sent to Ohio, and placed in the school at Worthington, then under the charge of his uncle, Bishop Chase, where he remained a few years; when he came to Cincinnati, whither his uncle had removed, and became a student of Cincinnati college, under the Bishop's presidency. He entered Dartmouth college as Junior, in 1824, and was graduated in 1826.

After his graduation, he repaired to Washington, D. C., where he commenced the study of law, in the office of William Wirt; and while thus pursuing his legal studies, a friendship was formed between the preceptor and the pupil, which terminated only with the decease of Mr. Wirt. While thus a student in Mr. Wirt's office, at the request of a respectable member of the Society of Friends, he drafted a memorial to Congress, praying for the abolition of slavery and the slave trade, in the District of Columbia. This memorial having been revised and modified, was signed by about eleven hundred citizens of the district, and presented to Congress in 1828, by whom it was received, and referred to the committee, for the district of Columbia.

Having completed his preparatory legal studies, Mr. Chase was admitted to the bar by the Circuit Court of the United States, for the District of Columbia; and shortly after his admission, he returned to Ohio, where he was admitted to practice, by the Supreme Court of the State, and then commenced his practice in Cincinnati, in 1830.

The leisure which usually attends the earlier years of a young lawyer's practice, did not, in his case, pass away unemployed. Finding that his own studies had been retarded by the confused state of the statutes of Ohio, he conceived the idea of embodying, in one work, all the general laws of the state, as well those which had been, as those which were in force. This purpose was carried into effect, and in the short space of three years, he gave to his profession, a work of two thousand three hundred royal octavo pages, which at once established his reputation for diligence and fidelity of research, and ability of production. This work, enriched by annotations of all the decisions bearing upon the statutes, and by an able and accurate sketch of the history of Ohio, still stands a monument to his fame. His "years of leisure" soon passed away, and these were followed by years of unceasing toil and complete success. In 1837, he made his first forensic effort for freedom, in the case of Matilda, who was claimed as a fugitive slave by a person from Missouri; but his effort was unavailing in her case, and the court remanded her to slavery. He afterward defended James G. Birney, upon an indictment for harboring a fugitive slave; and although unsuccessful in the inferior Court, he succeeded in the Supreme Court, in obtaining a reversal of the judgment, and the acquittal of Mr. Birney.

These efforts were followed by his masterly defense of John Vanzandt, in the Supreme Court of the United States, who also was charged with harboring and concealing fugitive slaves; by his argument in Ohio, in the case of Samuel Watson, claimed as a slave; and by his public speeches and reports, made to the numerous state and national conventions, held with reference to the great question of human liberty, within the last ten years. In 1841, he became a conspicuous member of the Liberty party, to the democratic principles of which, as promulgated at Buffalo, in 1848, he still adheres.

In February, 1849, he was called from his office labors, by the voice of the General Assembly of Ohio, to a seat in the senate of the United States, for the full term of six years; a position to which, although placed there from the walks of private life, his previous training, had peculiarly fitted him.

As a lawyer, Mr. Chase is diligent, patient, and accurate, and as an advocate, he takes rank among the first in the country. In politics he is a democrat; and if, in his political action, he has not fully harmonized with the great party bearing that name, it is because of his conviction, that to nationalize, extend, and perpetuate slavery, is irreconcilable with democratic principles.

For twenty-three years past, he has been a member of the Episcopal Church, and his character is without a stain. Of the various public and benevolent movements of the day, he has ever been a steadfast supporter, and to the poor and oppressed, he has always proved a disinterested friend.

The fine mezzotint portrait of Senator Chase, in these pages, will be recognized at once, as a faithful and striking likeness.

FARMERS' COLLEGE.

BOARD OF INSTRUCTION.

THE Faculty consists of the following members:—

President.—F. G. Cary, Professor of Moral Philosophy and Rhetoric, and Superintendent of Buildings, Grounds, and Finance.

R. H. Bishop, D. D., Professor of History and Political Economy.

R. S. Bosworth, Professor of Chemistry, and its application to Agriculture and the Arts.

J. S. Henderson, Professor of Mathematics, Natural Philosophy, and Astronomy.

J. S. Whitwell, Professor of Ancient Languages and Belles Lettres.

C. Sheferstein, Teacher of Modern Languages.

G. S. Ormsby, Professor of Preparatory Course.

BOARD OF DIRECTORS.

President.—E. M. Gregory; Secretary—J. W. Caldwell; Treasurer—S. F. Cary.

Robert Crawford, Giles Richards, Timothy Kirby, Rev. John Covert, W. A. Bagley, James Huston, Joseph Longworth, Sylvester Ruffner, Thomas B. Wetherby, Paul C. Huston, J. P. Reznor, Samuel Wiggins.

This institution, which is situated on a beautiful summit, six miles north from Cincinnati, and is fast rising in public estimation, had its origin in the seminary, called from the name of its founder and proprietor, Cary's Academy.

Near the site of the present college, F. G. Cary, in the spring of 1833, commenced, with only four pupils, a boarding-school, which, at the expiration of eight years, numbered more than a hundred students. This institution was carried on until 1845, extensively by individual enterprise, when a rapidly increasing patronage made an enlargement and re-modification necessary. For this purpose, a joint-stock company was formed, thirty dollars constituting a share; and subsequently a charter was procured, granting the usual college rights and privileges.

In the fall of 1846, the building, under the name of Farmers' College, was completed, and the college organized. Mr. Cary, merging into the establishment, his private interests, was appointed President, and invested with the power of conducting the internal arrangements of the institution.

Since the organization, there have been annually, over two hundred students connected with its various departments; and in the eighteen years of its existence, one thousand young men have gone forth from its walls into the business of life.

Six instructors have been employed, who have hitherto been remunerated, exclusively, from the fees of tuition. A good chemical and philosophical apparatus, have been procured, comprising a telescope with a reflector of six and one-fourth inches aperture, made by Bruno Hasert, of Cincinnati.

An effort is now being made, fully to endow this institution, and place it upon a permanent basis; and the success which has hitherto attended this educational enterprise, gives encouragement to expect its speedy accomplishment.

The prominent characteristic of this institution, has ever been the practical character of its course of instruction. To assert the dignity of labor, has been its object.

MARKETS AND MARKET-HOUSES.

THERE are six market-houses in Cincinnati, all spacious, and well arranged for the exposure and sale of fresh meat and vegetables. These are Lower Market, Canal, Pearl, Fifth, Sixth, and Wade street market-houses. The last named is two hundred and fifty feet long; the others range from three hundred and seventy to three hundred and ninety-five feet each, in length, except the Pearl street, which is three hundred and forty feet; most of these houses are thirty-six feet wide. But meat may be bought extensively in quarters outside of the stalls, and vegetables are sold in wagons and carts, and at stands, outside of, and beyond the market-houses, to equal extent with that sold inside. The supply to these markets is such as might be expected from the fertility of the Great and Little Miami and Mill creek farms. As high as seven hundred wagons have been enumerated in one day, at a single one of these markets; most of these wagons, also, carried full loads for two horses. As many as nineteen hundred and fifty market-wagons carts, &c., have attended our various markets in the same day.

Cincinnati has long enjoyed pre-eminence in putting up pork, but is little known abroad for the extensive beef operations of which this city is the theatre. There are no means at hand of comparing the magnitude of the beef business here with that of Chicago or other important beef-packing points; but there is one remarkable feature of our beef, the quality of it, which has not only no superior, but no rival in the world for excellence.

Christmas-day is the great gala day of the butchers of Cincinnati. The parade of stall-fed meat, on that day, for several years past, has been such as to excite the admiration and astonishment of every stranger in Cincinnati—a class of persons always here in great numbers. The exhibition, this last year, has, however, greatly surpassed every previous display in this line.

A few days prior to the return of this day of festivity, the noble animals which are to grace the stalls on Christmas eve, are paraded through the streets, decorated in fine style, and escorted through the principal streets with bands of music and attendant crowds, especially of the *infantry*. They are then taken to slaughter-houses, to be seen no more by the public, until cut up and distributed along the stalls of one of our principal markets.

Christmas falling last year on Tuesday, the exhibition was made at what is termed our middle or Fifth street market-house. This is three hundred and eighty feet long, and of breadth and height proportionate—wider and higher, in fact, in proportion to length, than the eastern market-houses. It comprehends sixty stalls, which, on this occasion, were filled with steaks and ribs alone, so crowded, as to do little more than display half the breadth of the meat, by the pieces overlapping each other, and affording only the platforms beneath the stall and the table, behind which the butcher stands, for the display of the rounds and other parts of the carcass. One hundred and fifty stalls would not have been too many to have been fully occupied by the meat exhibited on that day, in the manner beef is usually hung up here and in the eastern markets.

Sixty-six bullocks, of which probably three-fourths were raised and fed in Kentucky, and the residue in our own State; one hundred and twenty-five sheep, hung up whole at the edges of the stalls; three hundred and fifty pigs, displayed in rows on platforms; ten of the finest and fattest bears Missouri could produce, and a buffalo calf, weighing five hundred pounds, caught at Santa Fé, constituted the materials for this Christmas pageant. The whole of the beef was stall-fed, some of it since the cattle had been calves, their average age being four years, and average weight sixteen hundred pounds, ranging from 1388, the lightest, to 1896, the heaviest. This last was four years old, and had taken the premium every year at exhibitions in Kentucky, since it was a calf. The sheep were Bakewell and Southdown, and ranged from ninety to one hundred and ninety pounds to the carcass, dressed and divested of the head, &c. The roasters or pigs would have been considered extraordinary anywhere but at Porkopolis, the grand emporium of hogs. Suffice to say, they did no discredit to the rest of the show. Bear meat is a luxury unknown at the East, and is comparatively rare here. It is the *ne plus ultra* of table enjoyment.

The extraordinary weight of the sheep will afford an idea of their condition for fat. As to the beef, the fat on the flanks measured *seven and one-quarter inches,* and that on the rump, *six and one half* inches through. A more distinct idea may be formed by the general reader, as to the thickness of the fat upon the beef, when he learns that two of the loins, on which were five and a half inches of fat, became tainted, because the meat could not cool through in time; and this, when the thermometer had been at no period higher than *thirty-six degrees,* and ranging, the principal part of the time, from *ten to eighteen degrees above zero.* This fact, extraordinary as it appears, can be amply substantiated by proof.

Specimens of these articles were sent by our citizens to friends abroad. The largest sheep was purchased by F. Ringgold, of the St. Charles, and forwarded whole to Philadelphia. Coleman of the Burnet House, forwarded to his brother of the Astor House, New York, nine ribs of beef, weighing one hundred and twenty pounds; and Richard Bates, a roasting piece of sixty-six pounds, by way of New Year's gift, to David T. Disney, our representative in Congress.

The Philadelphians and New Yorkers confessed that they never had seen anything in the line to compare with the specimens sent to those points.

The beef, &c., was hung up on the stalls early upon Christmas eve, and by twelve o'clock next day, the whole stock of beef—weighing 99,000 pounds—was sold out; two-thirds of it at that hour being either preparing for the Christmas dinner, or already consumed at the Christmas breakfast. It may surprise an eastern epicure to learn that *such beef* could be afforded to customers for *eight cents* per pound, the price at which it was retailed, as an average.

Engraved by F. E. Jones from a Daguerreotype

Yours Truly
A. Morrell Jr.

No expense was spared by our butchers to give effect to this great pageant. The arches of the market-house were illuminated by chandeliers and torches, and lights of various descriptions were spread along the stalls. Over the stalls were oil portraits—in gilt frames—of Washington, Jackson, Taylor, Clay, and other public characters, together with landscape scenes. Most of these were originals, or copies by our best artists. The decorations and other items of special expense these public-spirited men were at, reached in cost one thousand dollars. The open space of the market-house was crowded early and late by the coming and going throng of the thousands whose interest in such an exhibition overcame the discouragement of being in the open air at unseasonable hours, as late as midnight, and before day-light in the morning, and the thermometer at fifteen degrees.

We owe this exhibition to the public spirit of Vanaken and Daniel Wunder, John Butcher, J. & W. Gall, Francis and Richard Beresford, among our principal victualers.

No description can convey to a reader the impression which such a spectacle creates. Individuals from various sections of the United States and from Europe, who were here—some of them Englishmen, and familiar with Leadenhall market — acknowledged they had never seen any show of beef at all comparable with this.

BIOGRAPHY.—A. MORRELL, JR.

Abm. Morrell, Jr., son of Judge Morrell, of Albany, New York, was born November 18, 1819, and emigrated to the West at the age of seventeen years, under charge of Thos. G. Gaylord, a relative. He became a partner, in 1839, with Mr. G., in the rolling-mill business; which connection subsisted until 1850, when the firm of Morrell & Jordan—in the same line of business—was formed, by the co-partnership of A. M., Junr. and Richard Jordan, of the late firm of Bush & Jordan, of Covington, Kentucky. To the skill, industry, and activity of Mr. Jordan, whose talents as a manager of iron works are unsurpassed anywhere, as well as to the financial and salesman tact of Mr. Morrell, this firm is indebted for its marked success. This establishment has since become, Morrell, Jordan & Phillips, by the introduction of Thomas Phillips, of Cincinnati.

THE HOG AND ITS PRODUCTS.

THE want of ready and cheap access to foreign markets, led the settlers of the western states, to raising hogs and distilling whisky, as a convenient means of taking corn, their great staple, in these shapes, to market.

To comprehend this subject fully, it may be remarked, that from the year 1791, in which Indian corn was first exported to foreign markets, until 1847, the annual export of that article, never exceeded two millions of bushels, and did not average half that quantity. This, in the comparison with the entire product of the United States, fell short of one per cent., and did not constitute, probably, ten per cent. of what was needed for domestic subsistence. In 1847—the great year of European famine, the export of corn reached, almost, to eighteen millions of bushels. It has sensibly declined from these figures since, although still greatly exceeding the export of years, prior to that date. But the large shipment of 1847 did not constitute more than *three* per cent., of the entire crop, of 1846, which had been a year of unexampled productiveness. It became, therefore, manifest, that a very small share of this, our most important cereal product, finds its way outside of the home market, and the farmer must feed his corn to hogs, or distill it, as the only means of disposing of an article so bulky and heavy, to its value, as Indian corn.

The corn raised, in reference to the whisky market, is independent of that which is fed to hogs; no price that can be paid by the distillers, affording adequate remuneration to growers of corn, who have to transport it far by land carriage.

Cincinnati, being the business centre of an immense corn-growing and hog raising region, is, in fact, the principal pork market in the United States, and, without even the exceptions of Cork or Belfast, Ireland, the largest in the world.

The business of putting up pork here, for distant markets, is of some twenty-six years' standing; but it is only since 1833, that it has sprung into much importance.

The following tables furnish a list of hogs put up in Cincinnati each year since, including that of 1833, and in Ohio since 1843. The season begins in November and ends in March. Each year refers to that in which business closed:

TABLE—A.

Year.	No. of Hogs.	Year.	No. of Hogs.	Year.	No. of Hogs.
1833	85,000	1840	95,000	1847	250,000
1834	123,000	1841	160,000	1848	498,160
1845	162,000	1842	220,000	1849	310,000
1836	123,000	1843	250,000	1850	401,755
1837	103,000	1844	240,000	1851	324,529
1838	182,000	1845	213,000		
1839	199,000	1846	287,000		

TABLE—B.

Year.	Hogs packed in Ohio.	Per cent. in Cin'ti.	Year.	Hogs packed in Ohio.	Per cent. in Cin'ti.
1844	560,000	43	1848	742,212	66
1845	450,000	47	1849	600,316	71
1846	425,000	68	1850	563,645	80
1847	325,000	70	1851	388,556	80

The hogs raised for this market, are generally a cross of *Irish Grazier, Byfield, Berkshire, Russia and China,* in such proportions as to unite the qualifications of size, tendency to fat, and beauty of shape to the hams.

They are driven in at the age of from eleven to eighteen months old, in general, although a few reach greater ages. The hogs run in the woods until within five or six weeks of killing time, when they are turned into the corn-fields to fatten. If the acorns and beech nuts are abundant, they require less corn; but the flesh and fat, although hardened by the corn, is not as firm as when they are turned into the corn-fields, in a less thriving condition, during years when mast, as it is called, is less abundant.

From the 8th to the 10th of November, the pork season begins, and the hogs are sold by the farmers direct to the packers, when the quantity they own justifies it. Some of these farmers drive, in one season, as high as one thousand head of hogs into their fields. From a hundred and fifty to three hundred, are more common numbers however. Where less than a hundred are owned, they are bought up by drovers, until a sufficient number is gathered for a drove. The hogs are driven into pens, adjacent to the respective slaughter houses. As soon as the drover or farmer sells to the packer, the hogs are put into small pens, where they are crowded as thick as they can stand, and a hand walks over the drove, knocking them on the head successively, with a two pointed hammer adapted to the purpose. They are then dragged out by hooks into the sticking room, where their throats are cut, the blood passing through a drain or sewer below, into large tanks prepared to receive it. The blood is saved, to be sold, together with the hoofs and hair, to the manufacturers of prussiate of potash and prussian blue. Adjacent to the sticking room, are the scalding troughs, which are heated by steam. These troughs are of one thousand gallons capacity each. After being scalded, the hogs are tossed, by machinery, on to a long bench; as many persons getting to work on a hog as can get round it. One cleans out the ear, which work must be done while the hog is reeking with steam, others pull off the bristles and hair, which are thrown on the floor, others again scrape the animal. When these operations are through, his hind legs are stretched open with a stick called a gambril, and the hog is borne off by three men, two of whom carry the front part on their crossed hands, and the other seizes the gambril. The hog, thus carried to the proper place, is slung to a hook, which suspends him beyond the floor. Here the animal falls into the hands of the gutter, who tears out the inside, stripping at the rate of three hogs to the minute.

The slaughter houses of Cincinnati are in the outskirts of the city, are ten in number, and fifty by one hundred and thirty feet each in extent, the frames being boarded up with movable lattice-work at the sides, which is kept open to admit air, in the ordinary temperature, but is shut up during the intense cold, which, occasionally, attends the packing season, so that hogs shall not be frozen so stiff that they cannot be cut up to advantage. These establishments employ, each, as high as one hundred hands, selected for this business, which requires a degree of strength and activity, that always commands high wages.

The slaughterers formerly got the gut fat for the whole of the labor thus described, wagoning the hogs more than a mile to the pork houses, free of expense to the owners. Every year, however, enhances the value of the perquisites, such as the fat, heart, liver, &c., for food; and the hoofs, hair, and other parts for manufacturing purposes. For the last two years, from ten to twenty-five cents per hog have been paid as a bonus for the privilege of killing.

The hauling of hogs from the slaughter house to the packers, is itself a large business, employing fully fifty of the largest class of wagons, each loading from sixty to one hundred and ten hogs at a load.

The hogs are taken into the pork houses from the wagons and

piled up in rows as high as possible. These piles are generally close to the scales. Another set of hands carry them to the scales, where they are usually weighed singly, for the advantage of the draught. They are taken hence to the blocks, where the head and feet are first struck off, no blow needing its repetition. The hog is then cloven into three parts, separating the ham and shoulder ends from the middle. These are again divided into single hams, shoulders and sides. The leaf lard is then torn out, and every piece distributed with the exactness and regularity of machinery, to its appropriate pile. The tender-loins, usually two pounds to the hog, after affording supplies to families, who consume probably one half of the product, are sold to the manufacturers of sausages.

The hog, thus cut up into shoulders, hams and middlings, undergoes further trimming to get the first two articles in proper shape. The size of the hams and shoulders varies with their appropriate markets, and with the price of lard, which, when high, tempts the pork packer to trim very close, and indeed, to render the entire shoulder into lard. If the pork is intended to be shipped off in bulk, or for the smoke house, it is piled up in vast masses, covered with fine salt in the proportion of fifty pounds of salt to two hundred pounds weight of meat. If otherwise, the meat is packed away in barrels with coarse and fine salt in due proportions—no more of the latter being employed than the meat will require for immediate absorption, and the coarse salt remaining in the barrel to renew the pickle, whose strength is withdrawn by the meat, in process of time.

The different classes of cured pork, packed in barrels, are made up of the different sizes and conditions of hogs—the finest and fattest making clear and mess pork, while the residue is put up into prime pork or bacon. The inspection laws require that clear pork shall be put up of the sides, with the ribs out. It takes the largest class of hogs to receive this brand. Mess pork—all sides, with two rumps to the barrel. For prime—pork of lighter weight will suffice. Two shoulders, two jowls, and sides enough to fill the barrel, make the contents. Two hundred pounds of meat is required by the inspector, but one hundred and ninety-six pounds, packed here, it is ascertained, will weigh out more than the former quantity in the eastern or southern markets.

The mess pork is used for the commercial marine and the United States navy. This last class, again, is put up somewhat differently, by specifications made out for the purpose. The prime is packed for ship use and the southern markets. The clear pork goes out to the cod and mackerel fisheries. The New Englanders, in the line of pickled pork, buy nothing short of the best.

Bulk pork is that which is intended for immediate use or for smoking. The former class is sent off in flat-boats for the lower Mississippi. It forms no important element of the whole, the great mass being sent into the smoke-houses, each of which will cure a hundred and seventy-five thousand to five hundred thousand pounds at a time. Here the bacon, as far as possible, is kept until it is actually wanted for shipment, when it is packed in hogsheads containing from eight hundred to nine hundred pounds, the hams, sides, and shoulders put up each by themselves. The bacon is sold to the iron manufacturing regions of Pennsylvania, Kentucky and Ohio—to the fisheries of Pennsylvania, Maryland and Virginia, and to the coast or Mississippi region above New Orleans. Large quantities are disposed of also, for the consumption of the Atlantic cities. Flat-boats leave here about the first of July, and they all take down more or less bacon for the coast trade.

For the purpose of farther illustrating the business thus described, let us take the operations of the active season of 1847–48. There is little doubt that an estimate of five hundred thousand hogs, by far the largest quantity ever yet put up in Cincinnati, is not beyond the actual fact. This increase partly results from the growing importance of the city as a great hog-market, for reasons which will be made apparent in a later page, but more particularly to the vast enlargement in number and improved condition of hogs throughout the west, consequent on that season's unprecedented harvest of corn. What that increase was, may be inferred from the official registers of the hogs of Ohio, returned to the auditor of state as subject to taxation, being all those of, and over, six months in age. These were one million seven hundred and fifty thousand; being an excess of twenty-five per cent., or three hundred and fifty thousand hogs, over those of the previous year. Those of Kentucky, whence come most of our largest hogs, as well as a considerable share of our supplies in this article, exhibit a proportionate increase, while the number in Indiana and Illinois greatly exceed this ratio of progress.

Of five hundred thousand hogs cut up here during that season, the product, in the manufactured article, will be :—

Barrels of Pork	180,000
Pounds of Bacon	25,000,000
" Lard	16,500,000

These are the products, thus far, of the pork-houses' operations alone. That is to say, the articles thus referred to, are put up in these establishments, from the hams, shoulders, sides, leaf lard, and a small portion of the jowls—the residue of the carcasses, which are taken to the pork-houses, being left to enter elsewhere into other departments of manufacture. The relative proportions, in weight of bacon and lard, rest upon contingencies. An unexpected demand and advance in price of lard would greatly reduce the disparity, if not invert the proportion of these two articles. A change in the prospects of the value of pickled pork, during the progress of packing, would also reduce or increase the proportion of barreled pork to the bacon and lard.

The lard made here is exported in packages for the Havana market, where, beside being extensively used, as in the United States, for cooking, it answers the purpose to which butter is applied in this country. It is shipped to the Atlantic markets also, for local use, as well as for export to England and France, either in the shape it leaves this market or in lard oil; large quantities of which are manufactured at the east.

There is one establishment here, which, beside putting up hams, &c., extensively, is engaged in extracting the grease from the rest of the hog. Its operations have reached, in one season, as high as thirty-six thousand hogs. It has seven large circular tanks—six of capacity to hold each fifteen thousand pounds, and one to hold six thousand pounds—all gross. These receive the entire carcass, with the exception of the hams, and the mass is subjected to steam process, under a pressure of seventy pounds to the square inch; the effect of which operation is to reduce the whole to one consistence, and every bone to powder. The fat is drawn off by cocks, and the residuum, a mere earthy substance, as far as made use of, is taken away for manure. Beside the hogs which reach this factory in entire carcasses, the great mass of heads, ribs, back-bones, feet, and other trimmings of the hogs, cut up at different pork-houses, are subjected to the same process, in order to extract every particle of grease. This concern alone turned out, the season referred to, three millions six hundred thousand pounds lard, five-sixths of which, was No. 1. Nothing can surpass the purity and beauty of this lard.

which is refined as well as made, under steam processes. Six hundred hogs per day pass through these tanks, one day with another.

We follow now to the manufacture of lard oil, which is accomplished by divesting the lard of one of its constituent parts—stearine. There are probably thirty lard oil factories here, on a scale of more or less importance. The largest of these, whose operations are probably more extensive than any other in the United States, has manufactured, heretofore, into lard oil and stearine, one hundred and forty thousand pounds monthly, all the year round.

Eleven million pounds of lard were run into lard oil that year, two-sevenths of which aggregate made stearine; the residue, lard oil, or in other words, twenty-four thousand barrels of lard oil, of forty to forty-two gallons each. The oil is exported to the Atlantic cities and foreign countries. Much the larger share of this, is of inferior lard, made of mast-fed and still-fed hogs, and the material, to a great extent, comes from a distance, making no part of these tables. Lard oil, beside being sold for what it actually is, enters largely, in the eastern cities, into the adulteration of sperm oil, and in France, serves to reduce the cost of olive oil. The skill of the French chemists enables them to incorporate from sixty-five to seventy per cent. of lard oil with that of the olive. The presence of lard oil can be detected, however, by a deposit of stearine; small portions of which always remain with that article, and may be found at the bottom of the bottle.

We now come to the star candles, made of the stearine expressed from the lard in manufacture of lard oil. The stearine is subjected to hydraulic pressure, by which three-eighths of it is discharged as an impure oleine. This last is employed in the manufacture of soap. Three million pounds of stearine, at least, have been made, in one year, into star candles and soap in these factories, and they are prepared to manufacture thirty thousand pounds star candles per day. The manufacture of 1847–48, embracing stearine from foreign lard, probably reached one-half that quantity.

From the slaughterers, the offal capable of producing grease, goes to another description of grease extractors; where are also taken hogs dying of disease or by accident, and meat that is spoiling through unfavorable weather or want of care. The grease tried out here, enters into the soap manufacture. Lard grease is computed to form eighty per cent. of all the fat used in the making of soap. Of the ordinary soap one hundred thousand pounds are made weekly, equal, at four cents per pound, to two hundred thousand dollars per annum. This is exclusive of the finer soaps, and of soft soap, which are probably worth twenty-five per cent. more.

Glue, to an inconsiderable amount, is made of the hoofs of the hogs.

At the rear of these operations, comes bristle dressing for the Atlantic markets. This business employs one hundred hands, and affords a product of fifty-five thousand dollars.

Last of all is the disposition of what cannot be used for other purposes, the hair, hoofs and other offal. These are employed in the manufacture of prussiate of potash, to the product of which, also, contributes the cracklings or residuum left, on expressing the lard. The prussiate of potash is used extensively in the print factories of New England, for coloring purposes. The blood of the hogs is manufactured into prussian blue.

A brief recapitulation, of the various manufactures out of the hog, at this point and date, present:

TABLE—D.

Barrels Pork..........	180,000	Pounds Star Candles...	2,500,000
Pounds Bacon........	25,000,000	" Bar Soap......	6,200,000
" No. 1 Lard...	16,500,000	" Fancy Soap, etc.	8,800,000
Gallons Lard Oil......	1,200,000	Prussiate of Potash....	60,000

Five hundred thousand hogs exhibit, including seven pounds of gut-fat to each, one hundred million pounds, carcass weight, when dressed. This is distributed thus:

TABLE—E.

180,000 bbls. Pork, 196 lbs. net, is........................	35,280,000
Bacon..	25,000,000
No. 1 or Leaf Lard......................................	16,260,000
Common Lard or Grease for oil, stearin and olein...........	6,000,000
Inferior Grease for Soap.................................	1,200.000
Evaporation, shrinkage, waste, cracklings and offal for manure.	16,260,000
	100,000,000

The value of all this depends, of course, on the foreign demand. In 1847 the pork, bacon, lard, lard oil, star candles, soap, bristles, &c., exceeded six millions of dollars in value. For 1848, it had, probably, reached eight millions. But for the reduced prices which a greatly increased product always creates, it must far exceed that value.

The buildings in which the pork is put up, are of great extent and capacity, and in every part thoroughly arranged for the business. They generally extend from street to street, so as to enable one set of operations to be carried on without interfering with another. There are thirty-six of these establishments, beside a number of minor importance.

The stranger here, during the packing, and especially the forwarding season, of the article, becomes bewildered in the attempt to keep up with the eye and the memory, the various and successive processes he has witnessed, in following the several stages of putting the hog into its final marketable shape, and in surveying the apparently interminable rows of drays, which, at that period, occupy the main avenues to the river, in continuous lines, going and returning, a mile or more in length, excluding every other use of those streets, from daylight to dark. Nor is his wonder lessened when he surveys the immense quantity of hogsheads of bacon, barrels of pork, and kegs of lard, for which room cannot be found on the pork-house floors, extensive as they are, and which are, therefore, spread over the public landing, and block up every vacant space on the sidewalks, the public streets, and even adjacent lots otherwise vacant.

It may appear remarkable, in considering the facilities for putting up pork which many other points in Illinois, Indiana, Ohio, and Kentucky possess in their greater contiguity to the neighborhoods which produce the hogs, and other advantages which are palpable, that so large an amount of this business is engrossed at Cincinnati. It must be observed, however, that the raw material in this business—the hog—constitutes sixty per cent. of the value, when ready for sale, and being always paid for in cash, disbursements so heavy, are required in large sums, and at a day's notice, that the necessary capital is not readily obtainable elsewhere in the west. Nor, in an article, which in the process of curing runs great risks in sudden changes of weather, can the packer protect himself, except where there are ample means in extensive supplies of salt, and any necessary force of coopers or laborers, to put on in case of emergency or disappointment in previous arrangements. More than all, the facilities of turning to account in various manufactures, or as articles of food in a populous community, what cannot be disposed of to profit elsewhere, renders hogs to the Cincinnati packer worth at least, five per cent. more, than they will command at any other point in the Mississippi valley.

As a specimen of the amazing activity which characterizes all the details of packing, cutting, &c., here it may be stated, that two hands in one of our pork-houses, in less than thirteen hours, cut up eight hundred and fifty hogs, averaging over two hundred pounds each, two others placing them on the blocks for the purpose. All these hogs were weighed singly on the scales, in the course of eleven hours. Another hand trimmed the hams,—seventeen hundred pieces,—in Cincinnati style, as fast as they were separated from the carcasses. The hogs were thus cut up and disposed of, at the rate of more than one to the minute.

Those who are cognizant to the importance of the domestic market, will not be surprised to learn that our export of pork to foreign countries, bears but a small proportion to the quantity packed.

Few persons at the east can realize the size, and especially the fatness to which hogs arrive in the west, under the profuse feeding they receive.

The following are specimens of hogs and lots of hogs, killed in Cincinnati, this season and the last.

Hogs.	Average weight—lbs.
7	720
5	640
22	403
52	377
50	375

Of these were nine—one litter—weighing respectively, 316, 444, 454, 452, 456, 516, 526, 532.

320 hogs	325
657 "	305

Few, if any of these hogs, were over nineteen months old. The last lot is extraordinary—combining quantity and weight—even for the west. They were all raised in one neighborhood in Madison county, Kentucky, by Messrs. Caldwell, Campbell, Ross, and Gentry, the oldest being nineteen months in age.

The value of these manufacturing operations to Cincinnati, consists in the vast amount of labor they require and create, and the circumstance that the great mass of that labor furnishes employment to thousands, at precisely the very season when their regular avocations cannot be pursued. Thus, there are perhaps, fifteen hundred coopers engaged in and outside of the city, making lard kegs, pork barrels, and bacon hogsheads: the city coopers, at a period when they are not needed on stock barrels and other cooperage, and the country coopers, whose main occupation is farming, during a season when the farms require no labor at their hands. Then there is another large body of hands, also agriculturists, at the proper season, engaged getting out staves and heading, and cutting hoop poles, for the same business. Vast quantities of boxes of various descriptions, are made for packing bacon, for the Havana and European markets. Lard is also packed to a great extent, for export in tin cases or boxes, the making of which, furnishes extensive occupation to the tin-plate workers.

If we take into view, farther, that the slaughtering, the wagoning, the pork-house labor, the rendering grease and lard oil, the stearin and soap factories, bristle dressing, and other kindred employments, supply abundant occupation to men, who, in the spring, are engaged in the manufacture and hauling of bricks, quarrying and hauling stone, cellar digging and walling, bricklaying, plastering, and street paving, with other employments, which in their very nature, cease on the approach of winter, we can readily appreciate the importance of a business, which supplies labor to the industry of, probably, ten thousand individuals, who, but for its existence, would be earning little or nothing, one-third of the year.

The last United States census, gave 26,301,293, as the existing number of hogs of that date. The principal increase since, is in the west, owing to the abundance of corn there; and that quantity may be now, safely enlarged to forty-five millions. This is about the number assigned to entire Europe, in 1839, by McGregor, in his Commercial Dictionary; and there is probably no material increase there since, judging by the slow advance in that section of the world, in productions of any kind.

The number of hogs cut up in the valley of the Mississippi, will reach, for recent years, as an average, one million seven hundred thousand; of this, it will be seen, that twenty-eight per cent., or over one-fourth of the whole quantity, is put up for market in Cincinnati alone.

From a Dag^{ype} by Plumbe. by T. Doney.

D. T. Disney

MEMBER OF CONGRESS FOR OHIO

BIOGRAPHY.—DAVID T. DISNEY.

The subject of these memoirs was born in Baltimore, in August, 1803, at which place, his father, William Disney, one of our oldest citizens resided at the time. Not the least remarkable circumstance in the history of D. T. Disney, is, that he was placed at school in the third year of his age. His teacher, Luther Griffin, in a note which lies before me, observes, "In the course of my teaching, I have had several thousand scholars under my charge, and do not recollect of but one, that in every respect was equal to young Disney." In 1817, the family, including David, at that date a lad of fourteen years, removed to Cincinnati, when his father opened a shop for the sale of paints, carrying on the house-painting business also, and the youth became assistant in the store, devoting his days to the business, and his evenings to mental improvement, partly in the acquisition of general knowledge, and partly in mathematical and legal reading and study. In this last pursuit he was liberally aided by the advice and oral instruction of Charles Hammond, on whose competency in that line, it is unnecessary, in Cincinnati, to insist. Hammond was so deeply interested in the young student, as to propose a business connection between the parties; but the young man was not willing, at this time, to assume the law as a profession, and continued to aid his father at home. In 1825, he made his debut as a writer, contributing regularly to one of our eastern city journals.

In 1829, Mr. Disney, then twenty-six years of age, commenced that political career, which, with brief exceptions, constitutes the residue of this narrative. At the October election of that year, Mr. Disney ran against Elijah Hayward, for the office of representative of Hamilton County, to the General Assembly, and triumphed over his competitor, who had represented the county for a series of years. The next fall, the democratic party, on whose ticket Mr. Disney had been nominated, was defeated, owing to dissensions among themselves. In 1831, Mr. Disney was once more returned to the State Legislature. In 1832, he was again brought forward as a candidate, and succeeded in so close a struggle, that a share of the ticket on which he ran, was defeated. On this occasion W. H. Harrison, afterward President of the United States, was on the whig ticket.

At the ensuing meeting of the Legislature, Mr. Disney was elected Speaker, by a vote of sixty-two to eight, although his competitor,

Mr. Campbell, had been a distinguished member of congress. At the ensuing election of 1833, he was a successful candidate for the senate, of which, upon its meeting, he became speaker, without an opposing vote. In the senate he presided with the same ability he had exhibited in the house of representatives as speaker. A speech, on the doctrine of instruction, which he delivered at this session, contributed to make him more extensively and favorably known at home and in the other sections of our republic.

At the ensuing session, the whigs were in majority in the senate, and elected one of themselves, as speaker. But at the next—an extra session—his political friends being again in the ascendant, Mr. Disney was once more called to preside over the deliberations of the senate. At the close of that session, he was appointed one of the commissioners, on the part of Ohio, to repair to Washington city, for the settlement of the points in issue between the states of Ohio and Michigan, on which, an appeal to arms, by the parties, seemed impending. In 1840 Mr. Disney was made a member of the board of equalization, charged with the duty of equalizing the taxes of the state, among the respective counties, and, at its meeting, was unanimously chosen its presiding officer. In 1843 he was again nominated for the state senate, and, after an ardent canvass, was elected by the largest majority ever given in the district. Mr. Disney remained in private life, from 1844 to 1848, at his own desire. He was chosen by the state convention, at Columbus, held the latter year, its president, and made senatorial delegate to the national convention, at Baltimore. At the fall election, having been nominated for congress, he was elected by nearly three thousand majority. In 1850 he was re-elected to the same office without opposition, although a spirited contest marked the canvass for the residue of the tickets, on both sides.

It is confidently believed that Mr. Disney has drawn up more committee reports, during the course of his legislative life at Columbus, than any public man in the state; nor does the thorough research which marks their preparation, indicate less labor, than the mere writing them out, although this last effort is usually considered the most exhausting task, in ordinary cases.

Mr. Disney's first effort in the national legislature, was upon the power of congress over the territories. This was admitted, by common consent, for research and cogency of argument, to be the ablest speech of the session, and elicited the commendation of some of the ablest lawyers of the republic, and warm complimentary notices from all parties. His report upon the Galphin claim, has stamped that iniquitous measure with an immortality of infamy. In the face of the legal opinion of the United States Attorney-General, the house of representatives indorsed the report by overwhelming majorities. Mr. D. sustained his report by a speech of such extraordinary research, and strength, as well as clearness of argument, as to impress itself upon professional minds, in congress, as an invincible legal argument. As such, it was requested for publication; but Mr. Disney being unexpectedly summoned home, by a family bereavement, which detained him in Cincinnati several days, was unwilling to keep the subject, or himself in connection with it, any farther before the community.

One chapter on the history of David T. Disney, ought not to be left out. To him, and one or two other patriotic spirits, Texas, in its darkest hours, was indebted for the impulse given her struggle for liberty, and for aid in men, arms and munitions of war, reaching just in time to aid her in winning the battle of San Jacinto, which was fought with Cincinnati muskets, powder, cannon and cannon balls. The service thus rendered, was made at a heavy sacrifice, pecuniary and otherwise. Arraigned before our courts; amerced in a heavy penalty, which hung over him and his property thirteen years; and vilified by numbers, who would now gladly change positions with him, he has the proud consolation of having done more than any individual, out of Texas, to have accomplished the final results, which have given Mexico to our forces, and California to our territory.

No individual in congress, represents so large a constituency as Mr. Disney; the entire population of his district, exceeding one hundred and seventy thousand. If the intelligence and enterprise of that community, and the commercial, manufacturing, political and social importance of Cincinnati, be taken into view, and the fact remembered, that he obtained the position he occupies, by a unanimous vote at one of the fullest polls ever held in the district, he has just reason to be gratified at the distinction conferred by the recent choice.

STATISTICS OF STRAWBERRIES, ETC.

As Cincinnati has for several years enjoyed a high reputation for the abundance and excellence of its strawberries, the statistics of this article may be of public interest.

Four thousand bushels of this berry were raised in this vicinity, and sold in our market-houses during the season of 1845, which was rather an unusually productive one. Twenty per cent. must be added, as the quantity delivered at steamboats, hotels, private dwellings, and confectionaries, or sold at stands or agencies in various parts of the city. In 1846, this quantity was increased to four thousand two hundred bushels, with an addition of twenty-five per cent. to the sales specified above. This was a cold and wet season, and unfavorable to their growth—the increase in quantity springing from supplies afforded by newly-bearing patches, which are added every year in the vicinity. In 1847, the first ascertainment of daily sales was commenced; it has been continued in 1848, and the table follows:

1847.	Bushels.	1848.	Bushels.
May 24	10	May 19	6
25	15	20	15
26	20	22	20
27	20	23	30
28	40	24	60
29	50	25	75
31	50	26	198
June 1	296	27	313
2	250	29	211
3	50	30	450
4	249	31	589
5	489	June 1	307
7	200	2	352
8	514	3	310
9	411	5	145
10	237	6	450
11	250	7	418
12	385	8	260
14	100	9	244
15	321	10	156

1847.	Bushels.	1848.	Bushels.
June 16	220	June 12	60
17	176	13	80
18	151	14	50
19	55	15	30
21	12	16	20
22	5	17	10
	4576	19	6
			4865

In 1847 and 1848, large quantities were sent off by railroads; and for these two years, additions must be made to the quantity sold at hotels, steamboats, private dwellings, confectionaries, &c., in the consumption of strawberries on the spots where they are raised, by pleasure parties from Cincinnati and other places in their vicinity. The entire product of the strawberry, therefore, should be put down in 1847, at 6500 bushels, and in 1848, at 7000 bushels; each successive year increasing the proportion of strawberries sold directly to purchasers at their homes, &c., over that disposed of in markets.

It will be observed that the Monday of each week, exhibits lighter sales than the previous Saturday or succeeding Tuesday. In general, however, these tables present a regular ascending and descending grade of production, during the twenty-six days which ordinarily constitute the season. What disparity in supplies exists, is occasioned either by the weather being unfavorable for picking, or very heavy stocks so reduce the price, as to make the expense of gathering too great to be profitably borne at current rates of sale.

The strawberries are brought in cases of five to eight drawers; each drawer containing thirty to forty quarts, which lie an average depth of two or two-and-a-half inches. They are delivered in Cincinnati, in time for sale, as early as four to five o'clock in the morning, when disposed of at the market-houses. A considerable share are sold in tin boxes of a quart each, or wooden ones of two quarts each, which fill up the same kind of drawers. These usually command a better price, not only on account of more perfect keeping of the article, but because they measure out more than when filled into the ordinary quart measure.

In former years, they were brought in wagons. A four horse wagon was once backed up to our market, with *two tons of strawberries,* packed in cases of drawers.

We cultivate strawberries here with reference to their sexual distinctions, and find this treatment very successful.

A good pistillate or female plant, is selected, such as the Hudson or Hovey's seedling, and the plants set out in rows fifteen inches apart, and the rows about fifteen inches from each other; then a path two or three feet wide; then a row of male or staminate plants, such as will bloom about the same time as the female; and then a path as before. Then another bed of three rows of female plants, with paths and rows of male plants, until the patch is completed. The object is to keep the male plants separate from the female, so that the latter shall be impregnated without being overrun by the male. This can easily be done, by hoeing the latter when they run into the paths.

In field culture, the plants are set out in rows eighteen inches or two feet apart from each other, and a male for about every ten or twelve female plants—all in the same row. Either one or two rows are planted in this way, leaving three feet between the lands, or room enough to plow and keep them clean. They are cultivated with the plow between the lands or beds, and with the hoe in the beds, to keep down the weeds and grass.

Field culture.

The lands or beds clear across the field—beds three feet wide, then a furrow.

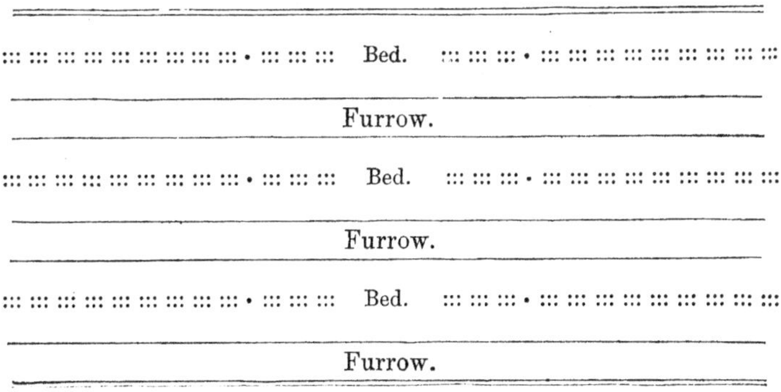

::: ::: ::: ::: ::: ::: ::: ::: ::: • ::: ::: ::: Bed. ::: ::: ::: • ::: ::: ::: ::: ::: ::: ::: ::: :::

Furrow.

::: ::: ::: ::: ::: ::: ::: ::: ::: • ::: ::: ::: Bed. ::: ::: ::: • ::: ::: ::: ::: ::: ::: ::: ::: :::

Furrow.

::: ::: ::: ::: ::: ::: ::: ::: ::: • ::: ::: ::: Bed. ::: ::: ::: • ::: ::: ::: ::: ::: ::: ::: ::: :::

Furrow.

Plants from eighteen to twenty four inches apart in a single row; every tenth plant, male.

Garden culture.

Path three feet wide.

Female bed, with three rows of pistillate or female plants.

Path.

Male bed, with one row of staminate or male plants.

Path.

Female bed, with three rows of pistillate or female plants.

Path.

Male bed, with one row of staminate or male plants.

Path.

Female bed, with three rows of pistillate or female plants.

Path.

Earliest, as in the order of ripening: 1st. Early Scarlet—tart, but high flavored—requiring much sugar. 2d. Necked Pine—highest flavored. 3d. Hovey's—sweetest variety in general culture, requiring but little sugar. 4th. Hudson—firmest and best adapted for carrying to market. There are cultivated here about as many of the latter variety as of all the first three named, or, it might safely be said, all others.

The largest berries produced at the Cincinnati Horticultural Society have been from Hovey's; but the general average of the whole crop, as to size, would probably be in favor of the Hudson.

Our horticultural society has stimulated a spirit of improvement that has afforded specimens of extraordinary size and quality otherwise. Strawberries measuring five to five and one-quarter inches in circumference, have been repeatedly exhibited at its exhibitions or fairs. In one or two instances specimens have been exhibited reaching to five inches and three-quarters in measurement.

The prices of strawberries vary, of course, with the character of the season, and the different periods of sale. They usually open at 20 to 25 cents per quart, a price which they command only for a day or two, and soon fall to 15, 12½, 10, and 8⅓ cents. When abundant, they obtain 5 to 6¼ cents, and occasionally fall to from 3 to 4 cents.

The season sales will not average higher than 7 cents, unless the season itself has proved unfavorable. No year is known in which strawberries have averaged as high as 10 cents per quart.

At least two-thirds of the strawberries sold here are raised on the banks of Licking river, a few miles above its mouth, which is just opposite Cincinnati. This affords the facility of water carriage, obviously of great advantage to the transportation of ripe fruit of a character so delicate as the strawberry. The entire quantity of ground on both sides of the Ohio which supplies this market cannot be short of two hundred and fifty acres. Much of this is in small patches of one, two, three, or five acres; the smaller the spot, in general, the more productive — proportionally — being the yield. One of the Culbertsons, a family which raises more largely of this berry than any other, has some sixty acres in three patches. One of these comprehends a field of thirty-five acres.

Just as the supply of strawberries is through, in this market, it is succeeded by that of the raspberry, which, in the course of a few years, will, probably, be raised to equal extent. At present, the supply of raspberries is about one-sixth that of strawberries. They are of various species—the cane, yellow, black, red Antwerp, and ever-bearing; of these, the red Antwerp is the general favorite. Raspberries average 8⅓ cents per quart, during the season. The raspberry culture of 1847, is as follows:

June	19	30 bush.	June	24	55 bush.	June	30	50 bush.
"	21	14 "	"	26	100 "	July	1	30 "
"	22	81 "	"	28	40 "	"	2	18 "
"	23	95 "	"	29	85 "			
								598 "

This includes only what is sold in our markets.

This article ought not to close, without reference to the moral aspect of the cultivation of these fruits, on such an extensive scale, as to bring their use within the reach of every individual, how limited soever his means.

In our Atlantic cities, and still more in Europe, these articles command a price, which denies their use to thousands whose appetites they tempt, and for whom they would form a wholesome refreshment in seasons of sickness for themselves or families. It is needless to point out the bitter feelings toward the rich, which such and other privations engender in the minds of these masses. Whatever tends to remove such distinctions in society, and place enjoyment and comfort alike within the reach of all the industrial classes, is so much gained to the general happiness of society at large. No one in Cincinnati feels that he cannot afford to buy his family everything he wishes, which is sold in its markets.

BIOGRAPHY.—G. W. COFFIN.

George W. Coffin, was born at Brownsville, Pennsylvania, November 17, 1814. His parents were from Nantucket. He resided in his native place until he reached the age of twenty-one, when he determined to change his residence to some more thriving spot. As he had a brother already in Cincinnati, he naturally directed his way to this city, where he has ever since dwelt. He engaged in the foundery of D. A. Powell, as pattern maker, at first, but after the lapse of one year, changed his employer, by taking charge of the bell foundery branch of Lyon, Thomas & Co.'s establishment; after remaining here six months, he engaged in business, with T. B. & H. B. Coffin, as bell and brassfounders, under the firm of G. W. Coffin & Co.; which firm still exists, although composed of different individuals.

Mr. Coffin is one of those ingenious men, who are constantly simplifying and improving the operations of whatever business they may be engaged in; and the bell business of this city has greatly advanced in character and extent from his labors and suggestions. His own establishment is the only one in the United States, in which bells are constructed on scientific principles, nothing being left by him to accident, in the quality and tone of the article which leaves "the Buckeye Foundery."

MEDICAL COLLEGE OF OHIO.

On the site of the existing building, which has so long borne this name, the erection of a new edifice is in process of being made, and will doubtless be completed and occupied in time for the ensuing course of lectures. A front view of the building is to be found in these pages, which may convey a correct notion of the external appearance it will present. The style of architecture is what is called the Collegiate Gothic, combining elegance and chasteness in a high degree. The front will be of brick, finished with cast-iron, painted in imitation of free-stone. The interior arrangements are such, that in adaptedness to its appropriate purposes, this building will not be second to the best college edifice in the United States.

This edifice will be of one hundred and five feet front, with a depth of seventy-five feet, and a height of fifty-five feet. The lower story on each side of the principal entrance to be occupied with stores. In the rear of these will be the library and general lecture room; this last fifty-four by forty-eight feet, and twenty-two feet in height, and lighted by a skylight twenty feet in diameter. In the rear of the lecture room, are two laboratory rooms, twenty-one feet by twelve each, which, with two in the story above, will be occupied by the Professor of Chemistry; and two rooms for the janitor; also one in the rear of the library room.

In the second story, there will be six offices to rent to physicians or other professional individuals. In the rear, on the right wing, is the museum, thirty-seven feet by forty-six, and fourteen feet high. On the third floor, in front, are to be four Professors' rooms. In the left wing will be the Anatomical lecture room, fifty-two feet in diameter, and twenty-seven feet in height; this will be lighted by a skylight fourteen feet in diameter.

On the fourth story, the front will be divided into six dissecting rooms and a room for the Professor of Anatomy. In the right wing will be the lecture room on Anatomy, thirty-nine feet in diameter, a circular amphitheatre, and twenty feet high, also lighted by skylight.

The lecture rooms will be occupied with seats, ranged in an oblong semicircular form, and rising at the same time amphitheatrically. This arrangement of seats in these lecture rooms affords every advantage alike for seeing and hearing, to the classes. The laboratory will communicate by sliding doors with the general lecture

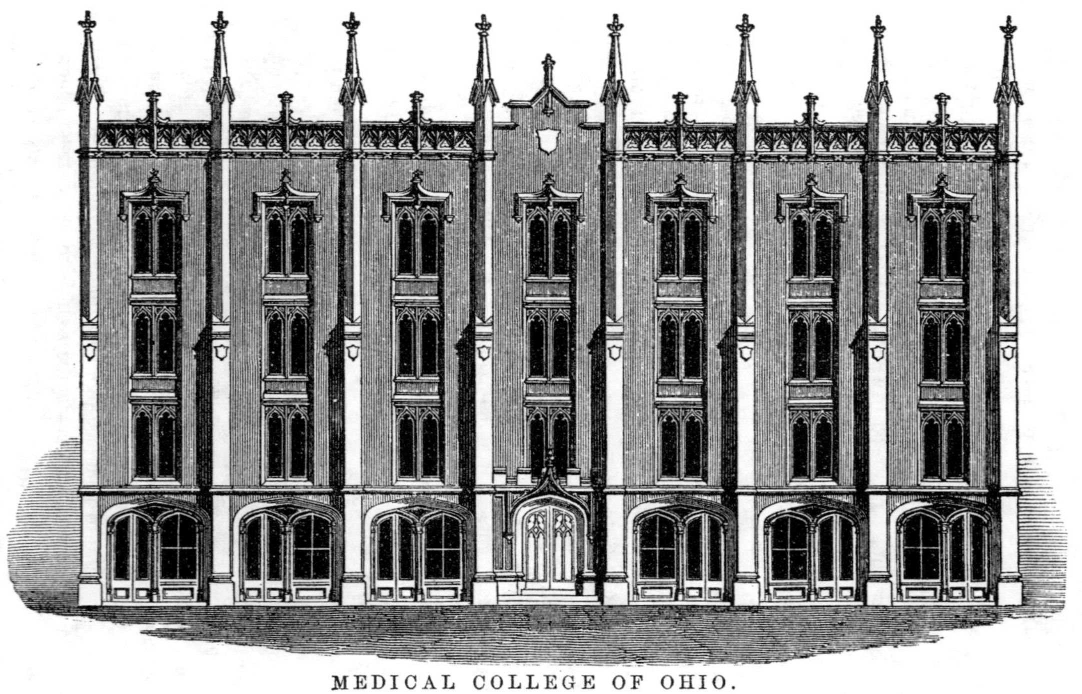

MEDICAL COLLEGE OF OHIO.

ENGRAVED BY F. E. JONES FROM A DAGUERREOTYPE.

Yours respectfully
John D Jones

room, so as to permit the Professor of Chemistry to refer to and illustrate his subjects, just as they stand in the laboratory.

Finally, the entire building is to be warmed by steam apparatus, in the basement, which will have the effect of diffusing an equable temperature throughout the whole edifice.

BIOGRAPHY.—JOHN D. JONES

WAS born December 9, 1797, in Conestoga valley, forty-five miles west of Philadelphia, and near the village of Morgantown, Berks county, Pennsylvania, where, until his 17th year, he was raised a farmer. Mr. J. is of Welsh descent, on the paternal line, his great grandfather, David Jones, emigrating to Pennsylvania in 1725. His maternal great grandfather—Graham—was from the north of Ireland, and arrived in America about the same period. Both branches were farmers, and many of their descendants took up arms during the war resulting in the establishment of American independence. Mr. Jones was engaged five years as clerk in a grocery house in Philadelphia, and came to Cincinnati in 1819, where he has resided ever since; being the only merchant here, who has been engaged in business thirty years and more. He is of the firm of J. D. & C. Jones & C.; the other members consisting of his brothers Caleb, and Michael, and his son G. W. Jones.

Mr. Jones married, in 1823, Elizabeth, daughter of the venerable John Johnston, a name long and intimately connected with the early pioneer history of Ohio. Mr. J. has been selected as an illustration of the mercantile class, and a biographical subject for this publication, as an example, if any were wanting, that application to business, sound sense, and probity, will always establish, for any individual, one of the highest positions in society—the esteem, confidence and attachment of those who know him best. If Mr. Jones has not achieved political distinction, it has resulted from the fact, that he has always had his own special mission to fulfill in the business community; and he has fulfilled it with honor to himself and family, and to the public advantage, in the lessons and example his life has given the community. Of the many individuals here, who have been successful in business, there are few who have expended so little upon their own personal indulgences, and so much in behalf of other deserving objects, public and private.

THE ELECTRO-CHRONOGRAPH.

The invention of the electro-chronograph, by Professor Locke of our city, may be properly noticed in connection with Cincinnati. This instrument being an invention in an abstruse department of science, can with difficulty be made intelligible in a popular work like this. The invention has been fully recognized in the Report of the Superintendent of the United States coast survey to congress, in 1848; by Congress itself; by the National Observatory; by the authors of the New Inventions in the United States, of 1849; and by Professor Loomis in his history of the recent improvements in Astronomy. The invention consists in such a combination of a suitable clock and electro-telegraph circuit, that the clock shall print its beats on paper or other material at the greatest distance to which telegraphic operations may be extended; at the same time permitting an observer, at any part of the circuit, to interprint his observations truly among the current time marks of the clock. Thus recording accurately and permanently the fraction of a second at which the event observed occurred. As often happens in similar cases, there has been some controversy. It has been represented that Prof. Locke had merely invented a new species of "electrical interrupter." Prof. Locke claims, however, to have invented the means, of accurately subdividing a second of time electro-telegraphically, and of making such a permanent record of this subdivision, by an observation, as greatly to improve the means of determining longitude, and accuracy of astronomical observations generally. This can be popularly understood by supposing that Dr. Locke had added a new hand to a clock, which would facilitate the subdivision and reading of a second into parts as much as the second-hand itself facilitates the accurate subdivision of a minute. The inventor did even more than this;—he not only added, in effect, this new hand, but he made it indicate the subdivision of a second at any telegraphic distance from the clock, and made it also record permanently that subdivision; the kind of electrical interrupter by which this is accomplished, is not very material. The committee, in Congress, had, upon representations made to them, that "magnetic clocks" had been before invented, stricken out the proposed appropriation to the inventor; but when they had satisfied themselves fully of the novelty and utility of the above improvement of the subdivision of the second of time, and the manner of recording the same, they restored it.

BIOGRAPHY—O. M. MITCHEL.

All men have a mission or destiny to fulfill, but all men have not the instinct to discern at the commencement of their business course, what that mission is. Happy the man who does not spend life, like Horne Tooke, in finding out that he was fitted for anything at all, rather than for what he had been all that life employed at. It was the mission of Columbus to discover a new and important continent on this earth of ours—it is the destiny of Mitchel to explore the skies, and if he should never discover a new planet, his labors and achievements thus far, in astronomical science, will secure a position among savans, of infinitely higher consequence.

O. M. Mitchel, was born in Union county, Kentucky, in July 1810. His father and mother were Virginians, who had emigrated to the west in 1800. His father died when the subject of this memoir was but two years old, leaving no property but unproductive lands. In 1816, the family removed to Lebanon, Ohio; and young Mitchel, then seven years old, commenced his education at a school. He read Latin and Greek fluently, at the age of twelve, and at thirteen, commenced the world on his own account. He entered a store at Piqua, which he left on the score of bad treatment, and started for Cincinnati. On the way, he was engaged by a merchant at Lebanon, to assist, at four dollars per month, in a new store opening at Xenia. Here he remained six months, when the store was removed to Lebanon; and here ended Mitchel's merchandising life. In 1825, he applied for, and through the assistance of Wm. McLean, member of Congress, for the Piqua district, Judge McLean, General Findley, and other members of Congress, from Ohio, obtained a cadet appointment at West Point.

Young Mitchel, less than fifteen years old at this time, immediately started off, in company with Indian traders—went with them to Upper Sandusky—thence forty miles through the wilderness, to Lower Sandusky, with an Indian guide; thence to Sandusky city in a small sloop; thence to Buffalo, deck passenger, on the old "Henry Clay;" thence on foot, with hunters, to Lockport; thence by canal, to Albany; and in June, 1825, reached West Point with a knapsack on his back, and twenty-five cents in his pocket. Here he studied, how assiduously, may be judged by his subsequent history, until June, 1829, when he graduated in the artillery corps.

In September, 1829, when only nineteen years of age, he received the appointment of assistant professor of mathematics, at the United States Military Academy at West Point, the duties of which, kept him there two years. In June, 1831, he was employed in the survey of the Philadelphia and Norristown railroad, and in the September following he married, and took charge of the survey of the Pennsylvania and Ohio railroad, which was completed, and report made in November of the same year. He then went to his post at St. Augustine—Florida, where he remained until his resignation, in June, 1832. In October, following, he came to Cincinnati, and engaged in the practice of the law, having been admitted to the bar in Florida. After practicing law for two years, in 1834, he opened a scientific school here, and in 1836, entered the Cincinnati College as professor of mathematics, philosophy, and astronomy. In 1837, he undertook the survey of the Little Miami railroad, which he finished and reported, and organized the company in six weeks.

At the college, as professor of astronomy, Mitchel had found his appropriate sphere, and his exercises there, doubtless, prepared the way for his great enterprise, the establishment of an observatory, with appropriate instruments, at Cincinnati. This was apparently as wild a project as was ever entered into by enthusiast. There was no individual beside himself, that felt much interest in the subject—no site or funds for the building, either in possession or in prospect. The whole public sentiment to sustain the enterprise had to be created, and thirty-two thousand dollars was the lowest figure required for the building and instruments. How all these means of accomplishing this great result were provided, may be discovered in the article in this volume, on the Observatory. Every man in this community, will confess, that the enterprise would have broken down in its every stage of progress, had Professor Mitchel withdrawn his hand, but for one day, from its prosecution and support.

In June, 1842, he went to Europe, and finished his studies with Professor Airy, astronomer royal, at Greenwich, England, and returned to Cincinnati, October, 1842. In 1845, the observatory building being finished, he took up his quarters there. His first observation was upon the transit of Mercury, May, 1845.

The attention of literary and scientific men at the east, being directed by these movements and results to the astronomical science of Cincinnati, Professor Mitchel has been repeatedly solicited to lecture, almost every year since, at intervals withdrawn from his observations, in our principal Atlantic cities, and at the more important towns of New England. These lectures have always commanded crowded houses of intelligent and highly interested auditors.

In October, 1848, he brought out his magnetic clock, and in the winter succeeding, surveyed the Ohio and Mississippi railroad, from Cincinnati to St. Louis. His new declination apparatus was invented, May, 1849. His first report on this machinery, was made to the American Association for the Advancement of Science, Aug., 1849, and his report of results, at its next annual session in August, 1850. A committee, of which Professor Pierce of Cambridge was chairman, was appointed by that body to examine the apparatus, which reported that the claims made in its behalf, of accuracy and facility in recording observations, had been substantiated to the entire satisfaction of every member of the committee. This report was made to the association at its recent meeting in this city, and adopted without a dissenting voice, several of the members taking occasion to compliment the professor in the highest terms.

Professor M. is engaged in prosecuting his astronomical labors with an intensity which is provoked by the important results which he feels are almost within his grasp, and to the acquisition of which, he has hitherto sacrificed offers of position and emolument elsewhere, more than adequate to his desires or his wants, and which few men in his circumstances, would have been able or willing to resist. Like all the distinguished men of the past, who have conferred honor on their places of birth or residence, but whose labors are undervalued or left unremunerated by those whom they most benefit, it will be the office of posterity to attest the value of those services to the cause of science, of which the envy of some, and the indifference of others, withholds the present acknowledgment.

If life be spared him, a bright perspective of fame, if not fortune, assuredly lies along the vista of the Professor's course. His motto for the future and for the past, will be, "Ich ersteige."

CINCINNATI—ITS DESTINY.

The law of gravitation or centralization—or as some designated it, the serial law, is now known to be one of the laws of nature. Formerly, "the major controls the minor," was a trite aphorism—regarded as almost an abstraction, and applicable to physical bodies only. The learned talked of it, especially astronomers, while descanting upon the movements of the heavenly bodies, as a law of the solar system ; it was spoken of as the law under, and in pursuance of, which, natural forces operated, such as the winds, the electrical fluids, descending bodies, etc.; but that it controlled, or affected in any manner, the results of artificial powers; or that its influence extended beyond the physical world, is a discovery wholly of modern times.

It is now known, that everything gravitates—that the larger controls the smaller, and that just in proportion to its density, ponderosity, and momentum—whether it be mentally, morally, or physically, is the lesser affected by the greater; and that when there is action—natural or artificial, it matters not—under the operations of this law will the greater influence control the lesser, exactly in the proportion they bear to each other.

The evolvement of artificial motive power, and its subjugation to the human will, which is the achievement of modern times, has elevated this *latent* law of nature to a position of first importance. The astonishing results which the steam-engine, the railroad, and the telegraph, are producing upon the world and the human condition, are such as to lead us into the shadowy future, to inquire what other and more remarkable effects are to flow from these new and great causes, operating under this law. But the mind is startled and becomes lost in its contemplation—the utmost outstretch of human penetration is baffled in its efforts, to estimate what lies before us in the immediate future. It is hardly possible even to approximate the result. Let us try it by analogy—a brief comparison with the past.

I ask to be indulged, only while I speculate upon the destinies of the western region of this continent, and more especially of our own city. Leaving the results to be produced, elsewhere, by the mighty agencies to which I have alluded to be investigated by others, my ambition will be satisfied, if I can, by analogy and comparison, foreshadow some of the consequences which may occur to our own section and people, and realize in part, what the future has in store for us.

Fifty years ago, where were we? Five millions of people inhabiting that tract of country, which lies between the eastern slope of the Alleghanies and the Atlantic ocean—with an occasional band of pioneers, who had scaled the mountains and cloven their way through the forests of the west, to some fair spots of earth on the margin of its streams, composed this nation.

It is sufficient for my purpose, that I state the condition of the country and its people, at that period, thus briefly. A few scattered settlements—a military post here and there—two or three small villages, of which this was one, surrounded by hostile savages, were all the lodgments which the white man had then made, in this now mighty region of the west. Many of the first settlers were soldiers; others had been led hither by the wild spirit of adventure, and a few, with their families, in pursuit of richer land. The suffering and privation which attended these early adventurers, are familiar histories in the families of their descendants.

Nothing distinguished the period to which I am referring, from others which preceded it, save the daring of the enterprise. The same slow movements and stagnation which characterized earlier times, attended this; the natural forces alone were operating; nothing moved by any other power.

Nations during preceding centuries had arisen, flourished and fell, scarcely crossing an imaginary boundary—cities were walled, and isolation and inertion marked the earth and its inhabitants, almost everywhere. What each produced each consumed; commerce was hardly known; a few crazy vessels on the sea, and caravans on the land, served all the purposes of trade. The mariner had no chart, and the muleteer no road; language, and laws, and customs, all differed; nothing was homogeneous; nations and people stood apart; they were estranged; their sympathies did not mingle, and hence they were enemies, and ravaged each others lands, and slew each other.

But this is a digression; let me return to the subject, and descend one decade of time. I have said that a little more of energy—of the spirit of adventure, which perhaps is a characteristic of our race, is all that distinguished the people and the period I was considering from any others that preceded them. That was our condition forty years ago. The interval exhibits progress according to the ordinary momentum. Comforts were provided under the instincts of necessity; the church, the school, the court-house, and the road, each appeared in its turn, and, having overcome the hardships of pioneer life, glowing accounts go back of happy western homes. Others are stimulated thereby, and the almost impassable road which traverses the mountain, is thronged with rude vehicles, covering the household and worldly gear of the new adventurous emigrant. Having reached the river, his own hands construct the bark with which he and his descend it, to his future home; slowly, wearily, expensively, the journey is made.

An infant commerce has sprung up, which was floated on the ark, the keel, and the barge, the history of which, is familiar to us all.

The genius of Bolton and Watt, had evolved the new motive power of steam, and this is the period at which Fitch, and Rumsay, and Fulton, had commenced applying it to its great use, but so imperfectly, that confidence in its success, was slowly and reluctantly yielded. A single steamer during that year, announced the mighty achievement to this vast western region.

Another decade—thirty years ago, where were we then? This is the period which dates an era. The magic influence of steam had been felt, and everywhere acknowledged. New life, new energy, new hope, new vitality, new action, were everywhere visible. The settlements were no longer isolated. There was the mill, the factory, the forge; all bore testimony to the new vivifying principle; but its great use in the west, was vindicated by the cheapened cost and expedition of locomotion and transportation—we had subdued the rivers and lakes, and made them subservient to our will; but looking east, there stood the frowning Alleghanies.

Let us come down another period, and then look. Twenty years ago—ah! there is the stage coach and ponderous Conestoga wagon, rolling over the scientifically built turnpike; there waves the rich harvest in the west where the forest waved ten years before; there rises the stately mansion, where the primitive cabin stood; there the opulent city, once the village site; and mark the fleets of noble steamers, which swarm our lakes and rivers.

But descend with me again—ten years ago—and where? why, we had risen to the rank of a mighty people, doubling in number the entire population when the nation sprang into being. Our voice was heard with attention in the halls of national legislation. The tide of emigration, at first feeble and slow, had now swollen and was rolling toward us in a mighty volume. The news of our wondrous march had gone booming across the water to the old world, and had stirred the nations; like bees, they had swarmed, and were emigrating. Our giant strides had astonished our eastern brethren, and they were reaching out their hands in friendly salutations. Turnpikes and canals were stretched out toward us, from all directions, with tenders of intercommunication and traffic. At a bound, we covered the land with population, from river to lake, and from lake to river. Instead of struggling feebly toward the west, as we had struggled to this point, by adding settlement to settlement, and county to county, we marshaled into line by platoons of states.

But we must pass the last decade, and then pause and meditate. *Where are we now?*

The chief feature which distinguishes this period from others which preceded it, is the clear development of that law of gravitation to which I have referred, and of the operation of the new forces under it, which the last decade has principally introduced. It will probably be known in coming time, as the railroad and telegraph period. Although the locomotive had been partially in use before, yet the full development of its capacity and uses, which has been chiefly achieved in this, will probably assign it as the one to which it properly belongs. Its claim to the telegraph is exclusive and undoubted.

It is a very difficult task to classify the various influences which mold and fashion the human condition; and it becomes doubly difficult when these influences themselves change, grow greater or less, or are disturbed by the introduction of new influences not in use before. The law of these influences can, perhaps, be made most clear by exhibiting the results of their operation, as far as they have appeared. Man, by nature, is a gregarious creature; but in the settlement of new countries, necessity and stronger instincts control this natural law; the desire for better land or health, or more comfortable provision for offspring, often draws him away from social comforts, and plants him in the wilderness. It was thus, that settlements were first made in this region of the west—isolation and dispersion characterized them; while under the pressure of more urgent wants, the emigrant felt not the discomfort of solitude; but soon these were provided for, and he longed for social intercourse. Provision for this, exhibits the operations of natural forces under the serial law. The village is the nucleus, and results from necessity; *this grows naturally in the middle of the settlement,* each one making his own road thereto. First comes the blacksmith, then the wheelwright, then the flouring-mill, then the carding machine, then the store, then the tavern, the church, &c., until its outline is completed; and there stands the village; and thus grow other villages in other settlements; it is the first circle in the serial law. Then these settlements desire intercourse one with another, so a road is made from village to village; but one improves faster than the others, some local advantage is the cause; then all the other villages construct their roads to it, and this makes the second circle. But among these villages of larger growth, one better situated than the rest advances with more rapidity, and the city soon stands in the centre of the third circle. Now, I pretend not to say, that this is the process of development always in a new country; I simply declare it to be the law, always more or less affected by neutralizing or counteracting forces.

Too much space is consumed, perhaps, in these details, but they illustrate a principle; the commercial, the monetary, and the social systems are controlled by the same law; they all operate in circles; and to save further time in elaboration, the reader is trusted, to run out the parallel.

We now come to the great disturbing forces, which have come into use within the past ten years, the railroad and the telegraph. Measuring by time, we are nearer to Boston now than we were to Columbus, in this state, at the latter period; this is the difference in actual locomotion, measuring by time; and as to mental communica-ation, it is now instantaneous, whereas at that time, the process consumed many days. These are the first great results which strike us—the almost entire annihilation of space by the one, and of time by the other.—In the one case the circle is widened in proportion as the distance from this to Columbus bears to the distance from this to Boston; while in the other, it is blotted out altogether, and the circle indefinitely widened or as far as the wires extend. The entire relationships of the country—its business, its monetary operations, its social intercourse, its values and productions,—even its fashions and tastes—if not wholly revolutionized, are very greatly changed. A bushel of wheat is worth more to-day, on the land which produces it, in the centre of Ohio, by fifty per cent., than the same article was worth, relatively, at the same point ten years ago. *This is the case now*—and with reference to social intercourse, thirty years ago an individual in Boston, designing to visit Cincinnati, arranged his business and took leave of his friends, preparatory to making a long and fatiguing journey; while now he deems it scarcely of sufficient importance to mention such a trip, even to his family.

It is not possible to estimate with entire accuracy the ultimate effects which the new influences we are considering, are to produce on our condition. We can, as I have said, only approximate them. Their introduction into our region is so recent, and the effects so few, that reliable conclusions cannot be drawn therefrom. By applying the law of the circles, we may be much aided in our conclusions. I have shown that with reference to that main element, time, the circle is extended so as to embrace Boston, that reached but to Columbus before.

The railroad is a costly structure, and therefore, unsuited to the isolated neighborhood — its true and legitimate use is the extended trunk line between great points, furnishing large amounts of travel and transportation. In the first experiments with this medium of intercommunication, efforts were made to bend and mold it so as to suit existing interests; but the instincts of capital soon discovered that the advantages of straight lines and easy grades, more than counterbalanced any which could be furnished by the way-side; so local interests are left at this time to adjust themselves to the new and more important interests. This seriously disturbs and interferes with the neighborhood village interests. The first circles may be said to be almost broken up, and their weight and influence, in business points of view, transferred to the intersection points, or termini of the great lines; where the railroad is in more extended use than here, this effect is much more apparent. But while this effect is produced on the neighborhood village, another class is found to start into successful and rapid existence, the centralizing tendency of the railroad, which brings large cities into being, carries along with it the suburban town, and the manufacturing village. It classifies the uses of things. The cheapness and rapidity of locomotion brings the homes of people ten, twenty, or thirty miles away from their business, as close as they were, by former modes of locomotion, at one or two,—and the products of the workshops at Lowell are as near the sale-room in Boston now, as they formerly were at Chelsea or Cambridge, although the first is forty miles away, and the others but two or three.

The large cities of the east and south have been and are still engaged in a vigorous struggle for the business of the west. The utmost ability of each has been, and is, at this moment being exerted in the construction of trunk lines of railroad of the best class reaching toward the western valley. This is being done under the influence of the serial law; each city is aiming to extend the circle of its business and influence, and each is achieving it. They are competing cities of the same grade of circles. *The next circle beyond is a central city—a city which shall have all these cities as satellites or outposts — Where shall that city stand?* Will my reader take a map, and trace with me the lines of the great trunk roads, as they will appear upon it? In the first place, if he will trace the coast-line from Boston to New Orleans, he will find that cutting across the Florida peninsula, it forms a crescent or semicircle. The road lying highest north, which touches Buffalo, may be denominated the Boston road, and comes first. This road, which has been some time in operation, has produced important results, although, for the want of competition, not those of speed and cheap transportation, it possesses the ability to yield. Then comes the New York and Erie; a magnificent work, just about being put into use. These roads connect with the Cleveland and Sandusky roads, reaching to Cincinnati by a short lake navigation—soon to be superseded by a direct connection along the lake shore. Next south, we have the Philadelphia road, stretching west, and connecting,—about November next,—with the Cleveland, at Gallion, some sixty miles south of Cleveland. Then comes the Baltimore road, to be completed during the ensuing year, to connect with this city, in almost a direct line, and without any water connection, by way of Belpré, in this state.

Let us pause here, and examine the probable effects of these four lines of communication. Here are four trunk roads each terminating at a great commercial point on the Atlantic sea-board. Now, leaving out of view the termini, here are four competitors for business, lying so far apart, and running through such distant districts of country, that a union of their interests, for the purpose of a monopoly, would seem totally out of the question. The manner of their construction forbids it; individual, corporate, and state interests are so interwoven, that a union for that purpose seems impossible. But then come in the cities which lie at the eastern termini—these cities have contributed largely in the construction of these works; their outlays were made—not for the revenues which the roads might yield, but for the purpose of securing business. Is there then, I ask, any possibility of a union, for the purpose of monopoly?

Then what will be the effect upon transportation and travel? I confidently predict that within five years—certainly within ten—passengers will be transported from Cincinnati to the Atlantic seaboard, and *vice versa,* for the sum of five dollars, and merchandise in the same proportion; and if the business of the road will not justify these reductions, the deficiency will be supplied by the cities at which they terminate. The next effect will be a general reduction on the margin of profit in commercial operations—a system of cut-under, will be pursued between the several eastern cities, until each will find its interest served by going nearer to the market of consumption of their wares with branch commercial houses. A new distributing point will be established, where their customers can resort, and save a journey to the east.

The next, or a cotemporaneous result, will be a reduction of the margin of profit to the manufacturing interest; indeed, at this time this effect is being rapidly evolved; competition does it. Ingenuity is at this time most effectively stimulated in the development of new principles in mechanics and chemistry;—daily and hourly almost, are new inventions being displayed, throwing out of use old machinery, and old modes of combination—the economies of the workshop — the close working of material — the methodizing of labor—and the perfecting of skill, by assigning to the operative a distinct part of the work—all at this time are operating to cheapen the cost of production down to its lowest possible point. A Yankee clock is now produced for sixty cents, that formerly cost three dollars; and Collins produces a better axe, to day, for seventy cents, than he previously did for a dollar and a half. When a point is reached, below which the producer cannot go, and live, what is the next move?—He must seek cheaper food—expenses must be lessened.—How is this to be done?—By going where the food is produced, and thus saving the cost of its transportation. The operative must emigrate, and now he *can* emigrate, for the cost of locomotion has declined as his labor has declined in value. The beginning of this movement shuts up nearly all the workshops of New England; for a margin of profit here, which leaves none there, will oblige all to emigrate whether willing or not, or give up the business.

The next great effect will be, the general up-rising of the labor class in agriculture—the tenant farmers at the east. The federal government promises cheap land soon; indeed, its enactments already make it cheap; one hundred dollars now buys as much land as two did formerly, and the prospect is, that it will still be less. What is the difference, intrinsically, between the value of land in this valley, and land of the same quality, east of the Alleghenies?—I can see none, but the cost of placing its surplus product at the same shipping point with the product of eastern land. Will the population then, not emigrate, if the land costs fifty dollars in the one section, and fifty cents in the other? cheap food is the great human want and this is the cereal region. Is it extravagant to say that under the influences which soon will conspire to invite settlers to our western lands, that this valley will contain twenty millions of inhabitants at the end of the next decade?

But let us take up the map again — other railroads from the Atlantic shore, point in this direction, and others again from the Gulf of Mexico. A road from Charleston, already penetrates the interior, until it passes the south-western boundary of South Carolina; so also does one leading from Savannah in Georgia; these roads connect and form the Chattanooga; which at this moment is being finished rapidly in the direction toward Knoxville and Nashville; both will probably be completed within the ensuing eighteen months. Then there is the road from Mobile to Cairo, at the junction of the Ohio and Mississippi rivers, and thence to Chicago, to which alternate sections of land, three sections deep on each side, have been dedicated by the general government. One section of this road is already contracted to be built, and the probabilities are that the others soon will be. Then there is the New Orleans road, by way of Jackson, Mississippi, and Florence, Alabama, in the direction of Nashville—a donation of land similar to that made to the Mobile and Chicago road, has been asked for this from the general government, and will be granted, probably, at the next session of Congress, which will undoubtedly secure its construction. Then there is the St. Marks road, leading from Apalachicola in Florida, which crosses the western section of that state, and leads up through western Georgia; a similar grant of land is asked for this, and will undoubtedly be made. Then there is the road from Memphis, leading in a north-easterly direction through the southern tier of counties in Tennessee, in the direction of Abingdon in Virginia—and points one branch by way of the valley of Shenandoah to Harper's Ferry, and another toward Richmond and Norfolk. A large portion of this line is under contract and progressing with great rapidity toward completion. This road crosses all the roads I have enumerated, which point from the south and south-west in this direction. A road is now in process of construction from this point to Lexington, in Kentucky, and another from the latter point to Danville, in the direct line to Knoxville, leaving, perhaps, one hundred miles to make the connection between those two points; another line is also in process of construction from Nashville to Louisville, by way of Bowling Green, leaving a hiatus of probably one hundred and twenty miles to connect Bowling Green with Lexington—but say that this connection shall not be made—we still have railroad connection with Louisville by two routes, the one by way of Lexington and Frankfort, the other by way of the Jeffersonville road, running to the Ohio and Mississippi road.

We will pause again, and take another survey. Here are six more great trunk roads; three leading from the Atlantic sea-board, and three from the Gulf of Mexico, all pointing toward this city, from Norfolk, Charleston, Savannah, St. Marks, Mobile, and New Orleans. When these roads are completed, we shall be in connection with each of these points, by two days of travel. It is well known that the sea-board cities of the south and south-west, have not given up the contest for at least a portion of the foreign commerce. They say, and say truly, that their region furnishes much the largest portion of the export trade of the nation, and that the import trade has been diverted from them by causes which are yet entirely within their control. Ship building has been carried on principally at the north, while the south furnishes the material. The north has been most active in penetrating the interior with thoroughfares, while the south possesses the same facilities for doing so, but has not. The south has been lulled into security by her reliance on natural thoroughfares; she has now awoke, and is preparing to resume the contest. Already do we hear of lines of ocean steamers, from Norfolk, Charleston, and Savannah, to ply between those cities and some of the ports of Europe. While New Orleans now enjoys, and will doubtless continue to enjoy, much the largest portion of the Gulf, the West India, and the South American trade.

The cities of Norfolk, Charleston, and Savannah, were they provided with suitable inland connections, would undoubtedly enjoy many advantages over cities situated farther north, in conducting a European commerce. In addition to furnishing the largest proportion of our exports, they have the advantage of a milder climate, enabling the sea voyager to reach their ports during the inclement winter months in greater safety. Railroad connections through to the cereal region of the free states, at the same charge for fare, as by the northern routes, would undoubtedly, through the inclement months of the year, at least, secure a vast amount of the emigrant travel from Europe. The reason of this, is plain—the tonnage required to transport the cotton, tobacco, etc., from the Atlantic planting states, now comes in, in ballast; whatever, therefore, could be added from this source, would be net gain. Will not, then, these roads from the south and south-west, be pushed through to their legitimate termini, with all possible expedition; and will they not, when so completed, engage at once, in the contest for western business?

Another inducement, to push with energy these works to completion, is found in the facilities they would afford the south and south-west, in the procurement of the supplies which they now derive by circuitous routes from this region, and the readiness with which they could return us their raw material to be worked up in our manufacturing establishments. The advantages to both sections, that would result, are of an importance difficult to estimate.—Contemplate, for a moment, the new facilities and vast increase of business that must result, from a connection with this great web-work of southern railroads. Ours is a climate in which the human energies can be employed for the longest period of the year, perhaps, with the least exhaustion of any other on the continent; where the highest average health is enjoyed; it possesses an almost unlimited amount of natural motive power; it is the centre of one of the best mineral regions on the globe, with inexhaustible coal-fields; it is the region where subsistence is produced in the greatest abundance, perfection, and variety, and where every element of raw material is found in the greatest abundance. Is it too much, then, to say, that for manufacturing purposes of every variety, it has not its superior, if equal, at any point on the face of the globe? Will the southern region, then, not be greatly benefited by being enabled to procure their implements, their subsistence, and all other necessary supplies by these expeditions and economical avenues? And will not this region, also, find its interests greatly benefited by this new market for the products of its labor, as well as in the cheapened cost at which it can derive that important raw material, cotton?

But the effect of greatest magnitude, by far,—the one that shall startle both sections of the country, when it shall come into use, as in my judgment, it certainly will, remains yet to be considered.

I have undertaken to show, and think I have shown, that the influx of population to engage in agriculture in the western region, owing to the cheap land and cheap locomotion, will be sudden and vast—beyond the ability of the most sagacious to estimate, so soon as the causes which I have enumerated, shall be in full operation. Instead of coming by thousands, as they now do, they will then come by tens of thousands.

The time consumed in seeding, tending, and harvesting the cereal crops, embraces but about half the year; if not in idleness then during the remainder of it, the laborer has to seek other employment than on the land. The grain crop is sown and gathered, during the months of April, May, June, July, August, September, and part of October; this includes corn. The cotton crop is seeded in the spring, and gathered during the late fall and winter months. Now let the great reduction take place, which I predict in the cost of locomotion; let the passage between this and the city of Charleston come down, as I predict it will, to five dollars, and to intermediate points in the same proportion; and let the time consumed in the trip be within my estimate, say thirty-six hours to Charleston, who will gather the cotton crop? What becomes of slavery and slave labor, when these *northern hordes* shall descend upon the fair fields of the sunny south? No conflict, no interference with southern institutions need be apprehended; the unemployed northern laborer will simply underwork the slave during the winter months, and when the crop is gathered, return to his home. It is known that the labor required to gather the cotton crop, as compared with that to plant and tend, is, as about four to one; that is, one man can plant and tend as much as four will pick. Let half a million or a million of men pass over a railroad twice a year for this purpose, even at a cheap rate of fare, what an item of revenue does it furnish. The English harvest is generally gathered by Irish laborers, many hundred thousands of whom, cross the channel annually for that purpose.

Let us return once more to the map.

We have yet to show what part the great west and north-west have to perform in this centralizing operation. The first road which claims our attention, is the Ohio and Mississippi, leading from here to St. Louis, and indefinitely beyond. This is the trunk road commencing at Baltimore, and stretching on the same line of latitude across toward the west through Cincinnati, which I regard as the most important on the continent. I do not anticipate with much confidence, the speedy realization of Mr. Whitney's project, which is to pass the commerce of Asia and Europe across this continent, somewhere about this line of latitude; but I do expect that some line of communication by railroad, will be gradually constructed toward the Pacific Ocean, by the way of *El Paso del Norte;* and I quite incline to the opinion, that this will be that road. I think so, for the reason, that El Paso is said to be the only practicable pass of the mountain, and that this appears to be the only practicable road between this and that point. St. Louis thinks so, and has commenced the work beyond her. But leaving out of view anything beyond St. Louis, it is a vastly important road, the most so, perhaps, of any in the west. It must concentrate an amount of business to pass over it—and for a time, probably, through this city, of astonishing magnitude. Beside the through business, it must tap the river travel at Cairo, and pass it entire almost over this line. This single item, according to the estimate of good judges, will pay ten per cent., upon the entire cost of the work. Fifteen hours, will be the probable time between St. Louis and Cincinnati. In the direction of the north-west from this city, we have three lines pointing; two of which, are already far advanced toward completion, to wit: the one by way of Lawrenceburgh to Indianapolis; the other, by way of Hamilton, Eaton, and Richmond. From Indianapolis, branch roads radiate to the west, north, and north-west, so as to pass to and over almost every important region in those directions, upon many of which, the work of construction is rapidly progressing. One points to Michigan City, lying on the south-eastern bend of Lake Michigan, and another to Chicago, on the south-western, while others reach west in the direction of Alton and Rock Island, on the Mississippi. From Chicago, a road is far advanced toward completion, in the direction of Galena and Dubuque, the greatest lead region of the world, perhaps, and another to Milwaukie, on the western shore of Lake Michigan. That this latter road will be made, I regard as certain; because it is absolutely necessary, and its further extension in the direction of the north-west, until it shall strike the copper region on the southern shore of Lake Superior, I regard as equally certain, for the same sufficient reason. In the first place, it will be observed, that this great section of our country, is situated in a high northern latitude, and that having no mode of communicating other than by water, it is ice-bound for a large portion of the year, and navigation necessarily suspended. The people west of Lake Michigan, of Upper Michigan, of Wisconsin, of Iowa, and Northern Illinois, embracing one of the finest grain and mineral regions on the continent, are isolated—totally cut off from all communication with other portions of the country, for at least five months of the year, owing to this cause; and the only practicable connection which can be made, either with the east or south, is by passing around the southern bend of Lake Michigan. Lakes cannot be crossed by railroads; you must go round them. The people of the eastern cities have long had their eyes on this very important fact, and hence their efforts to reach Chicago, by way of the Erie lake shore, and across the peninsula of Michigan, with their railroads. But we are as nearly ready to connect with Chicago as they; and when these connections are made, what direction will business take? In the first place, we are in the enjoyment of a clear margin, of at least, half a cent per pound, over our eastern neighbors, on all necessaries of southern production, such as sugar, molasses, coffee, etc., which are required in the region we are considering. The cost of placing those articles on our landing, by way of the river, when we shall have the impediment removed from the navigation at the Falls of the Ohio, which will allow a suitable class of boats to navigate our southern waters, will not exceed fifteen cents per hundred, and the cost, hence, to the lake, by canal or railroad, will not exceed twenty cents. Now the cost on the same articles for transportation, delivered at the city of New York, coastwise, will be fully that sum; say thirty-five cents per hundred, and the transportation to the shore of Erie and Michigan, are yet to be provided for, which cannot certainly be less than fifty cents per hundred. These articles are the leaders, as they are called, in commercial transactions, with the west. Then there is our iron, glass, machinery implements, utensils, etc., all furnished at this point, cheaper than from the east, with an extensive market for the products of this north-western region. I ask, then, where will the trade go?

I now bring my survey of the railroad influences—those which now exist, and those in prospect—which are so materially to affect the destinies of Cincinnati, to a close. Had time and space allowed, many others, as well as other radiating points, would have been passed in review; but as I have said, the reader is trusted to trace and apply their influence.

This examination exhibits fourteen great trunk roads, radiating to every point of the compass, and each one terminating at either a great commercial point on the sea-board, or in a mineral or agricultural region, with all their influences converging to this centre. Our river connections, canals, and turnpikes, are not embraced, they being in use before. Nor have I alluded to the scientific, the social, the artistic, or the philanthropic influences, all of which operate under the same law of the spheres, in circles rising to the climax, which must centralize somewhere; and the political, monetary, and commercial so imperfectly, that I fear their weight in the scale, will not be appreciated. The great cities of the old world were the growth of centuries, each under the influence of some great, but sluggish force. Vienna, Berlin, and St. Petersburg, are forced cities, built under the iron rule of despotism, to decay, doubtlessly, upon the overthrow of arbitrary power. Fashion and taste, combined with national pride, built Paris. "Paris is France," because France yields everything for her greatness. Diplomacy, backed by the navies of England, built London. The statesmanship which centralized there, became the arbiter in continental quarrels, and constituted her the highest point of political influence; and capital, which is always timid, took shelter under the double guarantee of her political wisdom and physical power. This capital has so aggregated, that it controls the world's monetary affairs, and now defies all the influences which threaten London. And New York—what built her? without doubt, it was her commerce—carried on mainly through foreign agencies. The legitimate imports of a country, are made by cities lying nearest the consumers; but the forced trade, that is, the portion which comes not upon order, but is the unsold stock of the manufacturer, to be forced without limit—goes to the most noted sale point. New York had been made so before, by being the factor for New England; and hence the centralization of foreign agencies at that point; but when a more central distributing point offers, where go these agencies? But I think I have said enough to show that Cincinnati is the grand centre of the United States, not geographically, perhaps, but the centre of the forces and influences, which, when readjusted after the introduction of the great disturbing cause, the railroad, must settle and determine the destiny and relative position of the various cities or centres, which are now struggling for supreme ascendency on this continent.

BIOGRAPHY—GEORGE W. NEFF.

George W. Neff, was born at Frankford, a village near Philadelphia, on the 19th day of May, 1800. He was the youngest son of Peter and Rebecca Neff, and lost his father when only four years of age, and was left under the care of a pious mother, who early instilled into his mind, those principles of religious truth, which ripened into fruit of later years. At the village school he was instructed in the rudiments of a plain English education, and when twelve years of age, was sent to Basking Ridge, New Jersey, where he remained for several years, in the family of Mr. Southard, father of the late Hon. Samuel L. Southard, whose kindness made a lasting impression on his heart, and whose memory he ever cherished with filial regard. Mr. Finley, afterward the Rev. Dr. Finley, had charge of the academy at Basking Ridge, and fitted young Neff for the junior class at Nassau Hall, Princeton, New Jersey, which he entered in 1816, and where he graduated with distinguished honor in 1818, in the largest class that had ever passed through the college. He was also a member of the "Clio" society, which presented him with a gold medal, on his retiring. Soon after he left the college, he commenced the study of the law, with the Hon. Horace Binney, in Philadelphia, and was admitted to practice in 1821, and attended to the duties of his profession in Philadelphia, for three years, exhibiting talents, that in due time would have won for him a proud position as an advocate. More alluring prospects of wealth, were presented to him in the west, where his brothers were about establishing a mercantile firm. He became a partner with them in trade, and in 1824, removed to this city, where he resided during the remainder of his life. His public spirit and enterprising benevolence, became soon manifest, and every judicious project for the improvement of the city, found in him a warm friend and zealous advocate.

He founded the present fire department of the city; was the originator of the fire association, and its first president; and was the first president of the Independent Fire Engine and Hose Co.—Rovers—also of Independent Fire Co., No. 2.

He was the first president of the Little Miami Railroad Co. He drew up the charter of the Fireman's Insurance Co., and had it passed; and was the president from its foundation, until his death. He was for many years a director in the Lafayette bank; was president of the city council for a series of years, and took a warm interest in the various plans formed from time to time, for increasing the business and developing the resources of Cincinnati.

Deliberate in forming an opinion, he was not backward in avowing it; firm in maintaining his sentiments, he had the ability to present his thoughts in the most striking manner to the minds of others.

He was for many years, and until his death, a trustee in Lane Seminary, at Walnut Hills. He aided greatly in establishing Spring Grove cemetery. About three years before his death, a severe illness gave a shock to his system, from which, he never entirely recovered; although his health was tolerably good until a few months prior to his death, a severe attack of jaundice terminated in dropsy, and after an illness of about five months, the latter part of it at the Yellow Springs, in this State, he departed this life, on the 9th of August, 1850. His remains were brought to the city, and, although, at a time, when there was so much sickness, that nearly all his intimate friends were absent from Cincinnati, his funeral was one of the largest that our city has ever witnessed, the firemen all turning out, and on a very short notice; and having their different alarm bells tolled during the procession. His remains were deposited in *Spring Grove cemetery, where he had a beautiful lot.*

The "Independent Fire Co.," as a testimony of respect, appointed a committee, and had a lithograph likeness taken from a daguerreotype. These portraits are the basis of that which may be found in this volume.

SHIP BUILDING ON THE OHIO.

There has always been more or less, ship and steamboat building and finishing, here; but this business involves large disbursements in advance; and a deficiency, at Cincinnati, of bank capital and bank accommodations, which exist abundantly at other places, has induced many steamboat owners to build elsewhere. On these accounts, we are not building and finishing as many steamboats as in former years; but the construction and equipment of ship vessels, which had been commenced years ago, at Marietta and other points, seems likely to become a permanent, and finally, an extensive business, at this, and some other points on the Ohio.

Within the last six years, the barque Muskingum, burthen 350 tons, was built at Marietta, and being loaded at Cincinnati, made a voyage to Liverpool. Her arrival there was thus noticed in the Liverpool Times, of the 30th January, 1845:

"*Arrival direct from Cincinnati.*—We have received a file of Cincinnati papers, brought by the first vessel that ever cleared out at that city for Europe. The building of a vessel of 350 tons, on a river seventeen hundred miles from the sea, is itself a very remarkable circumstance, both as a proof of the magnificence of the American rivers, and the spirit of the American people. The navigating of such a vessel down the Ohio and the Mississippi, and then across the Atlantic, would, a few years ago, have been thought impossible. She brings a cargo of provisions; and we trust, that the success of this first adventure, will be such as to encourage its frequent repetition. The name of the vessel is the Muskingum."

The building of the Muskingum was followed by that of various others; and John Swasey, of the firm of J. Swasey & Co., a public spirited citizen here, has taken a deep interest in, and as rank a hold of this subject, as any individual can do, whose active capital is embarked in other business pursuits. The following letter was written by that firm, in answer to inquiries made of them by the author of "Cincinnati in 1851," and affords an intelligent view of this enterprise, so deeply interesting to the west.

"In regard to the building of sea-going vessels at this point—Cincinnati—our experience convinces us that the business can be carried on here to as good advantage as in any of the eastern cities, and at less cost than vessels of equal quality can be built anywhere on the sea-board. Within the last eighteen months, we have built and completed three vessels; one full-rigged brig, the Louisa, of 200 tons, and two barques, the John Swasey and Salem, of 300 and 350 tons, measurement burthen. The Louisa and John Swasey took in full cargoes at this port for Salem and Boston, proceeded down the river, in tow of Steamers, for New Orleans, with battened hatches and royal masts on end, and put right out to sea, stopping at New Orleans only long enough to bend sails and ship a crew. These craft have proved themselves fine vessels and fast sailers. The Louisa lately returned to Salem from a six months' trading voyage to the west coast of Africa; and the Captain reports her sailing and weather qualities to be of the highest order. The last named vessel, the Salem, which was launched about a month ago, left this port light, in the expectation of being able to procure, at

New Orleans, a profitable freight, for California, eastern ports, or Europe. Three years ago, we built at Marietta, on the Muskingum, two schooners, the Grace Darling and Ohio, of 150 tons burthen; both of these vessels we loaded at this port, with provisions and other produce for Salem. These vessels have ever since been engaged in the African trade, and are in no respect behind any vessels of their class. About three years ago the Minnesota, a ship of 850 tons burthen, was built at this place, for Captain Deshon, of New Orleans, by Messrs. Litherbury & Co. She was intended for the cotton carrying trade, but has since made several voyages to different parts of the world, and proved herself a good ship. We are now getting out the timber for another ship of 350 tons, to be built at Covington, and ready to launch in the early part of next fall. The timber for this vessel we procure from the neighborhood of Point Pleasant, on the Kanawha.

"There is nothing to prevent vessels built on the Ohio river, being equal in every respect of material, model, construction, &c., to vessels built in any of the eastern cities, or elsewhere. The principal advantage we have, consists in the abundance of excellent oak timber, with which the country on both sides of the Ohio abounds; and an incidental advantage in the certainty of being able to obtain, at this place, a full cargo of provisions, breadstuffs, &c., for eastern ports or Europe, at any time during the winter season.

"The disadvantages consist in the obstruction to navigation at the Falls of the Ohio, and in being able to get out when loaded, only at high stages of the river. There are other minor disadvantages, which, as the business increases, will be done away with altogether, such as being obliged to procure from the east, a number of articles necessary in the full equipment of the vessels."

Eastern ship-builders are also becoming interested in this subject. In a letter dated from this city to his friends at home, a practical ship-builder from the state of Maine, says,—"I have now been engaged in ship building, upon the margin of the Ohio river, for the last two years. I have built two barques and a brig, and have another on the stocks. I find timber abundant, of good quality, of easy access, and the cost not one-fourth of New York prices; copper, iron, and cordage, at eastern prices—rents and boarding, far below. Ship plank, worth forty dollars per thousand in New York, are placed upon the banks of the Ohio from five to eight dollars. Floor timbers, worth in New York forty-five cents per cubic foot, are here furnished

ENGRAVED BY E E. JONES FROM A DAGUERREOTYPE

for seven to ten cents; and so of knees and other products of the forest."

With these facts before them, the lumbermen and the ship builders of New York have not been sleeping on their posts. A committee has been dispatched to secure the most eligible site for an extensive ship-building community, or colony, from New York. This committee have in part discharged their duty by the purchase of twenty-five square miles of territory, clothed with millions of the most valuable timber, and possessing numerous advantages which will be set forth by a report, now soon to be laid before the stockholders.

The forests of white oak, interspersed with groves of yellow and hard pine, in the Kanawha and Big Sandy region, will furnish, for years to come, a sufficient supply to build the navies of the world.

NEW PUBLIC BUILDINGS.

A NUMBER of buildings for various purposes of a public character, are in process of erection, or will shortly be commenced. Among these, are the German Protestant Orphan Asylum, and the Widows' Home, on Mount Auburn; an Engine house, on Vine, near Front street; public school houses in the Eleventh and Twelfth wards, and on Mount Adams; a spacious Hotel, on the corner of Walnut and Sixth street, and another at the corner of Front and Broadway; an Episcopal church on Sycamore street, north of the canal; St. John's—Episcopal, corner of Plum and Seventh streets; First Presbyterian church, Fourth, near Main street, and Seventh Presbyterian church, Broadway, between Fourth and Fifth streets. These last three, will be magnificent structures, internally and externally. A City Hall is expected to be shortly put up, on Plum, between Eighth and Ninth streets; as also, a spacious building for the United States public offices here, such as the custom-house, depository of public moneys, and post-office, at the south-west corner of Fourth and Vine street. A new county court-house, with public offices, has been commenced, on a scale and in conformity to a plan, which justifies the expectation that it will prove an ornament to Cincinnati.

ST. PETER'S CATHEDRAL.

This fine building, belonging to the Roman Catholic Society, is completely finished, excepting the portico in front, after being ten years in progress of construction; and is worthy of all the labor and expense it has cost, as an architectural pile and an ornament to our city. It is the finest building in the west, and the most imposing, in appearance, of any of the cathedrals in the United States, belonging to the Roman Catholic church, the metropolitan edifice in Baltimore not excepted.

St. Peter's Cathedral is a parallelogram of two hundred feet in length, by eighty in breadth. It is fifty-five feet from floor to ceiling. The roof is partly supported by the side walls, which, as well as the front, average four feet in thickness, but principally upon eighteen free-stone pillars, nine on each side, which are of three-and-a-half feet diameter and thirty-three feet in height. The ceiling is of stucco-work, of a rich and expensive character, which renders it equal in beauty to that of any cathedral in the world, as asserted by competent judges, although executed, in this instance, by J. F. Taylor, a Cincinnati artist, for a price less than one-half of what it would have cost in Europe. The main walls are built of Dayton marble, of which this building furnishes the first example in Cincinnati. The basement is of the blue limestone of the Ohio river, and forms an appropriate contrast with the superstructure. The bells, not yet finished, which will be a chime of the usual number and range, played by machinery, such as is employed in musical clocks, are in preparation for the edifice. The steeple is two hundred and twenty-one feet in height. The cathedral is finished with a centre aisle of six feet, and two aisles for processional purposes, eleven feet each, adjoining the side-walls. The residue of the space forms one hundred and forty pews ten feet in length. The roof is composed of iron plates, whose seams are coated with a composition of coal-tar and sand, which renders it impervious to water.

An altar of the purest Carrara marble, made by Chiappri, of Genoa, occupies the west end of the Cathedral. This is embellished with a centre piece, being a circle with rays, around which, wreaths and flowers are beautifully chiseled. It is of exquisite design and workmanship. At the opposite end, is put up an immense organ, of forty-four stops and twenty-seven hundred pipes, lately finished bv

Schwab, of our city, which cost $5,400. One of these pipes alone is thirty-three feet long, and weighs four hundred pounds. There is no doubt, that this is an instrument superior in size, tone and power, to any on this continent.

The following paintings occupy the various compartments in the Cathedral:

St. Peter liberated by the Angel.

Descent from the Cross.

Annunciation of the Blessed Virgin.

St. Jerome in the attitude of listening to the trumpet announcing the final judgment.

Christ in the Garden.

Flight into Egypt.

The St. Peter is by Murillo, well known as the head of the Spanish school; and was a present to Bishop Fenwick, by Cardinal Fesch, uncle to Napoleon. The others are by some of the first artists in Europe.

The two windows next the altar are of stained glass, and serve to give us, of the west, an idea of that style of imparting light, through edifices devoted to religious purposes, in the old world.

Not a drop of ardent spirits was consumed in the erection of the Cathedral, and, notwithstanding the unmanageable shape and size of the materials, not an accident occurred in the whole progress of the work. Every man employed about it, was paid off every Saturday night; and, as the principal part of the labor was performed at a season of the year when working hands are not usually employed to their advantage, much of the work was executed when labor and materials were worth far less than at present. The Dayton marble alone, at current prices, would nearly treble its original cost. The heavy disbursements have proved a seasonable and sensible benefit to the laboring class. The entire cost of the building is $120,000.

The plate of the Cathedral, in this publication, represents its finished state.

OHIO FEMALE COLLEGE.

This institution is located at College Hill, Hamilton county, Ohio, five miles north of the city.

The corner-stone of the main edifice was laid on the 21st of Sept., 1848, and the institution went into operation in the fall of 1849. In 1851, the college was chartered by the Legislature, with the same powers of conferring degrees upon its graduates and awarding diplomas as are usually possessed by male colleges. The course of studies is extensive and thorough, including a wide range of scientific, mathematical and classic learning, and equal, in respect to variety and extent, to that pursued in our best male colleges. The institution has a library, philosophical, chemical and astronomical apparatuses, for the illustration of the natural sciences; a cabinet of minerals, and a good refracting telescope. Four buildings have already been erected for the accommodation of the pupils, the principal of which, is a magnificent structure, four stories high, and for beauty, adaptation and architectural taste, is unsurpassed by any school building in the west. A beautiful chapel, and two other buildings used as study rooms and dormitories, complete the group occupied at present for college purposes. Other buildings will doubtless soon be added. The location is one of the very best that could have been selected. It is central, accessible, elevated, and healthy, surrounded by pleasant groves and picturesque scenery, and sufficiently far from the city to be free from its temptations and dissipating tendencies, yet near enough to enjoy its privileges. The design of its founders has been to establish an institution of learning, centrally, in the west, where their daughters might enjoy advantages equal to those of their sons for acquiring the imperishable treasures of knowledge, where by intellectual and moral culture, they may be fitted for teachers of seminaries, missionaries, or to fill with honor and usefulness any station in life. The college is under the supervision of an efficient board of trustees, of which board, the Hon. John McLean is president, and Samuel F. Cary, secretary. All letters of inquiry relative to the institution, should be addressed to the secretary of the board, or to Rev. John Covert, president of the college, College Hill, Hamilton county, Ohio.

OHIO FEMALE COLLEGE.

NATIONAL ARMORY IN THE WEST.

The establishment of an armory by the national government, at what shall be adjudged the most appropriate point in the west, is a measure which has been loudly called for, a length of time; and although the claims of the west to its due share in the disbursement of the public moneys by our national legislature have been long slighted with impunity, there can be no doubt, that under the apportionment of representatives to Congress, created by the census of 1850, this mighty section of the republic will be strong enough to insist on that measure of justice due to her interests, her rights and her numbers.

The following propositions, in relation to the armory, may be regarded of such weight, that their mere statement supersedes any elaborate argument.

1. That the west has a just claim to the next armory that may be established, the other great sections of the United States, each possessing one.

2. That the central position of Cincinnati to the whole country, and its ready communication with the entire west, already existing to a great extent, and about to be spread more widely by the network of railroads which will connect us shortly with every important point, claims for the vicinity of this city, a decided preference in the location of that armory.

3. That the low price of the necessaries of life in this immediate region; the abundance of the best quality of iron, coal, and other materials, almost at our doors; and the fact, that competent workmen to any necessary extent, already trained to the use of tools, can be found in Cincinnati, are advantages that can be combined at no other place.

4. Lastly, that the cheap and abundant hydraulic power at Hamilton, twenty-one miles north of Cincinnati, points out that precise spot as the proper point for such armory.

What the United States government requires for this purpose, are:

I. An abundant supply of water-power, for present and future use.

II. That this power shall be free from interruption by high or low water.

III. That the constancy of an ample supply, shall not be liable to frequent interruptions from breaches, repairs of locks, tumble dams, and other works connected with navigable canals; and,

IV. That the expenses of such water-power, should be moderate. All these circumstances exist at Hamilton, to a degree that cannot be found anywhere else.

The water-power obtainable at Hamilton, is five times the quantity necessary for an armory on the same scale, as that of Springfield or Harper's Ferry—a power equal to thirty run of stones being amply sufficient for an armory at this point.

At Hamilton, a sufficient quantity can be furnished for an armory, which will be liable to no interruption from high or low water, or other ordinary causes. Nothing is hazarded in the assertion, that the expenses of water-power and the cost of land, upon which to construct the armory, would be far below what it would cost at any place in the west, offering equal advantages.

The Cincinnati, Hamilton, and Dayton railroad, which will be opened for travel and transportation, before Congress can be called on to act upon this subject, will afford every facility to transport all the manufacturing materials requisite, which are not already on the spot, and at a mere trifle of expense.

In view, therefore, of

The extent, safety, and low price of water-power:

The eligibility of Hamilton, as a site for the favorable location of machine shops and the application of power:

The advantages of cheapness of site, and of cost in the improvements, low rates of rent, and of the necessaries of life: and,

The facilities afforded for the distribution of arms, and the purchase and delivery of materials:

There can be no doubt, in the mind of any candid and intelligent individual, that Hamilton is the spot, in the western states, which possesses such controlling and commanding advantages as to supersede all others in adaptedness to the great object referred to—the establishment of a National Armory in the West.

In many aspects of this subject, the establishment of an armory at Hamilton, would be of equal advantage to Cincinnati with its location here.

BIOGRAPHY—NICHOLAS LONGWORTH.

Nicholas Longworth, the subject of this memoir, was born in Newark, N. J., on the 16th of January, 1783. He came to Cincinnati, which has been his residence ever since, in May, 1804. He engaged at once in reading and studying law in the office of Judge Burnet, then and always, the first lawyer in the city, in point of ability and standing, and after a briefer space than would now be allowed by the courts, was admitted to the bar. He followed his law practice until 1819, when he left the pursuit of the legal profession to newer or younger members. His earnings and savings had been, during the period alluded to, invested in lands and lots in and adjacent to Cincinnati, under the conviction that no other investment of his funds, would prove so profitable. This may seem insufficient to account for the amount of property he has since accumulated from these investments; but it should be remembered that property here was held at low values, in early days, many of his city lot purchases having been made for ten dollars or less, each. It must also be recollected, that Mr. Longworth was a regular lot and land dealer, selling as well as buying, and his profits constantly furnished the means of extending his investments. Nor should it be forgotten, that dealing in property in a rising market, which Cincinnati has always afforded, is a business in which all is gain and nothing loss; differing in this respect from ordinary trade, both in the certainty of profit as well as the security of its debts, which are always protected by mortgage. As an example of the facility with which small amounts, comparatively, secured what has since become of immense value, it may be stated, that Mr. Longworth once received as a legal fee, from a fellow accused of horse stealing, and who had nothing else to give, two second hand copper stills. These were in charge of Joel Williams, who kept a tavern adjacent to the river, and who was a large property holder here in early days. On presenting his order, Mr. Williams told Longworth he could not let the stills go, for he was just building a distillery in Butler county, but he would give him a lot of thirty-three acres on Western Row, in lieu of the article. Mr. Longworth, whose view of the value of property here, was always in advance of public opinion, gladly closed with the proposal. These thirty-three acres occupied a front on Western Row from Sixth to Seventh street, running west for quantity, and this transaction alone, taking into view the prodigious advance in real estate here, would of itself have furnished the basis of an immense fortune, the naked ground being now worth nearly two millions of dollars.

Mr. Longworth went on adding lot to lot, acre to acre, in this mode, until, although he has sold more lands and lots than any man in Cincinnati, he is still the largest landholder in the city.

What Mr. Longworth's property is worth, is rather difficult to determine; but as his taxes for 1850 were upward of seventeen thousand dollars, the largest sum paid by any individual in the United States, William B. Astor excepted, whose taxes for the same year was twenty-three thousand one hundred and sixteen dollars, the presumption is, that there are few individuals of higher reputed wealth in the United States. If, however, he were a man of wealth, and nothing more, this notice would not have appeared in these pages.

Longworth is a problem and a riddle; a problem worthy of the study of those who delight in exploring that labyrinth of all that is hidden and mysterious, the human heart, and a riddle to himself and others. He is a wit and a humorist of a high order; of keen sagacity and shrewdness in many other respects than in money matters; one who can be exact to a dollar, and liberal, when he chooses, with thousands; of marked peculiarity and tenacity in his own opinions, and yet of abundant tolerance to the opinions, however extravagant, of others—a man of great public spirit and sound general judgment. All these things rarely accompany the acquisition and the accumulation of riches.

In addition to all this, it would be difficult to find an individual of his position and standing so perfectly free from pride—in the ordinary sense. He has absolutely none, unless it be the pride of eccentricity. It is no uncommon circumstance for men to become rich by the concentration of time, and labor, and attention, to some one object of profitable employment. This is the ordinary phase of money getting, as closing the ear and pocket to applications for aid is that of money saving. Longworth has become a rich man on a different principle. He appears to have started upon the calculation that if he could put any individual in the way of making a dollar for Longworth, and a dollar for himself at the same time, by aiding him with ground for a lot, or in building him a house on it—and if, moreover, he could multiply cases of the kind by hundreds, or perhaps thousands, he would promote his own interests just in the same measure as he was advancing those of others. At the same time, he could not be unconscious, that while their half was subdivided into small possessions, owned by a thousand or more individuals, his half was a vast, a boundless aggregate, since it was the property of one man alone. The event has done justice to his sagacity. Hundreds, if not thousands, in and adjacent to Cincinnati, now own houses and lots, and many have become wealthy, who would in all probability have lived and died as tenants under a different state of case. Had not Mr. Longworth adopted this course, he would have occupied that relation to society which many wealthy men now sustain, that of getting all they can, and keeping all they get. There are men, even in Cincinnati, who do not deserve the very ground which forms their last resting-place.

Every man of extensive means, who does not give freely to every object to which that disinterested individual, the public, thinks he ought to contribute, is, of course, branded as penurious, or at least, destitute of liberality of spirit. It would be impossible for Nicholas Longworth to form an exception to this rule, since it is one of the very few general rules that have no exceptions. There is a story told of the rich Duke of Newcastle having been applied to for aid, by an individual claiming to be a poor relation. "What is the relationship?" inquired the duke. "We are both descendants of Noah," replied the applicant. "A very just claim," rejoined the duke, and giving him a penny, added, "There, take that, and if every one of your relations gives you as much, you will be a richer man than the Duke of Newcastle." If Mr. Longworth were to contribute to every application made here, it would leave him as poor a man as the most necessitous applicant at his doors.

Mr. Longworth has his own views and his own ways, as regards relief of, and assistance to, the necessitous. That he is governed by conscientious motives, no one ought to doubt, who learns, as he easily may, that Longworth is a supernumerary township trustee, whose office is crowded at regular hours with twenty, thirty, or fifty miserable objects, whose cases he examines into, and disposes of at a cost of time and patience, which most men would, ordinarily, not submit to. Relief is then provided for, on a system which protects itself from being made a means of fostering idleness or mendicity. All this is done obviously on principle, since he must be a loser pecuniarily, as well as in precious time, by such a course.

Many instances might be cited to show that Mr. Longworth is, for a rich man, an uncommonly liberal one. I shall refer to the Observatory case, alone.

Mr. Longworth, on application to him to know whether he would part with the Mt. Adams property, and on what terms for an observatory, promptly made a donation of the ground—four acres in extent, for that purpose. After the building had been erected, an assertion was made in one of our city papers, and as Mr. Longworth believed and charged in his reply, by an individual who had property equally suitable for this purpose, that Longworth was governed by interested motives, the value of Mr. Longworth's property contiguous, being enhanced by that improvement. Every intelligent person who read the article, must have felt that an imputation of the kind, in this case, was supremely ridiculous. But Longworth was piqued, and in his own caustic language, retorted with an offer, that if the individual who wrote that piece, would deed the same quantity of ground for an observatory, he would himself put up a building equal to that which had been erected upon Mount Adams, and appropriate the spot thus vacated, for promenade grounds for the benefit forever, of the citizens of Cincinnati. In this way he suggested to the writer, that he might appropriate to himself all the benefits which such an improvement would secure to his adjacent property, and at the same time, be the means of conferring a lasting public benefit on the citizens of Cincinnati. No reply was made, and perhaps had not been expected.

The original gift of the four acres, all within the heart of the city, was a very liberal act, and the proposition to put up an observatory at his own cost, rendered the proposal thus made, a munificent one.

If the fact, that a community has been made the better or worse, by an individual having existed in it, be, as a standard writer considers it, an unerring test of the general character of that individual, there is no hazard in saying that Cincinnati is the better off for Nicholas Longworth having been an influential citizen of its community, and that putting him to this test, he has fulfilled his mission upon earth, not indeed, as fully as he might have done, but perhaps as fully as one would have done, who might have stood in his shoes.

Nor ought it to be forgotten, that by Mr. Longworth's labors in the introduction of the grape, and improved cultivation of the strawberry, on which objects he has spent thousands of dollars, he has made these fruits accessible to the means of purchase of every man, even the humblest among us. How much more manly and spirited is this, than tempting the poor man with the sight of luxuries he may look at, but can never expect to taste.

Mr. Longworth is a ready and a racy writer, whose vein of thinking and expression is always rich, and who blends pleasantry and wit with grave arguments and earnest purposes. His writings on the strawberry and the grape, and his various contributions to the press abound with examples of this kind, recognizable here, as his, at a single glance. His bon-mots and quizzicalities are like his own sparkling champagne, brilliant and evanescent. Few of these can be referred to on the spur of this occasion; two or three, however, may suffice as a sample, if even inferior to the average. They are taken from "Cist's Advertiser," the editor of which, relates them upon his own knowledge.

"During the war with Mexico, one of our city dailies stated that Mr. Longworth had offered a contribution of ten thousand dollars, as advance pay and equipment of the Ohio volunteers, a large share of which were from Cincinnati—a difficulty having arisen as to the State of Ohio furnishing the necessary advances. I was somewhat surprised at this, believing Mr. Longworth no friend to the war with Mexico, and when I next met him, congratulated him on his public spirit, referring at the same time to the statement in the journals. "Not a word of it true! not a word of it true!" observed Longworth. "I might have said, and believe I did say, that I would give ten thousand dollars as a contribution to a regiment of volunteers, but it was on condition—on the express contingency that I should have the picking out who among our citizens should go, and I believe I would make money by the offer, yet—but recollect, I am to have the say who are to go."

While the Presidential struggle of 1844 was raging, Mr. Longworth was applied to for a contribution of one hundred dollars for campaign expenses. "Don't know whether I shall give a cent," he replied. "I never give something for nothing. We might fail to elect Clay, as we did before, and I should fling away the hundred dollars." The applicant, a President of one of our banks, assured him there was no doubt of Mr. Clay's election—there could be none. "Well," said Longworth, "I can tell you what I will do. I will give you the hundred dollars, but mind, you shall be personally responsible to me for its return if Clay is not elected." The politician, finding he could make no better bargain, and never dreaming of defeat, acceded to these terms. The funds all went into the common purse, and when the hundred dollars had to be made good, the banker had to pay the amount out of his own pocket—*multa gemens.*

The other day, I had occasion to make up a contribution to relieve the wants of a destitute, but deserving widow residing in the Sixth ward. Among othér persons, I applied to Longworth. "Who is she? Do you know her? Is she a deserving object?" I assured him that she was; I had good reason, I said, to believe that she bore an excellent character, and was doing all in her power to support a large family of small children. "Very well, then," said Mr. Longworth, "I shan't give a cent. Such persons will always find plenty to relieve them. I shall assist none but the idle, drunken, worthless vagabonds that nobody else will help. If you meet with such cases call upon me." That this was not a mere pretense I find in the success of an application made here, in behalf of the Mormons, after they had been driven from Illinois. A committee of that people visited Cincinnati and applied to a friend of mine who said he had no money to give, but wrote a note to Mr. Longworth, in which he stated that he had sent these persons to him, as having a claim on him, *they not being Christians!* Mr. Longworth gave them accordingly ten dollars.

BOWLDER PAVEMENT.

OUR limestone pavements have long been an annoyance and reproach to the community. Of friable material and irregular shape, they soon break into inequalities, where water lies after heavy rains, increasing and extending the irregularity of the surface. It is easy to perceive, to what extent this must affect the comfort as well as the health of our citizens.

Of late years, we owe to the public spirit of D. L. De Golyer, the introduction of bowlder pavement, which is gradually changing the whole surface of the city. Properly laid, these require neither repaving nor repairing, for fifty years or more. Indeed this material, is nearly indestructible. Our bowlders are smaller than those used in the Atlantic cities, which circumstance renders the surface here, comparatively smooth. When this species of pavement shall be spread over the whole city, we may hope to escape those clouds of dust, which in dry summer weather, constitutes our greatest street nuisance.

HOTEL FOR INVALIDS.

THE CINCINNATI OBSERVATORY.

This temple of astronomical science occupies, already, its appropriate department, in this volume; but the statement of its establishment, comprehends a history so remarkable, and a lesson so valuable, as to justify a more extended narrative. It is an example of what may be accomplished, by the public spirit of a community, when its energies are stimulated into activity, by the enthusiasm, intelligence, vigor, and perseverance of any one man, of competent ability, to direct it to a successful issue.

The Observatory, either as respects the building, or its scientific instruments and machinery, is the only one in the world constructed and put into operation by the people—the masses. How this was done, cannot be more clearly stated, than in the language of Professor Mitchel, himself, in one of his lectures.

On the 9th of November, 1843, the corner-stone of the Observatory was laid by John Quincy Adams, in the presence of a vast multitude, with appropriate ceremonies, and followed by the delivery of an address replete with beauty and eloquence. The season was too far advanced to permit anything to be done toward the erection of the building during the fall; and, indeed, it was not the intention of the Board of Directors to proceed with the building, until every dollar, required in the payment for the great telescope, should have been remitted to Europe. At the time of laying the corner-stone, but three thousand dollars, out of nine thousand five hundred, had been paid. This was the amount required in the contract, to be paid on signing, and the remaining sum became due on finishing the instrument.

The contract having been made, conditionally, in July, 1842, it was believed that the great Refractor would be shipped, for the United States, in June, 1844, and, to meet our engagements, the sum of six thousand five hundred dollars, must be raised.

This amount was subscribed, but, in consequence of commercial difficulties, all efforts, hitherto made to collect it, had been unavailing, and in February, 1844, the Board of Control solicited the Director of the Observatory, to become the general agent of the Society, and to collect all old subscriptions, and obtain such new ones as might be necessary to make up the requisite sum. The accounts in the hands of the previous collector, were, accordingly, turned over to me, and a systematic effort was made to close them up. A regular journal was kept of each day's work, noting the number of hours employed, the persons visited, those actually found, the sums collected, the promises to pay, the positive repudiations, the due-bills taken, payable in cash and trade, and the day on which I was *requested to call again.* These intervals extended from a week or ten days, to four months. The hour was in general fixed, and when the day rolled round, and the hour arrived, the agent of the Society presented himself, and referred to the memoranda. In many cases another and another time was appointed, until, in some instances, almost as many calls were made as there were dollars due. By systematic perseverance, at the end of some forty days, the sum of three thousand dollars was paid over to the treasurer, as the amount collected from old subscribers. Nearly two thousand dollars of due-bills had been taken, payable in carpenter work, painting, dry-goods, boots and shoes, hats and caps, plastering, brick-laying, blacksmith work, paints and oils, groceries, pork barrels, flour, bacon and lard, hardware, iron, nails, &c., in short, in every variety of trade, materials, and workmanship. The due bills, in cash, brought about five hundred dollars in the course of the next thirty days, and a further sum of three thousand dollars was required for the last remittance to Europe.

It was determined to raise this amount, in large sums, from wealthy and liberal citizens, who had already become members of our Society. The list first made out, and the sums placed opposite the names of each person, is now in my possession. On paper the exact amount was made up in the simplest and most expeditious manner; eight names had the sum of two hundred dollars opposite them, ten names were marked one hundred dollars each, and the remaining ones, fifty dollars each. Such was the singular accuracy in the calculation, that, when the theory was reduced to practice, it failed in but one solitary instance. One person, upon whom we had relied for two hundred dollars, declined absolutely, and his place was filled by another.

I called on one of the eight individuals marked at two hundred dollars, and, after a few moments' conversation, he told me, that in case one hundred dollars would be of any service to me, he would gladly subscribe that amount. I showed him my list, and finding his name among those reckoned at two hundred dollars, he remarked that he would not mar so beautiful a scheme, for the sum of one hundred dollars, and accordingly entered his name in its appropriate place.

At a meeting, held in May, of the Board of Control, the treasurer reported that the entire amount was now in the treasury, with the exception of one hundred and fifty dollars. The board adjourned to meet, on the same day, of the following week, when the deficiency was reduced, by the agent, to twenty-five dollars, and on the same day, an order was passed, to remit the entire amount to Barings & Brothers, London, to be paid to the manufacturer, on the order of Dr. J. Lamont, of Munich, to be given on the packing of the instrument. The last twenty-five dollars was obtained, and placed in the treasurer's hands, immediately on the adjournment of the Board. Thus was completed, as it was supposed, by far the most difficult part of the enterprise. All the cash means of the Society had now been exhausted, about eleven thousand dollars had been raised, and to extend the effort, yet farther, under the circumstances, seemed to be quite impossible. Up to this time, nothing had been done toward the building; and, after paying for the instrument, not one dollar remained in cash, to commence the erection of a building which must cost, at the lowest estimate, five or six thousand dollars.

Some two or three thousand dollars had been subscribed, payable in work and materials. Owing to a slight change in the plan of the building, the foundation walls, already laid in the fall of 1843, were taken up and relaid. Finding it quite impossible to induce any master workman to take the contract for the building, with the many contingencies by which our affairs were surrounded, I determined to hire workmen by the day, and superintend the erection of the building personally. In attempting to contract for the delivery of brick, on the summit of Mount Adams, such an enormous price was demanded for the hauling, in consequence of the steepness of the hill, that all idea of a brick building, was at once abandoned, and it was determined to build of limestone; an abundant supply of which, could be had on the grounds of the Society, by quarrying. Having matured my plans, securing the occasional assistance of a carpenter, about the beginning of June, 1844, I hired two masons, one of whom was to receive an extra sum for hiring the hands, keeping their time, and acting as the master workman. One tender to these workmen, constituted the entire force with which I commenced the erection of a building, which, if prosecuted in the same humble manner, would have required about twenty years for its completion. And yet our title bond required that the building should be finished in the following June, or a forfeiture of the title by which we hold the present beautiful site, must follow. My master mason seemed quite confounded, when told that he must commence work with such a force. In the outset, difficulties were thick and obstinate. Exorbitant charges were made for delivering lime. I at once commenced the building of a lime-kiln, and, in a few days, had the satisfaction of seeing it well filled, and on fire; true, it caved in once or twice, with other little accidents, but a full supply of lime was obtained, and at a cheap rate.

Sand was the next item, for which the most extravagant charges were made. I found this so ruinous that an effort was made, and finally, I obtained permission to open a sand-pit, which had long been closed, for fear of caving down a house, on the side of the hill above, by further excavation. An absolute refusal was at first given, but systematic perseverance again succeeded, and the pit was re-opened. The distance was comparatively short, but the price of mere hauling was so great, that I was forced to purchase horses, and in not a few instances fill the carts, with my own hands, and actually drive them to the top of the hill, thus demonstrating practically, how many loads could be fairly made in a day.

Another difficulty yet remained—no water could be found nearer than the foot of the hill, half a mile distant, and to haul all the water so great a distance would have cost a large sum. I selected one of the deepest ravines on the hill-top, and throwing a dam across, while it was actually raining, I had the pleasure of seeing it fill rapidly from the hill-sides; and in this way an abundant supply was obtained for the mixing of mortar, at a very moderate expense of hauling.

Thus prepared, the building was commenced, with two masons and one tender, during the first week; at the close of the week I had raised sufficient funds to pay off my hands, and directed the foreman to employ, for the following week, two additional masons and a tender; to supply this force with materials, several hands were employed in the quarry, in the lime-kiln, and in the sand-pit, all of whom were hired by the day, to be paid half cash and the residue in trade. During all this time, I may remark, that I was discharging my duties as professor of Mathematics and Philosophy in the Cincinnati College, and teaching five hours in each day. Before eight o'clock in the morning, I had visited all my workmen in the building, in the lime-kiln, sand-pit and stone quarry—at that hour my duties in the college commenced, and closed at one. By two o'clock,

P. M., I was again with my workmen, or engaged in raising the means of paying them on Saturday night. The third week the number of hands was again doubled ; the fourth week produced a like increase, until finally, not less than fifty day laborers were actually engaged in the erection of the Cincinnati Observatory. Each Saturday night exhausted all my funds, but I commenced the next week in the full confidence that industry and perseverance would work out their legitimate results. To raise the cash means required, was the great difficulty. I have frequently made four or five trades to turn my due-bills, payable in trade, into cash. I have not unfrequently gone to individuals and sold them their own due-bills payable in merchandise, for cash, by making a discount. The pork merchants paid me cash for my due bills, payable in barrels and lard kegs, and in this way, I managed to obtain sufficient cash means, to prosecute the work vigorously during the months of July and August ; and in September, I had the satisfaction to see the building up and covered, without having incurred one dollar of debt. At one period, I presume, one hundred hands were employed, at the same time, in the prosecution of the work. More than fifty hands on the hill, and as many in the city in the various workshops, paying their subscriptions by work for different parts of the building. The doors were in the hands of one carpenter, the window-frames in those of another—a third was employed on the sash—a painter took them from the joiner, and in turn delivered them to a glazier, while a carpenter paid his stock by hanging them, with weights purchased by stock, and with cords obtained in the same way. Many locks were furnished by our townsmen in payment of their subscriptions. Lumber, sawing, flooring, roofing, painting, mantles, steps, hearths, hardware, lathing, doors, windows, glass, and painting, were in like manner obtained. At the beginning of each week my master carpenter generally gave me a bill of lumber and materials wanted during the week. In case they had not been already subscribed, the stock-book was resorted to, and there was no relaxing of effort until the necessary articles were obtained. If a tier of joists was wanted, the saw-mills were visited, and in some instances the joists for the same floor came from two or three different mills.

On covering the building, the great crowd of hands employed, as masons, tenders, lime-burners, quarry-men, sand and water men, were paid off and discharged ; and it now seemed that the heavy pressure was passed, and that one might again breathe free, after the responsibility of such heavy weekly payments was removed.

Having used as much space as is admissible, I conclude, for the present, by referring to the following table, which will give, perhaps, a more correct idea of the organization of the Cincinnati Astronomical Society, than a labored description.

The members of the Society, so far as known, are divided as follows:

Judges	6	Lumber Merchants	18
Physicians	25	Livery Stable Keepers	3
Magistrates	6	Hardware Merchants	7
Lawyers	33	Steamboat Owners	5
Officers of Insurance Offices	8	Engineers	2
Persons living from rents	34	Engraver	1
Blacksmiths	8	Plumbers	2
Iron and Brass Founders	17	Lockmakers	2
Wholesale Grocers	39	Paperhangers	7
Retail "	17	Stonemasons	3
Editors	5	Brick " and Plasterers	2
Teachers	25	Sawyers	7
Clergymen	5	Butchers	3
Dry-Goods Dealers	30	Bookseller	1
Bankers and Brokers	21	Hatters	3
Clerks	13	Horticulturists	3
Leather Dealers and Tanners	6	Millers	2
Iron Merchants	16	Tinners	2
Pork Merchants	16	Ice Dealer	1
Book Publishers	2	Architects	2
Druggists	16	Painters	4
Watchmakers	4	Farmers	2
Carpenters and Joiners	23	Cooper	1
Tailors and Clothiers	6	Brickmaker	1
Saddlers	2	Lamp Dealers	2
Crockery Merchants	7	Mattress Makers	2
Hotel Keepers	6	Manufacturers of White Lead	3
Printers	7	" " Saleratus	1
Shoemakers	5	" " Cotton Yarn	2
Cabinetmakers	6	" " Oil-Cloth	1
Ship Builders	4	" " Plows	2
Stone Cutters	3	" " other articles	9
Wire Workers	1	Carriage Makers	4
Lockmakers and Bell Hangers	3	Remainder unknown.	

REEDER'S BUILDING, THIRD, WEST OF WALNUT STREET.

COAL.

So extensive has been the consumption, or rather waste of timber in the vicinity of our western cities, within the last fifty years, as to render the use of mineral coal, as fuel, a strict necessity.

On the first introduction of coal for that purpose, twenty-five or thirty years since, it was sold at twenty to twenty-five cents per bushel, while fire-wood could be purchased at two dollars and fifty cents per cord; making ten or twelve bushels of coal as costly as one cord of wood. The relative value of these fuel materials, has altered so greatly since, in the advanced price of wood and the reduced price of coal, that we can hardly realize the fact that even at the rates thus named, and including the price of sawing and splitting, the coal was the cheaper article for family use.

The early supplies of coal were brought here by Ephraim Jones, from Wheeling and Pittsburgh; and for years these were the only varieties consumed here.

But the great superiority of coal over wood, for families, in the facility of putting it away in a small space; the convenience of taking it through a dwelling; the readiness with which its fires can be shut down at night, and rekindled in the morning—in a cold morning, a great point of advantage—the superior degree of safety of coal over wood, as regards accidental fires resulting from their use, and more than all, the changed relation of value—coal now costing hardly more than one-fourth the price of firewood, have rendered the coal popular, alike to the employer and those he hires. Wood, except for cooking purposes, is fuel here no longer.

The principal objection to the use of coal, is the presence of sulphur and of bitumen to such excess, as to render its use unpleasant and unhealthy in chambers, as well as a nuisance in the streets; defiling the persons of individuals, and the fronts of the buildings. Most of us have visited Pittsburgh and Wheeling, and can comprehend the force of these objections.

Fortunately for us, we have coal mines opened and opening constantly for the supply of this market, which promise to obviate the objection alluded to. These are:

1. The Pomeroy mines, in Meigs county, Ohio.
2. The Peach Orchard field, on Sandy, Virginia.
3. The Cannel coal, on Kanawha.

4. The coal on the Monongahela and Youghiogeny, of the Cincinnati Coal-mine Company, and lastly:

5. The new mines at South Point, Lawrence county, in Ohio, and the Rock Grove mines in Virginia, just commencing to supply this market.

These varieties burn free from sulphur, and consume every portion to ashes, as any one will find on making the test.

The consumption of coal in 1840, was one million nine hundred thousand and fifty bushels. It has increased since, to nearly eight million bushels; the regular decline in price, and our business enlargement stimulating a constantly increasing consumption of the article.

GLENDALE.

This is a village, and once a series of fine farms, amounting in the aggregate to five hundred and sixty-five acres. It is situated on the line of the Cincinnati, Hamilton and Dayton railroad, and twelve miles from our own city. The property has been purchased by a joint-stock company of thirty persons, who propose, after selecting their own lots out of the premises, to lay off the residue into building lots of various sizes, confining their sales to actual residents, at least for the summer season, and of a description of persons who will be desirable neighbors to each other. A series of improvements are in progress, which will make Glendale a delightful residence. An artificial lake of four acres surface, and seventeen feet depth, has been created, by running a dam three hundred feet long just below four or five permanent and abundant springs; which will secure inexhaustible supplies of water for washing and bathing.

Glendale will be a station for wooding and watering, and passengers and freight for the Cincinnati, Hamilton, and Dayton railroad.

An arrangement will be made to establish regular morning and evening trains to and from Cincinnati, in addition to the through trains. This will afford unrivaled facilities to accommodate the dwellers at Glendale.

There will be three hundred lots or more, laid out, for future purchasers.

WOODRUFF HOUSE,

P. E. & G. P. TUTTLE, ... PROPRIETORS.

CENSUS OF OHIO—1850.

COUNTIES.	WHITE.	COLORED.	TOTAL.	1840.
Adams	18,890	53	18,943	12,775
Allen	12,100	16	12,116	9,079
Ashland*	23,824	2	23,826	
Ashtabula	28,727	40	28,767	23,723
Athens	18,137	80	18,217	19,109
Auglaize*	11,278	63	11,341	
Belmont	33,914	685	34,599	30,901
Brown	26,648	686	27,334	22,715
Butler	30,439	355	30,794	28,173
Carroll	17,635	50	17,685	18,108
Champaign	19,278	465	19,743	16,720
Clark	21,872	302	22,174	16,832
Clermont	30,056	393	30,449	23,100
Clinton	18,268	569	18,837	15,719
Columbiana	33,437	164	33,601	40,378
Coshocton	25,631	40	25,671	21,500
Crawford	18,167	10	18,177	13,152
Cuyahoga	47,776	329	48,105	26,506
Darke	20,038	239	20,277	13,282
Defiance*	6,947	19	6,966	
Delaware	21,682	132	21,814	22,060
Erie	18,436	142	18,578	12,457
Fairfield	30,002	255	30,257	31,924
Fayette	12,457	279	12,736	10,984
Franklin	41,327	1553	42,880	25,049
Fulton	7,779	1	7,780	
Gallia	15,885	1179	17,064	13,444
Geauga	17,816	7	17,823	16,297
Greene	21,339	608	21,947	17,528
Guernsey	30,295	177	30,472	27,748
Hamilton	153,356	3494	156,850	80,145
Hancock	16,753	21	16,774	9,981
Hardin	8,237	14	8,251	4,598
Harrison	19,901	259	20,160	20,099
Henry	3,432		3,432	2,503
Highland	24,909	872	25,781	22,269
Hocking	13,990	129	14,119	9,741
Holmes	20,457	1	20,458	18,088
Huron	26,184	19	26,203	22,661
Jackson	12,376	348	12,724	9,744
Jefferson	28,469	664	29,133	25,030
Knox	28,828	42	28,870	29,579
Lake	14,619	36	14,655	13,740
Lawrence	14,944	303	15,247	9,725
Licking	38,738	107	38,845	35,096
Logan	18,671	497	19,168	14,015
Lorain	25,834	257	26,091	18,467
Lucas	12,255	126	12,381	9,382
Madison	9,922	90	10,012	9,025
Mahoning*	23,680	53	23,733	
Marion	12,536	18	12,554	20,852
Medina	24,396	37	24,433	18,352

COUNTIES.	WHITE.	COLORED.	TOTAL.	1840.
Meigs	17,921	39	17,960	11,452
Mercer	7,319	393	7,712	8,277
Miami	24,391	566	24,957	19,688
Monroe	28,306	61	28,367	18,521
Montgomery	38,007	210	38,217	31,038
Morgan	28,515	78	28,593	20,852
Morrow*	20,239	1	20,240	
Muskingum	44,460	593	45,053	38,749
Ottawa	3,309	1	3,310	2,248
Paulding	1,765	1	1,766	1,034
Perry	20,751	23	20,774	19,344
Pickaway	20,720	390	21,110	19,725
Pike	10,337	618	10,955	7,626
Portage	24,331	56	24,387	19,688
Preble	21,708	40	21,748	19,482
Putnam	7,221		7,221	5,189
Richland	30,823	54	30,877	44,532
Ross	30,263	1821	32,084	27,460
Sandusky	14,495	34	14,529	10,182
Scioto	18,562	167	18,729	11,192
Seneca	26,995	110	27,105	18,139
Shelby	13,573	383	13,956	12,154
Stark	39,789	99	39,888	34,605
Summit	27,375	106	27,481	22,562
Trumbull	30,504	36	30,540	25,700
Tuscarawas	31,658	74	31,732	25,631
Union	12,081	124	12,205	8,422
Vanwert	4,748	45	4,793	1,577
Vinton*	9,252	101	9,353	
Warren	25,024	536	25,560	23,141
Washington	29,139	373	29,512	20,823
Wayne	33,024	21	33,045	35,808
Williams	8,018		8,018	4,995
Wood	9,147	18	9,165	5,458
Wyandot*	11,121	48	11,169	
Totals	1,957,465	23,495	1,980,960	1,519,467

* Erected since 1840

Note.—Since the earlier pages of this publication went to press, the Cincinnati Female Institute, under charge of Professor Zachos and Miss M. Cox, has been removed to Dayton, and merged in the Cooper Female Institute of that city.

This change serves only to enlarge its recommendations to those desirous of sending pupils, in the measure of advantage, Dayton possesses over Cincinnati as respects abundant range of exercise, as well as purer air to breathe.

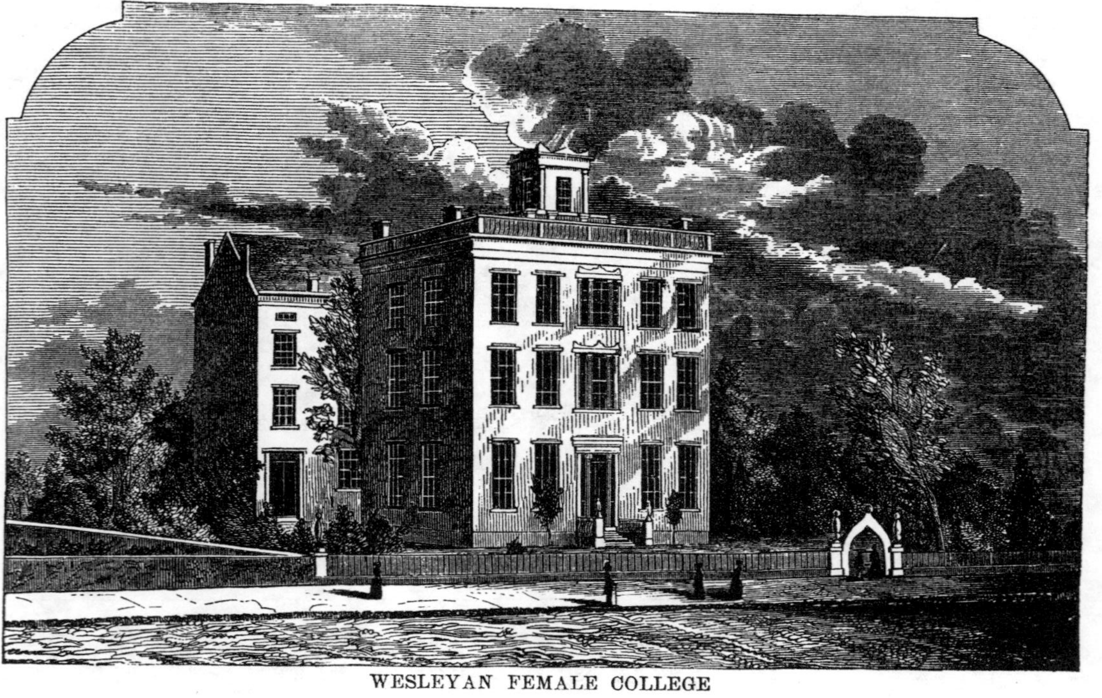

WESLEYAN FEMALE COLLEGE

THE PROTESTANT UNIVERSITY OF THE UNITED STATES.

This Institution was incorporated by the Legislature of Ohio, in the year 1845, and is under the management of a competent board of trustees. The following is the second section of its charter, which fixes its location, defines its object, and secures to it the most unlimited academic powers, viz: "The said university shall be located *in*, or *near* to, the city of Cincinnati; and its object and purpose are hereby declared to be the promotion and advancement of education, the cultivation and diffusion of literature, science, and the arts, in all their departments and faculties." It is not *Sectarian*. Thus, in the ninth and eleventh sections, it is expressly "provided that in the rules and regulations governing the admission of students, there shall be no preference on account of religious sects, or any other cause, except good moral character, and the promise of superior scholarship," and "that the corporation shall have no power at any time to establish a sectarian religious test, as a condition of enjoying the honors and privileges of the university." But it is *Protestant*. And this name was given to it, by the Legislature, because of the provision in the eleventh section of its charter, "That it shall always be conducted in subserviency to the True, Reformed, Protestant Christian Religion, as taught in the Holy Scriptures of the Old and New Testaments." Its general corporate powers are correspondingly liberal in their character. This outline, as it is due to our citizens, will sufficiently explain, for the present, the nature and scope of the institution.

The university has not yet been opened for instruction, but much has been done in preparation for this. The Rev. William Wilson, of this city, who is about to sail for Europe in its interest, is its chancellor. It has recently been endowed, by the munificent bequest of an enlightened, spirited, and patriotic protestant, in the eastern section of our country. The whole Protestant world, as well as the republic of letters and science, are deeply interested in the success of this university.

The Officers of the Board of Trustees, are:—

BAPTIST THEOLOGICAL SEMINARY, AT FAIRMOUNT.

FARMERS' COLLEGE, HAMILTON COUNTY, O.

Prices of Jones' Hand-Presses.

Double medium, with boiler apparatus, $240; imperial, 220; super royal, 200; medium, 190; Cap, without boiler apparatus, 75.

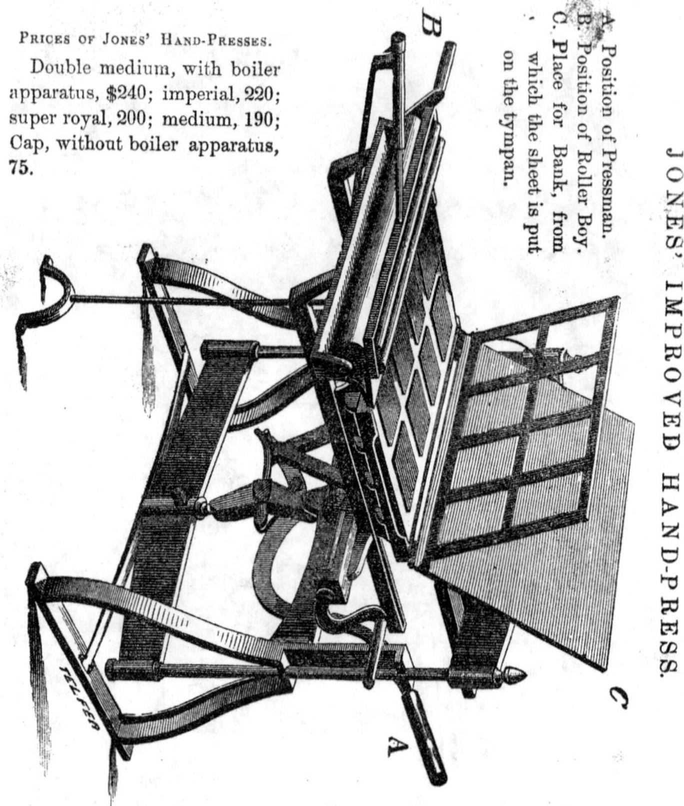

JONES' IMPROVED HAND-PRESS.

A. Position of Pressman.
B. Position of Roller Boy.
C. Place for Bank, from which the sheet is put on the tympan.

Guilford & Jones, 41 Second street, who have the exclusive right for the manufacture and sale of this valuable hand-press, are now prepared to fill orders for medium and double medium sizes. By this press, an increase of at least fifty per cent. of work is obtained, with a great reduction of labor. Its peculiar advantages over the old consist:—1. In the saving of time in putting on and taking off the sheet. 2. In the saving of time in running the bed under and out from the platin. 3. In the flying the frisket, as it is self-acting. 4. In the application of the leverage, by which means a very heavy impression is obtained by a small expenditure of physical force. 5. In the saving of time and labor of stepping backward and forward by the pressman, as it is unnecessary for him to move out of his tracks while at work. 6. From the manner in which the points are attached, it being impossible for the blankets to full up as the form runs under the platin, which, in the ordinary press, renders the points liable to move.

WILSON'S PATENT STEAM RENDERING TANKS.

LOTZE'S NEW PATENT WARM AIR FURNACE OF 1850,

FOR HEATING CHURCHES, DWELLINGS, STORES, AND OTHER PUBLIC BUILDINGS.

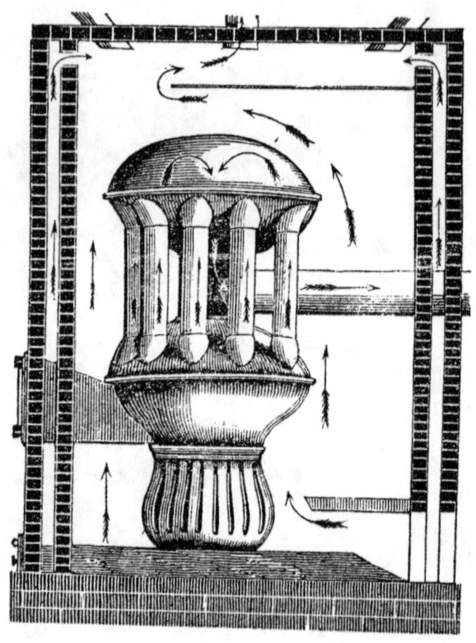

FURNACE, WITH BRICK AIR-CHAMBER, FOR BURNNG COAL.

FURNACE STOVE, FOR BURNING WOOD.

www.ingramcontent.com/pod-product-compliance
Lightning Source LLC
LaVergne TN
LVHW020114110826
845151LV00001B/153

9781425543051